The Behavior of Federal Judges

THE
Behavior
OF
Federal Judges

**A THEORETICAL AND EMPIRICAL STUDY
OF RATIONAL CHOICE**

Lee Epstein

William M. Landes

Richard A. Posner

Harvard University Press

Cambridge, Massachusetts · London, England

2013

Library of Congress Cataloging-in-Publication Data

Epstein, Lee, 1958–
The behavior of federal judges : a theoretical and empirical study of
rational choice / Lee Epstein, William M. Landes, and Richard A. Posner.
p.   cm.
Includes bibliographical references and index.
ISBN 978-0-674-04989-5 (alk. paper)
1. Judicial process—United States. I. Landes, William M.
II. Posner, Richard A. III. Title.
KF5130.E46 2013
347.73'14—dc23   2012008907

Contents

Figures

Tables

I often say that when you can measure what you are speaking about, and express it in numbers, you know something about it; but when you cannot measure it, when you cannot express it in numbers, your knowledge is of a meagre and unsatisfactory kind: it may be the beginning of knowledge, but you have scarcely, in your thoughts, advanced to the state of *science,* whatever the matter may be.

—Baron William Thomson Kelvin, "Electrical Units of Measurement"
(May 3, 1883), in Kelvin, *Constitution of Matter* (vol. 1 of his *Popular Lectures and Addresses*), 73–74 (1889) (emphasis in original)

For the rational study of the law the black-letter man may be the man of the present, but the man of the future is the man of statistics and the master of economics.

—O. W. Holmes, "The Path of the Law," 10 *Harvard Law Review*
457, 469 (1897)

General Introduction

In the continuing drama of American law the judge still holds the center of the stage, down in front of the footlights. . . . Much of our finest intelligence is engaged in studying what judges do and say and in guessing at their inmost sensations.

—John P. Dawson[1]

J**UDGES INDEED PLAY** a central role in the American legal system—more so than in most others. But the behavior of American judges, and in particular the determinants of their decisions, are not well understood, including by lawyers, law professors, and even many judges (we'll explain that paradox in due course). In part this is because judges in our system are permitted to be, and most are, quite secretive.[2] Indirect methods must be employed to understand their behavior. Beginning more than half a century ago but accelerating in recent decades, social scientists—political scientists in particular, but also economists and psychologists, and, increasingly, academic lawyers knowledgeable about social science—have used ever more sophisticated theoretical concepts and quantitative tools to penetrate self-serving judicial rhetoric, go beyond judges' limited self-understanding, and place the study of judicial behavior on a scientific ba-

1. *The Oracles of the Law* xi (1968). Still true, almost half a century later.
2. With exceptions, of course. See, for example, William Domnarski, *Federal Judges Revealed* (2009), a study based on oral histories of a number of federal district and circuit judges. See also books based on the private papers of Supreme Court Justices, such as Lee Epstein and Jack Knight, *The Choices Justices Make* (1998); Forrest Malzman, James F. Spriggs II, and Paul J. Wahlbeck, *Crafting Law on the Supreme Court* (2000); and Walter F. Murphy, *Elements of Judicial Strategy* (1964).

sis. Yet this literature is not well known to the legal community,[3] apart from the small sliver that without pretension to doing social science research takes an interest, whether sympathetic or critical, in what social scientists might have to say about judges.[4] That separation is unfortunate, because many conventional legal scholars, abetted by judges, have promoted an unrealistic but influential theory of judicial behavior in which careerism and ideology play no role in judicial decisions, while some social scientists and some journalists have sponsored the opposite but also unrealistic conception of judges as merely politicians in robes.

The theory of judicial behavior in which careerism and ideology play no role in judicial decisions we call "legalism," though the more common term is "formalism."[5] In its simplest form, judges are said merely to apply law that is given to them to the facts; their task is mechanical, at best a form of engineering (but not "social engineering"), and involves no exercise of discretion. In a more complex version, judges (especially Supreme Court Justices) apply to cases an intellectual system—a methodology—adopted on politically neutral grounds to generate objective decisions. These systems are called by such names as "originalism," "textualism," "the Constitution in exile," "the Constitution as common law," "the living Constitution," "active liberty"—the list goes on and on.

Some academic lawyers have sponsored the opposite conception of judges—that their legalist pretensions are mere rhetoric, designed to conceal the political character of their rulings. About those systems these academic critics might say with Kierkegaard that "in relation to their systems most systematizers are like a man who has built a vast palace while he himself lives nearby in a barn; they themselves do not live in the vast systematic edifice."[6] The skeptical theory of judicial behavior was taken

3. Frank B. Cross, "Political Science and the New Legal Realism: A Case of Unfortunate Interdisciplinary Ignorance," 92 *Northwestern University Law Review* 251 (1997); Gerald Rosenberg, "Across the Great Divide (Between Law and Political Science)," 3 *Green Bag* (second series) 267 (2000).

4. For a recent, and very good, example, see Charles Gardner Geyh, "Can the Rules of Law Survive Judicial Politics?" 97 *Cornell Law Review* 191 (2012).

5. For an illuminating discussion of legalism (formalism), see Paul N. Cox, "An Interpretation and (Partial) Defense of Legal Formalism," 36 *Indiana Law Review* 57 (2003).

6. Søren Kierkegaard, *Papers and Journals: A Selection* 212 (Alastair Hannay trans. 1996).

to an extreme by such "realists" as Fred Rodell of Yale and by the votaries of "critical legal studies," a revival of Rodell-style extreme legal realism that flourished in the 1970s and is now defunct, although some of its avatars, such as feminist legal theory and critical race theory, continue to have a following among academic lawyers.

Properly understood, legal realism is an attempt to be realistic about judicial behavior, and an attempt with a distinguished pedigree (Jeremy Bentham, Oliver Wendell Holmes, Benjamin Cardozo, Learned Hand, moderate legal-realist scholars such as Karl Llewellyn, and other luminaries[7]). But the school of legal realism lacked both an articulated model of judicial behavior and the data and empirical methodology required to test such a model. These tools are now available and we build with them in this book, hoping to augment the existing social-scientific literature on judicial behavior.

There is an important difference between traditional legal realism and the concept of realism that shapes our analysis. The traditional realism was, like legalism, a jurisprudential theory—a theory about the legitimacy and character of particular judicial outcomes. It was not a theory of how judicial behavior is shaped by incentives and constraints. Legal realists, notably Jerome Frank, offered conjectures about judicial psychology, but realist analysis was largely limited to the influence of a judge's ideology, or, what was believed to be correlated with it, social class, on judicial votes. There is more influencing a judge than class and ideology, and the "more" includes, but importantly is not exhausted in, legalist reasoning. This is brought out in a striking passage by Llewellyn, the foremost academic legal realist:

> Those phases of human make-up which build habit in the individual and institutions in the group . . . [are] laziness as to the reworking of a problem once solved; the time and energy saved by routine, especially under any pressure of business; the values of routine as a curb on arbitrariness and as a prop of weakness, inexperience and instability; the social values of predictability; the power of whatever exists to produce expectations and the power of expectations to become norma-

---

7. Such as Ambrose Bierce, who in *The Devil's Dictionary* (1911) defined "lawful" as "compatible with the will of a judge having jurisdiction."

tive. The force of precedent in the law is heightened by an additional factor: that curious, almost universal sense of justice which urges that all men are properly to be treated alike in like circumstances. As the social system varies we meet infinite variations as to what men or treatments or circumstances are to be classed as "like"; but the pressure to accept the views of the time and place remains.[8]

These are shrewd observations. They are paralleled from outside the legal profession by remarks to us (which we have edited slightly) by the economist Andrei Shleifer, in correspondence:

Consider common law judges who face few prospects of promotion, are not so high in the judicial hierarchy that they are making law, and cannot be fired or voted out. These judges face almost no incentives. They need to move cases through, and they need to be not so utterly random that they get overturned very much. But these are not enormously strict constraints. So what consequences follow? I think that in this context just about any external or internal motivation can prove decisive. Of course, one motivation might be to try to figure out what the law is and to apply it, but this is only one of them. Judicial politics is one that the legal literature focuses on; abuse of lawyers to humor oneself is another. But one needs to take a much broader view: that just about anything can move these judges when incentives are so weak.

Right/left politics is only one source of judicial bias. Other sources might be much more important. Judges can be pro-dog or anti-dog. More importantly, judges can be pro-government or anti-government. If many judges are former prosecutors or believe that "prosecutors don't get names out of a phone book," this might be a more significant bias than right/left politics. Judges may have their own philosophies on all kinds of matters, in other words. There may be a very important interaction between the judicial branch and the media. If judges are really not particularly constrained, presumably they will try to get at-

8. K. N. Llewellyn, "Case Law," in *Encyclopedia of the Social Sciences,* vol. 3, p. 249 (E. R. A. Seligman ed. 1930).

tention, be liked, be popular. Since media intermediates a lot of information, they might choose to do what the media want.

Building on such insights, we aim in this book to present a realistic model of judicial behavior that is sufficiently simple and definite to be testable empirically, and then to test it.

Chapter 1 presents the model. Using concepts from labor economics, it models the judge as a participant in a labor market—the judicial labor market—and defends the model against legalist objections. We explain that a judge conceived of as a participant in a labor market can be understood as being motivated and constrained, as other workers are, by costs and benefits both pecuniary and nonpecuniary, but mainly the latter: nonpecuniary costs such as effort, criticism, and workplace tensions, nonpecuniary benefits such as leisure, esteem, influence, self-expression, celebrity (that is, being a public figure), and opportunities for appointment to a higher court; and constrained also by professional and institutional rules and expectations and by a "production function"—the tools and methods that the worker uses in his job and how he uses them. We rebut the formidable challenge that Judge Harry Edwards of the U.S. Court of Appeals for the District of Columbia Circuit has mounted to the realist approach to judicial behavior.

We call ours "the" realist approach, but other such approaches are possible and are found in the scholarly literature, approaches that emphasize the influence on judging of personal characteristics, such as race and sex, religious upbringing, temperament, cognitive limitations, education—even law-school grades.[9] Those approaches are fruitful, but in order to make our analysis manageable we employ a simpler model, though we do from time to time touch on personal-identity characteristics, which influence ideology and through ideology judicial outcomes.

Ours is strictly a positive analysis. We do not ask how judges should decide cases but how they do decide them—more broadly, how they do

---

9. These approaches are discussed in Richard A. Posner, *How Judges Think*, ch. 1 (2008). See also Lawrence Baum, *The Puzzle of Judicial Behavior* (1997); Eileen Braman, *Law, Politics, and Perception* (2009); Frank B. Cross, *Decision Making in the U.S. Courts of Appeals* (2007).

their judicial work (which is not limited to casting votes in cases). That doesn't mean our book is of purely academic interest. The better that judges are understood, the more effective lawyers will be both in litigating cases and, as important, in predicting the outcome of cases, thus enabling litigation to be avoided or cases settled at an early stage. And judges who understand their motivations and those of other judges are likely to be more effective judges. A realistic understanding of judges should also improve legal education and enable the design of realistic proposals both for continuing judicial education and for judicial reform. We have therefore worked hard to make a book largely of statistical analysis intelligible to lawyers and judges who have no familiarity with such analysis. To that end we follow this general introduction with a technical introduction that defines statistical terms and explains the statistical methodologies employed in the book. It is very important to us that lawyers and judges who are unfamiliar with statistical analysis be able to understand the entire book, because our findings are of greater potential importance to them than to any other segment of our intended audience.

Chapter 2 seeks to introduce the legal profession, including law professors and judges, to a substantial social-scientific literature about judges of which much of the profession is ignorant. We show that it is a literature richer in data than in theory and that it is heavily focused on the U.S. Supreme Court and to a lesser extent on the lower federal courts, though recently it has begun paying increased attention to state and foreign courts as well. We review the history of the empirical studies that relate to our model of the judge, noting a fourfold division: studies of individual decision-making (the effect of a judge's ideology, life experiences, personality, etc., on his judicial votes); of collegial and other group effects (such as panel composition, dissent aversion, and opinion assignment by presiding judges); of hierarchical effects (the relations between lower and higher courts); and of interactions between the judiciary and other branches of government. This last division of the literature plays almost no role in our analysis, however.

A particular focus of chapter 2 is on the methodological problems that empirical studies of judicial behavior have encountered and tried to overcome. These problems primarily involve determining the ideology of judges and the ideological character of judicial votes, with the further complication that a judge's ideology when he is appointed (what we call his ex ante ideology) may differ from the ideology reflected in his judicial votes (his ex post ideology). Both are important, and the methods of determining ex ante ideology may not be appropriate for determining ex post ideology, and vice versa. The various methods, as we explain, all have their strengths and weaknesses, and we use all to a greater or lesser extent.

The remaining chapters present the results of original empirical research conducted by us. Data availability and a desire to keep the book to a manageable length have persuaded us to limit our analyses to the federal judiciary, and specifically to the Article III federal judiciary, consisting of Supreme Court Justices, court of appeals judges, and district judges. There are other federal judicial officers, primarily federal magistrate judges and bankruptcy judges (all bankruptcy judges are federal), but they are not appointed by the President or confirmed by the Senate, and have fixed terms of office rather than life tenure. Their appointment is authorized by Article I of the Constitution rather than by Article III, the latter being the provision authorizing a federal judiciary consisting of judges who are appointed for life by the President subject to Senate confirmation.

Chapters 3 through 8 propose and test a variety of hypotheses concerning judicial behavior. A major focus is on the relative weight of ideology and legalistic analysis in decision-making in the different tiers. But we also measure more mundane, though we think very important, influences on judicial behavior, such as effort aversion (which includes but is not exhausted in leisure preference), that are predicted by our labor-economics model of judicial incentives and constraints. Effort aversion includes both reluctance to work "too" hard—that is leisure preference—and reluctance to quarrel with colleagues (conflict aversion). Both are aspects of the "quiet life" that is especially valued by persons in jobs that offer little upward mobility—and in the case of a federal judgeship involve virtually no downward mobility—and few opportunities for increasing their pecuniary income other than by quitting and, in the case of judges, having quit, going into the private practice of law.

Regarding the appellate tiers—the Supreme Court and the courts of appeals—we explore in addition a variety of social or collegial phenomena that may influence judicial votes, such as conformity (an aspect of conflict aversion—the desire to "go along"), group polarization (the tendency of a faction to become more extreme as it grows relative to other factions—the opposite of the conformity effect), and what we call political polarization (the tendency, distinct from group polarization, for an increase in the size of one factional group to produce more extreme voting by all the factions). Relations with coworkers are an important influence on workplace behavior—and remember that we're treating courts as workplaces.

In the case of the Supreme Court (chapter 3), we find that our evaluation of ideology, utilizing several measures, tracks pretty closely what "everyone knows" is the ideological rank order of the Justices who served between the 1937 and 2009 terms, the period to which we limit our study. Consistent with many other studies, we find that Justices appointed by Republican Presidents vote more conservatively on average than Justices appointed by Democratic ones, with the difference being most pronounced in civil rights cases and least pronounced in federalism, privacy, and judicial power cases. These findings support the realist understanding that many cases that reach the Supreme Court tend both to be highly charged politically and to be indeterminate from a legalist standpoint, forcing the Justices back on their priors—which often have an ideological component—to resolve the case.

We find that the ideology of some Justices changes during their time on the Court. They may become more liberal or more conservative than when they were appointed (we follow the previous literature on judicial behavior in calling this "ideological drift") or relative to the ideology of the President who appointed them. The second phenomenon, which we dub "ideological divergence," shows that Justices aren't merely agents of the President who appointed them—which is no surprise, because once appointed they are free from any control by him.

The chapter includes a separate analysis of the Court's unanimous decisions, a subject that the existing literature has rather neglected. Unanimity in an ideologically divided court, as the Supreme Court is and has been, has been thought to undermine the theory that the Court's decisions are ideologically driven. We interpret the substantial percentage of unanimous decisions—more than 30 percent—to mean that the ideological stakes in many of the Court's cases are small enough to be overcome by mild dissent aversion of Justices; and yet we find that discernible traces of ideological influence do remain in those decisions.

We look for group effects in the Court—and do not find any. Members of a liberal or conservative minority on the Court are no more likely to go along with the majority if the majority grows. That is, we find no conformity effect, common in many workplaces, where a worker who bucks the office consensus may find himself ostracized. We attribute its absence to the absence of strong dissent aversion in the Court, as well as to the Justices' secure tenure and (with exceptions, none recent) lack of ambition for higher office, which encourages greater independence than in an ordinary workplace. We find no group polarization or political polarization effects, either; these absences may also be related to the Justices' secure tenure.

In analyzing the courts of appeals, in chapter 4, we find that the judges of these courts are less ideological than Supreme Court Justices on average, but not that ideology plays a negligible role in their decisions. Because the ideological stakes are greater in Supreme Court than in court of appeals decisions (the courts of appeals have a mandatory jurisdiction, and as a result can't insist on a diet of ideologically charged cases and anyway don't have the last word in such cases, or indeed in any cases that the Supreme Court might decide to hear if the losing party petitioned for certiorari), and because the courts of appeals have heavier workloads than the Supreme Court, we expect effort aversion to play a greater role. Effort aversion further reduces the influence of ideology by placing a premium on unanimity, which reduces effort (no dissents, and no revision of majority opinions to counter dissents) both in time and in strained relations among judges. We thus attribute panel composition effects—the well-documented tendency of the ideological direction of a court of appeals judge's votes to be influenced by the opposing ideology of another judge, or other judges, on the panel—in part to dissent aversion, as explained at length in chapter 6.

We also find a conformity effect, which is the other side of dissent aversion, in the courts of appeals. As a result, there is a double effect when a judge appointed by a President of one party is replaced by a judge appointed by a President of the other party (the party of the appointing

President being a proxy for the appointee's ideology) and the newly appointed judge is part of the majority bloc on the court. If, for example, in a court in which the majority consists of judges appointed by Republican Presidents, a more conservative judge replaces a less conservative one, the majority bloc will vote more conservatively, of course—but so will the minority.

Also in chapter 4 we use a new method of assessing the ex ante ideology of federal judges (the ideology they bring with them to the court, before they begin to hear cases) and compare it with their ex post ideology (the ideological direction of their judicial votes). We apply the method both to court of appeals judges and, for the sake of comparison, to Supreme Court Justices as well. We find substantially greater divergence between ex ante and ex post ideology in the courts of appeals and attribute it to the greater influence of legalistic considerations in those courts. The weightier such considerations are, the less likely a judge of conservative inclinations is to vote consistently conservatively or a judge of liberal inclinations consistently liberally.

Federal district courts, the subject of chapter 5, are the trial level of the federal judiciary, though nowadays the vast majority of their cases are decided without a trial and often without any significant judicial proceedings, being settled or abandoned early in the litigation. Cases in these courts, unlike cases in the courts of appeals, are unfiltered, whereas the courts of appeals hear only cases that a party who lost in the district court has chosen to appeal.[10] District courts therefore hear a higher percentage of cases that can be disposed of readily by the application of legalist concepts than courts of appeals do. Indeed, a high percentage of cases filed in the district courts lack even arguable merit.

Moreover, legalist concepts such as standing, ripeness, and mootness, and doctrines that allow early dismissal of weak cases, are designed in part to reduce judicial workloads (for the concepts have largely been created by judges), and workloads are heavier in trial courts than in appellate courts. So we expect those concepts to play a greater role in decision-

---

10. The courts of appeal also hear cases that originate in administrative agencies and are appealed directly to the court of appeals, skipping the district courts—immigration and many labor cases, for example.

making in the district courts than in the courts of appeals or the Supreme Court. And so we find, and conclude that there is indeed less ideology in district court decision-making than in that of either of the higher levels of the federal judiciary.

We relate this phenomenon to the concept in organization theory of "management by exception," whereby the simplest questions are answered at the bottom of a decisional hierarchy and only the most difficult at the top. In the case of the federal judiciary, this implies that the role of ideology in decisions will increase as cases rise through the judicial hierarchy from the district court to the Supreme Court. Because both the district courts and the courts of appeals have a mandatory rather than a discretionary jurisdiction, they decide (the district courts particularly) a great many one-sided cases. The Supreme Court decides more evenly balanced—typically because they are more indeterminate legalistically—cases than the courts of appeals because the Court's decisional capacity is so limited in relation to the number of decisions by those courts and also by state courts, which decide many cases that involve a federal issue that the losing party might want to raise in the U.S. Supreme Court. Also, legalistically indeterminate cases tend to give rise to conflicts between federal courts of appeals, and only the Supreme Court can resolve those conflicts.

The contrast between the federal appellate tiers is especially pronounced in criminal cases. Most criminal appeals are by defendants rather than by the government, are subsidized, and are so lacking in merit that even liberal court of appeals judges usually vote to affirm. The Supreme Court hears criminal appeals only if they have substantial merit. Thus we expect and find that the fraction of conservative votes (a vote to uphold a criminal conviction is scored as a conservative vote) is substantially higher in courts of appeals than in the Supreme Court, even in the case of court of appeals judges appointed by Democratic Presidents.

Yet mention of criminal cases suggests a possible objection to the proposition that the ideological influence in judicial decisions increases as one moves from the lowest to the highest rung of the judicial hierarchy. Sentencing is traditionally an area of almost untrammeled exercise of discretion by district judges—a discretion that was, it is true, curtailed by the Sentencing Reform Act of 1984 but that has largely been restored by the

Supreme Court. Appellate review of many other types of ruling by district judges is also supposed to be deferential.

To the extent that appellate judges defer to district court rulings, we might expect district judges to have the scope and inclination to engage in ideological decision-making. We test this hypothesis in chapter 5 but find only limited support for it, even with regard to sentencing, where the decision-making autonomy of the district judge is at its highest. We attribute this negative finding to the fact that many appellate judges accord only quite limited discretion to district court rulings, and this in turn triggers reversal aversion by district judges—they cannot be confident that the appellate court will defer to an ideologically colored exercise of discretion by them.

The last three chapters, like the section of chapter 5 that discusses the judicial hierarchy, deal with topics that cut across two or even all three tiers of the federal judiciary, although data availability limits our analysis in chapter 7 to the Supreme Court.

Chapter 6 analyzes the phenomenon of dissent in both the Supreme Court and the courts of appeals. We stress the existence and significance of a reluctance by some judges to dissent publicly even when they disagree with their colleagues' decision. Dissent aversion is an example of a behavior that neither legalism nor legal realism in its jurisprudential sense can explain, but that a richer model of judicial incentives and constraints—our model, emphasizing effort aversion—can.

We find pronounced dissent aversion in the courts of appeals but not in the Supreme Court. We trace this difference to differences in the size of the appellate panel (nine Justices in the Supreme Court unless there are vacancies or recusals, but except in cases heard en banc three judges at the court of appeals level—and the larger a panel, the likelier disagreement is) and in workload (the Supreme Court's workload is lighter). We show that panel composition and judicial workload (and, as a consequence of workload, adherence to precedent) influence the costs and benefits of dissenting and hence the prevalence of dissent. We also explore, though with rather inconclusive results, the effects of senior status (for which federal judges, depending on how long they have served, are eligible between the ages of 65 and 70 and which allows them to take a lighter caseload without any diminution in pay) and of age on the propensity to dissent, assuming that effort aversion increases with age.

Chapter 7 examines the goals of Supreme Court Justices in questioning lawyers at oral argument. We suggest that those goals are strategic rather than just a matter of trying to get at the truth in order to facilitate legalist decision-making. We relate patterns of questioning at argument to limitations of judicial deliberation, to personality, and, counterintuitively, to leisure preference. Regarding personality, we consider extroversion a characteristic likely to impel a Justice to ask many questions at oral argument and/or to participate in many public events.

In chapter 8 we study the behavior of federal judges who have a realistic prospect of promotion. Desire for promotion is a significant motivating factor in many workplaces, and federal district judges are not infrequently (though not routinely) promoted to courts of appeals, while court of appeals judges are sometimes, though rarely, promoted to the Supreme Court; at this writing, eight of the nine Supreme Court Justices are former federal court of appeals judges, although they are a tiny minority of all court of appeals judges. We ask whether aspirants for promotion within the judiciary alter their judicial behavior in order to improve their promotion prospects—in other words whether they "audition" for appointment to a higher court. Comparing the voting behavior of court of appeals judges when they are realistically in the promotion pool and thus potential auditioners with their behavior after age eliminates their prospects for promotion and with the behavior of court of appeals judges who were never in the pool, we find that potential auditioners do tend, though only on average, to alter their behavior in order to improve their prospects for appointment to the Supreme Court. We conduct a similar analysis of district judges' auditioning for promotion to the court of appeals, with similar though weaker results. Auditioning behavior by judges is important evidence of the role of self-interest in the judicial utility function.

The conclusion sums up briefly but also suggests a number of promising topics for future study by ourselves or others.

We seek in this book to make four contributions. First, we present and test empirically a more realistic theory of judicial behavior than either the traditional legalist theory—still beloved of the legal professoriat and of the

judiciary in its public-relations mode—or the dominant theory in political science, which exaggerates the ideological component in judicial behavior. Although the bulk of our analysis consists of hypothesis testing by
means of statistical analysis, the hypotheses themselves are generated by
theoretical reflection on likely judicial behavior; the book thus contains a
good deal of interstitial qualitative analysis.

Second, we revise some of the coding of U.S. Supreme Court and (especially) federal court of appeals decisions in the U.S. Supreme Court
Database (which covers the 1946 to 2010 terms)[11] and the U.S. Appeals
Court Database (1925 to 2002).[12] These are the principal databases that
have been used in previous studies, and we use them extensively as well.
We have also updated a dataset created by Sunstein and his colleagues[13]
on the votes of court of appeals judges in ideologically sensitive subject-
matter areas, and we use this dataset in our study, as we do a database of
judicial sentencing in chapter 5 and four databases that we have created
ourselves: an ex ante ideology measure that we use in chapters 3 and 4, a
dismissal dataset that we use in chapter 5, a database of individual court
of appeals judges' dissent rates that we use in chapter 6, and a judges'
background dataset that we use in chapter 8.

Third, we make extensive use of regression analysis, rather than just
simple correlation (though we use simple correlation extensively as well),
to isolate variables that our model predicts should influence judicial behavior in specific ways. Claims about judicial behavior based on simple
correlation are commonly made in law journals and reported in the media, but studies that do not control for potentially relevant variables, as
regression analysis enables us to do, often produce unsound results.[14]

The structure of the federal judiciary facilitates cross-sectional statisti-

11. http://supremecourtdatabase.org (visited Dec. 9, 2011), commonly referred to as the
Spaeth database. The database is updated by its managers at the end of each Supreme Court
term.

12. www.cas.sc.edu/poli/juri/appct.htm (visited Dec. 9, 2011), commonly referred to as
the Songer database.

13. See Cass R. Sunstein, et al., *Are Judges Political? An Empirical Analysis of the Federal
Judiciary* (2006).

14. See Lee Epstein and Gary King, "The Rules of Inference," 69 *University of Chicago
Law Review* 1 (2002)

cal analysis. At both the court of appeals and the district court level, though of course not at the Supreme Court level, the structure is regional (except for the Federal Circuit, which we exclude from our analysis because its case mixture is so different from that of the other courts of appeals). Circuits and districts, while differing from one another in caseload and number of judges and the ideological composition of the court, exhibit sufficient similarities (in mode of appointment and terms of employment, for example) to minimize noise in the data. And because the output of federal judges is contained in public documents almost all of which are online, modern electronic search techniques make it feasible to create and analyze large databases of judicial activity.[15]

The technical introduction that follows this general introduction explains the rudiments of regression analysis. But as it also sets forth some terminological conventions that we employ in the book, even our statistically sophisticated readers will want to read it (it is very short).

A fourth point, related to the comprehensive character of our model of judicial behavior, is that the scope of our analysis is broader than that found in most of the existing literature. That literature is concerned almost exclusively with either votes cast by individual judges or case outcomes, in the Supreme Court and to a lesser extent in the courts of appeals. We too test hypotheses related to voting in these courts, but we study judicial behavior in the federal district courts as well, plus such other dimensions of judicial behavior as opinion length, citations, dissents, and questions asked by Supreme Court Justices at oral argument.

15. All the data used in our statistical analyses are available online at http://widefeetdesigns.com/client/epsteinBook/.

Technical Introduction

THE ANALYSIS IN THIS BOOK is largely though not entirely statistical, and we have thought it might be helpful to introduce at the outset some technical concepts and terms in statistics that may be unfamiliar to many readers.[1] As we emphasize in the general introduction, we want this book to be accessible to judges, lawyers, law professors, law students, and others who are not adept at statistical analysis, as well as to those members of the legal profession who are, and of course to social scientists. We also explain conventions we use to make our analysis at once clear and compact.

A good deal of our analysis involves testing hypotheses about the relations between a dependent variable (what we are trying to explain—for example, the ideological valence of judicial votes) and an independent variable or variables (what our theory suggests may explain the dependent variable—for example, judges' ideological leanings, workloads, and interactions with colleagues). Sometimes we summarize the strength of the relation with a statistic called the correlation coefficient (r) or, more

---

1. For a good, short introduction to statistical analysis (although longer than this glossary), oriented toward the use of such analysis in law, see David Cope, *Fundamentals of Statistical Analysis* (2005).

commonly, r-squared (that is, r multiplied by itself—usually, and by us in this book, written R^2). An r of .5 or, equivalently, an R^2 of .25 between judges' ideology and their votes would indicate that judges' ideology explained 25 percent of the variation in votes.

Multiple regression analysis, which we use extensively, enables the separate effect of each independent variable on the dependent variable to be estimated. Thus we can estimate, for example, whether judges' ideology affects judicial votes separately from the effect of other variables on their votes, such as workload.

Linear Regression

Regression models take various forms. One is linear regression—an equation for determining the straight line that provides the best fit for the data being analyzed. When the regression model perfectly predicts the dependent variable, the R^2 is 1—all the observations fall precisely on the regression line. That is rare, however, because of errors in the data, because in most regressions not all independent variables are identified and included, and because some observations are, for various reasons, idiosyncratic.

The "best fit" in regression analysis is the line that minimizes the sum of the squares of the distance between each data point and the line (that distance is called the "residual"). Why the square rather than the absolute distance? One answer is that least-squares regression is an unbiased estimate of the true regression line, so that as the sample size increases, the coefficients on the independent variables converge to their true value. Also, squaring amplifies the effect of outliers on the regression estimation and so imparts a conservative bias to the estimate.

A regression is easily visualized if the data are two-dimensional—for example, a scatter of points on a graph. The regression line is the straight line the points are closest to, as in Figure TI.1, which regresses salary (the dependent variable) on job experience (the independent variable). The intercept (the point at which the regression line crosses the vertical axis) is 29.9, and thus predicts salary when experience is zero. (In the tables in the book, the term "constant" refers to the value of the dependent

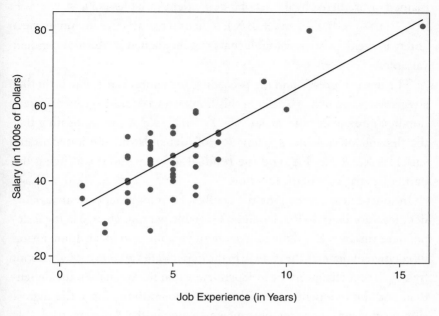

Figure TI.1   Linear Regression

variable at the intercept.) The slope of the regression line is 3.3, meaning that for every additional year of experience the expected increase in salary is $3300 (because salary is in thousands of dollars on the vertical axis). The R^2 is .60 and the correlation is statistically significant at the .05 level of significance, explained below.

A regression line can also be visualized in a three-dimensional scatter; think of a straight line through a cube. People cannot visualize more than three dimensions, but a linear regression can determine the straight line that minimizes the sum of the squared residuals (the square of the distances of the data points from the regression line) in a multidimensional scatter of data.

We can write a regression equation as $Y = a + b_1X_1 + b_2X_2 + B_3X_3 + \ldots + B_tX_t + u$, where Y is the dependent variable, a is the intercept, the X's are independent variables, the b's are the regression coefficients of the independent variables (that is, numbers indicating the relation between a dependent variable and an independent variable), and u is the regression residual—the part of the dependent variable that is not explained or predicted by the set of independent variables (so $u = Y - a + b_1X_1 + b_2X_2 + B_3X_3 + \ldots + B_tX_t$), or in other words the amount of variability in the dependent variable that is not explained by the independent variables.

The linear regression in the preceding paragraph is just one form that a regression can take. Usually in this book we write the regression equation in a more general form, such as $Y = f(X_1, X_2, X_3, u)$, indicating that the dependent variable is a function of (depends on) the independent variables X_1, X_2, and X_3 and the residual u, but without specifying the particular structure of the function.

In most linear regressions the coefficient of an independent variable denotes the change in the dependent variable per unit change in the independent variable. But if the independent variable is in logarithmic form,[2] its coefficient denotes the change in the dependent variable brought about by a 1 percent change in the independent variable. And if both the dependent and the independent variables are in logarithmic form, the regression coefficient equals the percentage change in the dependent variable brought about by a 1 percent change in the independent variable. Either way, the larger the absolute size of the coefficient ("absolute" meaning regardless of whether the coefficient is a positive or a negative number), the bigger the effect of a change in the independent variable on the dependent variable.

The statistical significance of a regression coefficient—which is to say the likelihood that it would not be observed as a matter of pure chance—is important, as is its size. We report the two most widely accepted tests of statistical significance: significance at the .01 level, which we indicate in the tables by two asterisks, and significance at the .05 level, which we indicate by one asterisk. To say that a result is significant at the .05 level is to say (roughly) that the probability that the observed result is attributable to chance alone is 5 percent or less, and at the .01 level that it is 1

---

2. A logarithm is a mathematical device for transforming an exponential number into a nonexponential (linear) number. For example, since $1000 = 10^3$, the log of 1000 = $\log_{10} = 3$, because 3 is the exponent that increases 10 to 1000. The logarithms dealt with in this book transform the exponential term into what is called the natural logarithm (base ≈ 2.71828) as distinct from the base 10 log in our previous example. The natural logarithm of 1000 is 6.91.

percent or less. Often we say that a variable is statistically significant or just that it's significant. This means that the variable is statistically significant at least at the .05 level.

To give a more precise measure of significance, we generally print what is called a "t-statistic" (called a "z-statistic" in logistic regressions, discussed in the next section) in parentheses under the coefficient of each independent variable. The t-statistic is the ratio of the coefficient to its standard error, which is a measure of the variance in the estimated regression coefficient compared to the true value of the coefficient. Ninety-five percent of the data in a normal distribution (that is, a distribution that can be graphed as a bell-shaped curve, where the horizontal axis is a range of characteristics, such as IQ or blood pressure, and the vertical axis is the number of observations of each characteristic in the range) are within 1.96 standard errors of the estimated mean of the distribution. So if the t-statistic is greater than 1.96, this means that there's less than a 5 percent chance that the true value of the estimated regression coefficient is zero. For example, if the coefficient is 4 and the standard error 2, so that 95 percent of the estimated regression coefficients are between 0.08 and 7.92, we can be confident (though of course not certain) that the true coefficient is positive.[3] In some tables we note that we have calculated "robust" standard errors, which adjust for statistical problems that might invalidate ordinary estimation of standard errors.

The tables indicate the results of our statistical analyses even when the results are not statistically significant, for the failure to attain statistical significance in a regression can be *analytically* significant as indicating an absence of reliable support for the hypothesis that the regression was testing. And sometimes two or more independent variables are jointly statistically significant even though none is significant in itself; the implication is that the variables are causally related to the dependent variables, but only when they are, as it were, working together.

---

3. To calculate the 95 percent confidence interval, we first subtract from the mean 1.96 times the standard error to obtain the lower bound. So: $4 - (1.96)(2) = .08$. To obtain the upper bound we add the mean to 1.96 times the standard error, yielding $4 + (1.96)(2) = 7.92$.

Logistic Regression

If the dependent variable that we are interested in explaining is dichoto-mous—for example, whether an appellate judge voted to affirm or to re-verse the lower court decision—linear regression is inappropriate. Instead we use logistic regression. Although there are measures of R^2 for logistic regression, they are all "pseudo" and cannot be interpreted in the same way as in linear regression models. We therefore do not report them. This is not a fatal shortcoming, because in regression analysis we are more in-terested in the effects of the individual independent variables on the de-pendent variable (as measured by their regression coefficients), and whether the independent variables are statistically significant, than in how much of the variance in the data the regression equation as a whole explains.

The coefficient of an independent variable in a logistic regression is the percentage change in the log of the odds ratio. Because these coeffi-cients are harder to interpret than in ordinary linear regressions, we trans-form them into marginal effects—the change in the dependent variable brought about by a unit change in the independent variable. We do this by setting each of the other independent variables equal to its mean value. Since we do this every time we report a logistic coefficient, we will not repeat each time that we are doing it. These marginal effects reported for logit regressions are comparable in terms of units and magnitudes to the coefficients in linear regressions.

The meaning of the constant term is obscure in logistic regression, and anyway it disappears when we present marginal effects. There can be no change in the dependent variable as a result of change in the constant term, because that term, unlike the independent variables, by definition does not change (that's what "constant" means).

In estimating a logistic regression, we are interested in the probability of one of two possible outcomes—for example, whether the probabil-ity that a court of appeals judge having certain characteristics that enter the regression equation as independent variables will or will not be ap-pointed to the Supreme Court. We report these probabilities ("predicted probabilities," they are called, because they are predicted from the regres-sion equation) where relevant to our analysis, but they are not observable in the tables.

Miscellaneous Points

1. In our linear regressions we sometimes calculate an expected value for the dependent variable by varying one of the independent variables while holding the other independent variables constant at their means. Again, we won't bother to repeat the qualification ("holding the other independent variables constant at their means") every time we vary an independent variable.

2. Many of our independent variables are "dummy" variables; that is, they are dichotomous and hence coded as 1 and 0—for example, 1 might be conservative and 0 might be liberal, defined as not conservative. The regression coefficient then equals the change in the dependent variable as the independent variable changes from 0 to 1 (a one-unit change).

When a variable is broken up into a set of dummy variables, as when the different regional circuits of the federal courts of appeals are each treated as a separate dummy variable (for example, 1 = Second Circuit and 0 = not Second Circuit, and a similar dummy for the Third Circuit, and so on), one of the variables is left out of the regression equation, with the result that the coefficients of the other variables indicate their relation to that one. (We always indicate which variable has been omitted from the set of dummy variables.) Sometimes the effects of one or more dummy variables in a series of such variables, such as circuit dummies, are not statistically significant but the group or subgroup of dummies taken as a whole has a statistically significant effect on the dependent variable; in that event the dummies in the group or subgroup are jointly significant.

3. Sometimes we aggregate—that is, treat a body of data as if it were a single datum. For example, if we're interested in a judge's ideological consistency over time, it would be misleading to treat each of his votes as a separate independent observation—that would create an exaggerated picture of the consistency of his voting, because most of his votes would be chronologically proximate to each other. Instead we average his votes over one term of court and treat that average as a single observation.

A related technique is clustering. We might treat each vote as a separate dependent variable rather than aggregating them into one variable, but then in estimating the standard errors of the regression coefficients cluster the observations by judge. (Thus aggregation is done before the regression is estimated and clustering is done as part of the estimation.) By reducing the number of separate observations in calculating standard errors, clustering produces higher standard errors and therefore lower estimates of statistical significance—and rightly so, for otherwise we would fool ourselves into thinking that we had many more independent observations than we do.

4. We try to avoid a potential confusion between the level of a probability and a change in that probability. Suppose the probability that judges appointed by Republican Presidents will vote for a particular outcome is 40 percent; then something happens and it rises to 45 percent. In one sense that is an increase of 5 percent, but in another and more meaningful sense it is an increase of 12.5 percent (.05/.40)—the percentage increase relative to the base probability. To avoid confusion we express a change in probability by fractions rather than percentages. So in the example we would say that the probability had increased by .05, signifying a 12.5 percent increase over the base percentage.

5. In tables we often carry fractions to three decimal places and in text often round them off to two.

CHAPTER 1

A Realistic Theory of Judicial Behavior

Judicial responsibility . . . connotes the recurring choice of one policy over another.

—Roger J. Traynor[1]

The courts must address themselves in some instances to issues of social policy, not because this is particularly desirable, but because often there is no feasible alternative.

—Henry J. Friendly[2]

IN A RECENT BOOK one of us listed and summarized nine theories of judicial behavior,[3] but then proceeded to integrate them into a single theory, that of the judge as a participant in a labor market—that is, as a worker.[4] That is the approach we take in this book to creating a model of judicial behavior that generates hypotheses testable with data.

What kind of worker is a judge? Well, he is not a freelance writer, a proprietor, a composer or other independent artist, or an entrepreneur; he is a government employee. In economic terms he is an agent; the government is the principal. To understand an agent's behavior requires understanding his incentives and constraints, some personal and others imposed by the principal.

1. "The Limits of Judicial Creativity," 63 *Iowa Law Review* 1, 12 (1977).
2. "The Courts and Social Policy: Substance and Procedure," 33 *University of Miami Law Review* 21 (1978).
3. Richard A. Posner, *How Judges Think*, ch. 1 (2008).
4. Id., ch. 2.

Empirical research cannot be conducted in a vacuum. The researcher has to have an idea of what facts about a matter are interesting, and theory may help him to identify those facts. We think the most fruitful theory to guide empirical study of judicial behavior is one of self-interested behavior, broadly understood, in a labor-market setting. Our premise is that judges, at least in case law systems, which are characteristic of nations that derive their legal system from England, are not calculating machines. Judges in a system that allows them a good deal of discretion, by granting them (in the case of federal judges) secure tenure but not providing rules of decision that make judging the mechanical application of rules to facts in all cases, are best understood as imperfect agents of a diffuse principal.

Three Concepts of Legal Realism

It has long been understood that American judges exercise, at least occasionally (and at the Supreme Court level much more than occasionally), a legislative or policymaking role, as acknowledged by Henry Friendly and Roger Traynor, the authors of the epigraphs that open this chapter. They were two of the most distinguished American judges of the modern era, and the passages we quoted state a position that was orthodox when they wrote them. Similar passages could be quoted from distinguished predecessors of Friendly and Traynor, such as Oliver Wendell Holmes, Louis Brandeis, Benjamin Cardozo, Learned Hand, and Robert Jackson, from leading academics and practitioners, and from presidents such as Franklin Roosevelt and philosophers such as John Dewey. The antecedents go as far back as Plato's dialogues, before there was a legal profession. In the *Apology* Socrates notes that each judge (really juror—there were no professional judges) "has sworn that he will judge according to the laws and not according to his own good pleasure"—but in *Gorgias* Socrates predicted that his trial would be the equivalent of the trial of a doctor prosecuted by a cook before a jury of children, and in the *Republic* Thrasymachus powerfully argues that justice is simply the will of the stronger. That is a common view of the legislative process (and therefore a view likely to be descriptive of judges when they exercise legislative powers), memorably articulated and embraced by Holmes when he said, "All that can be expected from modern improvements is that legislation should easily and quickly, yet not too quickly, modify itself in accordance with the will of the *de facto* supreme power in the community. . . . The more powerful interests must be more or less reflected in legislation, which, like every other device of man or beast, must tend in the long run to aid the survival of the fittest."[5]

The first full articulation of the realist conception of judging can be found in Jeremy Bentham's *Introduction to the Principles of Morals and Legislation* (1780). A century later Holmes gave it a slogan on the first page of his book *The Common Law* (1881): "The life of the law has not been logic; it has been experience." The same conception was articulated by Cardozo and Roscoe Pound, and by the self-described legal realists of the 1920s and 1930s, such as Jerome Frank and Karl Llewellyn, and it has been refined by political scientists, economists, psychologists, and sociologists, and also by lawyers—increasingly, law professors who have degrees in other fields as well as in law—who adopt a social-scientific approach to law.

Every competent observer knows that American judges at the appellate level create rules of law, both explicitly in common law fields and implicitly by interpretation of constitutional and statutory provisions, and that this is inevitable, given the nature of American government. Not only constitutional law—obviously—but also antitrust law, labor law, securities law, pension law, and so on are largely the result of discretionary judgments made by judges. That is why confirmation hearings for federal judges are often so contentious, why judicial elections (common at the state level) attract large campaign contributions, and why proposals to make state judges appointed rather than elected are strongly opposed. Judges like to refer to Congress and the Presidency as the "political branches" of government, implying self-servingly that the judiciary is apolitical. That is almost true if "politics" is equated with partisan politics, but it should not be. Decisions influenced by a political ideology are political, and many judicial decisions are so influenced.

The term "legal realism" is sometimes used to denote a jurisprudential approach rather than judicial behavior as such—a jurisprudential approach that has regard only for the consequences of a decision for the parties to the case before the court, and thus that ignores systemic conse-

5. Anonymous [Oliver Wendell Holmes, Jr.], "The Gas-Stokers' Strike," 7 *American Law Review* 582, 583 (1873).

quences, such as the effect on the efficacy of law if precedent, clear statutory text, or other conventional sources of legal meaning are disregarded. Legal realism so regarded is a brand of shortsighted pragmatism that inflects the consequences for the parties with the judge's political preferences or personal sentiments. Legal realism in this sense has strongly influenced the approach of political scientists to judicial behavior—naturally; political scientists are students of politics and study government agencies and officials as political organs and actors, and judges are government officials.

The defensible realisms—realism about the judge as a human being exercising discretionary authority, and realism as a jurisprudential theory that emphasizes the judge's legislative or policymaking role (the indefensible concept of judicial realism is the assumption that judicial behavior in the American system is guided *entirely* by political, religious, sentimental, or other personal, subjective factors)—are linked. If the judge has to exercise discretion, implying that he cannot in all cases just mechanically apply rules to facts to yield a decision (even assuming unrealistically that fact-finding, at least, is mechanical and unproblematic), then to decide a case he is bound sometimes to have to fall back on intuitions of policy; and often they will be intuitions generated by ideology. He cannot just throw up his hands and refuse to decide a case on the ground that the "law" in some narrow sense yields no clue to how to decide.

But it would be more precise to describe judicial decision-making in areas in which mechanical application of rules that have been given to rather than made up by judges is infeasible as subjective rather than as ideological, because nonlegalistic factors other than ideology influence decisions, such as the judge's mood, his energy,[6] his idiosyncratic reaction to the parties or their lawyers, or his lack of interest in the case. Ideology (or, more broadly, "values") may be the subjective influence on judges that is most significant for the society, but other subjective influences should not be ignored and we do not ignore them, but have called in economics to help us understand them.

6. A study of parole decisions by Israeli judges found that the judges were more favorable to parole applicants early in the day and after their food breaks. Apparently the judges tire as the day wears on, as do most workers. Shai Danziger, Jonathan Levav, and Liora Avnaim, "Extraneous Factors in Judicial Decisions," 108 *Proceedings of the National Academy of Sciences* 6889 (2011).

Economics has already contributed to the development of a realistic theory of judicial behavior by emphasizing the judge as a rational actor—a maker of rational choices—in the standard economic sense.[7] In this theory the ideological and the legalist approaches to deciding cases are not posited, but instead are derived from a judicial utility function—a model of rational response to preferences and aversions not limited to legalism and ideology. This book refines and extends that approach.

Other social-scientific research on judicial behavior has tended to be empirical to the virtual exclusion of theory—in other words, it has tended to lack "microfoundations." It has tended to posit, rather than to derive from a utility function, such propositions as that the goal of Supreme Court Justices is to produce outcomes that coincide with the Justices' ideological preferences, which the Justices can do because they control their docket, have life tenure, are not subject to reversal by a higher court, and are not ambitious for higher office, and so, being minimally constrained, can pursue that goal by voting in cases in accordance with their ideological preferences.[8] That is too simple an account of the Justices' behavior, because it neglects factors that deflect Justices from the wholehearted pursuit of their goals.

An empirical literature adds complexity by emphasizing the strategic

---

7. See Matthew C. Stephenson, "Legal Realism for Economists," *Journal of Economic Perspectives* 191 (Spring 2009); Posner, *How Judges Think*, note 3 above; Gilat Levy, "Careerist Judges and the Appeals Process," 36 *RAND Journal of Economics* 275 (2005); Ahmed E. Taha, "Publish or Paris? Evidence of How Judges Allocate Their Time," 6 *American Law and Economics Review* 1 (2004); Gordon R. Foxall, "What Judges Maximize: Toward an Economic Psychology of the Judicial Utility Function," 25 *Liverpool Law Review* 177 (2004); Andrew F. Daughety and Jennifer F. Reinganum, "Stampede to Judgment: Persuasive Influence and Herding Behavior by Courts," 1 *American Law and Economics Review* 158, 165–167 (1999); Christopher R. Drahozal, "Judicial Incentives and the Appeals Process," 51 *SMU Law Review* 469 (1998); Thomas J. Miceli and Metin M. Coşgel, "Reputation and Judicial Decision-Making," 23 *Journal of Economic Behavior and Organization* 31 (1994); Richard A. Posner, "What Do Judges and Justices Maximize? (The Same Thing Everybody Else Does)," 3 *Supreme Court Economic Review* 1 (1993); Richard S. Higgins and Paul H. Rubin, "Judicial Discretion," 9 *Journal of Legal Studies* 129 (1980). Cf. Frederick Schauer, "Incentives, Reputation, and the Inglorious Determinants of Judicial Behavior," 68 *University of Cincinnati Law Review* 615 (2000).

8. These are the basic premises of the "attitudinal" model of judicial behavior, as influentially articulated in Jeffrey A. Segal and Harold J. Spaeth, *The Supreme Court and the Attitudinal Model Revisited* 92–94 (2002). We discuss that model in the next chapter.

interactions of judges (including Supreme Court Justices) who are connected either collegially (as members of the same appellate court or panel) or hierarchically (as lower court and higher court judges). We examine those issues in this book but set others aside, such as "strategic retirement"—the idea that Justices accelerate or delay their retirement in order to maximize the probability that their successors will be ideologically akin to them.[9] We also set aside strategic interaction between the courts (especially the U.S. Supreme Court) and other branches of government. The Constitution creates a system of checks and balances among the branches, and the courts both engage in and are subject to checking and balancing. To keep this book within reasonable bounds we do not discuss that form of judicial strategizing, though in the next chapter we cite some of the pertinent literature.

Political scientists were the first social scientists to study judicial behavior; economists, and academic lawyers influenced by economics, are Johnny-come-latelies. Although some of the political science literature now borrows from economics, we'll see that economics can further enrich political science by relating political behavior by judges to incentives and constraints, in the spirit of economic analysis of rational behavior, and by doing so can enable, among other things, a more precise understanding of the role and character of ideology in the behavior of American judges.

The Labor-Market Theory of Judicial Behavior

Consider the benefits and costs of work as they appear to a worker. Rarely are they only pecuniary. A worker will care about what he is paid, of course, but a paycheck is not the full measure of a worker's "income" in a real as distinct from a solely pecuniary sense of that word. Nor are readily

9. The subject of an inconclusive scholarly literature. See, for example, Albert Yoon, "Pensions, Politics, and Judicial Tenure," 8 *American Law and Economics Review* 143 (2006); David C. Nixon and J. David Haskin, "Judicial Retirement Strategies—The Judge's Role in Influencing Party Control of the Appellate Courts," 28 *American Politics Quarterly* 458 (2000); Deborah J. Barrow and Gary Zuk, "An Institutional Analysis of Turnover in the Lower Federal Courts, 1900–1987," 52 *Journal of Politics* 457 (1990); Peverill Squire, "Politics and Personal Factors in Retirement from the United States Supreme Court," 10 *Political Behavior* 180 (1988).

monetizable fringe benefits such as health insurance and a pension the only components of real income besides wages. Some benefits of work are difficult to monetize, such as tenure or other forms of job security. Others have no monetary dimension at all, unlike job tenure, which affects expected earnings. Nonmonetizable benefits, which are important in jobs such as a judgeship that attract persons who could generally earn more money in a different branch of the legal profession, include the intrinsic interest of the work and the power or prestige and pride or self-esteem (for example, the sense of satisfaction at being employed in a socially useful job) that the job confers on him. The social dimension of work—interactions with colleagues, staff (for example, law clerks), and customers (lawyers and litigants are rough analogs, in judicial work, of customers—though not of customers who can invoke the slogan "The customer is always right")—can also be a source of pleasure, though also of pain. Promotion prospects may be important too; the value of a job to a worker includes the prospect of higher pay or more satisfying work as he climbs the promotion ladder. And for judges, as for some other classes of public employee, there is the "revolving door" option to consider.

And the costs of work? One cost—the risk of losing one's job (and perhaps having great difficulty finding another, comparable one) or of suffering a pay cut—is just the obverse of the benefit of job security, which eliminates or reduces such risks. Other costs of work include the forgone value of leisure, the expenditure of energy in working, and adverse working conditions, such as long commutes or heavy travel (except for court of appeals judges in some of the circuits that embrace a large geographical region), boring or physically strenuous or even dangerous work, and criticism by superiors or members of the public. Leisure preference can make work costly in nonpecuniary terms by increasing the opportunity costs of work (the benefits of leisure that are forgone when one is working). So can effort aversion (the desire for a "quiet life"), which is a broader concept. Effort aversion is affected not only by hours worked but also by the intensity of the work—the effort invested in it—plus anything else that makes it harder or less agreeable, such as physical or emotional strain. Like the nonpecuniary satisfactions of work, effort aversion can be expected to play a particularly large role in the utility function of a securely tenured worker—such as a federal judge—who can slack off without paying a heavy penalty.

The obverse of fruitful relations with colleagues are tense, competitive, even antagonistic ones. These are not uncommon in appellate courts (the relations of the members of which have been analogized to arranged marriage with no divorce option), but they are minimized in the federal courts of appeals by clever rules governing the power structure within the court. One is the role assigned to seniority in the allocation of power. The court's chief judge is neither elected nor appointed; he is simply whichever judge in active service (that is, not yet a senior-status judge[10]) has served longest on the court but is not yet 65. (He can refuse the appointment, and if so the next most senior active-service judge is offered it.) Therefore judges do not scheme or campaign to become chief judge, which would cause bruised feelings.[11] In addition, the judge who presides at oral argument and therefore assigns the majority opinion (and thus occupies a position of modest power vis-à-vis the other judges on the panel) is, again, simply the active judge who has served the longest of any of the judges on the panel (unless the chief judge is on the panel, in which event he presides).

Determining who is chief judge strictly on the basis of seniority means that he or she often will not be the best person for the job. The response to this problem has been to limit chief judges to a nonrenewable seven-year term (which probably should be shorter, however). The system thus trades off competence against the danger of infighting, which is acute in a system in which the members of a group, who must work together, are chosen by different appointing authorities (different Presidents, often of different parties and different ideologies) on the basis of differing criteria, serve long terms, and are subject to very little in the way of discipline. Holmes likened the Supreme Court Justices to nine scorpions in a bottle.

The rational worker will want to have as great a surplus of benefits

10. Federal judges, upon reaching the age of 65 with 15 years of service or 70 with 10, have the option of taking "senior status," which allows them to work part-time at full pay, in lieu of retirement (also at full pay).

11. The method of appointing chief district judges is the same. In contrast, the Chief Justice of the United States (who is of course the chief judge of the Supreme Court, though he also has administrative responsibilities with respect to the entire federal judiciary) is appointed by the President when the position becomes vacant, rather than being selected automatically on the basis of seniority.

from work over costs as he can obtain. This may require him to make difficult tradeoffs—for example, between on the one hand money and satisfactions generated by a job that requires long hours of work and high risks of failure and on the other hand leisure and avoidance of stress; or between a job that promises riches but obscurity and a job that pays much less but confers power and the possibility of a measure of fame. The employer has a different objective—to maximize the worker's net contribution to the value of the employer's output. Insofar as that contribution is positively related to the costliness of working to the worker (for example, to how hard he works) and negatively related to the worker's expense to the employer, there is a conflict of interest. The employer will want to adopt rules and practices intended to align the worker's incentives with the employer's. The worker will resist—sometimes successfully, as when the workplace is unionized, or when management and ownership are divided, as in large publicly traded corporations, whose top executives frequently are overcompensated in the sense that their services could be bought more cheaply if only the shareholders controlled hiring and compensation.

These principal-agent tensions are present in all jobs, including that of a judge. They may seem, and indeed may be, particularly acute in the federal judiciary, because many of the traditional ways in which principals seek to align their agents' incentives with their own have been taken off the table in the interest of assuring the judges' independence not only from the other branches of government but also from the other judges. Federal judges[12] cannot be fired, or even forced to retire, except for egregious misconduct or complete inability to perform. They cannot be demoted, either, and their pay cannot be docked. Nor do they receive bonuses for superior performance; the only raises permitted are uniform raises for all the judges of the same rank.[13]

---

12. We limit our attention to Article III judges—that is, judges who are confirmed by the Senate for life—and thus exclude other federal judicial officers: bankruptcy judges, magistrate judges, administrative law judges (including immigration judges), and members of administrative boards that review the decisions of administrative law judges.

13. There are only four ranks in the case of Article III judges: district judge, circuit judge (that is, court of appeals judge), Associate Justice of the Supreme Court, and Chief Justice of the United States. Chief judges of courts of appeals and district courts are not a separate grade

A higher court can reverse decisions by a lower court but has no control over that court's personnel, budget, or other management functions. The judges of the district courts and courts of appeals thus don't "work for" the Supreme Court, though they are subordinate to it. It's as if in a private company the only authority of one's boss were to correct one's work. And as we've said, authority within the federal courts is determined by seniority rather than by decisions made by superiors.

It may seem from this description that the "agents" in the federal judiciary (that is, the judges) are completely autonomous and so might as well be considered the real principals. Not so. Some behavioral constraints are imposed on judges by their principal—a collective principal consisting of the appointing authorities, the judges' judicial superiors, and, to a degree, their colleagues; members of the legislative and executive branches of government; and even the public—the ultimate principal in democratic government. (Franklin Roosevelt's unsuccessful Court-packing plan is the *locus classicus* of a power struggle involving the Supreme Court, Congress, the President, and the general public.[14]) There are also constraints that would operate on judges even if they were principals (realistically, they are semiprincipals) rather than agents. We have mentioned professional criticism, which includes criticism by other judges, who may or may not be the judicial superiors of the judge they are criticizing, and criticism by lawyers, law professors, and journalists. The possibility of such criticism, along with the other constraints that we have discussed, affects a judge's labor-leisure tradeoff. A judge can work at a leisurely pace or intensely. If the leisurely pace, by reducing the quality or quantity of a judge's work, generates criticism, the judge may decide to shift his effort-leisure boundary closer to the effort end of the spectrum.

Organization theorists discuss the creation of a "high commitment" culture as a method of motivating agents when the usual incentives and constraints are inoperative—a way of getting the agents to identify with

---

because, unlike the Chief Justice vis-à-vis the Associate Justices, they aren't paid more than the other judges of their courts.

14. For an excellent treatment, see Jeff Shesol, *Supreme Power: Franklin Roosevelt vs. the Supreme Court* (2010). For an empirical analysis of the public's response to the Court-packing plan, see Gregory A. Caldeira, "Public Opinion and the U.S. Supreme Court: FDR's Court-Packing Plan," 81 *American Political Science Review* 1139 (1987).

the mission.[15] The professional military is a high-commitment culture. The judiciary has long aspired to be (or, cynics would say, pretended to be) one. Borrowing from the myth that ermines would rather die than get their lovely white fur dirty, English judges trimmed their robes with ermine to signify purity.

Consistent with endeavoring to create a high-commitment culture in the federal judiciary, the White House generally attempts (though within limits defined by politics) to recruit persons who will be highly committed to their judicial job. Candidates for a federal judgeship undergo an elaborate screening process, in conformity with the economic principle that where it is difficult to evaluate the quality of a producer's output, the buyer will perforce scrutinize the quality of the producer's inputs. That is the basis on which a person might choose a surgeon or a lawyer and it is one reason why federal judging is a lateral-entry career. As we'll see in chapter 8, a federal judge is rarely appointed before the age of 40, and often he is in his fifties and occasionally even in his early sixties. He will have had a substantial career in another branch of the legal profession and thus have acquired habits of work and demonstrated traits of character that provide some evidence that he will perform the duties of his judicial office competently.

The threat of reversal by a higher court, and in extreme cases of discipline (usually in the form of a reprimand, but in cases of criminal conduct or abandonment of office, removal by impeachment by the House of Representatives and conviction by the Senate or, in the case of incapacity, removal by a circuit's judicial council), is a constraint. As are professional criticism and even public opinion; for as tenured academics know, when the heavier constraints of termination or demotion are inoperative with respect to an employee, the lighter constraint of criticism can weigh heavily.

There is also the carrot of promotion—promotion of district judges to the court of appeals and of court of appeals judges to the Supreme Court. About 11 percent of district judges are promoted to the courts of appeals, a percentage high enough to influence a district judge's behavior if he as-

15. See, for example, John Roberts, *The Modern Firm: Organizational Design for Performance and Growth* 173–176 (2004).

pires to be a court of appeals judge. Not all district judges do, though the
pay is slightly higher, the staff slightly larger, the prestige slightly greater
(because there are many fewer court of appeals judges than there are district judges), threats by angry litigants fewer, and the work somewhat less
demanding.

Although the probability that a court of appeals judge will be promoted to the Supreme Court may seem minuscule, this is misleading.
Most court of appeals judges, whether because of advanced age or other
disqualifying characteristics, have no chance of being promoted. A small
number are realistically eligible; each of them has a probability of promotion that, while still low, is not minuscule, at least in recent decades, when
most Supreme Court Justices have been former federal court of appeals
judges. The 11 percent figure for promotion from the district court to the
court of appeals similarly underestimates the promotion prospects of the
subset of district judges who are plausible candidates for promotion. We
test the effect of promotion prospects on the behavior of federal judges in
chapter 8. We study whether they wait for lightning to strike or audition
for a star role.

We expect leisure preference to play a greater role in judicial than in
most other employments because of life tenure and the invariability of the
judicial salary to performance. One should not be surprised that the rate
at which federal courts of appeals reversed district courts' judgments in
civil cases fell in the Second and Ninth Circuits, relative to the other circuits, when those circuits (but not the others) were inundated by immigration cases in the early 2000s as a result of efforts by the Justice Department to clear the backlog of immigration cases at the administrative
level.[16] Less time and effort are involved in affirming than reversing a decision, whether by a district court or by an administrative agency such as
the Board of Immigration Appeals. Especially as judges age, and either
their energy wanes or boredom sets in, or they realize that further effort
will do little to alter their career achievements or reputation, we can ex-

---

16. Bert I. Huang, "Lightened Scrutiny," 124 *Harvard Law Review* 1109 (2011). For
other evidence of effort aversion by judges, see Eric Helland and Jonathan Klick, "The Effect
of Judicial Expedience on Attorney Fees in Class Actions," 36 *Journal of Legal Studies* 171
(2007).

pect them to delegate more of their work to law clerks and other staff, and perhaps to dissent less (see the last section of chapter 6), because a dissent is always added work—a judge does not get credit against his opinion-writing assignments by writing dissents.

A possible example of leisure preference is the increasing public extra-judicial activity of Supreme Court Justices. Courts throughout the world publicize their decisions, issue press releases, and maintain websites describing their procedures and publishing their opinions and brief biographies of their members.[17] What is new for the Court are the book tours, mock trials of fictional and historical figures, ethnic pride activities, autobiographies and memoirs, authorized biographies, talks to high school students, debates with each other on television, speechifying all over the world, and even the making of rather unguarded public statements on controversial legal and political issues.[18] "There are no more wallflowers on the Supreme Court."[19] Even as dignified and reserved a Justice as Ruth Bader Ginsburg consented to preside, wearing a Civil War uniform, at a mock public court-martial of General Custer for losing the Battle of the Little Big Horn.[20] In the past, Justices engaged with the media primarily when the Court was embattled, which it is not at present and hasn't been since the Reagan years (and then only mildly).[21] No more. "It seems that

17. Jeffrey K. Staton, *Judicial Power and Strategic Communication* (2010).

18. See Richard Davis, *Justices and Journalists: The U.S. Supreme Court and the Media* (2011). See also Lawrence Baum, *Judges and Their Audiences: A Perspective on Judicial Behavior* (2006); Elliot Slotnick and Jennifer A. Segal, *Television News and the Supreme Court* (1998); William Haltom, *Reporting on the Courts: How the Mass Media Covers Judicial Actions* (1998); Adam Liptak, "Justice Stevens Is Off the Bench But Not Out of Opinions," *New York Times*, May 31, 2011, p. A14; Liptak, "$1.175 Million to Sotomayor for Memoir, Forms Reveal," *New York Times*, May 28, 2011, p. A14; Jess Bravin, "An Ideal Trial?" *Washington Wire*, Apr. 12, 2011, http://blogs.wsj.com/washwire/2011/04/12/an-ideal-trial/ (visited Dec. 9, 2011). See also the discussion in chapter 7 of attention-seeking behavior by Supreme Court Justices.

19. Richard A. Posner, "The Court of Celebrity," *New Republic*, May 26, 2011, pp. 23, 25, reviewing Davis's book, note 18 above.

20. Jess Bravin, "Supreme Night Court: Judges Relax by Trying the Fictitious and the Dead," *Wall Street Journal*, Mar. 14, 2011, p. A1.

21. Some might point to the 2000 decision in *Bush v. Gore,* but the public's confidence in the Court did not drop as a result of the much-criticized decision in favor of Bush. See James L. Gibson, Gregory A. Caldeira, and Lester Kenyatta Spence, "The Supreme Court and the

everywhere you look, you see [a Justice] popping up: giving speeches, signing books, leading workshops, posing for pictures at charity functions. This is what law professors call 'extrajudicial activity,' and we have seen a spate of it lately, not only during the court's summer recesses, when justices fly the marble coop, but throughout the term that began last October and ended this week."[22] In an article about Justice Sotomayor we read that "the substance of what she says and stands for might be familiar, but her style in communicating that substance seem to be making it newly appealing. This bodes well for the liberal wing of the Court, which has been waiting years for an effective voice *to promote its views to the general public.* Here's hoping it has finally found a voice with staying power."[23]

The increase in the Justices' extrajudicial activities has coincided with a decline in their workload as a result of a reduction in the number of cases in which plenary review is granted and of the growth in the size and quality of the Justices' staffs. Both developments have given Justices more time for extrajudicial activity—stated differently, have reduced the opportunity costs of such activity.

Tables 1.1 through 1.3, which are based on the Justices' publicly available financial disclosure forms, give a partial glimpse of the amount of their current public extrajudicial activity.

Leisure preference may figure in judges' creation and embrace of doctrines that limit judicial workloads—doctrines such as harmless error, waiver and forfeiture, political questions, the plain-meaning rule of statu-

---

U.S. Presidential Election of 2000: Wounds, Self-Inflicted or Otherwise?" 33 *British Journal of Political Science* 535 (2003).

22. Jeff Shesol, "Should Justices Keep Their Opinions to Themselves?" *New York Times,* June 29, 2011, p. A21.

23. David Fontana, "Sonia Sotomayor: How She Became the Public Face of the Supreme Court's Liberal Wing," *New Republic Online,* June 29, 2011, www.tnr.com/article/poli tics/91013/sonia-sotomayor-supreme-court-liberal-voice?page=0,1&utm_source=The%20 New%20Republic&utm_campaign=89d7b35af8-TNR_Daily_062911&utm_medium= email (visited Dec. 9, 2011) (emphasis added). Sotomayor has appeared on *Sesame Street.* See "Sesame Street: Sonia Sotomayor: 'The Justice Hears a Case," *YouTube,* www.youtube. com/watch?feature=player_embedded&v=FizspmIJbAw (visited Feb. 7, 2012); "In the Case of Baby Bear v. Goldilocks," *Daily Report, ATLaw,* Jan. 29, 2012, www.atlawblog .com/2012/01/in-the-case-of-baby-bear-v-goldilocks/ (visited Jan. 30, 2012).

Table 1.1 Average Annual Number of Public Nonjudicial Events, by Justice, 2002–2009

Justice (Years on Court between 2002 and 2009)	Average Number of Events per Year	Total Events
Scalia (8)	23.13	185
Breyer (8)	16.50	132
O'Connor (4)	15.75	63
Kennedy (8)	15.00	120
Ginsburg (8)	12.25	98
Thomas (8)	8.38	67
Roberts (4)	8.00	32
Alito (4)	7.25	29
Rehnquist (3)	2.50	5
Stevens (8)	2.25	18
Souter (8)	0.38	3

Note: We exclude Sotomayor, who was not confirmed until August of 2009.

tory interpretation, the adoption of rules in lieu of standards, deferential standards of appellate review, plea bargaining, and, above all, the requirements of standing (federal courts may not adjudicate cases that are moot, may not issue advisory opinions, and so forth) and the principle of adhering to precedent *(stare decisis),* along with the correlative practice of distinguishing precedents (rather than either following them blindly or overruling and replacing them) in order to make the law a more precise and therefore more reliable guide.[24] These practices are big time-savers! For example, it's a lot easier to decide a case because it is materially identical to one previously decided (which might be a case that had distinguished an earlier precedent in an effort to fine-tune the law) than to analyze every new case afresh. Notice too that if appellate judges don't respect precedent, the law is less certain and this results in more appeals—so the appellate judges have more work to do. In chapter 5 we test the hypothesis that district judges with heavier workloads are more likely to accept the Supreme Court's recent invitations (in the *Twombly* and *Iqbal* decisions, discussed in that chapter) to require a plaintiff to conduct a more thorough precomplaint investigation in order defeat a motion to dismiss the complaint. We call these "invitations" rather than "directives" because

24. Nicola Gennaioli and Andrei Shleifer, "The Evolution of Common Law," 115 *Journal of Political Economy* 43 (2007).

Table 1.2   Justices' Total Public Events by Category, 2002–2009

Category	Number of Events	Percent of Events
U.S. Law School Event	311	41.4
U.S. Public Event	38	5.1
U.S. Private Event	270	35.9
International Event	133	17.7
Total	752	100.0

Note: "U.S. Law School Event" denotes events sponsored by law schools in the United States, including moot court competitions, lectures, and classes. "U.S. Public Event" denotes government-sponsored events, mostly speeches to other members of the federal judiciary. "U.S. Private Event" denotes events sponsored by private U.S. organizations, such as bar associations and interest groups. "International Event" denotes events sponsored by foreign governments, universities, or other organizations.

Table 1.3   Justices' Total Public Events by Year, 2002–2009

Justice	2002	2003	2004	2005	2006	2007	2008	2009
Rehnquist	0	2	3	—	—	—	—	—
Stevens	4	1	2	5	2	0	3	1
O'Connor	16	19	28	0	—	—	—	—
Scalia	15	21	15	24	25	33	30	22
Kennedy	15	16	11	16	20	12	19	11
Souter	1	0	0	1	0	0	1	0
Thomas	10	8	8	3	6	16	9	7
Ginsburg	14	14	13	10	10	12	16	9
Breyer	14	13	12	14	22	21	23	12
Roberts	—	—	—	—	6	10	7	9
Alito	—	—	—	—	2	11	11	5
Sotomayor	—	—	—	—	—	—	—	1
Total	89	94	92	73	93	115	119	77

rarely can the defendant appeal the ruling if a judge decides not to dismiss a case, so the case continues on to settlement or final judgment.

The doctrines that we have listed are more than just time-savers. That is why they can't be classified as products just of leisure preference or effort aversion. They are essential to the manageability of the federal judicial system. Because of the pyramidal structure of a judicial system, adding judges would not be an apt response to increased workload. As the bottom of the pyramid expanded, the judges at the top (the Supreme Court Justices), however hardworking, would be overwhelmed unless their number was increased—which would make it more difficult to keep the law coherent—or unless they dealt summarily with their cases, thereby reducing the quality of their output, or unless their jurisdiction was curtailed.

The workload-saving doctrines we've listed are sometimes defended as reducing the role of ideology in the judicial process by reducing the scope of judicial discretion.[25] But the effects of such doctrines are not substantively neutral. Reducing access to federal courts weighs most heavily on persons seeking to expand legal rights, and such expansions generally advance the liberal political agenda; examples are antidiscrimination, prisoner rights, immigrant rights, consumer protection, and environmental litigation.

Moreover, procedural doctrines that reduce judicial workload have only a short-run effect in curbing ideological judging. When the Supreme Court decides a novel case, the lower courts fall into line and dissenting and successor Justices may do so as well; but that does not detract from the novelty of the decision—which is to say that it was not itself based on a mechanical application of existing rules but created a new rule and thus was legislative in character. One has only to compare the existing body of constitutional doctrine with the slim text of the Constitution to see the point. The Supreme Court has *created* constitutional law, despite its embrace of doctrines designed to curtail its discretion as well as limit its workload and that of the lower courts.

A related point is that procedural doctrines (not limited to those designed to reduce judges' workloads or curtail judicial discretion) are not always applied neutrally. Conservative Justices tend to vote to deny plaintiffs seeking a liberal decision standing to sue, and liberal Justices to vote to grant standing to such plaintiffs.[26] Court of appeals judges in ideologi-

25. For evidence that rules indeed reduce the scope of judicial discretion and with it the role of ideology in judging, see Adam B. Cox and Thomas J. Miles, "Judicial Ideology and the Transformation of Voting Rights Jurisprudence," 75 *University of Chicago Law Review* 1493, 1516 (2008).

26. See Nancy Staudt, "Modeling Taxpayer Standing," 79 *New York University Law Review* 612 (2004); Richard J. Pierce, Jr., "Is Standing Law or Politics?" 77 *North Carolina Law Review* 1741 (1999); C. K. Rowland and Bridget Jeffery Todd, "Where You Stand Depends on Who Sits: Platform Promises and Judicial Gatekeeping in the Federal District Courts," 53 *Journal of Politics* 175 (1991); Gregory J. Rathjen and Harold J. Spaeth, "Denial of Access

cally heterogeneous circuits are more likely to invoke procedural limitations to avoid having to rule on the merits of disputes.[27] In chapter 5 we'll
see that even after one controls for the influence of Supreme Court precedent, the district court's workload, and the ideological predisposition of
the appellate judges in the district court's circuit, a district judge's ideological leanings are likely to influence his decision on whether to grant or
deny a motion to dismiss—and such motions usually are filed by defendants aligned with conservative interests.

In private employment the volume of work that an employee is required to do is determined by the employer; in the judiciary it is determined jointly by the "employer"—the elected branches of government,
which determine the number of judges—and by the employees (the
judges), who create rules, both procedural and substantive, for regulating
the volume and complexity of cases and therefore the amount of work per
judge. All the doctrines that we've listed that limit judicial workloads were
created by judges.

An example of an effort-versus-leisure choice that appellate judges
make is whether to write a dissenting opinion. A judge is committed to
writing the majority opinions that are assigned to him (and if he is the as-
signing judge, the norms of equal assignment require him to assign the
same number of opinions to himself as to the other judges). But the decision to write a dissenting opinion is discretionary, and since it requires
effort, we predict that the number of dissenting opinions that a judge
writes will be negatively influenced by effort costs (see chapter 6).

An important form of judicial effort aversion is avoiding the ill will of
one's judicial colleagues—wrangles with colleagues make for a harder job,
thus requiring more effort, than if collegiality reigns. The relation of ill
will to the decision to dissent comes from the fact that a dissent imposes
effort costs on the writer of the majority opinion, who, to hold on to a
majority, may have to revise his opinion to meet the points made by the

and Ideological Preferences: An Analysis of the Voting Behavior of the Burger Court Justices,
1969–1976," in *Studies in U.S. Supreme Court Behavior* 24 (Harold J. Spaeth and Saul
Brenner eds. 1990).

27. Shelley Murphey, "Going Procedural: Conflict Avoidance in the U.S. Courts of Appeals" (Northwestern University School of Law, Oct. 2010),www.law.northwestern.edu/sear
lecenter/papers/MurpheyPPT.pdf. (visited Dec. 9, 2011).

dissent. It is also a criticism of the judges in the majority for adopting a position that the dissent contends is wrong. Neither judges in the majority in a case nor putative dissenters much like dissents, and we infer from this that the number of dissenting opinions will overstate the actual unanimity of judicial opinion concerning the correct outcome of cases.

The desire for a good reputation, like the desire to avoid criticism (which for most judges is really just the obverse of the desire for a good reputation), affects a judge's effort-leisure tradeoff. But it affects another tradeoff as well: the creativity-continuity tradeoff. Judges are expected to maintain a reasonable degree of stability of law by meeting such role expectations as giving substantial weight in their decisions to legislative texts and prior judicial decisions. But they can obtain an enhanced reputation by seasoning their respect for continuity with a dash of creativity. As one moves up the judicial hierarchy, the weight of creativity in judicial reputation increases. Not only do the higher judges have greater power to change the law, but the percentage of novel cases rises as one moves up the ladder, and the uncreative judge, virtually by definition, cannot do justice to novel cases. So the higher judges are evaluated by their creativity and not just by their ability to apply clearly applicable statutory text and judicial precedent to new cases that do not differ materially from previous ones or to exploit gaps or ambiguities in the applicable statutory text. Traynor and Friendly, with whom we began, are notable examples of judges who achieved renown by being creative. But creativity comes at a cost in leisure forgone by a judge who strives to speak in a distinctive voice rather than edit law clerks' opinion drafts.

Related to creativity is power. When text and precedent do not dictate a decision, the judge has an opportunity to implement his view of desirable public policy, as if he were a legislator; and decisions affect behavior in the world outside the courthouse—precedents operate much as statutes do, constraining behavior. Judges trade off power against leisure and against other influences on reputation. A judge may feel very strongly about a policy issue; yet a fear of being criticized for "judicial activism," or fear of reversal by a higher court, by legislation, or in an extreme case by a constitutional amendment, may convince him that he cannot achieve his policy objective in the case at hand.

The power and creativity satisfactions of a judgeship bear on the propensity to dissent. A dissent unlikely to lead to an eventual change in law confers little benefit on the dissenter. And the busier a court is, the less likely it is to reexamine its precedents, because decision according to precedent is a big time-saver, and so the less likely a dissent is to herald future changes in law. Also the more cut-and-dried the courts' cases are, the less room there is for disagreement about proper outcomes and so the fewer will be the occasions for dissent. On both workload and novelty grounds we can expect dissents to be more frequent in the Supreme Court than in the courts of appeals. Workload pressures too, as we noted earlier, make the rate of dissenting understate the actual disagreement among judges, and those pressures diminish as one moves up the judicial ladder.

We must not limit our consideration of factors influencing judicial behavior to those that are external to the judge, such as the possibility of reversal or the reactions of colleagues. Other important influences are internal. One example is how the mind processes information; another is personality. We'll call these influences "psychological." They are both cognitive and emotional.

Judicial decisions in cases involving either factual or legal uncertainty (or both) can be expected to be heavily influenced by the preconceptions that a judge brings to a case.[28] Those preconceptions are likely to be influenced in turn by a host of background factors, including personal-identity characteristics such as race and sex, previous professional and life experiences, education, parental influence, personality or temperament, and (often as a function of such characteristics) moral or religious principles and political ideology. Judges are supposed to lay their preconceptions to one side when deciding a case, and usually they try to do so because it is one of the expectations of the role and a trait for which aspirants for a judgeship are self-selected or which is selected for by the appointing authorities. But when one must make a decision under uncertainty, it is impossible to banish preconceptions unless one decides to flip a coin or can

---

28. Judges are reluctant to acknowledge that preconceptions influence their decisions. For a notable exception, see Henry J. Friendly, "Reactions of a Lawyer-Newly-Become-Judge," in Friendly, *Benchmarks* 1, 14–21 (1967).

delay decision until the uncertainty is dispelled; neither is a permissible option for a judge.

When a case is novel in the sense that it can't be resolved by reference to the orthodox legal materials of authoritative legislative text and precedent, then beliefs and intuitions shaped by the judge's personal history, identity, and psychology may be decisive. Bayesian decision theory teaches that a good reasoner begins an inquiry with prior beliefs about its likely outcome but updates them as evidence accumulates.[29] The priors of a judge facing a novel case are likely to have a strong ideological component because ideology is a worldview that gives one an initial take on a new problem. (If the case is not novel, the judge's priors are likely to be legalistic rather than ideological.) So liberals are suspicious of the police, and before the terrorist attacks on the United States of September 11, 2001, opposed most wiretapping. They updated their view on the basis of the attacks, and so while remaining more suspicious of the police than conservatives became less suspicious than they had been.

Even if a case isn't particularly novel, judges sometimes (maybe often) engage in "motivated reasoning"—picking out unconsciously those facts, precedents or other authoritative texts, or secondary materials, that support a preexisting view (wherever it might come from) and discounting the materials that don't support that preconceived view.[30] Another name for this tendency is "confirmation bias"—the common tendency, when one has a preconception (and that is almost always), to look for evidence to confirm, not refute, it. Scientists are trained to look for evidence that refutes their hypotheses; lawyers and judges are not. "An attorney who treats a client like a hypothesis would be disbarred; a Ph.D. who advocates a hypothesis like a client would be ignored."[31]

Think of two extreme models of judicial decision-making. In one, the judge, giving up on reason, decides the outcome of a case by flipping a

---

29. See Richard A. Posner, *Frontiers of Legal Theory* 343–345 (2001).

30. See Eileen Braman, *Law, Politics & Perception* (2009).

31. Lee Epstein and Gary King, "The Rules of Inference," 69 *University of Chicago Law Review* 1, 9 (2002).

coin (Justice Bridlegoose in Rabelais's *Gargantua and Pantagruel*). In the other, the judge uses tools of logic and science to decide the outcome. Judges don't decide cases by coin flipping or some other aleatory method, and often they are both able and motivated to decide a case by something approaching a scientific or logical methodology. But sometimes they perforce just muddle through, using a "method," if one can call it that, that has been described in another context as "a tension between 'ingenious' and 'apodeictic' modes of cognition. The former is characterized by the contingency and instability of the self's cognitive encounter with the world, and by the self's readiness to 'invent' meaning through language, to adjust style and turn substance into metaphor; the latter by the attaching of the self to the illusory certainties and conclusions produced by such encounters."[32]

In light of this discussion it is easy to see how a judge can be ideological without having an ideology that conforms to standard notions of "liberal" and "conservative." In fact it's unclear what a "standard" liberal or, especially, conservative ideology is.[33] Most liberals place personal liberty far above economic liberty, but libertarians, though generally thought of as conservative, value both forms of liberty and so may combine laissez-faire economic views with support of gay marriage, legalized prostitution, and repeal of the drug laws. But they tend, in contrast to liberals, to be unsympathetic to the poor, to criminals (except for some white-collar criminals), and to members of minority groups—libertarians are individualists, often Social Darwinists, believing in sink or swim (another name for survival of the fittest). Most conservatives, however, are not libertarians; they tend to exalt executive power, especially in matters of national security, to be social conservatives, and to be religious, which liberals nowadays tend not to be.

Neglect of the variousness of ideology, and of factors influencing judicial decision-making that aren't limited to ideology but include personal-

32. Lorna Hutson, "One Thousand Times a Day," *Times Literary Supplement*, May 27, 2011, pp. 22–23.

33. See, for example, Jeffrey Rosen, "Disorder in the Court: Legal Conservatism Goes to War with Itself," *New Republic*, July 13, 2011, p. 7.

ity, animosities, resentments, and ambition, leads to the underestimation of the influence on judicial decisions of subjective factors—factors that are extralegal, at least in a narrow, legalistic sense of "legal." Such neglect suggests that classifying judges as liberal or conservative simply on the basis of whether a liberal or a conservative President appointed them is simplistic; yet we shall see throughout the book that it is a serviceable proxy, although we use other proxies as well. There are many conservatisms—on the present Supreme Court, Roberts, Scalia, Kennedy, Thomas, and Alito are differently conservative from each other—but there is enough overlap for these Justices to constitute a conservative bloc, though less cohesive than the liberal bloc.[34]

Moreover, while a judicial vote that would be coded conservative by all observers—for example, a vote to affirm a death sentence—might be cast by a conservative judge motivated by his conservative ideology, it might also be cast by a liberal judge pragmatically trading off the systemic bad consequences of a liberal ruling against the attraction of doing justice in the individual case, by a strategic liberal who doesn't want to anger colleagues by dissenting (or who is auditioning for appointment to a higher court), or by a lazy liberal. Only if the first cause were the operative one would the vote be a product of ideology. Ideology, legalism, pragmatism, strategy, and effort aversion all enter as preferences in the judge's utility function, with different weights depending on the judge (his personality, temperament, life and career experiences, and so forth) and the particulars of the case. It is out of such elements rather than out of logic and data that some judges (and more law professors) have built elaborate theories—law as the quest for original meanings, law as active liberty, law as libertarianism, law as integrity, and so forth—theories the realist regards as rationalizations of dispositions rather than as theories that actually guide decisions.

34. Of the Court's 14 5–4 decisions during the 2010 term, the four liberals were on one side and the four conservatives (the ninth Justice, Kennedy, is also conservative, but not as conservative as the other four—he is the swing Justice) on the other in all but two. The odds of this occurring by chance are minuscule. See Adam Liptak, "A Significant Term, with Bigger Cases Ahead," *New York Times,* June 28, 2011, p. A12.

The Judicial Utility Function

Drawing together the principal strands of the preceding discussion, and simplifying, we can formalize the judicial utility function (U) as follows:

$$U = U(S(t_j), EXT(t_j, t_{nj}), L(t_l), W, Y(t_{nj}), Z).$$

That is, the judge seeks to maximize his utility subject to a time constraint ($T = t_j + t_{nj} + t_l$) where T is his total available hours (24 hours per day), t_j is the number of hours he devotes to judicial activities, t_{nj} is the number of hours he devotes to nonjudicial work such as writing and lecturing, and t_l is the number of his leisure hours.

S denotes the satisfactions of the job and is expected to be a positive function of the hours the judge devotes to his judicial work. S includes the internal satisfaction of feeling that one is doing a good job, the prospect of being promoted within the judiciary, and the social dimensions of a judgeship, which can either add to or subtract from utility—productive working relations with judicial colleagues, law clerks, other staff, and lawyers add to utility, while animosities, usually from or toward judicial colleagues and usually resulting from disagreement, subtract from it.

EXT are external satisfactions from being a judge, including reputation, prestige, power, influence, and celebrity, which are positively related to the time devoted to both judicial and nonjudicial activities. L is leisure, and is a function of hours of leisure activities (so $t_l = T - t_j - t_{nj}$). W is the judicial salary, while $Y(t_{nj})$ is other earned income and is related to hours spent in nonjudicial work. Z is the combined effect of all other variables, including the cost of increasing the probability of promotion to a higher level of the judiciary (what we call auditioning).

Throughout the book we'll be examining factors that influence various arguments in the judicial utility function and as a result alter judicial behavior. The judicial workload is an obvious example; it is likely to have a negative effect on S, L, and $Y(t_{nj})$. Another is the cost, in time (for example, in forgone leisure hours and nonjudicial work hours) and in collegiality, of dissenting, a cost that also is likely to have a negative effect on S, L, and $Y(t_{nj})$.

A factor that might or might not affect judicial behavior is reversals. At the district court level reversals result in more work for judges because often the reversal is accompanied by a remand of the case to the district judge for further proceedings, which can increase *tj* and also decrease the time available for desired nonjudicial activities, including both leisure and nonjudicial work. These reversals reduce both *EXT* and *L* and by doing so can be expected to generate reversal aversion. By this we mean efforts by district judges to avoid being reversed and thus avoid the increase in *tj* devoted to rehearing a case or rebutting criticism that accompany a reversal.

We expect less or perhaps zero reversal aversion at the court of appeals level, because the Supreme Court reviews, and hence reverses, such a minute fraction of court of appeals decisions. At the Supreme Court level there is zero reversal aversion. Supreme Court decisions cannot be reversed, although in statutory as distinct from constitutional cases Congress can abrogate for the future the rule or principle declared by the Court. And while abrogating a rule of constitutional law adopted by the Court formally requires a constitutional amendment, which has become almost impossibly difficult, Congress has and sometimes deploys weapons that can prod the Court into reversing a constitutional decision—weapons such as jurisdiction stripping, impeachment threats, and threats to cut the Court's budget.[35]

It might seem that reversal aversion would be motivated at both the court of appeals and district court levels by their possible effect on *S* and *EXT,* including any negative effects on promotion. But, perhaps oddly, little attention is paid to reversal rates, even with respect to promotion. For example, Robert Bork had a perfect record—zero reversals as a court of appeals judge—yet was denied confirmation, whereas Alito and Sotomayor had been reversed frequently yet were confirmed easily. In some instances there may even be a Babe Ruth effect. Ruth during his career hit more home runs than any other baseball player, but he also struck out more and had a lower batting average than some players, such as Ty Cobb, who probably were less able than he. Ruth could have increased

35. See James Meernik and Joseph Ignagni, "Judicial Review and Coordinate Construction of the Constitution," 41 *American Journal of Political Science* 447 (1997); Gerald N. Rosenberg, "Judicial Independence and the Reality of Political Power," 54 *Review of Politics* 369 (1992).

his batting average and reduced his strikeouts by swinging less often for the fence, but his reputation would have suffered. (Think how much more famous he is than Cobb.) Similarly, the bolder judges may be courting reversal because the cost to their reputation and influence of being reversed is less than the benefit to their reputation and influence from their bold decisions that are not reversed.

The Legalist Countertheory of Judicial Behavior

The theory that we have sketched thus far of judicial behavior that is rational in the economic sense is opposed to the conventional theory of judicial behavior, in which judges decide cases strictly in accordance with orthodox norms of judicial decision-making. That theory allows no room for leisure preference, angling for promotion, worrying about engendering the ill will of colleagues by taking forthright positions, allowing policy preferences to influence decisions, or allowing ideological or other subjective preconceptions to contaminate the impartial application of legal rules and principles given to rather than invented by the current judges. On this account legal reasoning is impersonal, even algorithmic; judges are human computers. In an older metaphor, they are oracles, applying to the facts of new cases law found in orthodox legal sources, such as statutory or constitutional text, or judicial decisions having the status of precedents, and doctrines built from those decisions. The judges are like the oracle at Delphi, who was the passive transmitter of Apollo's prophecies. The analogy of judge to oracle was Blackstone's, who went so far as to argue that even common law judges were oracles, engaged in pressing immemorial custom into service as legal doctrines, rather than in creating doctrines.[36]

No one today thinks the judicial process *wholly* oracular. But lawyers and judges—particularly judges and law professors—cling to the idea (though how far they actually believe it may be questioned) that judicial decision-making is, at least primarily, an "objective" activity, producing decisions by analysis rather than by ideology or emotion. The idea of the judge as an analyst shares with the idea of judge as an oracle the assump-

---

36. William Blackstone, *Commentaries on the Laws of England,* vol. 1, p. 69 (1765).

tion that legal questions always have right answers, answers transmitted from an authoritative source, though in the modern view the transmission is not direct but is mediated by analysis. The judge remains an oracle in the sense that his personality does not count. The personality of the oracle at Delphi was no more important to her prophecies than the personality of a coaxial cable.

The legalist theory received its canonical modern expression by John Roberts at his Senate confirmation hearing for Chief Justice, when he said that the role of a Supreme Court Justice, which he promised to faithfully inhabit, was comparable to that of a baseball umpire. The umpire calls balls and strikes but does not pitch or bat or field[37]—or make or alter the rules of baseball. Roberts was echoed four years later by Sonia Sotomayor at her confirmation hearing.[38] Yet no competent observer of the judicial process actually believes that all judges, or even most judges, in our system are always legalists, or for that matter always realists. More cases fit the legalistic theory than the realistic one (notably appellate cases decided without a published opinion—which is now the majority of cases decided in the federal courts of appeals), but a greater number of *important* cases, the cases that shape the law, fit the realistic theory than the legalistic one.

Roberts can't have meant what he said. This is not to accuse him of hypocrisy. Judicial confirmation hearings are a farce in which a display of candor would be suicide (as Elena Kagan acknowledged at her confirmation hearing,[39] having earlier urged greater candor in these hearings[40]). It

37. "I will remember that it's my job to call balls and strikes and not to pitch or bat." *Confirmation Hearing on the Nomination of John G. Roberts, Jr. to Be Chief Justice of the United States: Hearing before the S. Comm. on the Judiciary*, 109th Cong., S. Hearing 158, p. 56 (2005).

38. "The task of a judge is not to make law—it is to apply the law." *Confirmation Hearing on the Nomination of Sonia Sotomayor to Be an Associate Justice of the Supreme Court of the United States: Hearing before the S. Comm. on the Judiciary*, 111th Cong., S. Hearing 503, p. 1344 (2009).

39. See "Senate Committee on the Judiciary Holds a Hearing on the Elena Kagan Nomination," June 29, 2010, www.washingtonpost.com/wp-srv/politics/documents/KAGAN HEARINGSDAY2.pdf (visited Dec. 9, 2011).

40. Elena Kagan, "Confirmation Messes, Old and New," 62 *University of Chicago Law Review* 919 (1995).

would be what philosophers call a "category mistake," as if a Shakespearean actor were to interrupt his recital of Hamlet's "To be, or not to be" soliloquy by saying that he didn't actually think that death was "a consummation devoutly to be wished"; he was just saying it because it was in the script he'd been given. Judicial confirmation hearings are theater.

And must be. Imagine if a nominee acknowledged that a high proportion of cases that reach the Supreme Court are indeterminate to legalistic analysis, so that in those cases the Justices perforce rely on intuition, often flavored by political ideology. The nominee would then have to answer questions about his ideology (of which he might be unaware, resulting in future embarrassment when he wrote an opinion that invited interpretation in ideological terms), and his willingness to do so would make agreement with that ideology the natural and legitimate touchstone for a Senator's vote for or against confirmation because the nominee would be acknowledging publicly that ideology *is* law at the Supreme Court level. By confining himself to purely technical issues the nominee enacts his belief that technical competence is the only consideration pertinent to confirmation.

Most proponents of one or another legalist theory of judging would if pressed acknowledge that it is less a rival to realism than a normative theory expressing the aspirations of an influential segment of the legal and political communities and one that resonates with the naïve conception of the judicial process held by much of the general public. There is a well-defined "official" judicial role, and many judges would experience cognitive dissonance if they acknowledged to themselves that really they were playing a different role in many cases, and those usually the most important. Many don't realize it or suppress the realization.

Beginning with chapter 3, we present our statistical evidence testing the realist versus legalist approaches. Not that statistical evidence is the only worthwhile evidence of judicial behavior. There is much to be learned from studies that compare a judicial opinion with the briefs and trial transcripts and other materials on which the judge based—or purported or was expected to base—his opinion.[41] And if impatient with aca-

---

41. See Gerald Caplan, "Legal Autopsies: Assessing the Performance of Judges and Lawyers through the Window of Leading Contract Cases," 73 *Albany Law Review* 1 (2009). See also Richard A. Posner, *Cardozo: A Study in Reputation,* chs. 3, 6 (1990).

demic studies, one has only to read the transcripts of Senate hearings on judicial nominees both to the Supreme Court and to the courts of appeals to realize the importance of ideology in the judicial process. The Senators pay less attention to legal skills or other technical qualifications to be a judge than they do to the nominee's ideology. Are the Senators deceived in thinking that ideology influences judges? Was then-Senator Obama mistaken when he voted against the confirmation of John Roberts to be Chief Justice, believing that Roberts would decide cases in accordance with his conservative ideology?[42] Were President Reagan and his advisers deceived when they tried to alter the ideological complexion of the federal courts of appeals by challenging "senatorial courtesy" and appointing conservative law professors?[43]

The decisions that invalidated the early New Deal statutes, the decisions that overruled those decisions, the decisions of the Warren Court, the decisions overruling or narrowing those decisions, the conservative activism of the Rehnquist and, even more, the Roberts Courts—how can such a cacophony of conflicting judicial voices be thought the result of judges' reasoning with the same tools learned in law school and honed in practice from the same constitutional language and the same precedents?[44]

Antirealism Personified: Judge Harry Edwards

Defenses of legalism tend to ignore the empirical literature, but an important exception is a long article by Judge Harry Edwards of the U.S. Court of Appeals for the District of Columbia Circuit.[45] Judge Edwards is the most pertinacious current critic of legal realism as a positive theory of ju-

---

42. See Editorial, "Why Obama Voted against Roberts," *Wall Street Journal*, June 2, 2009, at A21.

43. See David M. O'Brien, "Federal Judgeships in Retrospect," in *The Reagan Presidency: Pragmatic Conservatism and Its Legacies* 330–336 (W. Elliot Brownlee and Hugh Davis Graham eds. 2003).

44. See Robert Justin Lipkin, "We Are All Judicial Activists Now," 77 *University of Cincinnati Law Review* 181 (2008).

45. Harry T. Edwards and Michael A. Livermore, "Pitfalls of Empirical Studies That Attempt to Understand the Factors Affecting Appellate Decisionmaking," 58 *Duke Law Journal* 1895 (2009). The article was coauthored with Michael Livermore, executive director of the Institute for Policy Integrity at New York University School of Law, but key portions are by

dicial behavior,[46] and his article with Livermore is the fullest account of his position. It may help in clarifying our approach to indicate the respects in which we disagree with Edwards's critique of realism—though with the qualification that if his critique is representative, we are all realists now,[47] even Judge Edwards, though some of us don't know it.

Legalistically Indeterminate Cases Shape the Law. Edwards contends that realists exaggerate the degree to which judges are unable to achieve agreement through deliberation that, overriding ideological and other differences, generates an objectively correct decision. His main evidence is that even in the Supreme Court about a third of the decisions are unanimous even though the Justices are ideologically diverse. And the percentage of unanimous decisions is much higher in the courts of appeals.

That is no evidence. Realists do not deny that *most* judicial decisions are legalistic, though not in the Supreme Court. Legalism is a *category* of realistic judicial decision-making, as our labor-market model of judicial behavior, which emphasizes work pressures, can help us see. Doctrines such as plain meaning (a rebuttable presumption that statutes and constitutional provisions mean what they say) and *stare decisis* (deciding cases in accordance with precedent) enable judges not only to economize on their time and effort but also to minimize controversy with other branches of government by appearing to play a modest "professional" role (in the sense in which members of professions seek deference from the laity on the basis of their real or pretended specialized knowledge), and to provide a product—reasonably predictable law—that is socially valued and therefore justifies the judges' independence and other privileges.

The prevalence of unanimous decisions in the courts of appeals—almost 98 percent of their decisions are unanimous, as we'll see in chap-

Judge Edwards alone and to simplify exposition we'll treat him as the sole author, though without meaning to depreciate Livermore's contribution.

46. See his articles "Collegiality and Decision Making on the D.C. Circuit," 84 *Virginia Law Review* 1335 (1998), and "Public Misperceptions concerning the 'Politics' of Judging: Dispelling Some Myths about the D.C. Circuit," 56 *University of Colorado Law Review* 619 (1985).

47. See also Brian Z. Tamanaha, *Beyond the Formalist-Realist Divide: The Role of Politics in Judging* (2010).

ter 6, in contrast to the Supreme Court—is a common riposte to arguments for the realistic conception of judging, just as the existence of dissent is one of the most common ripostes to arguments for the legalistic conception. But the divergence is less than it appears to be. Unanimity exaggerates consensus, and dissent underestimates disagreement.

And cases that arouse no disagreement among the judges tend not to be the cases that shape the law. Of the 7183 cases decided by the Supreme Court in the 1946 through 2009 terms, 38 percent were unanimous but only 9 percent were reported on the front page of the *New York Times* the day after the Court issued it; the corresponding percentage of the 4488 non-unanimous cases was double that. Today's law is the product of decisions that were stabs in the dark when made rather than applications of settled law. Only a few of those cases were unanimous, such as *Brown v. Board of Education,* and that decision was not arrived at by legalistic analysis and could not have been. It was the product of ideological consensus among the Justices, reflecting elite opinion—a growing repugnance of enlightened Americans to racial segregation, viewed as antithetical to evolving American values.

This point undermines Judge Edwards's complaint that the principal court of appeals databases (including two we use, the Songer and Sunstein databases; see chapters 3 and 4) are limited to published court of appeals decisions, and the majority of court of appeals decisions nowadays are unpublished; if they are included in the denominator, the dissent rate is minuscule. The vast majority of unpublished decisions are affirmances, and as we show in chapter 5 this is a reflection of the signal lack of merit of most cases filed in the federal district courts. It doesn't cost much to file a case; the filing fee is low and the plaintiff is not required to be represented by a lawyer. There are also many incompetent lawyers, many potential plaintiffs who have very low opportunity costs of suing (prison inmates, for example), and many emotional plaintiffs with a deep sense of having been wronged who will sue even if there is no substantial legal ground for suing. These cases are losers and the unpublished decisions affirming their dismissal have little impact on the law, especially since most such decisions cannot be cited as precedents.

When he was a young poet T. S. Eliot had a day job as a banker, at which he probably spent more time than he did writing poetry at night and on weekends. And actors spend more of their working time reading scripts, auditioning, negotiating contracts, and simply waiting for another acting engagement than they spend acting. Should we say therefore that T. S. Eliot and Lawrence Olivier weren't primarily creative artists but rather were primarily drudges? To answer yes would be no sillier than to say that the dominant activity of court of appeals judges is applying settled law to uncontested facts. That may be what they spend a majority of their time on in some of the busier circuits, but it is not their principal work.

Judge Edwards estimates that 5 to 15 percent of cases decided by his court are indeterminate from a legalist standpoint.[48] And his is an intermediate, not a final, appellate court. If one cumulates those figures over many years and many courts, it is apparent that an immense number of decisions are legalistically indeterminate; and among them are the decisions that have made the law what it is today.

Granted, Judge Edwards's court, the U.S. Court of Appeals for the District of Columbia Circuit, has few criminal or civil rights cases; appeals in such cases bulk large in the other federal courts of appeals, and very few have merit. So in those courts the percentage of indeterminate cases is lower than in Edwards's court, yet it is high enough to change the law profoundly over a period of years, and this apart from the seismic changes brought about by Supreme Court decisions.

Edward Rubin, noting in the spirit of Edwards's 5 to 15 percent estimate of indeterminate cases that judges "generally say . . . that they perceive about 90 percent of the cases presented to them as controlled by [existing] law,"[49] remarks that this "sounds a bit like an urban legend." The judges "are almost certainly correct in their assessment that 90% of their cases do not elicit controversy" among them, but "this may only mean that virtually all federal judges share an ideology that determines 90% of the cases. . . . Moreover, . . . [the 10 percent] probably represent the growing edge of the law, the issues that determine its future contours. If two countries are fighting each other along a shared frontier, we would not say they are 90% at peace; rather, we would say that they are fully at

48. Edwards and Livermore, note 45 above, at 1898.
49. Edward Rubin, "The Real Formalists, the Real Realists, and What They Tell Us about Judicial Decision Making and Legal Education," 109 *Michigan Law Review* 863, 873 (2011).

war, but fighting in only 10% of each country's area."[50] And there is the Supreme Court to consider. It "takes the cases most likely to change [the law]," and "once the court has changed the law, lower federal courts will be heavily influenced by its decision. Thus, the Justices can answer as Aesop's lioness did when the rabbit asked her how many children she had: 'Only one, but that one is a lion.'"[51]

Proxy Problems. Judge Edwards points out that the standard realist variable in empirical studies of judicial behavior—the party of the President who appointed the judge who cast the vote in question—explains only a fraction of judges' votes. And that is true. One reason it's true is that the party of the appointing President is, as we've said, a crude proxy for ideological leanings.

Yet despite its crudeness, it has been found in numerous studies (see next chapter)—including many of the studies that we have conducted and report on in this book—to have significant explanatory value even after correction for other variables that might influence a judge's votes. The crudeness of the variable actually enhances the significance of its correlation with judicial votes classified by ideology; for there could be, and indeed doubtless are, many judges whose votes are motivated by ideology but just not the ideology of the party to which the President who appointed them belonged. And there are less crude proxies for a judge's ideology, which we and other students of judicial behavior employ—and find to have the predicted effect.

Judicial Self-Reporting. Judge Edwards gives great weight to what judges report about how they decide to vote as they do—in fact, to what Judge Edwards reports.[52] The premise is that judicial introspection is a valid source of knowledge. The premise is sound only if judges are introspective, only if introspection enables a judge to dredge up from the depths of his unconscious the full array of influences on his exercise of discretion, and only if judges are candid in their self-reporting. None of these as-

50. Id. at 873–874.

51. Id. at 875.

52. Edwards and Livermore, note 45 above, at 1950–1958.

sumptions is plausible. One expects judges in their public statements to down-pedal the creative or legislative element in judging, if only to avoid seeming to compete with the other branches of government in making policy. And of many a judge it can be said, as Goneril said of King Lear, "He hath ever but slenderly known himself."

Edwards argues from the secrecy of judicial deliberations that there is no alternative to taking the judges' self-reported motives at face value: "The deliberative process pursuant to which case inputs are transformed into a judicial decision cannot be observed by outsiders."[53] But secrecy is characteristic of political and business deliberation as well as judicial, yet Edwards doubtless believes, and rightly so, that he understands a good deal about political and commercial decision-making.

Is Judicial Rhetoric Evidence for How Judges Decide Cases?   Most judicial opinions are legalistic in style. They cite prior decisions as if those decisions really were binding, parade reasoning by analogy, appear to give great weight to statutory and constitutional language, delve into history for clues to original meaning, and so forth. But that is what one expects if most judges think of themselves as legalists, or wish to conceal the creative (often the ideological) element in judging; or if most judicial opinions are largely written by law clerks (they are), who are inveterate legalists because they lack the experience or confidence or "voice" to write a legislative opinion of the kind that judges like John Marshall, Oliver Wendell Holmes, Louis Brandeis, Benjamin Cardozo, Robert Jackson, Learned Hand, Roger Traynor, and Henry Friendly wrote.

The motive of concealment deserves particular emphasis. Judges have political reasons to represent creativity as continuity and innovation as constraint; and as there is no recognized duty of candor in judicial opinion writing, they cannot be accused of hypocrisy in writing (or having their law clerks write) that way even if they're aware that it doesn't always track their actual decisional process.

Law Suffused with Politics.   The rhetorically strongest move by legalists is to label the legalist approach "law" and the realist approach "politics."

53. Id. at 1903.

It is effective rhetoric because it makes a realist judge seem like someone who flouts his judicial oath—which requires a judge to uphold the law— and thus a usurper. Edwards states that "the hypothesis that law substantially influences outcomes in most cases certainly has not been disproved by the analyses offered in [the social-scientific literature]."[54] No one ever said it has been. But what is interesting is his suggestion that "law *substantially influences* outcomes in *most* cases." In other words, in some cases the law doesn't influence the outcome of the case at all and in the other cases it merely influences—it does not determine—the outcome. This statement, which if read literally would be an endorsement of legal realism in its most extreme form, is best understood as reflecting an impoverished conception of law. For what does Judge Edwards think the judge is doing in those cases in which "law" doesn't even influence the outcome? And in the rest of the cases, where it does influence the outcome, what else is going on?

A more coherent understanding of the word is that as long as the judge is acting within his jurisdiction he is doing "law."[55] The judge's duty is to decide cases. If the orthodox materials that guide decision do not point one way or the other in a particular case, is the judge to throw up his hands and say, "No law to apply, so I'm going home early today"? Edwards quotes approvingly a statement by Brian Tamanaha that "judges have acknowledged the openness of law and their frailty as humans, but steadfastly maintain that this reality does not prevent them from carrying out their charge to make decisions in accordance with the law to the best of their ability."[56] What does "law" mean when its "openness" is conceded? If law is open to the influence of ideology, and properly so as the quotation implies, then what is legalism in contrast to realism? Tamanaha goes on to state, in another passage quoted approvingly by Judge Edwards, that judges say "they follow the law in the substantial proportion

54. Id. at 1942.

55. See Hans Kelsen, *Pure Theory of Law* (Max Knight trans. 1967); Richard A. Posner, *Law, Pragmatism, and Democracy,* ch. 7 (2003).

56. Edwards and Livermore, note 45 above, at 1950–1958, at 1915, quoting Brian Z. Tamanaha, "The Realism of Judges Past and Present," 57 *Cleveland State Law Review* 77, 91 (2009). Is it really "frailty" not to be a thoroughgoing legalist judge? And is what judges "steadfastly maintain" good evidence of anything?

of the cases where the legal result is clear."[57] Again, what are they doing in the *other* cases?

Justice Scalia was not stepping out of his proper role as a judge when he said in an opinion that "the rule that juries are presumed to follow their instructions is a pragmatic one, rooted less in the absolute certitude that the presumption is true than in the belief that it represents a reasonable practical accommodation of the interests of the state and the defendant in the criminal justice process."[58] This is just as proper a judicial statement as the legalist assertions for which Justice Scalia (he of such pronouncements as the "rule of law" is the "law of rules") is more famous.

Judge Edwards does not make the mistake of thinking that ideology is external to law. He does state incorrectly that "empirical studies . . . assume . . . that ideology is invariably extrinsic to law,"[59] but what is significant about the statement is the implication that ideology is *intrinsic* to law—which is true, and is what realists think. Continuing in this vein, he acknowledges (albeit in tension with his "substantially influences" statement in the same article, and with his approval of the Tamanaha passage that we quoted) that "some play for inherently contestable political judgments is simply built into law and strikes us as a normal constituent of good judging"[60] and that the American conception of law "encompasses, at least in some circumstances, forms of moral or political reasoning."[61] The first acknowledgment gives the game away. The second assumes that judicial resort to moral and political considerations is a form of "reasoning," but such beliefs are less often the product of a reasoning process than of temperament, upbringing, religious affiliation, personal and professional experiences, and characteristics of personal identity such as race and sex.[62]

Edwards makes other concessions to realism. He says that law includes

---

57. Id. at 89, quoted in Edwards and Livermore, note 45 above, at 1943.
58. Richardson v. Marsh, 481 U.S. 200, 211 (1987).
59. Edwards and Livermore, note 45 above, at 1948.
60. Id. at 1946.
61. Id. at 1900. See also id. at 1898–1901.
62. Richard A. Posner, *The Problematics of Moral and Legal Theory* (1999), offers a skeptical account of moral reasoning.

what is "ideological in a law-like way,"[63] and that there are "situations in which ideological or political questions are intrinsic to law."[64] He doesn't indicate how common those situations are, however, and his article offers no example of a case in which ideology or politics influenced the outcome. One way to interpret his article is as claiming that *all* judicial decisions are proper, because ideology and politics are proper influences on law in difficult cases, at least in the American legal system, but that empirical students of judicial behavior deny this, define law as legalism, and so regard all traces of ideological or political influence in judicial decisions as showing that much of the time judges aren't doing "law"; they're politicians in robes. That is one possible reading of some of the early empirical studies of judicial behavior but is an inaccurate description of more recent studies.

The Significance of Deliberation. Recognizing that there is a considerable area of indeterminacy in law viewed from a legalistic perspective, Edwards falls back on the idea of deliberation as a way of overcoming indeterminacy.[65] We'll see in chapter 8 that this idea exaggerates the significance of judicial deliberation. Here we note merely that English judges until quite recently did not engage in deliberation at all—they were forbidden to do so by the rule of "orality": everything a judge did was to be done in public so that the public could monitor judicial behavior.[66] Yet the product of these nondeliberating judges was highly regarded; nor are we aware that the decline of orality in the English legal system—a product of increased workload—has improved the system. In fairness, however, we note that the leisurely pace of English appellate proceedings may have provided a substitute for deliberation; each judge on the appellate panel had much longer than his American counterpart to think about the case he was hearing.

Judicial deliberation in the American context is handicapped by the heterogeneity of American judges. Judges do not select their colleagues

63. Edwards and Livermore, note 45 above, at 1947.
64. Id. at 1943.
65. Id. at 1949.
66. Robert J. Martineau, Appellate Justice in England and the United States: A Comparative Analysis 101–103 (1990).

or successors; nor are all the judges on a court selected for the same reasons or on the basis of the same criteria. Even when all were appointed by the same President (which is uncommon), the appointments will have been influenced by considerations unrelated to the likelihood that the appointees will form a coherent deliberating entity—considerations such as the recommendations of a Senator, the quest for racial, ethnic, gender, and other forms of diversity, and political services.

Consider too the curiously stilted character of judicial deliberation, generally confined to the discussion of and voting on cases after oral argument (if the case is argued rather than submitted on the briefs). At the post-argument conference the judges speak their piece, usually culminating in a statement of the vote they are casting, either in order of seniority or in reverse order of seniority, depending on the court, and it is a serious breach of etiquette to interrupt a judge when he has the floor. This corseted structure of discussion reflects the potential awkwardness of a freewheeling discussion among persons who are not entirely comfortable arguing with each other because they were not picked to form an effective committee, and who as an aspect of the diversity that results from the considerations that shape judicial appointments may have sensitivities that inhibit discussion of issues involving race, sex, religion, criminal rights, immigrants' rights, and other areas of law that arouse strong emotions. Judicial deliberation can be productive when the issues discussed are technical in character, in the sense of ideologically and emotionally indifferent, in contrast to issues that carry a moral or ideological charge; frank discussion of such issues is productive of animosity. But cases that raise issues that all the judges agree are merely technical tend not to be the cases that shape the law in momentous ways.

Should Judges Be Expected to Be Legalists? Anyone who has studied professional behavior, including that of academics, knows that self-interest, along with personality and, yes, in many fields (including law!), politics, play a role in their behavior. Why would we not expect that to be true with respect to judges? Are they saints by birth or continuous prayer? Are they made saints by being appointed to the bench? Does a politicized selection process select for saints? Legalist theorists have not explained how it is that federal judges are made over into baseball umpires. Granted, there are expectations concerning the judicial role; there is a degree of self-selection into the career of a judge and anyway persons uncomfortable in the role are unlikely to seek a judgeship or remain a judge; and an appreciation for legal values is inculcated by legal training and reinforced by experience as a lawyer. So judges are not *just* like other people, or, in their "legislative" role, just like members of Congress. But remember that Judge Edwards has conceded that a nontrivial fraction even of intermediate appellate cases cannot be decided by legalist methods but require what he calls moral and political reasoning. In the cases that count, judges cannot be legalists even if they want to be or think they are. Presidents know this; the Senate knows this; much of the public knows this; and legalists, Judge Edwards not excepted, know it too but are reluctant, in part perhaps out of concern for the public image of the judiciary, to confront its full implications for the understanding of judicial behavior.

CHAPTER 2

The Previous Empirical Literature

History

In 1944 the *New York Times* published an article by Arthur Krock about a young political scientist, C. Herman Pritchett, who was keeping "box scores" of the votes and opinions of Justices of the Supreme Court.[1] Pritchett wanted objective evidence that the Justices' decisions were influenced by their ideology. He thought it no coincidence that two of Roosevelt's appointees, Hugo Black and William Douglas, almost always joined each other's opinions—both were very liberal—and almost never voted with the ultraconservative James McReynolds.

Krock pointed out that Pritchett's evidence "would not increase the respect in which certain members of the court may be held as judges and as lawyers." But potential pushback from the legal community did not

---

1. The original article was "Alignments and Disputes in the Supreme Court," *New York Times,* Jan. 14, 1944, p. 18; the term "box scores" appeared in a follow-up piece by Krock, "The Supreme Court's Dissent Record Grows," *New York Times,* Feb. 22, 1946, p. 24. Pritchett had published his "box scores" in his article "Divisions of Opinion among Justices of the U.S. Supreme Court, 1939–1941," 35 *American Political Science Review* 890 (1941). He amplified his analysis in his book *The Roosevelt Court* (1948).

keep Pritchett's counting project from catching on, initially among his fellow political scientists, later among a broader range of social scientists and eventually some academic lawyers as well. Since Pritchett blazed the trail, there have been hundreds of empirical studies of why judges make the decisions they do[2]—Justices of the U.S. Supreme Court, other federal judges, and increasingly state and foreign judges as well, although our book is limited to the federal courts, for which the data are abundant and uniform. We list a number of the previous studies in the appendix to this chapter.

The scholarly literature confirms Pritchett's insight that ideology plays a significant role in judicial behavior. But it also provides evidence of the existence of constraints—such as precedent and fear of reversal (not a fear felt by Supreme Court Justices, of course), or of retaliation by other branches of government—on freewheeling ideologically motivated judicial behavior. The literature regards judges as primarily seeking to conform the law to their policy preferences, but as being limited in doing so by a variety of factors and forces. Even so, it does not offer a complete model of judicial behavior. We proposed such a model in chapter 1 and test it in the chapters that follow this one.

Pritchett of course was not the first legal realist, or even the first quantitative student of judicial behavior.[3] But the scale of his research was unprecedented and he is rightly regarded as the founder of the quantitative

2. For reviews of the literature, see Richard A. Posner, *How Judges Think* (2008); Gregory C. Sisk, "The Quantitative Moment and the Qualitative Opportunity: Legal Studies of Judicial Decision Making," 93 *Cornell Law Review* 873 (2008); Frank B. Cross, "What Do Judges Want?" 87 *Texas Law Review* 183 (2008); Michael Heise, "The Past, Present, and Future of Empirical Legal Scholarship: Judicial Decision Making and the New Empiricism," 2002 *University of Illinois Law Review* 819 (2002); Lawrence Baum, *The Puzzle of Judicial Behavior* (1997). See also the recent collection of essays (with very good bibliographies) *What's Law Got to Do with It? What Judges Do, Why They Do It, and What's at Stake* (Charles Gardner Geyh ed. 2011).

3. Charles Grove Haines, "General Observations on the Effects of Personal, Political, and Economic Influences in the Decisions of Judges," 17 *University of Illinois Law Review* 96 (1922), had examined the outcomes in New York City's courts of 17,000 prosecutions for public intoxication. Forty-one magistrates heard these cases, and the results varied dramatically among them. One dismissed the charges against only one of the 566 defendants he tried; another dismissed 54 percent. Only a few social scientists tried to carry on Haines's work until Pritchett picked up the banner after the Supreme Court's challenge to the New Deal.

social-scientific study of judicial behavior.[4] Our review of the scholarly literature focuses on the mainstream research program initiated by Pritchett; some more specialized studies are cited in subsequent chapters. The principal relevance of this chapter to the rest of the book, however, will be found in our discussion of methods of assessing the degree to which judges' ideologies influence federal judicial decisions; we will come to that shortly.

Pritchett had become interested in ideological judicial voting by noticing that Supreme Court Justices were publishing dissenting opinions at an unprecedented rate. As shown in Figure 2.1, the rate of published dissents began a sharp rise in the 1930s; until then, the Justices had maintained the illusion of unity. And illusion it was: Chief Justice Morrison Waite's docket books, in which he recorded the private conference votes of the Justices, shows that the Justices of the 1870s and 1880s disagreed plenty; but they were disinclined to make their disagreements public.[5] Until the late 1930s, dissenting opinions were rarely filed in more than 10 percent of the Court's cases each term. By 1943 this figure had risen to 50 percent, and in only three terms since then has the percentage fallen below that.[6] The average has been close to 65 percent.

4. See, for example, Jeffrey R. Lax, "The New Judicial Politics of Legal Doctrine," 14 *Annual Review of Political Science* 131, 139 (2011). Glendon A. Schubert's books, *Quantitative Analysis of Judicial Behavior* (1960) and *The Judicial Mind: The Attitudes and Ideologies of Supreme Court Justices, 1946–1963* (1965), also played a big role in "accelerating the scientific treatment of judicial politics." Kenneth N. Vines, "Judicial Behavior Research," in *Approaches to the Study of Political Science* 125, 129–30 (Michael Haas and Henry S. Kariel eds. 1970). See also Nancy Maveety, "The Study of Judicial Behavior and the Discipline of Political Science," in *The Pioneers of Judicial Behavior* 1, 14 (Maveety ed. 2003).

5. Lee Epstein, Jeffrey A. Segal, and Harold J. Spaeth, "The Norm of Consensus on the U.S. Supreme Court," 45 *American Journal of Political Science* 362 (2001). Robert C. Post reached the same conclusion about the Taft Court in his article "The Supreme Court Opinion as Institutional Practice: Dissent, Legal Scholarship, and Decisionmaking in the Taft Court," 85 *Minnesota Law Review* 1267 (2001).

6. Those terms are 1996 (49 percent), 1997 (same), and 2005 (46 percent). On why the Justices began regularly filing dissenting opinions, see, for example, Gregory A. Caldeira and Christopher J. W. Zorn, "Of Time and Consensual Norms in the U.S. Supreme Court," 42 *American Journal of Political Science* 874 (1998); Stacia L. Haynie, "Leadership and Consensus on the U.S. Supreme Court," 54 *Journal of Politics* 1158 (1992); Thomas G. Walker, Lee Epstein, and William J. Dixon, "On the Mysterious Demise of Consensual Norms in the U.S. Supreme Court," 50 *Journal of Politics* 361 (1988). These papers and others claim that

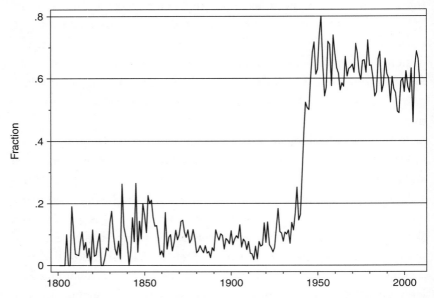

Figure 2.1   Fraction of U.S. Supreme Court Cases with at Least One Dissenting Opinion, 1801–2010 Terms

Note: Data are from Lee Epstein et al., *The Supreme Court Compendium: Data, Decisions and Development* 227–231 (2007), updated using the U.S. Supreme Court Database (supremecourtdatabase.org, visited Aug. 23, 2011), the source of the judicial data on which we base our empirical analysis of the Supreme Court.

The breakdown of consensual norms intrigued Pritchett. If, as orthodox jurists claimed, judges were merely "declaring" the law, reasoning by the same analytical methods from the same orthodox legal materials consisting largely of constitutional and statutory text and of judicial decisions deemed precedential, why did they disagree so often? Pritchett hypothesized that the legal realists were correct that judges are "motivated by their own preferences."[7] As he later wrote, "It is precisely because the Court's institutional ethos has become so weak that we must examine the thinking of individual justices."[8]

He created matrices showing the number of non-unanimous decisions in which pairs of Justices voted together, as well as left-right continua of

---

Chief Justices, particularly Stone, played the decisive roles in the sudden sharp increase in dissents (tabulated in chapter 6 of this book, where we offer a different explanation).

7. C. Herman Pritchett, *The Roosevelt Court: A Study in Judicial Politics and Values, 1937–1947* xiii (1948).

8. Pritchett, *Civil Liberties and the Vinson Court* 22 (1954).

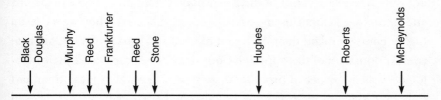

Figure 2.2   Pritchett's Continuum of Liberal and Conservative Voting on the U.S. Supreme Court, 1939–1941 Terms

Notes:

   1. Reproduced from C. Herman Pritchett, "Divisions of Opinion among Justices of the U.S. Supreme Court," 35 *American Political Science Review* 890, 894 (1941).

   2. Pritchett ordered the Justices from most liberal (Black and Douglas) to most conservative (McReynolds).

the sort displayed in Figure 2.2. Operating under the assumption that such comparisons revealed Justices' "'liberalism' and 'conservatism' as those terms are understood by the man on the street,"[9] he concluded that ideology strongly influenced the Justices' decisions.

Subsequent studies crystallized what came to be called the "attitudinal" model of judicial behavior, whereby Justices of the U.S. Supreme Court were hypothesized to cast their judicial votes on the basis of their personal political ideologies.[10] The Justices are uniquely able to do so because of their freedom, noted in chapter 1, from the usual constraints that operate on employees and other agents. Because most other judges in the United States and elsewhere[11] are more constrained, the attitudinal model cannot be expected to have uniform explanatory power. Not that other, more constrained judges wouldn't *like* to decide cases in a way that would promote their ideological preferences. And sometimes they can— and sometimes when they can't there may be a subtle ideological motive: judges may follow the precedents established by their judicial superiors

   9. "Divisions of Opinion among Justices of the U.S. Supreme Court," note 1 above, at 895.

   10. See, for example, Schubert, *The Judicial Mind,* note 4 above; S. Sidney Ulmer, "The Analysis of Behavior Patterns on the United States Supreme Court," 22 *Journal of* Politics 629 (1960); Harold J. Spaeth, *An Introduction to Supreme Court Decision Making* (1972); Jeffrey A. Segal and Harold J. Spaeth, *The Supreme Court and the Attitudinal Model Revisited* (2002).

   11. But see C. L. Ostberg and Matthew E. Wetstein, *Attitudinal Decision Making in the Supreme Court of Canada* (2007).

not only because reversal of their decisions would erase those decisions and perhaps be embarrassing as well, but also because they worry lest a higher court supplant their preferred rule with its least preferable alternative. And Justices of the Supreme Court may sometimes mask their ideological goals in order to promote them more effectively—mask them not only by disingenuous reasoning but also by occasionally voting or even writing against their ideological grain in an attempt to show that they are not ideological.

Ideology Measures

A potentially fatal weakness of Pritchett's methodology was the lack of a measure of judicial ideology based on information prior to the Justices' votes in particular cases. Some Justices vote more liberally and some more conservatively, as inferred from their votes, but the difference might reflect legalist rather than ideological values. For example, a liberal Justice committed to judicial self-restraint might in an era of conservative federal and state legislation vote to uphold such legislation, and so his votes would be coded conservative even though politically he was liberal. Measures of ideology were needed that didn't just assume that a judicial vote that could be located at a point on the ideological spectrum was actually generated by the judge's ideology.

Thus two kinds of ideology measure are needed—ex ante and ex post. By "ex ante" we mean measures that are based entirely on preappointment information about a judge or Justice and by "ex post" we mean measures, such as those used by Pritchett, that are based on postappointment information—mainly judicial votes.[12] Both types of measure are problematic, though in different ways.[13]

---

12. On measures of judicial ideology in general, see Lee Epstein et al., "Ideology and the Study of Judicial Behavior," in *Ideology, Psychology, and Law* (Jon Hanson ed., forthcoming); Joshua B. Fischman and David S. Law, "What Is Judicial Ideology, and How Should We Measure It?" 29 *Washington University Journal of Law and Public Policy* 133 (2009); Gregory C. Sisk and Michael Heise, "Judges and Ideology: Public and Academic Debates about Statistical Measures," 99 *Northwestern University Law Review* 743 (2002).

13. For description and critique, see Corey Rayburn Yung, "Judged by the Company You Keep: An Empirical Study of the Ideologies of Judges on the United States Courts of Appeals," 51 *Boston College Law Review* 1133, 1140–1153 (2010).

A common ex ante measure is the political party of the appointing President; it is ex ante because it is fixed at the time of appointment and thus abstracts from the possibility that the judge's ideology may change (or that he may not be ideological as a judge); a famous example is the gravitation of Justice Blackmun from right to left. Another drawback is that it assumes that all Republican Presidents are conservative—and uniformly so—and all Democratic Presidents uniformly liberal. Yet "Eisenhower [was] not Reagan,"[14] and Jimmy Carter was not Lyndon Johnson. A survey of political scientists who study the Presidency, asked to rank Presidents from 0 to 100 on the basis of their social and economic liberalism, placed Carter closer to Nixon than to Johnson on the spectrum of economic liberalism.[15]

The *R/D* ideology proxy further assumes that Presidents always want to appoint judges who share their ideology. Actually in making judicial nominations they seek to advance one or a combination of three agendas—personal, partisan, and policy.[16] Eisenhower's appointment of Earl Warren was not about promoting an ideology but about repaying a campaign debt. A prediction of Warren's votes that was based on Eisenhower's ideology would be that half his votes would be liberal—yet in fact three-fourths were. And Presidents are sometimes misinformed about a prospective judge's ideology; the first President Bush probably didn't realize that David Souter was a liberal.

Still another drawback of the *R/D* measure is that Presidents do not control judicial appointments fully. Their choices must be confirmed by

14. Michael Giles, Virginia Hettinger, and Todd Peppers, "An Alternative Measure of Preferences for Federal Judges," 54 *Political Research Quarterly* 623, 624 (2001). Susan B. Haire, Martha Anne Humphries, and Donald R. Songer, in their article "The Voting Behavior of Clinton's Courts of Appeals Appointees," 84 *Judicature* 274, 278 (2006), report that "in contrast to Reagan-Bush appointees, the Clinton appointees offered substantially more support to the liberal position in civil rights claims. When voting on criminal and economic issues, [however], Clinton judges generally adopted positions that were strikingly similar to those taken by judges appointed by moderate Republican [Presidents]."

15. Carter's economic-liberalism score was 60.3, Nixon's 47.7, and Johnson's 78.2. Jeffrey A. Segal, Richard J. Timpone, and Robert M. Howard, "Buyer Beware?: Presidential Success through Supreme Court Appointments," 53 *Political Research Quarterly* 557, 562 (2000). The higher the score, the more liberal the President.

16. Sheldon Goldman, *Picking Federal Judges* (1997). See the appendix to this chapter for other studies.

the Senate, and by appealing to the norm of senatorial courtesy even a Senator of the same party as the President can exert considerable and sometimes decisive influence in filling a lower court judgeship allocated to the Senator's state. Michael Giles and his colleagues have developed an ex ante judicial ideology measure based on senatorial influence.[17] They assign to the judge the ideology of the Senator of the judge's state who is of the same party as the appointing President. If both Senators are of the President's party, the judge is given the average of their ideology scores; if neither is, he is given the President's score. Senators' ideology is inferred from their roll-call votes and the President's from his position on bills pending in Congress.[18]

We use the senatorial courtesy measure in places in this book, while recognizing that, like the other ideology measures, it is imperfect. For example, Democrat Patrick Moynihan and Republican Alfonse D'Amato, when they were the Senators from New York, as they were for many years, agreed to split recommendations for judicial appointments between them, with the Senator of the President's party receiving three-quarters of the picks.[19] Yet under the senatorial courtesy scoring procedure all judges nominated during Republican administrations are given D'Amato's ideology score even if Moynihan picked them, and during Democratic administrations all judges picked by D'Amato receive Moynihan's score. To come closer to home, Judge Posner's senatorial courtesy score is only

17. See Giles, Hettinger, and Peppers, note 14 above. See also Lee Epstein et al., "The Judicial Common Space," 23 *Journal of Law, Economics, and Organization* 303 (2007). Recent applications are listed in the appendix to this chapter. The "judicial common space" method of determining judicial ideologies combines Giles's senatorial courtesy method of determining the ideology of court of appeals judges with the Martin-Quinn method of determining the ideology of Supreme Court Justices, in order to provide a measure of judicial ideology that is common to both court of appeals judges and Supreme Court Justices. It ignores the ex ante–ex post distinction. We use it in chapter 3 in analyzing ideological divergence between Justices and the Presidents who appoint them.

18. On most important pieces of legislation the President announces a "vote intention"— how he would vote on the bill if given the opportunity. See Nolan N. McCarty and Keith T. Poole, "Veto Power and Legislation: An Empirical Analysis of Executive and Legislative Bargaining from 1961–1986," 11 *Journal of Law, Economics, and Organization* 282 (1995).

19. See Kirk Johnson, "The Street Fighter and the Professor: Moynihan and D'Amato: A Loyal Pair," *New York Times*, March 15, 1993, p. B1.

barely conservative because he receives the ideology score of the moderate Republican Senator Charles Percy, the Republican Senator from Illinois when Posner was appointed. The implication is that Posner must have been a moderate, or else Percy would not have proposed him. In fact Percy did not propose him, and supported him only reluctantly, under pressure from the Reagan White House, which wanted to make the federal courts of appeals more conservative.[20]

An influential ex ante measure of judicial ideology, developed by Jeffrey Segal and Albert Cover (and now Segal with other collaborators), is based on the editorials published in four newspapers (two conservative and two liberal) about a nominee to the Supreme Court, from the time of nomination through the Senate's vote to confirm.[21] Each paragraph in each editorial is coded as indicating that the nominee is liberal ($+ 1$), conservative ($- 1$), or moderate (0). The fraction of paragraphs coded conservative is subtracted from the fraction coded as liberal and divided by the total number of paragraphs coded as liberal, conservative, and moderate. The resulting scale ranges from $- 1$ (unanimously conservative) to 0 (moderate) to $+ 1$ (unanimously liberal).

Segal-Cover scores are limited to Supreme Court Justices because there are few newspaper editorials about prospective appointees to other courts. Even with regard to Justices, the editorials are better measures of ideology in cases involving civil rights and civil liberties than in ones involving federal taxation and federalism,[22] because newspapers are less interested in a prospective Justice's inclinations in those fields.

There is something distinctly old-fashioned about thinking that only newspaper editorials can provide reliable information about a judge's preappointment ideology. There is a great deal of information about

20. Nancy Scherer, *Scoring Points* 110 (2005); Sheldon Goldman, *Picking Federal Judges* 299 (1997).

21. See Lee Epstein and Jeffrey A. Segal, *Advice and Consent: The Politics of Judicial Appointments* (2005); Jeffrey A. Segal and Albert D. Cover, "Ideological Values and the Votes of U.S. Supreme Court Justices," 83 *American Political Science Review* 557 (1989), updated in Segal et al., "Ideological Values and the Votes of U.S. Supreme Court Justices Revisited," 57 *Journal of Politics* 812 (1995).

22. Lee Epstein and Carol Mershon, "Measuring Political Preferences," 40 *American Journal of Political Science* 261 (1996).

judges online (including books and scholarly articles) that doesn't find its way into newspaper editorial columns. We use such information in chapter 4 to provide both a counterpart to Segal-Cover scores for court of appeals judges and an alternative measure for Supreme Court Justices in order to facilitate comparison between the Supreme Court and the courts of appeals.

Segal-Cover scores enable nominees to be placed in rank order, which is desirable, but its method of doing so can be questioned. An experienced teacher can give numerical scores to essay questions on an exam; if there are four questions and the teacher scores each 0, 1, or 2, there is a potential rank ordering of 0 to 8. But to score paragraphs in newspaper editorials makes the Segal-Cover method of ranking judges hostage to different newspapers' policies regarding length and number of paragraphs, policies liable to be arbitrary. The measure we use in chapter 4 avoids, or at least mitigates, this objection by dividing judges into four ideological classes (strongly conservative, moderately conservatively, moderately liberal, and strongly liberal) without attempting to rank judges within each class; and we find that our classification scheme generates fewer anomalies than Segal-Cover's.

The most common ex ante measure of judicial ideology (the most common measure of judicial ideology, period) is the party of the appointing President. It has several advantages over other measures: it is unambiguous, usable for all Article III judges (because all are appointed by the President), highly correlated with other measures of judicial ideology (including ex post measures), and easy to understand.[23]

Ex post measures of judicial ideology are usually based on an analysis of judges' or Justices' judicial votes. The simplest measure is each Justice's ratio of judicial votes coded conservative to those coded liberal. David Danelski, however, based his ex post analysis of judicial ideology on extracting from speeches by two Supreme Court Justices—Brandeis and Butler—clues to their political values, much as political scientists do content analysis of political documents.[24]

Andrew Martin and Kevin Quinn developed a "the company they

23. David Zaring, "Reasonable Agencies," 96 *Virginia Law Review* 135, 179 (2010).

24. David J. Danelski, "Values as Variables in Judicial Decision Making: Notes toward a Theory," 19 *Vanderbilt Law Review* 721 (1966).

keep" measure: it begins with ideological voting data for each Justice and uses voting alignments between Justices to get a more precise fix on each Justice's ideology.[25] Corey Yung has proposed a variant of the Martin-Quinn measure, designed for studying court of appeals judges.[26] He makes four principal adjustments. The first is to take account of reversal behavior by court of appeals judges: if one judge reverses conservative district court decisions more frequently than liberal ones and another judge does the opposite, this is evidence that the first judge is more liberal than the second. Second, because court of appeals judges are distributed across many different courts (there are 13 federal courts of appeals), with different dockets, Yung reduces the influence of the different case mixtures facing different judges by excluding judges of the D.C. and Federal Circuits, both of which (the Federal Circuit especially, which we exclude from our own analyses) face very different case mixtures from the 11 other courts of appeals. Third, he adjusts for panel composition effects (the influence that judges having different ideologies exert on each other in deciding a case). And fourth, he limits his sample to judicial votes cast in 2008, thus eliminating time effects, though at the cost of reducing the size of his vote sample. But it's still a large sample; it includes all judges who had at least 300 interactions with other judges, which means that each sat on panels that heard at least 100 appeals that year (almost all court of appeals cases are heard by three-judge panels).

We use the Martin-Quinn measure in chapters 3 and 4 and Yung's in chapters 4 and 5. In chapter 4 we also experiment with a simplified version of his measure—the ratio of court of appeals judges' votes to reverse liberal district court decisions to their votes to reverse conservative district court decisions, corrected only for panel composition effects.

The objection to ex post measures (other than Danelski's, which is not based on judicial voting) is circularity—classifying a judge or Justice as conservative on the basis of his judicial votes makes it impossible to say that a liberal judge has a conservative voting record (or vice versa); his

25. See Andrew D. Martin and Kevin M. Quinn, "Dynamic Ideal Point Estimation via Markov Chain Monte Carlo for the U.S. Supreme Court, 1953–1999," 10 *Political Analysis* 134 (2002); Martin and Quinn, "Can Ideal Point Estimates Be Used as Explanatory Variables?" http://adm.wustl.edu/research.php (visited June 10, 2012).

26. Yung, note 13 above, at 1153–1160.

voting record is the only datum about his ideology. But an ex post measure can elude circularity by first classifying votes ideologically in just a subset of areas of law (for example, by removing all First Amendment cases from the dataset for a particular judge) and then reestimating the judge's Martin-Quinn score on the basis of his votes in other cases to see whether those scores accurately predict his votes in First Amendment cases.

Recall that one of Yung's innovations is to compare judges' rates of reversing district court decisions in cases in which the standard of appellate review is deferential. If some judges reverse liberal district court decisions in such cases disproportionately, this is evidence that those judges are conservative, rather than that their votes are merely coded conservative and actually are generated by a nonideological jurisprudence.

A qualitative assessment of judicial ideology can cast light on ideology in a way that a mere count of liberal and conservative judges cannot. One of the methods of estimating the ideology of Supreme Court Justices that we use in chapter 3 divides the Justices into conservatives, moderates, and liberals on the basis of secondary literature. Most of that literature is not quantitative and infers the ideology of Justices not only from their votes (though that is a primary source) but also from the ideological attitudes displayed in their opinions and elsewhere.

Because ex post measures of judicial ideology (other than Danelski's) are based on the ideological valence of judicial votes, that valence has to be determined. Harold Spaeth, a lawyer and political scientist, provided the essential data for the Supreme Court by creating the U.S. Supreme Court Judicial Database.[27] The Spaeth database contains hundreds of pieces of information about each case, including whether the Court's decision (and each Justice's vote) was liberal or conservative. His classifications mostly comport with conventional understandings. "Liberal" votes, for example, are those in favor of defendants in criminal cases; of women and minorities in civil rights cases; of individuals in suits against the government in First Amendment, privacy, and due process cases; of unions and individuals over businesses; and of government over businesses. "Conservative" votes are the reverse. In chapter 3 we question some of

27. See supremecourtdatabase.org (visited Dec. 9, 2011).

the classifications, however, and for our empirical analyses of the Supreme Court use a corrected version of the Spaeth database.[28]

The primary databases of judicial votes for the courts of appeals that we use are the U.S. Courts of Appeals Database (the Songer database, created by Donald Songer)[29] and a database constructed by Cass Sunstein and his colleagues.[30] The first we have corrected (more extensively than we've done with the Spaeth database); the second we have updated and expanded, as explained in chapter 4.

Our data on district court decisions are drawn in part from the cases in our updated version of the Sunstein database (the database contains only court of appeals decisions, but they are deciding appeals from district courts), in part from a database that we created of district court decisions that dismiss a case for failure to state a valid claim, and in part from sentencing data collected by the Transactional Records Access Clearinghouse program (TRAC) of Syracuse University.

The Songer and Sunstein databases are limited to published (in the special sense of being citable as precedents) court of appeals decisions; we explained in chapter 1 why such a limitation is not troublesome.

Previous Studies of Judicial Ideology

Most studies of judicial ideology have been of Supreme Court Justices (see the list in the appendix to this chapter); we mention just a smattering here. Some studies ask whether conservative Justices are more likely to vote to overrule liberal precedents and invalidate liberal statutes and liberal Justices to vote to overrule conservative precedents; the answer is

28. For other criticisms of the database, see Anna L. Harvey and Michael Woodruff, "Confirmation Bias in the United State Supreme Court Judicial Database," *Journal of Law, Economics, and Organization* (forthcoming); Carolyn Shapiro, "The Context of Ideology: Law, Politics, and Empirical Legal Scholarship," 75 *Missouri Law Review* 75, 91–104 (2010); Shapiro, "Coding Complexity: Bringing Law to the Empirical Analysis of the Supreme Court," 60 *Hastings Law Journal* 477 (2009). We discuss the criticisms made by Shapiro in her 2010 article in the next chapter.

29. "Judicial Research Initiative," www.cas.sc.edu/poli/juri/appct.htm (visited Dec. 9, 2011).

30. Cass R. Sunstein et al., *Are Judges Political? An Empirical Analysis of the Federal Judiciary* (2006).

yes.[31] Similarly, liberal Justices have been found to be more likely to vote to invalidate conservative laws and conservative Justices more likely to vote to invalidate liberal ones.[32] This tendency has been increasing since the 1960s,[33] confirming a conjecture that judicial self-restraint has long been in decline.[34]

One study found a high positive correlation between how often Justices vote for the government in non-unanimous (hence "close") constitutional criminal cases and how often they vote for the government in non-unanimous statutory criminal cases.[35] Some Justices lean in favor of government, others in favor of defendants, and these leanings explain their votes in close cases whether the case arises under the Constitution or under a statute, despite huge textual differences, which might be expected to be decisive with legalists, between the Constitution and the statutes. Though based on judicial votes alone, the study provides persuasive evidence that ideology is influencing those votes.

Ideology has also been found to influence the Justices' votes on which cases to hear. Conservative Justices tend to vote to hear cases in which the lower court reached a liberal decision, liberal Justices the opposite;[36] the

31. Stefanie A. Lindquist and Frank B. Cross, *Measuring Judicial Activism* 129 (2009); Lori A. Ringhand, "Judicial Activism: An Empirical Examination of Voting Behavior on the Rehnquist Natural Court," 24 *Constitutional Commentary* 43 (2007); Jeffrey A. Segal and Robert M. Howard, "How Supreme Court Justices Respond to Litigant Requests to Overturn Precedent," 85 *Judicature* 148 (2001); Thomas G. Hansford and James F. Spriggs II, *The Politics of Precedent* (2006); Saul Brenner and Harold J. Spaeth, *Stare Indecisis* (1995).

32. Jeffrey A. Segal and Harold J. Spaeth, *The Supreme Court and the Attitudinal Model Revisited* 416 (2002); Lindquist and Cross, note 31, at 61, 80; Lee Epstein and Andrew D. Martin, "Is the Roberts Court Especially Activist? A Study of Invalidating (and Upholding) Federal, State, and Local Laws: 1969–2009 Terms," *Emory Law Journal* (forthcoming).

33. Lee Epstein and William M. Landes, "Was There Ever Such a Thing as Judicial Self Restraint?" 100 *California Law Review* 557 (2012).

34. Richard A. Posner, "The Rise and Fall of Judicial Self-Restraint," 100 *California Law Review* 519 (2012).

35. Ward Farnsworth, "Signatures of Ideology: The Case of the Supreme Court's Criminal Docket," 104 *Michigan Law Review* 67 (2005).

36. For example, Ryan J. Owens, "The Separation of Powers and Supreme Court Agenda Setting," 54 *American Journal of Political Science* 412 (2010); Ryan C. Black and Ryan J. Owens, "Agenda Setting in the Supreme Court: The Collision of Policy and Jurisprudence," 71 *Journal of Politics* 1062 (2009); Segal and Spaeth, note 32 above, at 265–267; Saul Brenner and John F. Krol, "Strategies in Certiorari Voting on the United States Supreme Court," 51 *Journal of Politics* 828 (1989).

effect on the Court's docket is noticeable.[37] Other research suggests that a Chief Justice is more likely to assign the preparation of the majority opinion in especially important cases to his ideological allies than to other Justices.[38]

Political scientists, who have dominated the social-scientific study of judicial behavior, have made far more studies of the Supreme Court than of other courts. Other courts play a smaller role in the political life of the nation; data relating to them are more difficult to collect and process; and ideology is less likely to influence the decisions of courts that are more constrained than the Supreme Court is—and ideology is what political scientists who study the courts tend to find interesting. But it would be a mistake to think ideology and other nonlegalistic factors absent from other courts. We seek to correct the balance—in this chapter by emphasizing studies of those courts—beginning with the federal courts of appeals.

An early study of the Second Circuit when Learned Hand was chief judge both exposed the infantile feud between two of the court's most distinguished members, Jerome Frank and Charles Clark (a warning about the importance and sometimes the difficulty of maintaining collegiality in an appellate court), and, in tables reporting each judge's scorecard of affirmances and reversals by the Supreme Court, demonstrated that liberal Second Circuit judges and liberal Supreme Court Justices tended to vote the same way; likewise conservatives on both courts.[39] Another early study found that federal court of appeals judges who were members of the Democratic Party when appointed were more likely than Republican judges to cast judicial votes in favor of unions in labor-management disputes and against corporations charged with antitrust violations.[40]

The Sunstein database reveals ideological voting in a number of areas of law, with the notable exception of criminal cases. One study, it is true,

37. See Gregory Caldeira and John Wright, "Organized Interests and Agenda Setting in the U.S. Supreme Court," 82 *American Political Science Review* 1109 (1988).

38. Forest Maltzman, James Spriggs, and Paul Wahlbeck, *Crafting Law on the Supreme Court* 48–51 (2000). The Chief Justice assigns the majority opinion when he is in the majority. If he is not, the senior Associate Justice in the majority assigns.

39. Marvin Schick, *Learned Hand's Court* (1970).

40. Sheldon Goldman, "Voting Behavior on the United States Courts of Appeals, 1961–1964," 60 *American Political Science Review* 374 (1966).

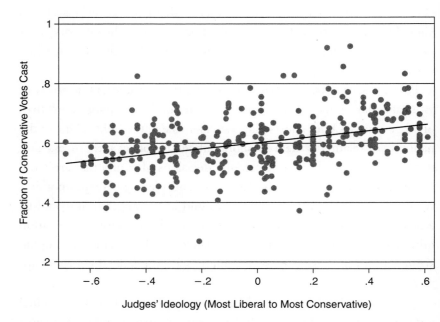

Figure 2.3   Relation between Ideology of U.S. Court of Appeals Judges and Their Votes

Notes:

1. The data are from Jeffrey A. Segal, "Judicial Behavior," note 44 above.

2. Each dot represents a judge. The closer a judge is to the regression (slanted) line, the more closely his ideology (as measured by the senatorial courtesy method) corresponds to his votes. The correlation is .40. Only votes by judges who voted in at least 20 cases are included.

found the same ideological split in criminal cases among court of appeals judges as among Supreme Court Justices.[41] But another study found that judges appointed by Republican Presidents ruled in favor of the government in 81.5 percent of criminal cases, compared to 76.2 percent for judges appointed by Democratic Presidents,[42] and while the difference was statistically significant it was not "nearly as stark" as in criminal cases in the Supreme Court.[43]

A study that used the senatorial courtesy method of scoring a judge's ideology also found, as shown in Figure 2.3, a much weaker relation be-

41. Ward Farnsworth, "The Role of Law in Close Cases: Some Evidence from the Federal Courts of Appeals," 86 *Boston University Law Review* 1083 (2006).

42. Jeffrey A. Segal, Harold J. Spaeth, and Sara C. Benesh, *The Supreme Court in the American Legal System* (2005).

43. Id. at 237–238.

tween judges' ideology and their votes in the courts of appeals than in the Supreme Court.[44] Another study separated court of appeals cases into seven categories (criminal, civil rights, First Amendment, due process, privacy, labor relations, and economic) and found in all but two (First Amendment and privacy) a small but statistically significant effect of ideology.[45] A survey of the empirical literature concludes that the effect is half as strong in the courts of appeals as in the Supreme Court, weaker still in the federal district courts, and almost nonexistent in state trial courts.[46]

Analysis of the adjudication of asylum claims (claims by refugees to be allowed to remain in the United States because they may be persecuted if deported) further illustrates the role of ideology in the courts of appeals.[47] Asylum claims are litigated before immigration judges (Article I judicial officers) with initial appeal to the Board of Immigration Appeals. If the BIA denies asylum, the alien can seek judicial review in the court of appeals for the region in which his claim was adjudicated by the immigration judge. Even though in asylum cases the courts of appeals are reviewing the decisions of the same agency (the BIA) and applying a uniform body of federal law, there is an extraordinary range of rates at which the different courts reverse denials of asylum: from 34 percent in the Seventh Circuit to 2 percent in the Fourth.[48] Such disparities, which persist even after adjustment for regional differences in the countries of origin of the asylum seekers,[49] cannot be explained by a legalist model of judicial decision-making. Different attitudes toward aliens must play a causal role

44. Jeffrey A. Segal, "Judicial Behavior," in *The Oxford Handbook of Law and Politics* 19–35 (Keith E. Whittington, R. Daniel Kelemen, and Gregory A. Caldeira eds. 2008).

45. Frank B. Cross, *Decision Making in the U.S. Courts of Appeals* 27 (2007).

46. Daniel R. Pinello, "Linking Party to Judicial Ideology in American Courts: A Meta-Analysis," 20 *Justice System Journal* 219 (1999).

47. Philip Schrag, Andrew J. Schoenholtz, and Jaya Ramji-Nogales, *Refugee Roulette: Disparities in Asylum Adjudication and Proposals for Reform* (2009).

48. Id. at 80.

49. Id. at 80–81. Cf. David S. Abrams, Marianne Betrand, and Sendhil Mullainathan, "Do Judges Vary in their Treatment of Race?" *Journal of Legal Studies* (forthcoming); Moses Shayo and Asaf Zussman, "Judicial Ingroup Bias in the Shadow of Terrorism," 126 *Quarterly Journal of Economics* 1447 (2011); Lisa Baldez, Lee Epstein, and Andrew D. Martin, "Does the U.S. Constitution Need an Equal Rights Amendment?" 35 *Journal of Legal Studies* 243 (2006).

in the difference in reversal rates, and such attitudes tend to have ideological roots, as indicated by current controversies over immigration policy, which pit liberals against conservatives.

A growing literature finds panel composition effects in the federal courts of appeals.[50] The judges studied by Sunstein and his colleagues voted to invalidate affirmative action in more than 50 percent of affirmative action cases, compared to 25 percent for judges appointed by Democratic Presidents—but the first figure rises to 67 percent when the panel consists of three appointees of Republican Presidents and the second falls to 20 percent when all three were appointed by Democratic Presidents. Panel composition effects are not limited to ideology, at least as proxied by the usual measures. When white judges sit on a panel with a black judge, the odds of the whites' voting in favor of liability in voting rights cases rise.[51] And men are significantly more likely to rule in favor of the plaintiff in a case alleging employment discrimination against a woman when the other member of the three-judge panel is a woman.[52]

A related finding is that, other things being equal, Supreme Court Justices are less likely to vote to grant certiorari when they think they'll wind up on the losing side of the case if certiorari is granted even if they would like to reverse the decision below (a "defensive denial").[53] There is also evidence of voting to hear a case when the Justice agrees with the lower court's decision, believes that the majority of his colleagues do too, and

50. Sunstein et al., note 30 above; Virginia A. Hettinger, Stefanie A. Lindquist, and Wendy L. Martinek, *Judging on a Collegial Court: Influences on Federal Appellate Decision Making* (2006); Frank B. Cross and Emerson H. Tiller, "Judicial Partisanship and Obedience to Legal Doctrine: Whistleblowing on the Federal Courts of Appeals," 107 *Yale Law Journal* 2155 (1998); Richard L. Revesz, "Environmental Regulation, Ideology, and the D.C. Circuit," 83 *Virginia Law Review* 1717 (1997).

51. Adam B. Cox and Thomas J. Miles, "Judging the Voting Rights Act," 108 *Columbia Law Review* 1 (2008); Sean Farhang and Gregory Wawro, "Institutional Dynamics on the U.S. Court of Appeals: Minority Representation under Panel Decision Making," 20 *Journal of Law, Economics, and Organization* 299 (2004).

52. Christina L. Boyd, Lee Epstein, and Andrew D. Martin, "Untangling the Causal Effects of Sex on Judging," 54 *American Journal of Political Science* 389 (2010). See also Jennifer L. Peresie, "Female Judges Matter: Gender and Collegial Decisionmaking in the Federal Appellate Courts," 114 *Yale Law Journal* 1759 (2005).

53. Gregory A. Caldeira, John R. Wright, and Christopher Zorn, "Strategic Voting and Gatekeeping in the Supreme Court," 15 *Journal of Law, Economics, and Organization* 549 (1999). See also H. W. Perry, *Deciding to Decide* (1991).

wants to give the ruling the weight of a Supreme Court decision ("aggressive grants"). Other studies have focused on efforts by Justices to influence one another through written communications.[54]

The fact that a judiciary is a hierarchy can be expected to generate additional effects arising from the group character of appellate decision-making. For example, threat of reversal might constrain lower court judges and administrative officers. Some might be embarrassed to be reversed, or, what is more likely, embarrassed to be reversed frequently, while others, not respecting their judicial superiors, might consider reversal a badge of honor and revel in their defiance of superior judicial authority. And if the rate of reversal were low, the threat of reversal might have no effect at all on the behavior of the lower court judges.

Evidence of "reversal aversion" by federal district judges is that liberal judges render more conservative decisions than they otherwise would and conservative judges the opposite.[55] District judges appointed by a Democratic President and reviewed by a court of appeals dominated by judges appointed by Democratic Presidents have been found to impose on average a prison sentence four months shorter than district judges also appointed by a Democratic President but who face the prospect of appellate review by a court dominated by judges appointed by Republican Presidents.[56] Reversal aversion thus blurs the ideological identity of district judges, which may explain why the empirical literature on ideological decision-making by those judges reaches mixed results.[57]

54. See, for example, Forrest Maltzman, James F. Spriggs II, and Paul J. Wahlbeck, *Crafting the Law on the Supreme Court: The Collegial Game* (2000); Wahlbeck, Spriggs, and Maltzman, "Marshalling the Court: Bargaining and Accommodation on the United States Supreme Court," 42 *American Journal of Political Science* 294 (1998); Lee Epstein and Jack Knight, *The Choices Justices Make* (1998).

55. Kirk A. Randazzo, "Strategic Anticipation and the Hierarchy of Justice in the U.S. District Courts," 36 *American Politics Research* 669 (2008).

56. Max M. Schanzenbach and Emerson H. Tiller, "Strategic Judging under the U.S. Sentencing Guidelines: Positive Political Theory and Evidence," 23 *Journal of Law, Economics, and Organization* 24 (2007).

57. See Denise M. Keele et al., "An Analysis of Ideological Effects in Published versus Unpublished Judicial Opinions," 6 *Journal of Empirical Legal Studies* 213 (2009); Kevin M. Clermont and Theodore Eisenberg, "CAFA Judicata: A Tale of Waste and Politics," 156 *University of Pennsylvania Law Review* 1553 (2008); Joseph L. Smith, "Patterns and Consequences of Judicial Reversals: Theoretical Considerations and Data from a District Court," 27 *Justice System Journal* 28 (2006); C. K. Rowland and Robert A. Carp, *Politics and*

Judicial review by a judge's colleagues, as distinct from review by a higher court, is illustrated by en banc proceedings in the courts of appeals. An analysis of all such proceedings between 1942 and 1999 found that the number declines as judges' average length of service increases. The authors speculate that as judges in a court's ideological minority learn about their colleagues' predispositions, they modify their decisions to reduce the likelihood that the decisions will be subjected to en banc review.[58]

Reversal aversion presumably is greater in the district courts than in the court of appeals, because the reversal rate of district court decisions is so much higher than the reversal rate of court of appeals decisions; although the Supreme Court reverses about two-thirds of decisions that it reviews, it reviews only a minute fraction of decisions of the courts of appeals (and of state courts). Nevertheless, a study of cases arising under the First Amendment's establishment clause concluded that court of appeals judges are in general "faithfully implementing" the Supreme Court's rulings,[59] by which the authors meant without reversal aversion. Judges averse to being reversed might be expected to pay less attention to liberal precedents when a majority of the Supreme Court Justices are conservative and to conservative precedents when the Court's majority is liberal, but the study found no such pattern. Yet a study of more than 10,000 citations by courts of appeals to 500 randomly selected Supreme Court decisions reached the opposite conclusion.[60] It found that when the composition of the Supreme Court that established a precedent and the Court's current composition were ideologically similar, the courts of appeals would follow the precedent in 70 percent of the cases and deviate in fewer

Judgment in Federal District Courts (1996); Orley Ashenfelter, Theodore Eisenberg, and Stewart J. Schwab, "Politics and the Judiciary: The Influence of Judicial Background on Case Outcomes," 24 *Journal of Legal Studies* 257 (1995); Mark A. Cohen, "The Motives of Judges: Empirical Evidence from Antitrust Sentencing," 12 *International Review of Law and Economics* 13 (1992); Cohen, "Explaining Judicial Behavior or What's 'Unconstitutional' about the Sentencing Commission," 7 *Journal of Law, Economics, and Organization* 183 (1991).

58. Michael Giles et al. "The Etiology of the Occurrence of En Banc Review in the U.S. Court of Appeals," 51 *American Journal of Political Science* 449 (2007).

59. Jennifer K. Luse et al., "'Such Inferior Courts . . .': Compliance by Circuits with Jurisprudential Regimes," 37 *American Politics Research* 75 (2009).

60. Chad Westerland et al., "Strategic Defiance and Compliance in the U.S. Courts of Appeals," 54 *American Journal of Political Science* 891 (2010).

than 15 percent. (By "deviating" the authors meant "distinguishing" a Supreme Court decision—that is, deeming it inapplicable to the current case. Lower court judges would not openly refuse to follow such a decision if they acknowledged that it was "on all fours" with their case.) But when the membership of the current Court was dissimilar ideologically from that of the Court that had created the precedent, the probability of compliance fell from 70 percent to less than 30 percent.

Other Influences

Studies find that influences on judges that legalists consider improper are not limited to ideology. Consider the influence on judges, including Supreme Court Justices, exerted by the President and Congress. Those branches affect the federal courts in a variety of ways—budget, appointments, implementation of judicial decrees, and legislation rejecting rules laid down in judicial decisions (provided they were not decisions interpreting the Constitution).[61] There is debate over how responsive judges and Justices are to the desires and concerns of legislative and executive officials.[62] Some political scientists have argued that there is no good reason to expect life-tenured federal judges to pay attention to such officials.[63] Other political scientists, regarding Justices as "single-minded seekers of legal policy,"[64] wonder why they would render a decision they knew Congress would overturn. And although one of the first major empirical studies[65] concluded that "the Court's reaction to the . . . revelation of congressional preferences is a collective

61. See Gerald N. Rosenberg, "Judicial Independence and the Reality of Political Power," 54 *Review of Politics* 369 (1992); Terri Jennings Peretti, *In Defense of a Political Court* (1999); Frank B. Cross and Blake J. Nelson, "Strategic Institutional Effects on Supreme Court Decision Making," 95 *Northwestern University Law Review* 1437 (2001); William N. Eskridge, Jr., "Overriding Supreme Court Statutory Interpretation Decisions," 101 *Yale Law Journal* 331 (1991).

62. See Pablo T. Spiller and Rafael Gely, "Strategic Judicial Decision Making," in *The Oxford Handbook on Law and Politics,* note 44 above, at 34–35.

63. See, for example, Segal and Spaeth, note 32 above.

64. Tracey George and Lee Epstein, "On the Nature of Supreme Court Decision Making," 86 *American Political Science Review* 323, 325 (1992).

65. Jeffrey A. Segal, "Separation-of-Powers Games in the Positive Theory of Congress and Courts," 91 *American Political Science Review* 28 (1997)

yawn,"[66] subsequent studies found that the other branches influence judicial decisions,[67] and the author of the first study has capitulated; he finds that the greater the ideological distance between the Court and the house of Congress that is ideologically closest to the Court, the less likely the Court is to strike down a federal law.[68] So the reason Congress rarely strips the Court's jurisdiction, reduces its budget, impeaches its members, or otherwise seeks to undermine its institutional legitimacy may be that the Justices sense danger and retreat.[69]

If judges respond to the preferences of elected officials, this implies at the least that they are responding at one remove to public opinion, since elected officials respond to public opinion. One expects a more direct relation in the case of elected judges,[70] and though early studies found little support for this expectation and concluded that voters were so unaware of and uninformed about judicial decisions that elected judges could ignore voters' preferences with impunity,[71] more recent ones find the oppo-

66. Spaeth and Segal, note 32 above, at 348.

67. See, for example, Anna Harvey and Barry Friedman, "Ducking Trouble: Congressionally Induced Selection Bias in the Supreme Court's Agenda," 71 *Journal of Politics* 574 (2009); Tom S. Clark, "The Separation of Powers, Court Curbing, and Judicial Legitimacy," 53 *American Journal of Political Science* 971 (2009); Mario Bergara, Barak Richman, and Pablo T. Spiller, "Modeling Supreme Court Strategic Decision Making: The Congressional Constraint," 28 *Legislative Studies Quarterly* 247 (2003); Lee Epstein, Jack Knight, and Andrew D. Martin, "The Supreme Court as a Strategic National Policymaker," 50 *Emory Law Journal* 583 (2001).

68. See Jeffrey A. Segal, Chad Westerland, and Stefanie A. Lindquist, "Congress, the Supreme Court, and Judicial Review: Testing a Constitutional Separation of Powers Model," 55 *American Journal of Political Science* 89 (2011).

69. There are many foreign parallels. For example, an analysis of the German Constitutional Court, one of the most powerful in Europe, finds that the judges take account of the parliament's (and public's) preferences and probable reaction to their decisions before issuing them. Georg Vanberg, *The Politics of Constitutional Review in Germany* 119–130 (2005).

70. See, for example, Melinda Gann Hall, "Constituent Influence in State Supreme Court: Conceptual Notes and a Case Study," 49 *Journal of Politics* 1117 (1987). Recent studies include Brandice Canes-Wrone, Tom S. Clark, and Jee-Kwang Park, "Judicial Independence and Retention Elections." *Journal of Law, Economics, and Organization* (forthcoming); Joanna M. Shepherd, "Money, Politics, and Impartial Justice," 58 *Duke Law Journal* 623 (2009), and "The Influence of Retention Politics on Judges' Voting," 38 *Journal of Legal Studies* 169 (2009); Richard Caldarone, Brandice Canes-Wrone, and Tom S. Clark, "Partisan Labels and Democratic Accountability: An Analysis of State Supreme Court Abortion Decisions," 71 *Journal of Politics* 560 (2009).

71. See, for example, Bradley C. Canon and Dean Jaros, "External Variables, Institutional

site[72]—for example that elected judges are reluctant to dissent[73] because they don't want to be "singled out for possible electoral sanction"[74] if their decisions are inconsistent with their constituents' desires. State supreme court justices have been found to be 13 percent less likely to reverse death sentences when the electorate supports capital punishment strongly,[75] while a study of all murders recorded by the Chicago police found that convicted defendants were significantly more likely to be sentenced to death in the sentencing judge's reelection year,[76] and a study of 7000 civil cases in 48 states found that elected judges are more likely than appointed ones to render decisions that redistribute wealth from out-of-state businesses to in-state plaintiffs.[77]

Whether federal judges, who are not elected, nevertheless follow elec-

Structure and Dissent on State Supreme Courts," 3 *Polity* 183 (1980); Victor Eugene Flango and Craig R. Ducat, "What Difference Does Method of Judicial Selection Make? Selection Procedures in State Courts of Last Resort," 5 *Justice System Journal* 25 (1979).

72. See, for example, Canes-Wrone, Clark, and Park, note 70 above; Caldarone, Canes-Wrone, and Clark, note 70 above; Alexander Tabarrok and Eric Helland, "Court Politics: The Political Economy of Tort Awards," 42 *Journal of Law and Economics* 157 (1999); Steven P. Croly, "The Majoritarian Difficulty: Elective Judiciaries and the Rule of Law," 62 *University of Chicago Law Review* 689 (1995); Daniel R. Pinello, *The Impact of Judicial Selection Method on State-Supreme-Court Policy: Innovation, Reaction and Atrophy* (1995).

73. Paul Brace and Melinda Gann Hall, "Integrated Models of Judicial Dissent," 55 *Journal of Politics* 919 (1993). Studies of state judges face tricky issues of measuring such judges' ex ante ideology. See, for example, Paul Brace, Laura Langer, and Melinda Gann Hall, "Measuring the Preferences of State Supreme Court Justices," 62 *Journal of Politics* 387 (2000); Lisa Baldez, Lee Epstein, and Andrew D. Martin, "Does the U.S. Constitution Need an ERA?" 35 *Journal of Legal Studies* 243 (2006). When, as is often the case, state judges are elected in nonpartisan elections, the political affiliation of the appointing authority cannot be used as a proxy for the judge's ideology and the judge himself may have no political affiliation.

74. Hall, note 70 above, at 1117.

75. Paul Brace and Brent D. Boyea, "State Public Opinion, the Death Penalty and the Practice of Electing Judges," 52 *American Journal of Political Science* 360 (2008).

76. Richard R. W. Brooks and Steven Raphael, "Life Terms or Death Sentences: The Uneasy Relationship between Judicial Elections and Capital Punishment," 92 *Journal of Criminal Law and Criminology* 609 (2002). Similarly, a study of 22,000 sentences in assault, rape, and robbery cases found that sentences become significantly longer as the judge's reelection campaign approaches. Gregory A. Huber and Sanford C. Gordon, "Accountability and Coercion: Is Justice Blind When It Runs for Office?" 48 *American Journal of Political Science* 48 (2004).

77. Tabarrok and Helland, note 70 above.

tion returns or strong currents of public opinion is difficult to determine, since the same forces that influence public opinion may influence judges simply because they are members of the public too. One study finds no support for the claim that federal judges are influenced by public opinion,[78] while other studies find that the attitudes of some Supreme Court Justices change, consciously or not, in response either to long-term shifts in the public mood or to the changing social forces that underlie them.[79] Uncertainty as to whether judges are responding to public opinion or to the same things that shape public opinion makes us skeptical of claims such as that "popular opinion [seems to] shape the broad contours of judicial policymaking."[80]

It's been found that when crises threaten the nation's security, the Supreme Court is substantially more likely to curtail rights and liberties than in normal times.[81] The courts of appeals have also been found to tend to defer to government litigants during wartime, but only in criminal cases.[82] The effect of the business cycle on judicial decisions has also been studied. When the government is the appellant and the economy is booming,

78. Helmut Norpoth and Jeffrey A. Segal, "Comment: Popular Influence on Supreme Court Decisions," 88 *American Political Science Review* 711 (1994).

79. Lee Epstein and Andrew D. Martin, "Does Public Opinion Influence the Supreme Court? Possibly Yes (But We're Not Sure Why)," 13 *Pennsylvania Journal of Constitutional Law* 263 (2010); Michael W. Giles, Bethany Blackstone, and Richard L. Vining, Jr., "The Supreme Court in American Democracy: Unraveling the Linkages between Public Opinion and Judicial Decision-Making," 70 *Journal of Politics* 293 (2008); William Mishler and Reginald S. Sheehan, "The Supreme Court as a Countermajoritarian Institution? The Impact of Public Opinion on Supreme Court Decisions," 87 *American Political Science Review* 87, 88 (1993).

80. Kevin T. McGuire and James A. Stimson, "The Least Dangerous Branch Revisited: New Evidence on Supreme Court Responsiveness to Public Preferences," 66 *Journal of Politics* 1018, 1019 (2004). See also Barry Friedman, *The Will of the People: How Public Opinion Has Influenced the Supreme Court and Shaped the Meaning of the Constitution* (2009); Robert Erikson, Michael B. Mackuen, and James A. Stimson, *The Macro Polity* (2002); Thomas R. Marshall, *Public Opinion and the Supreme Court* (1989).

81. Lee Epstein et al., "The Supreme Court during Crisis: How War Affects Only Non-War Cases," 80 *New York University Law Review* 1 (2005).

82. Tom S. Clark, "Judicial Decision Making during Wartime," 3 *Journal of Empirical Legal Studies* 397 (2006). See also Paul M. Collins, Jr., et al., "International Conflicts and Decision Making on the Federal District Courts," 29 *Justice System Journal* 121 (2008).

more than half the sitting Justices can be expected to vote in the government's favor, but the fraction falls to a third during a bust.[83]

These findings, especially those relating to national security crises, are ambiguous because the balance of competing interests that is acknowledged even by most legalists to properly influence judicial decisions may shift in favor of the government during crises. In that event the judicial response need not be evidence for a realist as opposed to a legalist theory of judicial behavior.

To conclude, the existing scholarly literature has not only created tools for determining the role of ideology in judicial decisions but also provided evidence that what in chapter 1 we called "realism" can explain a good deal of judicial behavior across a broad range of courts, although by no means all. But the literature, though its aperture is much wider than it used to be, remains heavily focused on the U.S. Supreme Court. Our empirical studies, presented in the chapters that follow, place equal emphasis on the lower federal courts. We also move beyond the existing literature's emphasis on ideology as the chief motivator of judges and therefore the proper focus of hypothesis testing. We build our empirical analysis on a model of judicial incentives and constraints and use sophisticated statistical methods to test its accuracy.

Appendix

Empirical Studies of Judicial Behavior[84]

Supreme Court

Influential studies include C. Herman Pritchett, *The Roosevelt Court* (1948); Robert A. Dahl, "Decision Making in a Democracy: The Su-

---

83. Thomas Brennan, Lee Epstein, and Nancy Staudt, "Economic Trends and Judicial Outcomes: A Macrotheory of the Court," 58 *Duke Law Journal* 1191 (2009). See also Nancy Staudt, *The Judicial Power of the Purse: How Judges Fund National Defense in Times of Crisis* (2011).

84. Empirical research can be quantitative or qualitative, but we focus on the former because most of the research we conducted for this book is quantitative.

preme Court as a National Policy Maker," 6 *Journal of Public Law* 279 (1956); Glendon A. Schubert, *The Judicial Mind* (1965); David W. Rohde and Harold J. Spaeth, *Supreme Court Decision Making* (1976); Jeffrey A. Segal, "Predicting Supreme Court Cases Probabilistically: The Search and Seizure Cases, 1962–1981," 78 *American Political Science Review* 891 (1984); H. W. Perry, *Deciding to Decide* (1991); Pablo T. Spiller and Rafael Gely, "Congressional Control or Judicial Independence: The Determinants of U.S. Supreme Court Labor-Relations Decisions, 1948–1988," 23 *RAND Journal of Economics* 463 (1992); Jeffrey A. Segal and Harold J. Spaeth, *The Supreme Court and the Attitudinal Model Revisited* (2002); Lee Epstein and Jack Knight, *The Choices Justices Make* (1998); Charles M. Cameron, Jeffrey A. Segal, and Donald R. Songer, "Strategic Auditing in a Political Hierarchy: An Informational Model of the Supreme Court's Certiorari Decisions," 94 *American Political Science Review* 101 (2000); Andrew D. Martin and Kevin M. Quinn, "Dynamic Ideal Point Estimation via Markov Chain Monte Carlo for the U.S. Supreme Court, 1953–1999," 10 *Political Analysis* 134 (2002).

Virtually no aspect of the work of the Supreme Court has escaped extensive, one might even say obsessive, analysis. To keep this appendix manageable we focus mainly on recent work in several areas, beginning with case selection. Studies include Ryan C. Black and Christina L. Boyd, "US Supreme Court Agenda Setting and the Role of Litigant Status," 28 *Journal of Law, Economics, and Organization* (forthcoming, 2012); Saul Brenner and John F. Krol, "Strategies in Certiorari Voting on the United States Supreme Court," 51 *Journal of Politics* 828 (1989); Ryan J. Owens, "The Separation of Powers and Supreme Court Agenda Setting," 54 *American Journal of Political Science* 412 (2010); Ryan C. Black and Ryan J. Owens, "Agenda Setting in the Supreme Court: The Collision of Policy and Jurisprudence," 71 *Journal of Politics* 1062 (2009); Anna Harvey and Barry Friedman, "Ducking Trouble: Congressionally Induced Selection Bias in the Supreme Court's Agenda," 71 *Journal of Politics* 574 (2009).

There are many studies of opinion assignment, such as Paul J. Wahlbeck, "Strategy and Constraints on Supreme Court Opinion Assignment," 154 *University of Pennsylvania Law Review* 1729 (2006); Forrest Maltzman and Paul J. Wahlbeck, "A Conditional Model of Opinion Assignment on the Supreme Court," 57 *Political Research Quarterly* 551

(2004). And numerous studies of opinion writing, including bargaining, methods, and citation practices, such as Jeffrey S. Rosenthal and Albert H. Yoon, "Detecting Multiple Authorship of United States Supreme Court Legal Decisions Using Function Words," 5 *Annals of Applied Statistics* 283 (2011); Jeffrey S. Rosenthal and Albert H. Yoon, "Judicial Ghostwriting: Authorship on the U.S. Supreme Court," 96 *Cornell Law Review* 1307 (2011); Pamela C. Corley, Paul M. Collins Jr., and Bryan Calvin, "Lower Court Influence on U.S. Supreme Court Opinion Content," 73 *Journal of Politics* 31 (2011); David S. Law and David Zaring, "Law Versus Ideology: The Supreme Court and the Use of Legislative History," 51 *William and Mary Law Review* 1653 (2010); Pamela C. Corley, *Concurring Opinion Writing on the U.S. Supreme* Court (2010); Frank B. Cross et al., "Citations in the U.S. Supreme Court: An Empirical Study of Their Use and Significance," 2010 *University of Illinois Law Review* 489 (2010); James H. Fowler et al. "Network Analysis and the Law: Measuring the Legal Importance of Precedents at the U.S. Supreme Court," 15 *Political Analysis* 324 (2007); Paul J. Wahlbeck, James F. Spriggs II, and Lee Sigelman, "Ghostwriters on the Court? A Stylistic Analysis of U.S. Supreme Court Opinion Drafts," 30 *American Politics Research* 166 (2002).

Another popular subject is Supreme Court review of the constitutionality of federal statutes, as well as Congress's response to such review. See Greg Goelzhauser, "Avoiding Constitutional Cases," 39 *American Politics Research* 483 (2011); Stefanie A. Lindquist and Frank B. Cross, *Measuring Judicial Activism* (2009); Tom S. Clark, "The Separation of Powers, Court Curbing, and Judicial Legitimacy," 53 *American Journal of Political Science* 971 (2009); Tom S. Clark and Keith E. Whittington, "Ideology, Partisanship, and Judicial Review of Acts of Congress, 1790–2006" (unpublished, Princeton University 2007); Lori A. Ringhand, "Judicial Activism: An Empirical Examination of Voting Behavior on the Rehnquist Natural Court," 24 *Constitutional Commentary* 43 (2007); Jeffrey A. Segal and Chad Westerland, "The Supreme Court, Congress, and Judicial Review," 83 *North Carolina Law Review* 1323 (2005); James Meernik and Joseph Ignagni, "Judicial Review and Coordinate Construction of the Constitution," 41 *American Journal of Political Science* 447 (1997).

There is also a substantial and varied body of work on Court-executive relations. See, for example, Nancy Staudt, *The Judicial Power of the Purse* (2011); Daniel E. Ho and Kevin M. Quinn, "Did a Switch in Time Save Nine?" 2 *Journal of Legal Analysis* 69 (2010); Connor N. Raso and William N. Eskridge, Jr., "*Chevron* as a Canon, Not a Precedent: An Empirical Study of What Motivates Justices in Agency Deference Cases," 110 *Columbia Law Review* 1727 (2010); Chris Nicholson and Paul M. Collins Jr., "The Solicitor General's Amicus Curiae Strategies," 36 *American Politics Research* 382 (2008).

On the effect of public opinion on the Justices, see, for example, Lee Epstein and Andrew D. Martin, "Does Public Opinion Influence the Supreme Court? Possibly Yes (But We're Not Sure Why)," 13 *University of Pennsylvania Journal of Constitutional Law* 263 (2010); Christopher J. Casillas, Peter K. Enns, and Patrick C. Wohlfarth, "How Public Opinion Constrains the U.S. Supreme Court," 55 *American Journal of Political Science* 74 (2011); Kevin T. McGuire and James A. Stimson, "The Least Dangerous Branch Revisited," 66 *Journal of Politics* 1018 (2008); Michael W. Giles, Bethany Blackstone, and Richard L. Vining, Jr., "The Supreme Court in American Democracy: Unraveling the Linkages between Public Opinion and Judicial Decision Making," 70 *Journal of Politics* 293 (2004); Roy B. Flemming and B. Dan Wood, "The Public and the Supreme Court: Individual Justice Responsiveness to American Policy Moods," 41 *American Journal of Political Science* 468 (1997); William Mishler and Reginald S. Sheehan, "Public Opinion, the Attitudinal Model, and Supreme Court Decision Making: A Micro-Analytic Perspective," 58 *Journal of Politics* 169 (1996); James A. Stimson, Michael B. MacKuen, and Robert S. Erikson, "Dynamic Representation," 89 *American Political Science Review* 543 (1995); Michael W. Link, "Tracking Public Mood in the Supreme Court: Cross-Time Analyses of Criminal Procedure and Civil Rights Cases," 48 *Political Research Quarterly* 61 (1995); Helmut Norpoth and Jeffrey A. Segal, "Popular Influence on Supreme Court Decisions," 88 *American Political Science Review* 711 (1994).

The role of interest groups (especially as amici curiae) in Supreme Court litigation has generated scores of interesting studies, including many by Paul M. Collins, Jr. See his *Friends of the Court: Interest Groups and Judicial Decision Making* (2008); "Counteractive Lobbying in the U.S. Supreme Court," 37 *American Politics Research* 670 (2009) (with

Lisa A. Solowiej); and "Amici Curiae and Dissensus on the U.S. Supreme Court," 5 *Journal of Empirical Legal Studies* 143 (2008). See also Joseph D. Kearney and Thomas W. Merrill, "The Influence of Amicus Curiae Briefs on the Supreme Court," 148 *University of Pennsylvania Law Review* 743 (2000); Lee Epstein and Ryan J. Owen, "Amici Curiae during the Rehnquist Years," 89 *Judicature* 127 (2005).

Many empirical studies focus on questions about precedent, including its creation and importance (or lack thereof). See, for example, Michael A. Bailey and Forrest Maltzman, "Does Legal Doctrine Matter? Unpacking Law and the Policy Preferences on the U.S. Supreme Court," 102 *American Political Science Review* 369 (2008); Tom S. Clark and Benjamin Lauderdale, "Locating Supreme Court Opinions in Doctrine Space," 54 *American Journal of Political Science* 871 (2010); Thomas G. Hansford and James F. Spriggs II, *The Politics of Precedent on the U.S. Supreme Court* (2006); Harold J. Spaeth and Jeffrey A. Segal, *Majority Rule or Minority Will: Adherence to Precedent on the U.S. Supreme Court* (1999); Mark J. Richards and Herbert M. Kritzer, "Jurisprudential Regimes in Supreme Court Decision Making," 96 *American Political Science Review* 305 (2002) (but see Jeffrey R. Lax and Kelly T. Radera, "Legal Constraints on Supreme Court Decision Making: Do Jurisprudential Regimes Exist?" 72 *Journal of Politics* 273 [2010]); Jack Knight and Lee Epstein, "The Norm of Stare Decisis," 40 *American Journal of Political Science* 1018 (1996); Tracey E. George and Lee Epstein, "On the Nature of Supreme Court Decision Making," 86 *American Political Science Review* 323 (1992); Glenn A. Phelps and John B. Gates, "The Myth of Jurisprudence: Interpretive Theory in the Constitutional Opinions of Justices Rehnquist and Brennan," 31 *Santa Clara Law Review* 567 (1991).

There are also studies of appointments both to the Supreme Court and to the lower federal courts. See Scott E. Graves and Robert M. Howard, *Justice Takes a Recess* (2009); Sarah A. Binder and Forrest Maltzman, *Advice and Dissent: The Struggle to Shape the Federal Judiciary* (2009); David M. Primo, Sarah A. Binder, and Forrest Maltzman, "Who Consents? Competing Pivots in Federal Judicial Selection," 52 *American Journal of Political Science* 471 (2008); Christine L. Nemacheck, *Strategic Selection: Presidential Nomination of Supreme Court Justices from Herbert Hoover through George W. Bush* (2007); Lee Epstein et al., "The

Changing Dynamics of Senate Voting on Supreme Court Nominees," 68 *Journal of Politics* 296 (2006); Stephen Choi and G. Mitu Gulati, "Choosing the Supreme Court: An Empirical Ranking of Judge Performance," 78 *Southern California Law Review* 23 (2004); Nancy Scherer, *Scoring Points* (2005); Lee Epstein and Jeffrey A. Segal, *Advice and Consent* (2005); Sarah A. Binder and Forest Maltzman, "The Limits of Senatorial Courtesy," 29 *Legislative Studies Quarterly* 5 (2004); Charles R. Shipan and Megan L. Shannon, "Delaying Justice(s): A Duration Analysis of Supreme Court Confirmations," 47 *American Journal of Political Science* 654 (2003); Sarah A. Binder and Forrest Maltzman, "Senatorial Delay in Confirming Federal Judges, 1947–1998," 46 *American Journal of Political Science* 190 (2002); Byron J. Moraski and Charles R. Shipan, "The Politics of Supreme Court Nominations: A Theory of Institutional Constraints and Choices," 43 *American Journal of Political Science* 1069 (1999); Gregory A. Caldeira and John R. Wright, "Lobbying for Justice: Organized Interests, Supreme Court Nominations, and the United States Senate," 42 *American Journal of Political Science* 499 (1998).

U.S. Courts of Appeals

Influential studies include Sheldon Goldman, "Voting Behavior on the United States Courts of Appeals, 1961–1964," 60 *American Political Science Review* 374 (1966); J. Woodford Howard, Jr., *Courts of Appeals in the Federal Judicial System* (1981); Donald R. Songer, "Consensual and Nonconsensual Decisions in Unanimous Opinions of the United States Courts of Appeals," 26 *American Journal of Political Science* 225 (1982); Frank B. Cross and Emerson H. Tiller, "Judicial Partisanship and Obedience to Legal Doctrine: Whistleblowing on the Federal Courts of Appeals," 107 *Yale Law Journal* 2155 (1998); Michael W. Giles, Virginia A. Hettinger, and Todd Peppers, "Picking Federal Judges: A Note on Policy and Partisan Selection Agendas." 54 *Political Research Quarterly* 623 (2001); David E. Klein, *Making Law in the United States Courts of Appeals* (2002).

More recent studies include Andreas Broscheid, "Comparing Circuits: Are Some U.S. Courts of Appeals More Liberal or Conservative than Others?" 45 *Law & Society* Review 171 (2011); Christina L. Boyd, Lee Epstein, and Andrew D. Martin, "Untangling the Causal Effects of Sex on Judging," 54 *American Journal of Political Science* 389 (2010); David Zaring, "Reasonable Agencies," 96 *Virginia Law Review* 135 (2010); Chad Westerland et al., "Strategic Defiance and Compliance in the U.S. Courts of Appeals," 54 *American Journal of Political Science* 891 (2010); Banks Miller and Brett Curry, "Expertise, Experience, and Ideology on Specialized Courts," 43 *Law and Society Review* 839 (2009); Jaya Ramji-Nogales, Andrew I. Schoenholtz, and Philip G. Schrag, *Refugee Roulette: Disparities in Asylum Adjudication* (2009); Robert J. Hume, "Courting Multiple Audiences," 30 *Justice System Journal* 14 (2009); Tom S. Clark, "A Principal-Agent Theory of En Banc Review," 25 *Journal of Law, Economics, and Organization* 55 (2009); Jennifer K. Luse et al., "'Such Inferior Courts . . .': Compliance by Circuits with Jurisprudential Regimes," 37 *American Politics Research* 75 (2009); G. Mitu Gulati and Stephen J. Choi, "Bias in Judicial Citations: A Window into the Behavior of Judges?" 37 *Journal of Legal Studies* 87 (2008); Todd A. Collins and Laura P. Moyer, "Gender, Race, and Intersectionality on the Federal Appellate Bench," 61 *Political Research Quarterly* 219 (2008); Jason J. Czarnezki, "An Empirical Investigation of Judicial Decisionmaking, Statutory Interpretation, and the Chevron Doctrine in Environmental Law," 79 *University of Colorado Law Review* 767 (2008); Stephen J. Choi and G. Mitu Gulati, "Trading Votes for Reasoning: Covering in Judicial Opinions," 81 *Southern California Law Review* 735 (2008); Frank B. Cross, *Decision Making in the U.S. Courts of Appeals* (2007); Micheal W. Giles et al., "The Etiology of the Occurrence of En Banc in the U.S. Courts of Appeals," 51 *American Journal of Political Science* 449 (2007); Cass R. Sunstein et al., *Are Judges Political? An Empirical Analysis of the Federal Judiciary* (2006); Virginia A. Hettinger, Stefanie A. Lindquist, and Wendy L. Martinek, *Judging on a Collegial Court: Influences on Federal Appellate Decision Making* (2006); Thomas J. Miles and Cass R. Sunstein, "Do Judges Make Regulatory Policy? An Empirical Investigation of *Chevron*," 73 *University of Chicago Law Review* 823 (2006); David S. Law, "Strategic Judicial Lawmaking: Ideology, Publication, and Asylum Law in the Ninth Circuit," 73 *University of Cincinnati Law Review* 817 (2005); Sean Farhang and Gregory Wawro, "Institutional Dynamics on the U.S. Court of Appeals: Minority Representation under Panel Decision Making," 20 *Journal of Law, Economics, and Organization* 299

(2004); David E. Klein and Robert J. Hume, "Fear of Reversal as an Explanation of Lower Court Compliance," 37 *Law and Society Review* 579 (2003); David E. Klein, *Making Law in the United States Court of Appeals* (2002); Sara C. Benesh, *The U.S. Court of Appeals and the Law of Confessions: Perspectives on the Hierarchy of Justice* (2002); Michael W. Giles, Virginia A. Hettinger, and Todd Peppers, "Picking Federal Judges: A Note on Policy and Partisan Selection Agendas," 54 *Political Research Quarterly* 623 (2001); John P. Kastellec, "Panel Composition and Judicial Compliance on the United States Courts of Appeals," 23 *Journal of Law, Economics, and Organization* 421 (2007).

U.S. District Courts

Influential studies include Michael W. Giles and Thomas G. Walker, "Judicial Policy-Making and Southern School Segregation," 37 *Journal of Politics* 917 (1975); Robert A. Carp and C. K. Rowland, *Policymaking and Politics in the Federal District Courts* (1983); C. K. Rowland and Robert A. Carp, *Politics and Judgment in Federal District Courts* (1996); Gregory S. Sisk, Michael Heise, and Andrew P. Morriss, "Charting the Influences on the Judicial Mind: An Empirical Study of Judicial Reasoning," 73 *New York University Law Review* 1377 (1998).

More recent work includes Joshua B. Fischman and Max M. Schanzenbach, "Do Standards of Review Matter? The Case of Federal Criminal Sentencing," 40 *Journal of Legal Studies* 405 (2011); Paul M. Collins, Jr. and Wendy L. Martinek, "The Small Group Context: Designated District Court Judges in the U.S. Courts of Appeals," 8 *Journal of Empirical Legal Studies* 177 (2011); Beth A. Freeborn and Monica E. Hartmann, "Judicial Discretion and Sentencing Behavior: Did the Feeney Amendment Rein in District Judges?" 7 *Journal of Empirical Legal Studies* 355 (2010); Ryan W. Scott, "Inter-Judge Sentencing Disparity after Booker: A First Look," 63 *Stanford Law Review* 1 (2010); Christina L. Boyd and David A. Hoffman, "Disputing Limited Liability," 104 *Northwestern University Law Review* 853 (2010); Christina L. Boyd and James F. Spriggs, "An Examination of Strategic Anticipation of Appellate Court Preferences by Federal District Court Judges," 29 *Washington University Journal of Law and Policy* 37 (2009); Denise M. Keele et al., "An Analysis of Ideological Effects in Published Versus Unpublished Judicial Opinions,"

6 *Journal of Empirical Legal Studies* 213 (2009); Kirk A. Randazzo, "Strategic Anticipation and the Hierarchy of Justice in U.S. District Courts," 36 *American Politics Research* 669 (2008); Max M. Schanzenbach and Emerson H. Tiller, "Strategic Judging under the U.S. Sentencing Guidelines: Positive Political Theory and Evidence," 23 *Journal of Law, Economics, and Organization* 24 (2007); Jeremy Buchman, "The Effects of Ideology on Federal Trial Judges' Decisions to Admit Scientific Expert Testimony," 35 *American Politics Research* 671 (2007); Brian A. Sutherland, "Whether Consent to Search Was Given Voluntarily: A Statistical Analysis of Factors That Predict the Suppression Rulings of the Federal District Courts," 81 *New York University Law Review* 2192 (2006); Ahmed E. Taha, "How Panels Affect Judges: Evidence from United States District Courts," 39 *University of Richmond Law Review* 1235 (2005); Gregory C. Sisk, Michael Heise, and Andrew P. Morriss, "Searching for the Soul of Judicial Decisionmaking: An Empirical Study of Religious Freedom Decisions," 65 *Ohio State Law Journal* 491 (2004); Nancy C. Staudt, "Modeling Standing," 79 *New York University Law Review* 612 (2004).

State Courts

Influential studies include S. Sidney Ulmer, "The Political Party Variable in the Michigan Supreme Court," 11 *Journal of Public Law* 352 (1962); Robert J. Sickels, "The Illusion of Judicial Consensus: Zoning Decisions in the Maryland Court of Appeals," 59 *American Political Science Review* 100 (1965); James Eisenstein and Herbert Jacob, *Felony Justice: An Organizational Analysis of Criminal Courts* (1977); James L. Gibson, "Judges' Role Orientations, Attitudes, and Decisions: An Interactive Model," 72 *American Political Science Review* 911 (1978); James H. Kuklinski and John E. Stanga, "Political Participation and Government Responsiveness: The Behavior of the California Superior Courts," 73 *American Political Science Review* 1090 (1979); Melinda Gann Hall, "Constituent Influence in State Supreme Courts: Conceptual Notes and a Case Study," 49 *Journal of Politics* 1117 (1987); Gregory A. Huber and Sanford C. Gordon, "Accountability and Coercion: Is Justice Blind When It Runs for Office?" 48 *American Journal of Political Science* 247 (2004).

For more recent work, see Brandice Canes-Wrone, Tom S. Clark, and

Jee-Kwang Park, "Judicial Independence and Retention Elections," *Journal of Law, Economics, and Organization* (forthcoming); Stephen J. Choi, G. Mitu Gulati, and Eric A. Posner, "Professionals or Politicians: The Uncertain Empirical Case for an Elected Rather than Appointed Judiciary," 26 *Journal of Law, Economics, and Organization* 290 (2010); Joanna M. Shepherd, "Money, Politics, and Impartial Justice," 58 *Duke Law Journal* 623 (2009); Richard P. Caldarone, Brandice Canes-Wrone, and Tom S. Clark, "Partisan Labels and Democratic Accountability: An Analysis of State Supreme Court Abortion Decisions," 71 *Journal of Politics* 560 (2009); Joanna M. Shepherd, "The Influence of Retention Politics on Judges' Voting," 38 *Journal of Legal Studies* 169 (2009); Theodore Eisenberg and Michael Heise, "Plaintiphobia in State Courts? An Empirical Study of State Court Trials on Appeal," 38 *Journal of Legal Studies* 121 (2009); Stephen J. Choi, Mitu Gulati, and Eric A. Posner, "Judicial Evaluations and Information Forcing: Ranking State High Courts and Their Judges," 58 *Duke Law Journal* 1313 (2009); Scott A. Comparato and Scott D. McClurg, "A Neo-Institutional Explanation of State Supreme Court Responses in Search and Seizure Cases," 35 *American Politics Research* 726 (2007); Lisa Baldez, Lee Epstein, and Andrew D. Martin, "Does the U.S. Constitution Need an ERA?" 35 *Journal of Legal Studies* 243 (2006); Eric Helland and Alexander Tabarrok, "The Effect of Electoral Institutions on Tort Awards," 4 *American Law and Economics Review* 341 (2002); Sara C. Benesh and Wendy L. Martinek, "State Court Decision Making in Confession Cases," 23 *Justice System Journal* 109 (2002); Laura Langer, *Judicial Review in State Supreme Courts: A Comparative Study* (2002); Paul Brace, Laura Langer, and Melinda Gann Hall, "Measuring the Preferences of State Supreme Court Judges," 62 *Journal of Politics* 387 (2000).

Foreign and International Courts

Influential studies include C. Neal Tate, "Social Background and Voting Behavior in the Philippine Supreme Court," 3 *Lawasia* 317 (1972); Alec Stone Sweet, *The Birth of Judicial Politics in France* (1992); Charles R. Epp, *The Rights Revolution* (1998); Tom Ginsburg, *Judicial Review in New Democracies* (2003); Gretchen Helmke, *Courts under Constraints*

(2005); Georg Vanberg, *The Politics of Constitutional Review in Germany* (2005).

Recent work includes Gretchen Helmke and Jeffrey K. Staton, "Courting Conflict: The Logic of Risky Judicial Decisions in Latin America," *American Journal of Political Science* (forthcoming); Keren Weinshall-Margel, "Attitudinal and Neo-Institutional Models of Supreme Court Decision Making: An Empirical and Comparative Perspective from Israel," 8 *Journal of Empirical Legal Studies* 556 (2011); James Meernik, "Sentencing Rationales and Judicial Decision Making at the International Criminal Tribunals," 92 *Social Science Quarterly* 588 (2011); Jeffrey A. Staton, *Judicial Power and Strategic Communication in Mexico* (2010); Sofia Amaral-Garcia, Nuno Garoupa, and Veronica Grembi, "Judicial Independence and Party Politics in the Kelsenian Constitutional Courts: The Case of Portugal," 6 *Journal of Empirical Legal Studies* 381 (2009); Raphaël Franck, "Judicial Independence under a Divided Polity: A Study of the Rulings of the French Constitutional Court, 1959–2006," 25 *Journal of Law, Economics, and Organization* 262 (2009); Paresh Kumar Narayan and Russell Smyth, "What Explains Dissent on the High Court of Australia? An Empirical Assessment Using a Cointegration and Error Correction Approach," 4 *Journal of Empirical Legal Studies* 401 (2007); Georg Vanberg, *The Politics of Constitutional Review in Germany* (2005); Jeffrey K. Staton and Georg Vanberg, "The Value of Vagueness: Delegation, Defiance, and Judicial Opinions," 52 *American Journal of Political Science* 504 (2008); Gretchen Helmke, *Courts under Constraints* (2005); Roy B. Flemming, *Tournament of Appeals: Granting Judicial Review in Canada* (2004); Stacia L. Haynie, *Judging in Black and White: Decision Making in the South African Appellate Division, 1950–1990* (2003); Lee Epstein, Jack Knight, and Olga Shvetsova, "The Role of Constitutional Courts in the Establishment and Maintenance of Democratic Systems of Government," 35 *Law and Society Review* 117 (2001).

CHAPTER 3

The Supreme Court

A T EVERY RECENT confirmation hearing, nominees to the Supreme Court have pledged undying fealty to what we are calling legalism. John Roberts compared judging in the Supreme Court to umpiring in baseball. Samuel Alito declared that Supreme Court Justices must "be careful not to inject their own views" into the interpretation of statutes or the Constitution.[1] Sonia Sotomayor retracted her public statements that had reflected a realistic understanding of the judicial role; backing off from her earlier statement that "a wise Latina . . . would more often than not reach a better conclusion,"[2] she said: "I believe my record of 17 years demonstrates fully that I do believe that law—that judges must apply the law and not make the law. Whether I've agreed with a party or not, found them sympathetic or not, in every case I have decided, I have done what the law requires."[3]

1. *Confirmation Hearing on the Nomination of Samuel A. Alito, Jr., to Be an Associate Justice of the Supreme Court of the United States: Hearing before the S. Comm. on the Judiciary,* 109th Cong., Sen. Hearing 277, p. 355 (2006).

2. Sonia Sotomayor, "A Latina Judge's Voice," 13 *Berkeley La Raza Law Journal* 87, 92 (2002).

3. *Confirmation Hearing on the Nomination of Sonia Sotomayor to Be an Associate Justice of the Supreme Court of the United States: Hearing before the S. Comm. on the Judiciary,* 111th Cong., Sen. Hearing 503, p. 70 (2009).

The Senate confirmed all three nominees, though no serious student of the Court could have believed their pledges of ideological neutrality. If such claims were taken at face value the Senate's votes would be very lop-sided either for or (less frequently) against the candidate, as they would reflect little more than an assessment of the candidates' professional quali-fications and personal character, which are rarely deficient (and deficien-cies in either regard are likely to result in the withdrawal of the candidate before he is voted on by the Senate). Yet since Nixon's appointment of Warren Burger as Chief Justice in 1969, 21 percent of the votes cast in the Senate on appointments to the Supreme Court have been in opposition to the nominee and 4 of the 21 nominees went down to defeat.[4] That is a small sample, but a 19 percent rejection rate is unprecedented for any other federal post, including other federal judgeships.[5]

When a Senator and a nominee are ideologically similar, the likelihood of the Senator's voting for the nominee is .91; when they are ideologically distant, it is only .07.[6] Senators, the President, interest groups, and many members of the general public as well realize that Justices are ideological and that this influences their judicial votes. Could Senators and Presi-dents, interest groups and the public, all be deceived?

The answer is no, as we can see by considering the utility function of a Supreme Court Justice. It is simpler than the generalized judicial utility function in chapter 1. We can ignore several of the variables when we con-

4. Calculated from http://epstein.law.usc.edu/research/Bork.html (visited Dec. 9, 2011). We include Harriet Miers but not Douglas Ginsburg. Although both nominations were with-drawn before the Senate voted on them, only Miers's nomination had been officially submit-ted to the Senate.

5. Sarah A. Binder and Forrest Maltzman, *Advice & Dissent: The Struggle to Shape the Federal Judiciary* 80 (2009) (tab. 4–1), claims that the confirmation rate for court of appeals judges fell to 48 percent between 2001 and 2008, compared to 90 to 100 percent before 1990. But they do not provide data on the fraction that the Senate actually rejected, either by vote or by filibuster, as distinct from withdrawals by candidates; many such withdrawals, however, are in anticipation of Senate rejection.

6. To calculate these predicted probabilities of voting for or against a nominee, we updated the analysis in Lee Epstein et al., "The Changing Dynamics of Senate Voting on Supreme Court Nominees," 68 *Journal of Politics* 296 (2006), which employs a regression model that includes as independent variables whether the President's party controls the Senate, whether the President and the Senator are of the same political party, the ideological distance between the Senator and the nominee, and the nominee's qualifications. We thank Chad Westerland for supplying us with later data.

sider the Supreme Court because Justices cannot be promoted to a higher court, few Justices have any realistic expectation of being promoted to Chief Justice, and the large size and quality of staff relative to the number of Justices and the Court's light caseload in recent years imply that a Justice's leisure activities and nonjudicial work activities are not significantly constrained by his or her judicial duties.

We can thus rewrite the judicial utility function, for Supreme Court Justices, as

$$U = f(S(t_j), Ext(t_j, t_{nj})).$$

Assuming that tj (the time devoted to judicial work) is a more or less fixed number based on the Justice's energy, work habits, and devotion to the job, the principal tradeoff a Justice makes is between time devoted to leisure activities and time devoted to nonjudicial activities that enhance the external satisfactions of his judicial job *(EXT)*—prestige, power, influence, and celebrity.

We can expect both S (the internal satisfactions of the judgeship) and *EXT* to be strongly influenced by a Justice's ideological leanings. The Supreme Court's principal role is to resolve large political controversies, and a Justice is likely to derive personal satisfaction, as well as reap prestige, exert power and influence, and achieve celebrity, from attempting to align the law with his ideological commitments; in contrast, caseload pressures, the threat of reversal or eventual overruling (and so of not having the last word), desire for promotion, a different case mix, and lower visibility combine to dampen the ideological ambitions of lower court judges.

The influence of a Justice's ideology on his voting behavior on the Supreme Court is therefore the principal focus of this chapter. After a brief description of our data and of problems with them (also discussed in the appendix to the chapter), we use a variety of measures of ideology to determine the correlation between a Justice's judicial voting and his or her ideological leanings. We find strong evidence that ideology does influence the Justices' judicial votes, and thus the Court's outcomes, in a variety of cases, and that this ideological influence has been growing. Turning next to changes in Justices' ideology over the course of their service on the Court, we distinguish between ideological drift—changes relative to the Justice's ideology when appointed—and ideological divergence— changes relative to the ideology of the appointing President. Such a study may seem more relevant to the behavior of the appointing authorities (for example, does the threat of drift or divergence influence the weight that a President will give to age in deciding whom to nominate for a position on the Court?) than of the Justices. But drift and divergence are behaviors of Supreme Court Justices, and we relate these behaviors to our model of the judicial worker.

The chapter then forks into separate analyses of unanimous and non-unanimous decisions in the Supreme Court. The former are thought to challenge the realist theory of judicial behavior because the Supreme Court has been ideologically divided throughout the period of our study. How then can it be unanimous in more than 30 percent of its cases? We show that unanimity is indeed inconsistent with an extreme realist model of the Justices' behavior. We trace the inconsistency to a combination of legalist commitment, absence of high ideological stakes in many Supreme Court cases, and modest effort aversion, which leads to reluctance to dissent at the drop of a hat. The second and third points, however, suggest that unanimity overstates actual agreement.

We find stronger ideological influence in non-unanimous decisions, but also moderating influences, such as a Justice's prior socialization as a judge of a lower appellate court (though the evidence of this is weak). We end with a discussion of group influences. In a non-unanimous decision, there are two groups of Justices: the majority and the minority, though the minority group may have only a single member. We inquire whether changes in the relative size of groups have an independent influence on Justices' votes and find they do not. We do find such influences in the courts of appeals, as discussed in the next chapter.

Data

Our data are drawn largely from the U.S. Supreme Court Database[7] (the Spaeth database), with modifications explained below and in the appen-

---

7. http://supremecourtdatabase.org (visited Dec. 9, 2011).

dix to this chapter. The database, updated each term, contains data on cases decided since the 1946 term. We supplement some of our analysis with a similar dataset for the 1937 through 1945 terms.[8] Our expanded dataset, which ends with the Court's 2009 term, includes 44 Justices (including 8 appointed prior to 1937) and 664 observations from the 1937–2009 terms.

The acid test of the role of ideology in Supreme Court decision-making is the ideological valence of Justices' votes. But some of the votes in the Spaeth database are improperly characterized as liberal or conservative because of the occasional mistaken attribution of ideology to an entire *category* of cases; an example is classifying all votes for plaintiffs in intellectual property or commercial speech cases as liberal, as the database does. We have made an effort to correct this problem, as explained in the appendix. The result has been to shift a relatively small number of votes by the Justices (about 1500 out of more than 42,000) into the unable-to-classify category that we call "other."

Our effort at correction may have fallen short. Carolyn Shapiro argues that the Spaeth coders are biased toward classifying every case as either liberal or conservative.[9] She read a random sample of 95 cases in the database, noted that only 3 had been classified by the coders as other, and judged that 38 belonged there.[10] The result was to change the ratio of conservative to liberal votes from 1.04 to .90. Judge Posner, recoding a random sample of 110 cases in the Spaeth database, agreed with Spaeth's coding in 75 percent of the cases; our recoding of some of Spaeth's categories has corrected some of the coding errors that Posner found (see appendix).

Table 3.1 summarizes the number of liberal, conservative, and unclassifiable votes in orally argued non-unanimous cases in the Supreme Court database, with and without our corrections.

---

8. Harold J. Spaeth (who created the U.S. Supreme Court Database), along with Lee Epstein and Jeffrey A. Segal, created this supplemental dataset. We cannot use it for all our analyses of the Court because it omits some variables available in the original Spaeth database.

9. Carolyn Shapiro, "The Context of Ideology: Law, Politics, and Empirical Legal Scholarship," 75 *Missouri Law Review* 75, 91–104 (2010).

10. See id. at 101 (tab. 1).

Table 3.1   Votes by Supreme Court Justices in Non-unanimous Cases, 1937–2009 Terms

	Civil Liberties	Economics/ Labor/Tax	All
Uncorrected			
Total	29,611	13,890	43,501
Other	9	0	9
Corrected			
Total	28,495	13,485	41,980
Other	1,125	405	1,530

Notes:

1. The Civil Liberties category includes criminal procedure, civil rights, First Amendment, due process, privacy, attorneys, federalism, and judicial power.

2. In both the corrected and uncorrected datasets, we excluded several hundred votes—the votes in the Interstate Relations and Miscellaneous cases—because we could not determine the issues in the cases.

3. "Other" includes cases in which the ideological direction of the Justice's vote was coded as "other."

Ideological Voting by Justices

Table 3.2, utilizing the ideological scoring of cases in the corrected Spaeth database, ranks the Justices in the 1937 through 2009 terms from most to least conservative on the basis of their judicial votes. Rehnquist and Thomas rank as the most conservative Justices and Sutherland, Alito, and McReynolds as the most conservative in economic cases (economic regulation, labor, and tax). At the other end of the ideological spectrum, Marshall, Douglas, Brennan, and Murphy rank as the most liberal Justices overall, although Black is the most liberal in the economic regulation category.

We present results in two subject-matter categories as well: civil liberties (all cases minus economic regulation, labor, and tax cases) and adjusted civil liberties, which excludes federalism and judicial power cases. Civil liberties account for 68 percent of all votes in non-unanimous cases. Although votes in the two civil liberties categories are highly correlated (.98), votes in the adjusted category are somewhat more ideological, indicating that issues of federalism and judicial power are less ideologically charged than issues of personal liberty.

The rankings in the table are generally consistent with what "everyone knows" to be the ideological differences among Supreme Court Justices.

Some of the specific rankings, however, cannot be taken seriously. For example, contrary to the table, Hughes was more conservative than Blackmun (after Blackmun's first few terms—true, his majority opinion in *Roe v. Wade* came early in his tenure, but it was not considered a radical opinion at the time; the vote was 7 to 2, with Burger in the majority), and McReynolds was more conservative than the second Harlan. Justices who served 70 years ago are difficult to place on the same ideological scale as current Justices, because the meaning of "liberal" and "conservative" has changed over this period. Yet even by the standard of his time McReynolds was a vicious reactionary and Harlan by the standards of *his* time a moderate conservative.

Table 3.2 adds three other ideology measures. One, which is limited to Justices appointed after 1937, is their Segal-Cover scores. They range from − 1 (most conservative) to 1 (most liberal), but we have transformed the scale to make 1 the most conservative and 0 the most liberal, to facilitate comparison with our other ideological rankings.

The Segal-Cover scores, as we know, are ex ante. The other two measures are ex post and thus based on judicial votes. They are the Martin-Quinn scores, which are based on votes in non-unanimous cases in the uncorrected Spaeth database, and calculations by Lee Epstein and colleagues, also using the uncorrected Spaeth database, of the fraction of conservative and liberal votes in both unanimous and non-unanimous cases in the adjusted civil liberties category in the 1946 through 2009 terms; we have backdated the calculation to 1937.

Table 3.3 presents a correlation matrix of the different ideology measures. Although all three of the additional measures are correlated with our basic measure (fraction of conservative votes)—and the Martin-Quinn and Epstein et al. measures are highly correlated with it—we need to consider how the anomalies that we noted are affected by the alternative measures. Table 3.4 compares judges' rankings on those three measures. It shows that anomalies are not avoided by using the Segal-Cover scores but if anything are multiplied; among other anomalies, Blackmun is ranked as more conservative than Thomas, Stevens than Souter, Breyer than Clark, and—strangest of all—Douglas than Harlan. The Martin-Quinn scores avoid the anomalies in fraction of conservative votes without introducing new anomalies. Epstein et al. rank Cardozo as more conservative than

Table 3.2 Fraction of Conservative Votes in Non-unanimous Cases for 44 Supreme Court Justices Ranked from Most to Least Conservative, 1937–2009 Terms

Justice	Fraction Conservative Votes					Other Ideological Measures		
	All	Civil Liberties	Economics	Adjusted Civil Liberties	Mean Votes per Term	Segal-Cover	Martin-Quinn	Epstein et al.
Rehnquist	0.850	0.894	0.685	0.917	67.32	0.955	2.85	0.913
Thomas	0.819	0.838	0.749	0.877	44.21	0.840	3.84	0.872
Burger	0.789	0.814	0.699	0.841	84.71	0.885	1.84	0.836
Scalia	0.774	0.796	0.693	0.822	52.25	1.000	2.73	0.818
Whittaker	0.757	0.739	0.781	0.756	61.17	0.500	1.25	0.756
Alito	0.756	0.747	0.791	0.825	39.40	0.900	1.77	0.823
Harlan	0.736	0.744	0.720	0.756	65.88	0.125	1.63	0.756
Sutherland	0.733	0.500	0.818	0.667	15.00	–	2.05	0.539
McReynolds	0.724	0.538	0.788	0.524	38.00	–	2.66	0.466
Roberts	0.702	0.699	0.711	0.724	41.60	0.880	1.70	0.725
Powell	0.695	0.700	0.675	0.711	81.50	0.835	0.93	0.706
O'Connor	0.692	0.691	0.695	0.708	58.44	0.585	0.89	0.705
Roberts, O.	0.660	0.573	0.710	0.617	55.88	–	1.60	0.512
Burton	0.660	0.742	0.555	0.746	63.21	0.720	1.03	0.721
Kennedy	0.655	0.664	0.623	0.690	48.30	0.635	0.83	0.687
Vinson	0.641	0.732	0.528	0.757	70.00	0.250	1.00	0.758
Butler	0.637	0.400	0.704	0.417	45.50	–	1.96	0.472
Minton	0.627	0.762	0.448	0.779	49.88	0.280	1.10	0.779
Jackson	0.605	0.630	0.579	0.657	65.17	0.000	0.74	0.608
Stewart	0.605	0.591	0.641	0.589	76.35	0.250	0.56	0.586
White	0.588	0.643	0.417	0.672	75.97	0.500	0.44	0.670

Frankfurter	0.582	0.600	0.563	0.544	62.50	0.335	0.53	0.518
Clark	0.560	0.709	0.343	0.735	63.83	0.500	0.49	0.735
Reed	0.542	0.687	0.412	0.727	58.20	0.275	0.36	0.639
Byrnes	0.518	0.609	0.455	0.733	56.00	0.670	−0.19	0.546
Blackmun	0.487	0.493	0.468	0.502	77.60	0.885	−0.12	0.497
Stone	0.442	0.544	0.387	0.546	56.78	0.700	−0.08	0.457
Hughes	0.439	0.439	0.438	0.318	42.75	—	0.09	0.412
Cardozo	0.375	0.800	0.182	0.800	16.00	—	−1.76	0.667
Sotomayor	0.368	0.310	0.556	0.261	38.00	0.220	−0.23	0.250
Brandeis	0.347	0.333	0.350	0.444	37.50	—	−0.53	0.455
Souter	0.333	0.299	0.464	0.283	45.47	0.675	−0.83	0.282
Breyer	0.327	0.315	0.381	0.302	42.06	0.525	−1.01	0.310
Stevens	0.313	0.287	0.409	0.267	61.34	0.750	−1.52	0.270
Fortas	0.300	0.253	0.415	0.193	56.75	0.000	−1.20	0.193
Goldberg	0.297	0.242	0.385	0.134	67.33	0.250	−0.79	0.134
Ginsburg	0.274	0.257	0.345	0.222	42.94	0.320	−1.16	0.228
Black	0.251	0.319	0.168	0.298	65.53	0.125	−1.76	0.312
Warren	0.247	0.275	0.206	0.234	66.44	0.250	−1.17	0.233
Rutledge	0.238	0.236	0.241	0.222	71.29	0.000	−1.39	0.249
Murphy	0.227	0.246	0.211	0.152	63.40	0.000	−1.60	0.208
Brennan	0.217	0.191	0.286	0.155	78.97	0.000	−1.94	0.156
Douglas	0.195	0.147	0.266	0.117	64.53	0.270	−4.12	0.139
Marshall	0.170	0.130	0.309	0.098	79.88	0.000	−2.83	0.099

Notes:

1. Fraction Conservative Votes is weighted by number of orally argued cases that the Justice voted in each term in each category. Civil Liberties is the same in the preceding table, but Adjusted Civil Liberties excludes federalism and judicial power cases. Economics includes economic, union, and tax cases.

2. Mean votes per term are in non-unanimous cases.

Table 3.3 Correlation Matrix of Ideology Measures

	Civil Liberties	Economics	Adjusted Civil Liberties	Segal-Cover Score	Martin-Quinn Score	Eps⬛ al. ⬛
All	.89	.88	.89	.62	.94	.⬛
Civil Liberties		.61	.98	.59	.78	.⬛
Economics			.63	.59	.86	.⬛
Adjusted Civil Liberties				.60	.78	.⬛
Segal-Cover Score					.60	.⬛
Martin-Quinn Score						.⬛

Note: The measures here correspond to those in Table 3.2.

Butler and McReynolds, but otherwise avoid the anomalies of the Segal-Cover scores.

It is no surprise that measures based on actual judicial votes are more highly correlated with each other than they are with the Segal-Cover scores; the latter are based on editorials, in four newspapers, that in effect predict, necessarily imperfectly, the Justice's judicial voting, before the Justice is appointed. Nevertheless the correlation between the Segal-Cover scores and the fraction of conservative Justices is high, and those scores will turn out to be useful in our regression analysis of the Justices' voting.

The anomalies in the scores are evidence that Presidents sometimes either lack good information about the ideological proclivities of Supreme Court candidates or make appointments to advance partisan or electoral goals rather than to create ideological legacies.[11] Stone, Brennan, Stevens, and Souter are notable examples of liberals appointed by Republican Presidents.[12] Yet as shown in Table 3.5, in each of the database's 11

11. See Sheldon Goldman, *Picking Federal Judges* (1997); Lee Epstein and Jeffrey A. Segal, *Advice and Consent* (2005). We examine the President's goals in greater detail in the next section of this chapter, and also examine there the phenomenon of Justices' ideological leanings changing (sometimes) over the course of their service on the Court.

12. We code Stone as a Republican because of his initial appointment by a Republican President, even though he was promoted to Chief Justice by a Democratic President and all our data come from his years as Chief Justice.

Table 3.4 Supreme Court Justices, 1937–2009 Terms, Ranked from Most to Least Conservative by Three Measures

Segal-Cover Score		Martin-Quinn Score		Epstein et al. Score	
Scalia	1.000	Thomas	3.840	Rehnquist	0.913
Rehnquist	0.955	Rehnquist	2.850	Thomas	0.872
Alito	0.900	Scalia	2.730	Burger	0.836
Burger	0.885	McReynolds	2.660	Alito	0.823
Blackmun	0.885	Sutherland	2.050	Scalia	0.818
Roberts, J.	0.880	Butler	1.960	Minton	0.779
Thomas	0.840	Burger	1.840	Vinson	0.758
Powell	0.835	Alito	1.770	Whittaker	0.756
Stevens	0.750	Roberts, J.	1.700	Harlan	0.756
Burton	0.720	Harlan	1.630	Clark	0.735
Stone	0.700	Roberts, O.	1.600	Roberts, J.	0.725
Souter	0.675	Whittaker	1.250	Burton	0.721
Byrnes	0.670	Minton	1.100	Powell	0.706
Kennedy	0.635	Burton	1.030	O'Connor	0.705
O'Connor	0.585	Vinson	1.000	Kennedy	0.687
Breyer	0.525	Powell	0.930	White	0.670
Whittaker	0.500	O'Connor	0.890	Cardozo	0.667
White	0.500	Kennedy	0.830	Reed	0.639
Clark	0.500	Jackson	0.740	Jackson	0.608
Frankfurter	0.335	Stewart	0.560	Stewart	0.586
Ginsburg	0.320	Frankfurter	0.530	Byrnes	0.546
Minton	0.280	Clark	0.490	Sutherland	0.539
Reed	0.275	White	0.440	Frankfurter	0.518
Douglas	0.270	Reed	0.360	Roberts, O.	0.512
Vinson	0.250	Hughes	0.090	Blackmun	0.497
Stewart	0.250	Stone	−0.080	Butler	0.472
Goldberg	0.250	Blackmun	−0.120	McReynolds	0.466
Warren	0.250	Byrnes	−0.190	Stone	0.457
Sotomayor	0.220	Sotomayor	−0.230	Brandeis	0.455
Harlan	0.125	Brandeis	−0.530	Hughes	0.412
Black	0.125	Goldberg	−0.790	Black	0.312
Jackson	0.000	Souter	−0.830	Breyer	0.310
Fortas	0.000	Breyer	−1.010	Souter	0.282
Rutledge	0.000	Ginsburg	−1.160	Stevens	0.270
Murphy	0.000	Warren	−1.170	Sotomayor	0.250
Brennan	0.000	Fortas	−1.200	Rutledge	0.249
Marshall	0.000	Rutledge	−1.390	Warren	0.233
		Stevens	−1.520	Ginsburg	0.228
		Murphy	−1.600	Murphy	0.208
		Cardozo	−1.760	Fortas	0.193
		Black	−1.760	Brennan	0.156
		Brennan	−1.940	Douglas	0.139
		Marshall	−2.830	Goldberg	0.134
		Douglas	−4.120	Marshall	0.099

Note: There are no Segal-Cover scores for Sutherland, McReynolds, Owen Roberts, Butler, Hughes, Cardozo, and Brandeis.

Table 3.5   Fraction of Conservative Votes in Non-unanimous Cases by Subject Matter and by Political Party of Appointing President, 1937–2009 Terms

	Fraction Conservative Votes			Ratio of R/D Fractions of Conservative Votes	Number	
	All Justices	Justices Appointed by Republican Presidents	Justices Appointed by Democratic Presidents	Votes	Observations	Votes
Criminal Procedure	0.544	0.611**	0.438	1.39	657	10,271
Civil Rights	0.484	0.563**	0.353	1.59	651	6604
First Amendment	0.491	0.543**	0.417	1.30	634	3504
Due Process	0.501	0.587**	0.384	1.53	545	1755
Privacy	0.520	0.546*	0.453	1.21	300	529
Attorneys	0.526	0.558*	0.439	1.27	271	390
Unions	0.452	0.576**	0.350	1.65	545	1841
Economic Activity	0.469	0.563**	0.384	1.47	661	9396
Judicial Power	0.561	0.596**	0.524	1.14	654	3621
Federalism	0.449	0.482**	0.402	1.20	618	1821
Federal Taxation	0.386	0.445**	0.342	1.30	530	2248
All Categories	0.496	0.569**	0.404	1.41	661	41,980
Civil Liberties	0.516	0.578**	0.424	1.36	661	28,495
Adjusted Civil Liberties	0.514	0.583**	0.407	1.43	661	23,053
Other	0.453	0.547**	0.372	1.47	661	13,485

Notes:

1. One asterisk signifies statistical significance at the .05 level and two asterisks at the .01 level. See technical introduction.

2. Fraction Conservative Votes is weighted by the number of cases in each category.

3. The number of cases in All Categories is equal to the sum of the Civil Liberties and Other cases, Adjusted Civil Liberties being a subset of Civil Liberties.

subject-matter categories the fraction of conservative votes cast by the entire set of Justices appointed by Republican Presidents is greater than that cast by the entire set appointed by Democratic Presidents. As a group, Justices appointed by Republican Presidents vote liberally more than they vote conservatively in only two of the subject-matter categories (federalism and federal taxation), while as a group Justices appointed by a Democratic President vote conservatively more than they vote liberally in only one category (judicial power).

The biggest ideological voting differences between Justices appointed by Presidents of different parties are found in union, civil rights, and due process cases and the smallest differences in judicial power, federalism, privacy, and federal tax cases. In the first group the average difference is about 20 percent, in the second between 7 and 10 percent. Privacy and judicial power are the two categories in which *D*s (Justices appointed by Democratic Presidents) vote most conservatively; criminal cases and judicial power are the categories in which *R*s vote most conservatively.

Table 3.6 classifies each Justice as conservative, moderate, or liberal on the basis of an assessment that we developed from secondary sources.[13] The ideological differences are substantially greater with this measure than with using the ideology of the party of the appointing President. Republican Presidents have sometimes appointed liberal Justices and Democratic Presidents have sometimes appointed conservative ones. Cardozo, Stone, Brennan, Warren, Stevens, and Souter were liberal Justices even though appointed by Republican Presidents, while McReyn-

---

13. Our assessment is based on a large number of studies, both quantitative and qualitative, mainly by political scientists, historians, and biographers, and is detailed in memoranda by our research assistant Xingxing Li posted on the website for this book, http://widefeetdesigns .com/client/epsteinBook/, and also the website of the Judicial Behavior Workshop, www.law .uchicago.edu/academics/judicialbehaviorworkshop/. Illustrative of the studies we used are Henry J. Abraham, *Justices, Presidents, and Senators: A History of U.S. Supreme Court Appointments from Washington to Bush II* (5th ed. 2008); Jeffrey A. Segal and Harold J. Spaeth, *The Supreme Court and the Attitudinal Model Revisited* 322 (2002); Melvin I. Urofsky, *The Warren Court: Justices, Rulings, and Legacy* (2001); Jeffrey A. Segal and Albert D. Cover, "Ideological Values and the Votes of U.S. Supreme Court Justices," 83 *American Political Science Review* 557 (1989); Edward V. Heck and Steven A. Shull, "Policy Preferences of Justices and Presidents: The Case of Civil Rights," 4 *Law and Policy Quarterly* 327 (1982).

olds, Reed, Burton, Vinson, Clark, and Minton were conservative Justices appointed by Democratic Presidents. Of the eleven moderates, Republican Presidents appointed seven (Hughes, Owen Roberts, Whittaker, Stewart, Blackmun, Powell, and O'Connor) and Democratic Presidents four (Frankfurter, Jackson, Byrnes, and White). In civil liberties cases the fraction of conservative votes by Justices whom we classify as conservative is 3 times the fraction for liberal Justices but only 1.36 times that of Justices appointed by Republican Presidents. The ratio is lower in the broad economic category—2.09 to 1.47—but still substantial.

Table 3.6 indicates that ideological voting has increased. In all categories the ratio of conservative votes by conservative Justices to conservative votes by liberal Justices increased from 2.73 in the period 1937–1979 to 3.02 in 1980–2009. (There is a similar increase in the adjusted civil liberties category, though not in the broader civil liberties category.) This increase may reflect the growing homogeneity of the political parties— the near disappearance of moderate Republicans and conservative Democrats.

The ratio of conservative votes by conservative Justices to conservative votes by liberal Justices decreased in the economic, tax, and union categories (from 2.10 to 1.87), because conservative and especially liberal Justices voted more conservatively in economic cases in the later period. This result is consistent with the general drift of U.S. public opinion in economic matters since the election of Ronald Reagan in 1980.

Sitting Supreme Court Justices, like nominees to the Court, are reluctant to acknowledge that any of their decisions are influenced by ideology.[14] Some of them may believe this; others may think it good public relations for the Court for Justices to forswear creativity, or may be reluctant to contradict the assurances they gave at their confirmation hearing. Or maybe when Justices first confront a new area of law they perforce vote

---

14. The qualification "sitting" is important. Since leaving the bench, Justices O'Connor and Souter have acknowledged that the job requires much more than simply applying the law to the facts in the case. Their new candor has led Dahlia Lithwick to ask "why it's only after they leave the court that justices are permitted to say that judging isn't simple. Is it some form of humility that requires sitting judges to downplay their intelligence or skills?" Dahlia Lithwick, "It's Complicated: David Souter Finally Tells Americans to Grow Up," *Slate,* June 9, 2010, www.slate.com/id/2256458 (visited Dec. 9, 2011). Whatever the answer is, it's not humility.

ideologically because the orthodox materials of legal decision-making cannot resolve the case, yet over time a body of precedent emerges and eventually all competent Justices, regardless of ideology, converge on case outcomes because they are committed to following precedent. There is no evidence of that in Table 3.6, however; on the contrary, there is, as we just noted, evidence of a secular increase in ideological voting. But our analysis does not exclude the possibility that there is convergence in particular areas but that new types of legal dispute arise all the time, so that

Table 3.6   Fraction of Conservative Votes in Non-unanimous Cases by Subject Matter and by Judge's Ideology, 1937–2009 Terms

	Proportion of Conservative Votes			Ratio of Proportions of Conservative Votes by C and L Justices
	Conservative Justices	Moderate Justices	Liberal Justices	
937–1979 Terms				
Civil Liberties	0.769**	0.630**	0.244	3.15
Adjusted Civil Liberties	0.794**	0.632**	0.207	3.84
Economics, Unions, and Tax	0.542**	0.582**	0.258	2.10
All Categories	0.679**	0.613**	0.249	2.73
980–2009 Terms				
Civil Liberties	0.790**	0.598**	0.226	2.64
Adjusted Civil Liberties	0.823**	0.619**	0.200	4.12
Economics, Unions, and Tax	0.675**	0.549**	0.361	1.87
All Categories	0.766**	0.588**	0.254	3.02
ll Terms (1937–2009)				
Civil Liberties	0.780**	0.617**	0.236	3.00
Adjusted Civil Liberties	0.809**	0.627**	0.204	3.97
Economics, Unions, and Tax	0.582	0.575**	0.279	2.09
All Categories	0.718**	0.604**	0.251	2.86

otes:

1. The conservatives are McReynolds, Sutherland, Butler, Reed, Burton, Vinson, Minton, Clark, Harlan, urger, Rehnquist, Scalia, Kennedy, Thomas, John Roberts, and Alito.

2. The moderates are Hughes, Owen Roberts, Frankfurter, Byrnes, Jackson, Whittaker, Stewart, White, ackmun, Powell, and O'Connor.

3. The liberals are Brandeis, Stone, Cardozo, Black, Douglas, Murphy, Rutledge, Warren, Brennan, Goldberg, rtas, Marshall, Stevens, Souter, Ginsburg, Breyer, and Sotomayor.

4. The level of statistical significance in the Conservative column refers to the difference between conservative d moderate Justices and in the moderate column to the difference between moderate and liberal Justices. The fference between the groups is in the expected direction except with respect to the conservative and moderates the economic category for the 1937–1979 terms—there the moderates are more conservative than the nservatives.

5. Proportion of Conservative Votes is weighted by the number of cases in each category.

the Court is continuously dealing with novel or fraught cases that it resorts to ideology to decide.

Changes in Justices' Ideology

A Justice's ideology might change during his time on the Court. That is true of other people; why not of Supreme Court Justices? Students of the Court call this "ideological drift." To study it we estimate separate regressions for each Justice appointed since 1937 who served at least 15 terms. The dependent variable is the fraction of the Justice's conservative votes in non-unanimous cases per term through 2009. The independent variable is the length of time he served (or has served, if a current Justice), where x equals 1 for his first term, 2 for his second term, and so on. We make the simplifying assumption that the Justice's judicial ideology either is constant over time (the regression coefficient is not statistically significant) or becomes more or less conservative at a constant rate, as shown by whether the regression coefficient is significantly positive or significantly negative.

The drift hypothesis is supported for 12 of the 23 Justices who served a minimum of 15 terms.[15] Blackmun, Brennan, Douglas, Marshall, O'Connor, Rehnquist, Stevens, and Souter became more liberal and Black, Frankfurter, Reed, and White more conservative.[16] Of the 8 Justices who became more liberal, Republican Presidents had appointed 6; Democratic Presidents appointed all 4 who became more conservative.

One cause of drift, though we can't test it adequately because we have only a single usable observation, is becoming Chief Justice. Our sample of one is Rehnquist. The only other Justice in the period covered by our

15. We used 15 terms as the cutoff to increase the reliability of our estimates. If we lower the cutoff to 10 terms, we find no change for Burton (14 terms), a significant negative coefficient for Murphy (10 terms), and a significant positive coefficient for Jackson (12 terms).

16. There is substantial overlap between our findings and those in Andrew D. Martin and Kevin M. Quinn, "Assessing Preference Change on the U.S. Supreme Court," 23 *Journal of Law, Economics, and Organization* 365 (2007), and in Lee Epstein et al., "Ideological Drift among Supreme Court Justices," 101 *Northwestern University Law Review* 1483 (2007). Martin and Quinn find that Black, Frankfurter, Jackson, Reed, and White became more conservative, while Blackmun, Brennan, Burger, Clark, Marshall, Powell, Warren, and Stevens became more liberal. Epstein et al. find liberal trends for Warren, Clark, and Powell.

data who became Chief Justice was Stone, and the Spaeth database does not contain enough of his votes as Justice and Chief Justice to enable a meaningful comparison between him and Rehnquist.

A Chief Justice has a greater interest than the other Justices in projecting a sense of a unified Court, for he'll be blamed for poor leadership if the Court is unusually divided, especially if he finds himself on the minority side of the divide. Hence we expect the Chief Justice to vote less ideologically than he did as an Associate Justice. This is not to say that his ideology will have changed, but only his incentive to express his ideology in his judicial votes.

Although the percentage of conservative votes by Rehnquist was higher before he became Chief Justice than afterward (89 percent versus 79 percent), if we add a dummy variable for the period in which he served as Chief Justice the regression coefficient is not significant, while the coefficient on the tenure variable remains significant. This suggests that his move leftward was attributable to a secular trend in his ideology rather than to his becoming Chief Justice.

The second type of ideological change we examine—one that, having received less attention in the empirical literature,[17] we emphasize in our study—is the tendency for the gap between the ideology of a Justice and the ideology of the President who appointed him to widen with the length of the Justice's service. This is what we are calling ideological divergence.

We doubt that the reason for this tendency is a sense of loyalty to the appointing President that diminishes the longer the Justice has served on the Court. Loyalty to the President is likely to be weak from the start. Not only can't the President retaliate against a Justice; a judicial vote motivated by loyalty to the President who appointed the Justice would advance the President's goals rather than the Justice's unless their goals were identical. The tendency to diverge is more plausibly explained not

---

17. Epstein and Segal, note 11 above, ch. 5, and Jeffrey A. Segal, Richard J. Timpone, and Robert Howard, "Buyer Beware? Presidential Success through Supreme Court Appointments," 53 *Political Research Quarterly* 559 (2000), compare the President's ideology with the Justice's career voting record, but provide only simple correlations regarding the divergence between the President's and the Justice's ideology over time, and only for four time periods.

by an erosion of loyalty but by the fact that some people's ideologies change over time, and the longer a Justice serves, the likelier such a change is. This tendency is support for a self-expression component of the judicial utility function.

Divergence between the ideological preferences of the President and his judicial appointee is also possible because the appointee may never have shared the President's ideology. Brennan, Stevens, and Souter are examples. The President may pick a Justice in order to advance his or his party's electoral interests, as when Eisenhower appointed Brennan to attract Catholic voters in the 1956 election.[18] And during periods of divided government the President may need to compromise with the Senate majority by appointing a candidate who is not his first choice,[19] as when the first President Bush picked Souter over Edith Jones.[20] And sometimes the President and his advisers may simply be mistaken about a candidate's ideological inclinations; Souter may be an example. Or a Justice may have been appointed because of a salient issue on which he agrees with the President, but later that issue fades and new issues emerge on which their views diverge.

To test for ideological divergence, we regress the ideological distance between Justice i and the appointing President in each term in which the Justice served on the following variables: the number of terms of the Supreme Court in which the Justice served *(Tenure)*; the Justice's age at appointment; District of Columbia (= 1 if he was a federal official, including a judge, in the District of Columbia when he was appointed to the Court[21]); and whether he was a federal court of appeals judge when appointed (= 1 if he was[22]). Since the President is likely to have better infor-

---

18. On the goals of Presidents in picking judges, see Goldman, note 11 above.

19. Brian Moraski and Charles Shipan, "The Politics of Supreme Court Nominations: A Theory of Institutional Constraints and Choices," 43 *American Journal of Political Science* 1069 (1999).

20. David Alistair Yalof, *Pursuit of Justices: Presidential Politics and the Selection of Supreme Court Nominees* 191–192 (1999).

21. We include Abe Fortas, who although not an employee of the federal government when appointed to the Court was (and remained) a key adviser to President Johnson and had an office in the White House and gave the White House as his address in his *Who's Who* entry.

22. We include Marshall, who had served as a court of appeals judge but was Solicitor General at the time of his appointment.

mation about potential appointees who are already working close by in the executive branch[23] or have served on a federal court of appeals or are older, we expect these variables to be negatively related to ideological drift. We use the absolute ideological distance as the dependent variable because our interest is in whether the Justice departs from the appointing President's ideology in any direction.[24]

For the President's ideology we rely on estimates by Keith Poole, based on the President's positions on bills before Congress.[25] Poole's scores range from −.485 for President Kennedy to .702 for the second President Bush. In order to have a comparable measure of judicial ideology so that we can compute the distance between the President's and the Justice's ideology beginning with the latter's appointment, we use the Martin-Quinn scores.[26] (For the Justice's first year, we use his Martin-Quinn score in his first term.) Our analysis ends with the 2008 (not 2009) term because at this writing Martin-Quinn scores are unavailable for subsequent terms.

The regression is based on 626 observations for the Justices who served on the Court for at least one term during the period that extends from the 1953 term to the 2008 term. For each Justice the number of observations equals the number of terms he served on the Court. We aggre-

23. See Lawrence Baum, *Judges and Their Audiences* (2006); Michael C. Dorf, "Does Federal Executive Branch Experience Explain Why Some Republican Supreme Court Justices 'Evolve' and Others Don't?" 1 *Harvard Law and Policy Review* 457 (2007); Linda Greenhouse, "Justices Who Change: A Response to Epstein et al.," 101 *Northwestern University Law Review* 1885 (2007).

24. For Rehnquist, the appointing President is Nixon through the 1985 term. Beginning in the 1986 term, when Rehnquist became Chief Justice, the appointing President is Reagan. We count Rehnquist as one Justice and treat Nixon as the appointing President, but counting Rehnquist as two Justices—an Associate Justice beginning in 1971 and Chief Justice beginning in 1986—would not alter our regression results. Stone was appointed by Roosevelt as Chief Justice in 1941. Since the data in the regression analysis begin in 1937, we measure Stone's ideological distance from Roosevelt rather than from Coolidge, who first appointed him to the Supreme Court.

25. See chapter 2, text at note 18.

26. Using a procedure outlined in Lee Epstein et al., "The Judicial Common Space," 23 *Journal of Law, Economics, and Organization* 303 (2007), Andrew Martin transformed for us the Justices' Martin-Quinn scores to enable us to compare them to Poole's scores for Presidents.

gate observations by term, because the ideological direction of a Justice's votes can be expected to be uniform in a given term, so that treating each vote of each Justice as a separate observation would create an exaggerated impression of the Justice's ideological consistency across terms.

The basic regression results are in column (1) of Table 3.7. The coefficient on *Tenure* is positive and implies that the ideological distance between Justice and President increases by an average of 2.9 percent a year. Equivalently, at the start of the Justice's career the correlation between the President's and the Justice's ideology is .65 but it declines to .42 after 10 years and .31 after 20 years.

The coefficient on the federal employment variable is negative—and large. The predicted ideological distance between Justice and President after one year is .24 if the appointee worked for the federal government in the District of Columbia but .48 if he did not. After 10 years the figures are .35 and .60 and after 20 years .48 and .72, which is the same gap after only one year for a Justice who did not work for the government at the time of his appointment.

The coefficients on age and on whether the Justice had been a court of appeals judge are not statistically significant.

Column (2) adds an interaction term to test whether ideological divergence is more gradual for Justices who worked for the federal government

Table 3.7   Regression of Ideological Divergence in Supreme Court, 1953–2008 Terms

	(1)	(2)	(3)
Tenure	0.013*	0.028**	0.011*
	(2.43)	(6.09)	(2.53)
First-Term Ideological Divergence	—	—	0.896**
			(5.84)
Age	0.006	0.004	0.008
	(0.90)	(0.60)	(1.51)
Former Federal Employment in	−0.243*	0.065	0.234*
District of Columbia	(2.43)	(0.64)	(3.43)
Former Judge	−0.085	−0.096	−0.023
	(0.84)	(1.06)	(0.34)
Interaction Term	—	−0.026**	—
		(4.18)	
R^2	.24	.35	.52

before being appointed. The answer is yes. The divergence of those Justices is predicted to be .37 after 10 years and .39 after 20 (a 5 percent increase), compared to .57 and .85 (a 49 percent increase) for the other Justices.

Any initial ideological difference between a President and a Justice he appoints should be known to the President; so any first-year difference in ideology between Justice and President would be evidence not of ideological divergence but of an ideological difference that existed when the Justice was appointed. We adjust by including the absolute ideological difference between the Justice and President in the Justice's first term as an independent variable. With this adjustment, the regression is based on 590 rather than 626 observations because we lose one observation per Justice. We also lose one Justice, because Byrne served only one term (1941).

The results are shown in column (3). We see that both length of service and first-term ideological divergence are highly significant predictors of divergence starting in the Justice's second term. The coefficient on first-term divergence is not significantly different from 1, implying that it persists throughout the Justice's career. This suggests a big potential ideological payoff to the President from learning a potential Justice's ideological inclination. The divergence (holding constant first-term divergence) is 3.9 percent per year (.011/.28, where .28 is the mean value of first-term divergence for the 35 Justices in the regression), compared to only 2.9 percent per year when first-term divergence is included. As before, service for the government before appointment to the Supreme Court has a powerful effect in reducing ideological divergence. The predicted divergence is almost the same for a Justice who had worked for the government and served twenty terms as a Justice (.44) as it is for a Justice who left the Court after two terms and had not worked for the government (.49). We added the interaction term from regression (3); as before, both it and length of service were significant, and again, for Justices who worked for the government, there is only a negligible increase in ideological divergence as length of service increases.

Ideological drift and ideological divergence have implications not only for Supreme Court appointments but also for appointments to the courts of appeals. Suppose a President as part of his legacy wants the Justices whom he appoints to perpetuate his ideology long after he has ceased to be President. This implies appointing Justices at a young age—which, however, increases the risk of ideological drift and divergence. To counter this risk a President might create a pool of possible Supreme Court appointees consisting of court of appeals judges, on the theory that a judge's performance on the court of appeals will provide better evidence of his ideological commitments than experience as a practicing lawyer.

Table 3.8 suggests that Republican Presidents beginning with Reagan followed such a policy (at least after they ran out of conservative academics to appoint—there were not and are not many conservative legal academics); it is one reason why today all but one of the Justices is a former federal court of appeals judge (another reason, however, is that Democratic Presidents appointed three Justices who had been court of appeals judges—Breyer, Ginsburg, and Sotomayor).

Table 3.8   Average Age of Court of Appeals Appointments, Eisenhower to Obama

	Average Age at Time of Appointment	Number of Appointees	Number ≤ 45 Years Old at Time of Appointment	Percent ≤ 45 Years Old at Time of Appointment
Eisenhower	56.6	45	3	6.7
Kennedy	54.7	20	2	10.0
Johnson	52.4	41	4	9.8
Nixon	54.0	45	4	8.9
Ford	52.6	12	1	8.3
Carter	52.3	56	10	17.9
Reagan	50.5	78	19	24.4
Bush I	50.0	38	9	23.7
Clinton	52.3	61	9	14.8
Bush II	51.0	59	13	22.0
Obama	55.0	15	1	6.7
1953–1980				
Democratic	52.7*	117	16	13.7
Republican	55.0	102	8	7.8
1981–2010				
Democratic	52.8*	76	10	13.2
Republican	50.4	175	41	23.4

Note: An asterisk indicates that the difference between Democratic and Republican appointees is significant in the 1953–1980 and 1981–2010 periods.

To implement such a policy and yet appoint Supreme Court Justices at a young enough age to create an ideological legacy implies appointing court of appeals judges at a young age—and Republican Presidents beginning with Reagan have done that. The average age of appointees to the courts of appeals by Republican appointees was 55 from the Eisenhower Administration through the Ford Administration but dropped nearly 5 years beginning with Reagan. In contrast, the average age of appointees to the courts of appeals by Democratic Presidents has remained about 53 over the past 50 years—except that Obama's 15 appointees (at this writing) were appointed at an average age of 55.[27]

Notice the difference in the table between Republican and Democratic Presidents since 1980 in appointments of persons no older than 45. Before 1980 a higher percentage of the judges appointed by Democratic Presidents were in that youthful age group; after 1980 the percentages reverse decisively. But we doubt that this method of minimizing ideological divergence is effective, since the age variable in Table 3.7 is not statistically significant—and indeed age is positively correlated with drift. We'll see in chapters 6 and 8 that dissent aversion and auditioning behavior may make the voting record of a court of appeals judge a poor predictor of his voting record in the Supreme Court.

The results in the table imply that a President who wants to minimize ideological divergence should favor Supreme Court candidates who have an ideology identical to his and about whom he can obtain good information because they are working for the federal government in the District of Columbia.

But changes in judicial ideology must be distinguished from differences, which may or may not be related to length of service, between the ideology that a Justice (or judge) brings with him to the bench (his ex ante ideology) and the ideology reflected in his judicial votes (his ex post ideology). These differences, examined in the next chapter for both the Supreme Court and the courts of appeals, provide insights into the balance between ideological and legalistic voting in the two appellate tiers.

---

27. See also Micah Schwartzman, "Not Getting Any Younger: President Obama's Penchant for Older Judges Scuttled Goodwin Liu," *Slate,* May 26, 2011, www.slate.com/id/2295597/ (visited Dec. 9, 2011).

Unanimous Decisions: The Role of Ideology

The Supreme Court is widely regarded, and not only by political scientists, as a political Court, an impression reinforced by the angry dissents in many controversial cases. Yet the fact that a substantial fraction of the Court's decisions are unanimous despite the Court's being ideologically divided suggests that legalism plays a role too. The unanimous decisions are therefore an important subject for study, but a rather neglected one.[28]

We define unanimous decisions as ones in which no Justice dissented, even if there were one or more concurring opinions. Concurring opinions are more common in unanimous decisions than in non-unanimous ones—41 percent of the unanimous decisions in the Spaeth database include concurring opinions, compared to 38 percent of the non-unanimous ones—although the reason may be arithmetical: in a 5–4 decision the maximum number of concurring opinions is 4; in a 9–0 decision it is 8.

Except in the 1969 term, when only eight Justices sat, we exclude unanimous cases in which one or more Justice was absent because we can't be certain that a ninth Justice would have agreed with the other eight.

About 29 percent of the Court's orally argued decisions in the 1946–2009 period were decided unanimously. Figure 3.1 shows that the percentage increased from 21 percent in 1946–1952 (the Vinson court) to 34 percent in 2005–2009 (the Roberts Court), with part of the increase being the result of an increasing fraction of unanimous decisions reversing the Ninth Circuit.[29] Over the entire period about 73 percent of Ninth Circuit decisions that the Supreme Court reviewed were reversed unani-

28. Not entirely, however. See Paul H. Edelman, David E. Klein, and Stefanie A. Lindquist, "Consensus, Disorder, and Ideology on the Supreme Court," *Journal of Empirical Legal Studies* (forthcoming); Pamela C. Corley, Amy Steigerwalt, and Artemus Ward, "Deciding to Agree: Explaining Consensual Behavior on the United States Supreme Court" (paper presented at 2008 annual meeting of the Midwest Political Science Association); Saul Brenner and Theodore S. Arrington, "Decision Making on the U.S. Supreme Court: Case Stimuli and Judicial Attitudes," 9 *Political Behavior* 75 (1987); Thomas R. Hensley and Scott P. Johnson, "Unanimity on the Rehnquist Court," 31 *Akron Law Review* 387 (1998).

29. On the "rogue" character of the Ninth Circuit, see Richard A. Posner, "Is the Ninth Circuit Too Large? A Statistical Study of Judicial Quality," 29 *Journal of Legal Studies* 711 (2000).

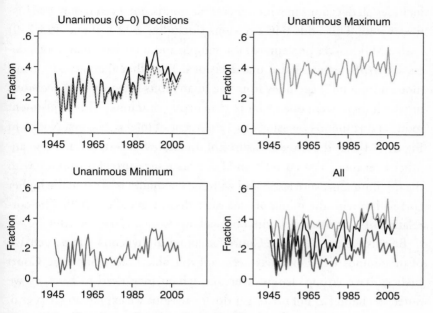

Figure 3.1   Unanimous Supreme Court Decisions, 1946–2009 Terms

Notes:

1. In the top left panel, the solid line shows unanimous 9–0 decisions except for the 1969 term, which includes 8–0 decisions because there were only eight Justices that term. The lighter dashed line shows 9–0 decisions excluding reversals of Ninth Circuit decisions.

2. Unanimous Maximum includes all orally argued decisions in which there was no dissenting opinion and thus adds to the unanimous category an additional 502 8–0 decisions, 124 7–0 decisions, 16 6–0 decisions, and 4 5–0 decisions.

3. Unanimous Minimum excludes unanimous decisions if there were one or more concurring opinions.

4. All includes all lines except unanimous reversals of Ninth Circuit decisions.

mously, compared to 63 percent for the other circuits. If we exclude reversals of the Ninth Circuit, the growth in unanimous decisions falls from 1.35 to 1.07 percent a year.[30] Even if we include them, there is no significant positive trend since Rehnquist's first term as Chief Justice, 25 years ago. The percentage peaked in 1997 at 51.1 percent (40.2 percent excluding Ninth Circuit reversals) and has declined since, to 37 percent.

Figure 3.1 presents alternative conceptions of a "unanimous" decision to the one we've been using. One alternative ("unanimous maximum")

---

30. We regressed the log of the percentage of unanimous decisions (with and without unanimous reversals of the Ninth Circuit) against time. The coefficients (and t-ratios) were .0135 (5.23) and .0107 (4.20) and were significantly different from each other.

includes all decisions in which there was no dissent, even if only five Justices voted. This adds 646 decisions (including 502 8–0 and 124 7–0) —an additional 32 percent—to the sample and increases unanimous decisions to 38 percent of the total decisions. The other alternative ("unanimous minimum") excludes from the unanimous category 836 decisions in which there were one or more concurring opinions. This adjustment reduces unanimous decisions to 17 percent of total decisions. Notice in Figure 3.1 that the three measures of unanimity generally track one another over time. The correlation of our main measure of unanimity with the minimum measure is .88 and with the maximum is .48, but the higher correlation with the minimum measure disappears after 1990. The correlation of both measures with our main measure is .76 since 1990.

Because of the Supreme Court's ideological divisions, the percentage of unanimous decisions may seem inexplicable unless Supreme Court Justices have strong dissent aversion, which they used to have, as we noted in chapter 2, but no longer do, for reasons we explain in chapter 6. An alternative explanation is that unanimous decisions are found only in cases that do not present ideological issues. A third possible explanation combines the first two: the ideological stakes are small in cases that are candidates for being decided unanimously, so even slight dissent aversion will generate a unanimous decision if the ideological stakes are small. A fourth explanation—the most plausible—adds to the third that when the ideological stakes are small, a combination of dissent aversion and legalistic commitments is likely to override Justices' ideological preferences.[31]

Supreme Court Justices are unlikely to be indifferent to such legalistic norms as *stare decisis;* a rampant disregard of precedent would unsettle the law and reduce the Justices' perceived legitimacy. (This doesn't necessarily mean that they "believe" these norms in some strong sense; they may just find them useful politically or because of their effect in reducing workload.) We predict therefore that few decisions overruling precedents

31. We derive this explanation from two papers by Paul H. Edelman, David E. Klein, and Stefanie A. Lindquist: "Measuring Deviations from Expected Voting Patterns on Collegial Courts," 5 *Journal of Empirical Legal Studies* 819 (2008), and "Consensus, Disorder, and Ideology on the Supreme Court," note 28 above. These articles find, as do we, that "disordered voting" (voting against the ideological grain) is unlikely in cases that overrule decisions of the Court.

will be unanimous (though there are some notable exceptions, such as *Brown v. Board of Education*), because a strong ideological conviction is likely to be required to override a commitment to *stare decisis.*[32]

Table 3.9 compares the number of unanimous and non-unanimous Supreme Court decisions that "formally alter" a Supreme Court precedent. The data come from the Spaeth database, which codes decisions as formally altering precedent if they say they're overruling a decision or use equivalent language, such as that the decision is "disapproved" or is "no longer good law." Notice that only 1.6 percent of unanimous cases formally alter precedent, while 2.3 percent of non-unanimous ones do. Stated otherwise, 22 percent of cases in which precedent is altered are unanimous compared to 29 percent in which it is not . These differences, however, are not statistically significant (the t-statistic is 1.75; to reach the .05 level it would have to be 1.96).

The number of unanimous cases that formally alter precedent drops sharply, from 33 in Table 3.9 to 16, when we use the "minimum" definition of unanimity (that is, where there is a concurring opinion). This suggests a weaker commitment to unanimity when a case formally alters precedent. But it's a weak suggestion. The presence of a concurring opinion in a case in which the vote is unanimous need not indicate disagreement with the reasoning of the majority opinion; it may indicate an attempt to bolster that reasoning or extend the scope of the decision.

We can derive additional evidence of the ideological stakes in unanimous Supreme Court decisions from the nature of the case (such as whether it is a civil liberties case or a tax case) and from the presence or absence of a dissent in the lower court. We do this by estimating the following regression equation for the probability of a unanimous decision:

$$P_u = f(Dissent, Reversal, CA\ Conflict, Other\ Conflict, Nonideological,$$
$$Ninth\ Circuit, Chief, Subject\ Area, u)$$

32. See, for example, Thomas G. Hansford and James F. Spriggs II, *The Politics of Precedent in the U.S. Supreme Court,* ch. 5 (2006). Hansford and Spriggs find that the Court is especially reluctant to overrule precedents that exhibit "vitality" as evidenced by the number of favorable references to them in Supreme Court opinions.

Table 3.9   Formal Precedent Alteration by Supreme Court, 1946–2009 Terms

	Unanimous		Non-unanimous	
	Cases	Percent	Cases	Percent
Alters Precedent	33	1.61	116	2.26
Does Not Alter Precedent	2017	98.39	5018	97.74
Total	2050	100.0	5134	100.0
	Precedent Alteration		No Precedent Alteration	
	Number of Cases	Percent	Number of Cases	Percent
Unanimous	33	22.1	2017	28.7
Non-unanimous	116	77.9	5018	71.3
Total	149	100.0	7035	100.0

The independent variables (all dummy variables) are *Dissent* (meaning that the majority opinion in the Supreme Court notes that there was a dissent in the lower court—it doesn't always, which means that we're underestimating the number of lower court opinions in which there was a dissent[33]); *Reversal* (Supreme Court reversed the lower court); *CA Conflict* (Court mentioned a conflict among federal courts of appeals on the issue on which certiorari was granted); *Other Conflict* (conflict among state courts or between a federal court [or courts] of appeals and a state court or courts[34]); *Nonideological* (ideological direction of the Supreme Court decision could not be specified—slightly more than 1 percent of the decisions in our sample could not be classified as either conservative or liberal, suggesting that ideological issues were not salient, and so we expect those cases to be disproportionately decided unanimously); *Ninth Circuit* (case came from the Ninth Circuit); *Chief* (a set of dummy vari-

33. In a dataset created by Lee Epstein and Jeffrey Segal consisting of a random sample of 907 cert. petitions in which certiorari was granted, the law clerk writing the cert-pool memo mentioned a lower court dissent in 334 cases, but in only 232 of the 334 did the Supreme Court's majority opinion mention the dissent.

34. Of the 1535 conflict cases, 1336 (87 percent) involve conflicts among the courts of appeals. The remaining 199 cases mainly involve conflicts between a federal and a state court or between state courts. Again there is underestimation. For example, in the random sample discussed in the preceding footnote, the Court gave no reason for granting cert. in 337 cases, but in 148 of them (44 percent) the cert-pool memo noted the existence of a conflict among federal or state courts.

Table 3.10 Description of Variables in Regressions of Unanimous Decisions, 1946–2009 Terms

	Mean (standard deviation)	
	All	Unanimous Only
Unanimous Decision: Coded 1 (yes) or 0 (no)	0.29	—
	(0.45)	
Direction: Ideological direction of Supreme Court decision	0.49	0.42
	(0.50)	(0.49)
Dissent: Dissent in court below	0.22	0.20
	(0.42)	(0.40)
Reversal: Reversal of court below	0.63	0.66
	(0.48)	(0.47)
CA Conflict: Conflict among federal appellate courts	0.22	0.27
	(0.42)	(0.45)
Other Conflict: Conflict among federal and state courts or among state courts	0.03	0.04
	(0.18)	(0.19)
Lower Court Ideological Direction: Ideological direction of lower court decision, coded 1 (conservative) or 0 (liberal)	0.56	0.57
	(0.50)	(0.50)
Nonideological: Ideological direction of Supreme Court decision unspecifiable	0.01	0.01
	(0.10)	(0.12)
Ninth Circuit: Case from Ninth Circuit	0.11	0.15
	(0.32)	(0.36)
Supreme Court Median: Ideology of the Court's median Justice each term as measured by Segal-Cover scores	0.52	0.55
	(0.23)	(0.22)
Fraction Republican: Fraction of Justices appointed by a Republican President	0.59	0.63
	(0.26)	(0.25)
Civil Liberties: (Adjusted) civil liberties case. Includes criminal procedure, civil rights, First Amendment, due process, attorney, and privacy cases.	0.51	0.44
	(0.50)	(0.50)
Economics: Economic case. Includes economic activity, union, and tax cases.	0.30	0.31
	(0.46)	(0.46)
Judicial Power: Judicial power case	0.13	0.19
	(0.34)	(0.39)
Federalism: Federalism case	0.05	0.05
	(0.23)	(0.22)
Number of Observations	7184	1728

Note: All regressions are limited to orally argued cases.

ables for the terms of the five Chief Justices in our sample—Vinson, Warren, Burger, Rehnquist, and Roberts, with Vinson the omitted variable); and *Subject Area* (a set of dummy variables denoting civil liberties, economic, and judicial power cases—the omitted category, which accounts for fewer than 6 percent of the cases, mainly federalism cases). Table 3.10 lists the variables and their means.

We predict a negative coefficient on *Dissent* and positive coefficients on *Reversal, CA Conflict,* and *Nonideological.* A dissent in the lower court suggests that the case has substantial ideological stakes; had they been insubstantial the lower court probably would have been unanimous (even if the panel was ideologically mixed), owing to the strong dissent aversion that we find in the federal courts of appeals in chapter 6. But we have not studied dissent aversion in state supreme courts, and many U.S. Supreme Court decisions come in appeals from such courts—of the 7159 orally argued cases that the Court heard in the 1946 through 2010 terms, 1619 (23 percent) came from state courts.

A unanimous decision is also more likely when the Court reverses rather than affirms the lower court, because some reversals are motivated just by error correction—to keep the lower courts in line on what may be technical issues with slight or no ideological stakes. The Court would have little reason to affirm a case involving a technical issue that the court of appeals had got right unless there was an intercircuit conflict. The Court feels some obligation to resolve such conflicts even if they don't present challenging issues—which are the issues that are likely to be ideologically charged, and so neither affirmances nor reversals in such cases are as likely to be ideologically motivated as other Supreme Court decisions. *Other Conflict* may be less likely to involve technical issues, in which event it would have a weaker effect on the likelihood of a unanimous decision than *CA Conflict.*

We expect a positive coefficient on *Ninth Circuit* because of the large number of unanimous reversals of Ninth Circuit cases. And since ideology is expected to play a larger role in civil liberties cases than in the other subject-matter areas, we predict a negative relation between the civil liberties variable and the likelihood of a unanimous decision.

The positive trend in the fraction of unanimous decisions should yield positive coefficients on the *Chief* dummy variables (since Vinson, who was Chief Justice when the unanimity rate was lowest, is the omitted variable). The effect should be largest in the Rehnquist and Roberts Courts, in view of the increase in the fraction of unanimous decisions in the last 25 years.

We experimented with two other variables: a rough measure of the

Court's ideological uniformity in each term and the Court's caseload. Neither was close to being statistically significant or affected the size or significance of the other variables—results contrary to expectations generated by our model.

Table 3.11 presents the results of the regression. The two regression equations are nearly identical except that (2) includes the two conflict

Table 3.11   Logit Analysis of the Probability of Unanimous Supreme Court Decision, 1946–2009 Terms

	Probability of Unanimous Decision	
	(1)	(2)
Dissent	−0.068**	−0.066**
	(4.86)	(4.22)
Reversal	0.054**	0.059**
	(4.39)	(4.45)
CA Conflict	—	0.057**
		(4.48)
Other Conflict	—	0.049
		(1.35)
Nonideological	0.042	0.085
	(0.99)	(1.19)
Ninth Circuit	0.016	0.016
	(0.95)	(0.92)
Warren Court (1953–1968)	0.044	0.048
	(0.81)	(0.84)
Burger Court (1969–1985)	0.066	0.065
	(1.32)	(1.28)
Rehnquist Court (1986–2004)	0.166**	0.158**
	(3.33)	(3.15)
Roberts Court (2005–)	0.139**	0.130**
	(2.93)	(2.74)
Civil Liberties	−0.082**	−0.104**
	(3.45)	(3.68)
Economics	−0.023	−0.050
	(0.90)	(1.67)
Judicial Power	0.076**	0.061
	(2.71)	(1.88)
Number of Observations	7184	6020

Notes:

1. The entries are marginal-effect coefficients.

2. Federalism and Miscellaneous are the omitted case categories.

3. Standard errors are adjusted by clustering on term of Court (so 64 clusters, 1 for each term).

variables and contains fewer observations (6020 instead of 7184) because our data on conflicts are based on the reasons the majority opinion gave for granting certiorari, and in 1164 cases no reason was given.

Dissent has a negative and highly significant effect in both equations. A lower court dissent produces a .068 decline in the probability of a unanimous decision, which is a 23 percent decline relative to the mean probability, .29, of a unanimous decision when there is no dissent in the lower court. *Reversal* and *CA Conflict* have positive and highly significant effects on unanimity; a reversal and a conflict in the lower courts raise the probability of a unanimous decision by .054 and .057 respectively (19 and 20 percent relative to the mean of .285). *Other Conflict* is insignificant, which is not surprising since we have no information on how often other conflicts involve nonideological issues. *Nonideological* and *Ninth Circuit* are also not significant.

The predicted probability of a unanimous decision is lower in civil liberties cases than in judicial power cases (21 and 36 percent respectively), as is to be expected, since civil liberties is a more ideologically charged field. In addition, cases are more likely to be decided unanimously by both the Rehnquist and Roberts Courts than by the Burger, Warren, and Vinson Courts.

If we add a dummy variable for whether the case was decided in a per curiam opinion rather than a signed one, the positive coefficient on the judicial power variable is no longer statistically significant. A disproportionate number of judicial power cases are decided per curiam—23 percent, versus only 5 percent on average for all other subject-matter areas—and per curiam decisions, even in orally argued cases (our sample is limited to such cases), are found generally in the less important or less contentious cases (though there are some famous exceptions[35]). Out of the 534 per curiam decisions in our Supreme Court sample of orally argued cases, 43 percent were unanimous, compared to 27 percent of the orally argued cases decided in a signed opinion. Sometimes a case is dis-

---

35. See, for example, Furman v. Georgia, 408 U.S. 238 (1972); Buckley v. Valeo, 424 U.S. 1 (1976); Bush v. Gore, 531 U.S. 98 (2000). A comparison of orally argued per curiams with all other orally argued cases on a common measure of case importance reveals that even orally argued per curiams are significantly less likely to be covered on the front page of the *New York Times* than signed opinions.

Table 3.12 Fraction of Unanimous Decisions across Fine Subject-Matter Classes

Subject Area	Fraction	Number of Cases
Interstate Relations	0.41	56
Judicial Power	0.41	943
Federalism	0.33	336
Attorneys	0.31	81
Unions	0.29	332
Economic Activity	0.29	1504
Civil Rights	0.29	1124
Privacy	0.28	90
Federal Taxation	0.28	290
Due Process	0.26	301
Criminal Procedure	0.20	1539
First Amendment	0.20	563

Notes:

1. We excluded the Miscellaneous category because it contained only 17 cases.

2. The total number of cases is 7159.

missed in a per curiam opinion because a jurisdictional flaw was discovered after the case had been argued, so there is no decision on the merits to classify as liberal or conservative.[36]

Table 3.12 lists the fraction of unanimous decisions in each subject-matter category, ranked from highest to lowest. Four of the five categories (all but taxation) in which the fraction of unanimous decisions is below the mean of .285—due process, criminal procedure, First Amendment, and privacy—are ideologically charged, but so are some of the categories in which the fraction of unanimous decisions is at or above the mean, such as civil rights, unions, and federalism.

We suggested earlier that if the ideological stakes in a case are small, even slight dissent aversion is likely to produce a unanimous decision. But the outcomes might still be correlated with the Court's overall ideology. We test that hypothesis using two measures of ideology: the fraction of Justices appointed by Republican Presidents and the Justices' Segal-Cover scores. We experimented with two other measures of the Court's

---

36. We also estimated the regressions in Table 3.11 substituting the alternative measures of unanimity (the minimum and maximum measures). The results were very similar. Although the magnitude of the regression coefficients differed, the direction of the effects and the levels of significant were the same.

ideology—the Martin-Quinn score and the fraction of Justices who identified themselves as Republicans when they were appointed (this fraction was identical to the fraction appointed by a Republican President in the 1990 to 2008 terms but not in the 1958 to 1989 terms—for example, Powell, appointed by Nixon, was a Democrat). These substitutions had only minor effects on the regression results.

Petitioners prevailed in 66 percent of the unanimous cases—meaning that the Court reversed the decision that had been appealed. We expect a negative coefficient on the variable for the ideological direction of the lower court decision because we expect reversals, which dominate the Court's decisions, to be heavily influenced by ideology, since the Supreme Court has neither the time nor the inclination to correct merely technical errors by the lower courts. Testing this hypothesis requires estimating separate regressions for unanimous decisions in which there is and those in which there is not a lower court conflict; for if there is a conflict that the Supreme Court wants to resolve, it is immaterial which side of the conflict the lower court is on in the case that the Supreme Court decides to hear.

Table 3.13 presents the results of the regression analysis. The ideological direction of the lower court decision is highly significant in regressions (1) and (2). The effects are large. For example, a conservative lower court decision reduces (and a liberal lower court decision increases) the probability of a conservative unanimous Supreme Court decision by between .42 and .44. This is, to repeat, because of the tendency of the Supreme Court to take cases in order to reverse the lower court decision.

The coefficients on the two ideological measures (*Fraction Republican* and *Segal-Cover*) are positive, but the first is not statistically significant in equation (1) and both have only small effects. The coefficients imply that a decline in the number of Justices appointed by a Republican President from 5 to 4 would decrease the fraction of conservative unanimous decisions by between .015 in equation (1), which holds constant the ideological direction of the lower court decision, and .026 in equation (3), which is limited to cases in which there was a conflict in the lower courts. Neither effect is large relative to the .41 fraction of unanimous Supreme Court decisions that are conservative. The predicted effects would be much greater if a Court consisting of eight Justices appointed by Republi-

Table 3.13 Logit Analysis of the Ideological Direction of Unanimous Decisions, 1946–2009 Terms

	Fraction Conservative Votes			
	No Conflict in Lower Courts		Conflict in Lower Courts	
	(1)	(2)	(3)	(4)
Ideological Direction of Lower Court Decision	−0.441** (10.92)	−0.417** (10.38)	—	—
Fraction Republican	0.138 (1.70)	—	0.236* (2.05)	—
Segal-Cover Median	—	0.339** (4.00)	—	0.465** (3.41)
Ninth Circuit	0.124* (2.51)	0.115* (2.28)	0.082 (1.36)	0.077 (1.28)
Civil Liberties	0.094 (1.33)	0.092 (1.31)	−0.036 (0.32)	−0.057 (0.50)
Economics	0.042 (0.60)	0.042 (0.62)	−0.139 (1.43)	−0.141** (1.41)
Judicial Power	0.502** (6.87)	0.500** (6.78)	0.034 (0.32)	0.023 (0.21)
Number of Observations	1189	1189	539	539

Notes:

1. The entries are marginal-effect coefficients at the mean values of all variables.

2. Federalism and Miscellaneous are again the omitted case categories.

3. The ideological direction of the 1189 9–0 decisions (8–0 for the 1969 term) is coded 0 = liberal; 1 = conservative.

4. Standard errors are clustered by term of Court (64 clusters, 1 for each term).

can Presidents and one appointed by a Democratic President changed to a Court of eight *D*s and one *R*. That would reduce the probability of a conservative unanimous decision by between .11 and .19 (27 and 46 percent respectively) relative to the mean of .41.

When we substitute Segal-Cover scores for *Fraction Republican,* the coefficients on the Court's ideology are more significant, as those scores avoid the obvious errors of classifying Brennan, Stevens, and Souter as conservative Justices just because Republican Presidents appointed them.

Of the remaining variables in Table 3.13, cases from the Ninth Circuit are significantly more likely to be decided conservatively when the ideological direction of the Ninth Circuit decision is held constant. But this effect is not significant when the Ninth Circuit decision involves an intercircuit conflict (equations (3) and (4)); this is consistent with our distinction between conflict and nonconflict cases. The subject-matter variables are generally not significant except for the increase in the probability of a conservative decision in judicial power cases in equations (1) and (2) but not in (3) and (4).

In short, we find that ideology plays only a small role in unanimous decisions. This is consistent with our theory, and with the indirect evidence presented in Table 3.13, that decisions are unanimous when the ideological stakes are not large enough to lead a Justice who disagrees with the majority to dissent.

Table 3.14 rounds off the analysis by presenting some voting characteristics of the current Justices, minus Kagan (too recently appointed to have enough votes) but plus Souter, who was appointed in the same general period as Thomas, Ginsburg, and Breyer; we exclude Stevens and O'Connor, who were appointed much earlier. The table reveals that the liberal Justices, plus Thomas, have the highest combined percentage of votes in unanimous decisions and dissenting votes. The implication (ignoring Thomas, an outlier in many respects) is that liberals are more inclined to join decisions that do not involve significant ideological stakes and are more inclined to dissent in cases that do because the Court is predominantly conservative. Justice Kennedy, the swing Justice, gets his way most of the time: he dissents the least among the Justices, and writes or joins concurring opinions rarely. Scalia—arguably the Court's intellectual

Table 3.14 Votes by Recently Appointed Justices (Beginning with Souter and Excluding Kagan)

Name	Percentage of Justice's Votes Cast in Unanimous Decisions	Percentage of Justice's Dissenting Votes in All Cases	Percentage of Justice's Concurring Votes in All Cases	Percentage Justice's Concu Votes in Unani Decisions
Alito	0.374	0.159	0.123	0.124
Breyer	0.421	0.207	0.118	0.112
Ginsburg	0.420	0.217	0.098	0.111
Kennedy	0.413	0.097	0.096	0.077
Roberts	0.391	0.122	0.063	0.056
Scalia	0.405	0.178	0.155	0.164
Sotomayor	0.424	0.227	0.106	0.107
Souter	0.419	0.182	0.094	0.109
Thomas	0.421	0.202	0.144	0.148

leader—writes or joins concurring opinions the most. Roberts is the least frequent dissenter after Kennedy and writes or joins the fewest concurring opinions, perhaps in order to signal that as Chief Justice he usually gets his way or that he seeks by his example to promote consensus.

Non-unanimous Decisions: The Role of Ideology

We turn now to the Court's non-unanimous decisions. Table 3.15 lists the variables in a regression analysis that we have done of those decisions. We estimate two regression equations:

$$SC = f(I, u) \tag{i}$$

$$Vote = f(I, u, LC, T, G, w) \tag{ii}$$

The dependent variable in equation (i) is the Justice's Segal-Cover score *(SC)*. The independent variables *(I)* are a set of ideological proxies and control variables: the party of the appointing President, the ideological composition of the Senate at the time of the Justice's appointment, the Justice's first term on the Supreme Court, and whether he had been an appellate judge before being appointed to the Supreme Court. The residual u in equation (i) is the difference between the Justice's actual and predicted Segal-Cover score. The dependent variable in equation (ii), *Vote,* is the ideological direction of the Justice's vote (1 = conservative and 0 = liberal) in each non-unanimous decision in the 1946–2009 terms. The independent variables are I and (crucially) the residual u from equation (i), plus LC (the ideological direction of the lower court decision—again 1 = conservative), T (a time trend), and G (group effects). The residual in (ii) is w.

The purpose of equation (i) is to generate an ideological variable, u, that is uncorrelated with the party of the appointing President, the composition of the Senate, the year of appointment, or the Justice's prior experience—that is therefore a pure measure of a Justice's own ideology. (Or nearly pure; prior experience may influence a person's ideology.). A positive u in equation (i) indicates that the Justice is even more conservative than one would predict from knowing the variables in I, and a nega-

Table 3.15 Definition and Means of Variables in Regressions of Non-unanimous Supreme Court Decisions, 1946–2008 Terms

	Definition	Mean
Vote	Justice voted conservatively (= 1) or liberally (= 0) in non-unanimous cases	0.506
Segal-Cover	Ex ante ideology (from 1 = most conservative to 0 = most liberal)	0.445
President	Party of appointing President: Republican (= 1) or Democratic (= 0)	0.486
Senate Republican	Fraction of Republican Senators at time of Justice's appointment	0.407
Residual (u_i)	Ideology not explained in Segal–Cover regression	0
Term	Term of court or time trend variable	1977.5
First Term	First Supreme Court term after Justice's confirmation	1965.4
Former Appellate Judge	Justice was appellate judge for at least two years prior to appointment to the Supreme Court	0.543
Fraction Other Republican	Fraction of other Justices appointed by Republican Presidents at time case decided	0.589
Ideological Direction of Lower Court Decision	Decision of court reviewed by Supreme Court was conservative (= 1) or liberal (= 0)	0.542
Adjusted Civil Liberties	Adjusted Civil Liberties case (= 1) if criminal procedure, civil rights, First Amendment, due process, attorney, or privacy; otherwise = 0	0.586
Economic	Economic case	0.284
Judicial Power	Judicial power case	0.087
Federalism	Federalism case	0.044

Notes:

1. Vote, Fraction Other Republican, Ideological Direction of Lower Court Decision, Adjusted Civil Liberties, Economic, Judicial Power, and Federalism were calculated for 37,420 observations, consisting of non-unanimous votes the ideological direction of which could be determined.

2. Segal-Cover, President, Senate Republican, Residual, First Term, and Former Appellate Judge were calculated for 35 observations (= number of Justices).

tive u indicates that he is more liberal than would have been predicted from those variables.

Suppose a Justice has a Segal-Cover score of 0, the most liberal possible such score, and yet had been nominated by a Republican President and confirmed by a Republican Senate. Then factors other than the political identity of the appointing authorities must have been responsible for the Justice's super-liberalism. The residual in equation (i) provides a purer estimate of the judicial candidate's ideology than his predicted Segal-Cover score, which is based on the party of the appointing President and other factors only indirectly related to the candidate's ideology.

The regression results are in Table 3.16. Regression (1) estimates equation (i) above, the equation in which the Justice's Segal-Cover score *(SC)* is the dependent variable. There are 35 observations in this regression—one for each Justice with a Segal-Cover score. The other three regressions estimate equation (ii), where *Vote* is the dependent variable.

The variables in regression (1) explain about 42 percent of the variance in Segal-Cover scores. Two of the four variables are statistically significant: Justices appointed by Republican Presidents have significantly higher conservative scores prior to confirmation than those appointed by Democratic Presidents, and even when the party of the appointing President is held constant, more recent appointees *(First Term)* tend to be more conservative.

We use u as an independent variable in regressions (2) through (4) to predict the ideology of the Justice's vote. Regression (2) analyzes the votes of the 35 Justices in the 1946–2009 terms. Regression (3) is limited to 17 Justices appointed by Republican Presidents and regression (4) to 14 Justices appointed by Democratic Presidents.

Regression (2) reveals that Justices appointed by Republican Presidents tend to vote conservatively in a higher fraction of cases than Justices appointed by Democratic Presidents, but the result is not statistically significant. That may seem surprising in light of Table 3.5, which showed highly significant differences between *R*s and *D*s in nearly all subject-matter areas even though Presidents have sometimes appointed Justices whose ideologies differed from their own. But the lack of significance is a statistical artifact rather than evidence that Justices are nonideological. The earlier table compared differences in voting without holding other variables constant, such as the Justice's ideology prior to his appointment. Whenever a regression includes two or more highly correlated independent variables, the significance level of each drops compared to what it would be without the correlated variables. (Suppose, for example, that the dependent variable was whether a person votes and the two variables were the person's income and his years of schooling. The positive correlation between income and years of schooling would make it difficult to estimate a separate effect of income and a separate effect of schooling on voter participation, which is positively correlated with both independent variables.) Thus, the fact that the party of the appointing

Table 3.16   Regression Analysis of Supreme Court Votes in Non-unanimous Cases, 1946–2009 Terms

		Vote (1 = Conservative, 0 = Liberal)		
	Segal-Cover Score (1)	All Justices (2)	Appointed by Republican Presidents (3)	Appointed by Democratic Presidents (4)
President	0.308*	0.137	—	—
	(2.55)	(1.84)		
Fraction Senate	−0.135	0.879	2.255**	0.496
Republican	(0.19)	(1.69)	(3.19)	(0.57)
Residual (u$_i$)	—	0.471**	0.529**	0.505
		(3.90)	(3.12)	(1.62)
Term	—	−0.007**	−0.009**	−0.003
		(3.11)	(4.75)	(0.61)
First Term	0.007*	0.008*	0.011*	0.005
	(2.60)	(2.54)	(2.55)	(0.79)
Former Appellate	−0.111	−0.218**	−0.204*	−0.158
Judge	(1.06)	(2.75)	(2.25)	(1.26)
Fraction Other	—	−0.142	−0.034	−0.147
Republican		(1.25)	(0.14)	(0.86)
Ideological Direction	—	−0.109**	−0.126**	−0.080*
of Lower Court		(6.18)	(7.29)	(2.21)
Decision				
Adjusted Civil	—	0.068	0.111	−0.001
Liberties		(1.43)	(1.88)	(0.01)
Economics	—	0.017	0.068	−0.058
		(0.54)	(1.80)	(1.26)
Judicial Power	—	0.120**	0.127**	0.084
		(3.80)	(2.85)	(1.88)
Constant	−13.392*	—	—	—
	(2.58)			
R^2	.42	—	—	—
N	35	37,420	21,985	15,435

Notes:

1. Equation (1) is a linear regression; equations (2)–(4) are logistic regressions.

2. Regression coefficients in equations (2)–(4) are marginal effects at mean values of all variables.

3. Standard errors in equations (2)–(4) are clustered by Justice. There are 35 clusters (Justices) in equation (2), 17 in equation (3), and 18 in equation (4).

4. Federalism is the omitted subject-matter category.

President and the composition of the Senate are highly correlated (.73) makes it less likely that both variables will be statistically significant in the same regression. They are jointly significant in regression (2), and if we exclude either the President or the Senate variable, the other is significant.

Regression (3) reveals that the Senate's political composition at the time of the Justice's appointment affects how conservative the judicial votes of an R are likely to be. Although we find no effect of Senate composition on votes of Justices appointed by Democratic Presidents (regression (4)), this is because every Justice appointed by a Democratic President was confirmed by a Senate that had a substantial majority of Democratic Senators, whereas only 5 of the 17 Justices appointed by a Republican President (Warren, Scalia, O'Connor, Roberts, and Alito) were confirmed by a Republican-controlled Senate. From regression (3) we can estimate that a change in the Senate lineup from 47 to 53 Republicans would increase the likelihood of a Justice's casting a conservative judicial vote from .55 to .71, because the more conservative the Senate is, the more conservative the nominees for the Court are likely to be.[37]

The personal-ideology variable *(u)* is statistically significant in regressions (2) and (3) but not in (4). Consider Justice Brennan, appointed by a Republican President and confirmed by a Democratic Senate. Although Brennan's Segal-Cover score is 0 (the maximum liberal score), his predicted ideology score in regression (1) is .47, so his u (the difference between his Segal-Cover score and its predicted value) is −.47. In equation (3) this implies that Brennan would vote liberally in 80 percent of the cases he heard, compared to 59 percent if the only factors one knew that might be relevant to his judicial ideology were the party of the appointing President, the composition of the Senate at the time of his appointment, and the values of the other independent variables in the regression during his tenure.

Here is an example at the other end of the ideological spectrum: President Truman appointed Harold Burton in 1945, when Republicans held only 40 percent of the seats in the Senate, so one might have expected

---

37. Estimated without issue-area dummies. We set all other variables at their means or modes for Justices appointed by Republican Presidents.

142 ~ The Supreme Court

Burton to be a liberal. But his Segal-Cover score is a conservative .72 (compared to Brennan's 0); his predicted Segal-Cover score is .21; and his u is .51, enabling us to predict that he would cast 58 percent more conservative votes than if u were zero (68 percent versus 43 percent).

Both the Brennan and Burton appointments were influenced by non-ideological factors—Eisenhower's desire to appoint a northeastern Catholic and Truman's to appoint a crony. It is not surprising, therefore, that the appointees turned out to be ideologically remote from the Presidents who appointed them. Our methodology enables such discrepancies to be predicted.

The regression analysis yields additional results worth noting:

1. Justices appointed more recently *(First Term)* are more likely to cast conservative votes, consistent with the ideological trend in American society as a whole. The result is significant in regressions (2) and (3) although not in (4).

2. *Term* (time trend) is negative, and is significant in the overall regression and in the regression limited to Justices appointed by Republican Presidents. The trend is slight—a .01 increase per year in the fraction of liberal votes by those Justices—but still it is surprising that liberal Justices appointed by Republican Presidents should become more liberal over time.

3. One might expect Justices who had been federal or state appellate judges for a significant period of time before their appointment to the Supreme Court to have become socialized into their judicial role and therefore as Supreme Court Justices to be more respectful of precedent than Justices lacking such experience. The variable *Former Appellate Judge* denotes a Justice who had served at least two years on another appellate court (federal or state) before being appointed to the Supreme Court. This definition excludes three Justices who had been federal court of appeals judges—Whittaker, Harlan, and Thomas. Whittaker and Harlan had been court of appeals judges for only about a year, and Thomas for less than a year and a half. With these exclusions, 18 of the 35 Justices in the 1946 through 2009 terms are classified as *Former Appellate Judge:* Alito, Blackmun, Brennan, Breyer, Burger, Ginsburg, Kennedy, Marshall, Minton, O'Connor, John Roberts, Rutledge, Scalia, Sotomayor, Souter,

Stevens, Stewart, and Vinson. It is true that Souter's career as a federal court of appeals judge was even shorter than Thomas's, but before that he had been a member of the New Hampshire Supreme Court for seven years.

If the socialization hypothesis is correct, the coefficient on *Former Appellate Judge* should be negative for Rs (equation (3)) and positive for Ds (equation (4)). That is, the former appellate judges are expected to be less ideological than the other Justices. *Former Appellate Judge* has the right sign (negative) in the R equation (3) and is statistically significant, but the wrong sign (for Ds—negative), though it is not significant, in the D equation (4). The effect in equation (3) is implausibly large, however: the predicted probability of a conservative vote is .71 if the R Justice had not been an appellate judge and .51 if he had been: 28 percent lower. The size of the gap may reflect the voting behavior of the 4 liberals (Blackmun, Brennan, Souter, and Stevens) who happen to be among the 13 Rs who had previous appellate court experience. Separating the Justices into conservatives and liberals (see note 39 below) and reestimating equations (3) and (4), we find that although the coefficient on *Former Appellate Judge* in equation (3) is still negative (though no longer statistically significant—the t-statistic is 1.78), its magnitude is much smaller—a predicted decline of .07, rather than .20 as in equation (3). The coefficient in the liberal equation is still negative, though not (quite) statistically significant (t-statistic of 1.84).

In equation (2), where Justices appointed by Republican and Democratic Presidents are combined, *Former Appellate Judge* has a significant negative effect, indicating that Justices who had been appellate judges tend to vote less conservatively than other Justices, independent of the party of the appointing President. That result, however, because it mixes Rs and Ds, does not support the hypothesis that former appellate judges tend to be more faithful to precedent than Justices who lack such a background. We suspect that, as before, the negative coefficient is picking up the liberal voting of the former appellate judges who, having been appointed by Republican Presidents, were erroneously (except perhaps in the case of Brennan) expected to vote conservatively.

4. The negative coefficients on *Ideological Direction of Lower Court*

Decision tell us that Justices are inclined to reverse. The Court's jurisdiction is discretionary, and except in the case of a conflict among lower courts, rarely is there an imperative reason for the Supreme Court to take a case to affirm the lower court decision. There is no change of law as a result of such an affirmance and hence relatively little value added by the Court's decision, though the decision will ensure that no lower court conflict will emerge concerning the issue resolved by the decision. Given the Court's propensity to reverse, we expect to find that the more liberal the lower court decision, the more likely a conservative vote in the Supreme Court is by Ds as well as Rs (this is indicated by the statistically significant negative coefficients in all three regressions), since reversal means voting contrary to the lower court.

The ideological direction of the lower court decision has predictive value. The probability predicted from equation (2) that a D will vote to reverse a liberal lower court decision in a civil liberties case is 50 percent, compared to 63 percent for an R. In economic cases the predicted probability of reversing a liberal decision is 45 percent for Ds and 58 percent for Rs; the corresponding percentages in judicial power cases are 55 and 68, and in federalism cases 43 and 57. In contrast, the predicted probability of a Justice's voting to reverse a conservative decision in economic cases is 66 percent for Ds and 52 percent for Rs; in judicial power cases the corresponding figures are 56 and 42 percent, and in federalism cases 67 and 54 percent.

Non-unanimous Decisions: Group Effects

By group effects or group influences we mean the influence of the ideological leanings of a judge or Justice on the judicial votes of his colleagues. We distinguish between the influence of a member or members of the group on other members and the efforts of group members to discover the preferences, inclinations, sensitivities, and other characteristics of the other members. We gave an example of the latter efforts in chapter 2—strategic behavior of individual Justices in voting to grant or deny certiorari. We confine our analysis to the influence effects of group membership.

Three such influences can be distinguished analytically, although the data do not always enable us to distinguish among them empirically. One is conformity—wanting to be "on board" with the majority,[38] so that, for example, as a conservative majority grows larger, the liberal minority becomes more conservative. We do not interpret this as a psychological phenomenon, although social psychologists discuss it in those terms; we relate it to (rational) dissent aversion, discussed in chapter 6.

Second is group polarization: the idea that deliberation among persons who lean in one direction is likely to make them lean even farther in that direction. The economic interpretation (again there is also a psychological one) is that a person who takes an extreme view among a group of like-minded persons is likely to seem in their deliberations the best-informed member because the least uncertain, and so it is rational for other members of the group to give disproportionate weight to his views. As the group grows, the probability that one of its members will be more extreme than the others also grows.

This is an unpersuasive theory. The extreme member may strike the others as a nut; moreover, they may exert a moderating influence on him. Worse from the standpoint of empirical analysis of Supreme Court behavior, since the size of the Court is constant an increase in the percentage of, say, Rs means a decrease in the percentage of Ds, implying that both the Rs and the Ds will become more conservative (the Ds because if they are more liberal the more of them there are, they are less liberal the fewer of them there are)—and that is identical to the conformity effect.

The third group effect we call political polarization. It builds on a different sense of the word "polarization"—the sense of two interacting groups growing farther apart, as when political scientists speak of the growing polarization of the American electorate. Political polarization would be found in the Supreme Court if, for example, after an increase in the fraction of Rs the Rs voted more conservatively but the Ds voted more liberally—the opposite of the group polarization effect. The idea is that the larger the majority is, the less it feels it has to accommodate the minority, and conversely the smaller the minority is, the less it bothers to try to accommodate the majority, because it cannot expect reciprocal concessions. A possible countervailing factor, however, is that the smaller the

38. See generally Lee Ross and Richard E. Nisbett, *The Person and the Situation: Perspectives on Social Psychology* 27–46 (1991).

minority, the greater the burden of dissent, as there are fewer Justices to divide dissent assignments among.

Fraction Other Republican in Table 3.16 (above) is our group effects variable. The conformity hypothesis predicts a positive sign in regressions (2)–(4)—that is, the higher the fraction of Justices appointed by Republican Presidents, the more conservatively each Justice (both *R*s and *D*s or maybe just *D*s) will vote. We find the opposite—negative signs in two of the three regression equations, although none is statistically significant. Thus we don't find a conformity effect. This is consistent with the absence of strong dissent aversion in the Supreme Court.

Fraction Other Republican does not allow us to test the group polarization effect, because an increase in the conservatism of a conservative bloc of Justices could be attributable simply to a new Justice's being more conservative than the existing conservative Justices rather than to his presence influencing their votes. A negative test is possible, however: if an increase in the size of a conservative in-group (say) has no significant effect on the fraction of conservative votes, this is evidence that there is no group polarization effect—and so we find in equations (3) and (4) in Table 3.16. We also find no evidence of political polarization.

We can, however, refine and extend our analysis of group effects in three different ways. First we can test alternative conceptions of group effects. We can define group polarization as the state in which members of a group or faction of Justices take a more extreme position as the membership increases, provided the group is already a majority. So *R*s will be more likely to vote conservatively as their number increases if there are at least five *R*s, and *D*s will be more likely to vote liberally as their number increases if there are at least five *D*s. To test this hypothesis we restrict the *R* regression to periods in which *R*s are a majority and the *D* regression to periods in which *D*s are a majority. Along similar lines we modify the conformity hypothesis so that it predicts that the pressure of a minority to conform becomes greater the smaller its size. So an *R* is less likely to vote conservatively as the number of *R*s declines, provided there are fewer than five *R*s (and the reverse with *D*s), and so we restrict the *R* regression to periods when *R*s are a minority and the *D* regression to periods when *D*s are a minority.

Second, we estimate group effects using both the Justice-specific variables (such as party of the appointing President and the residual from the Segal-Cover regression) used in Table 3.16, and a fixed-effects model that includes the independent variables from the table that are not Justice-specific (such as a time trend), while replacing the Justice-specific variables with dummy variables for each Justice, which abstract from the effect of other Justices on the Justice's votes. The aim is to hold constant effects on Justices' votes that are independent of group influences (hence "fixed effects"). In that way we isolate those influences on the Justices.

Third, we reestimate the regressions, replacing the R and D proxies for ideology because those proxies have obvious errors, such as classifying Brennan, Warren, Stevens, and Souter as conservatives because they were appointed by a Republican President, and because there has been little variation in the ratio of Rs to Ds since 1975, even though the ideology of the Court has changed over this period. Our replacement is the conservative/liberal breakdown in Table 3.6, based on secondary sources.

Table 3.17 presents the regression results. The dependent variable is the fraction of conservative votes in non-unanimous cases. To simplify the regression we eliminate the moderate group, reassigning each of its members to either the conservative or the liberal group,[39] and present the regression coefficients (and t-statistics) only for the group effects independent variables. The top half of the table identifies members of a group as Rs or Ds, the bottom half as Cs (conservatives) or Ls (liberals). The independent variables in the columns labeled (1) and (2) are the same as the independent variables in Table 3.16, while columns (3) and (4) use the independent variables in the fixed-effects regression model in order to isolate group effects. Rows (1) and (2) test the revised group polarization and conformity hypotheses for R and D Justices and rows (4) and (5) test the same hypotheses for Cs and Ls. (For purposes of comparison rows (3) and (6) borrow the regression coefficients on the group effects

---

39. In Table 3.6 the conservative Justices were Reed, Burton, Vinson, Minton, Clark, Harlan, Burger, Rehnquist, Scalia, Kennedy, Thomas, John Roberts, and Alito. From the moderate category we added Whittaker, Stewart, Powell, and O'Connor to the conservative group in Table 3.17. And to the liberals in the earlier table—Black, Breyer, Douglas, Murphy, Rutledge, Warren, Brennan, Goldberg, Fortas, Marshall, Stevens, Sotomayor, Souter, and Ginsburg—we added from the moderate group Frankfurter, Jackson, White, and Blackmun.

Table 3.17 Regression Analysis of Group Effects in Supreme Court, Justice-Specific and Fixed-Effects Models, 1946–2009 Terms

Group	Hypothesis	Justice-Specific Model		Fixed-Effects Model	
		R (1)	D (2)	R (3)	D (4)
(1) R or D Majority	Group Polarization	−0.565 (1.66) n = 19,311	−0.273 (1.10) n = 8490	−0.448* (2.40) n = 19,311	−0.07 (0.49) n = 84!
(2) R or D Minority	Conformity	−0.276 (0.59) n = 2674	−0.202 (0.80) n = 6945	−0.276 (0.59) n = 2674	−0.733 (2.93) n = 69
(3) R or D (Majority or Minority)	Unclear	−0.161 (0.51) n = 21,985	−0.147 (0.86) n = 15,435	−0.250* (1.96) n = 21,985	0.036 (0.30) n = 15,4
		C (1)	L (2)	C (3)	L (4)
(4) C or L Majority	Group Polarization	— n=5876	−0.014 (0.04) n = 15,890	— n = 5876	−0.35 (1.05) n = 15,8
(5) C or L Minority	Conformity	0.001 0.07) n = 10,948	— n = 4706	0.145 (1.32) n = 10,948	— n = 47!
(6) C or L (Majority or Minority)	Unclear	0.030 (0.40) n = 16,824	−0.140 (0.55) n = 20,596	−0.076 (0.97) n = 16,824	−0.49 (2.05) 20,59

Notes:

1. All regressions are logistic regressions; t-ratios in parentheses and n = number of observations = number of votes.

2. Standard errors are clustered by Justice. There are 18 clusters in the R regressions and 17 in the D regressions and 17 clusters in the C and 18 in the L regressions.

3. Regression coefficients are marginal effects at mean values of all variables.

variables from Table 3.16.) When we use the conservative/liberal classification, we can't test group polarization of conservative Justices because their number did not exceed five in any term in our sample, and so we cannot determine whether Cs would vote more conservatively if they had a larger majority. Likewise we can't test the conformity effect on Ls because they were never fewer than four.

The regression results do not support the group effects hypotheses. Only 4 of the 20 regression coefficients are statistically significant, and none of them supports any of the hypotheses. Consider, for example, the group polarization hypothesis for Rs in the fixed-effects model, which we test in row (1) of column (3). The statistically significant negative coefficient implies that as an R majority grows, each R tends to vote less conservatively—contrary to the hypothesis. We likewise find a significant negative coefficient in row (2) of column (4), which tests the conformity hypothesis for Ds using the fixed-effects model: Ds vote less—not more—conservatively as their minority bloc shrinks. The other two significant coefficients are found in the fixed-effects regressions that include either all Rs or all liberals. The first coefficient indicates that Rs vote less conservatively as their number increases and the second that liberals vote less conservatively as the number of Ls decreases. Both results are contrary to the group effect hypotheses. We also find, though we do not include the coefficients in Table 3.17, no systematic group effects if we substitute the threefold classification of conservatives, moderates, and liberals in Table 3.6 for the simpler twofold classification in Table 3.17. We conclude that group effects are unimportant in the Supreme Court.

To wrap up: utilizing an expanded and corrected dataset, our analysis establishes, we hope with rigor and precision, the existence of a substantial ideology effect in Supreme Court decisions. It also finds a self-expression component in the utility function of Supreme Court Justices, but it does not find group effects. It documents the role of ideology in unanimous decisions by the Supreme Court (a neglected topic), refines the understanding of ideological change over a Justice's career, and provides ideological profiles of individual Justices.

Appendix

The Corrected U.S. Supreme Court Database

The U.S. Supreme Court Judicial Database (the Spaeth database) contains data for all Supreme Court decisions beginning with the 1946 term in which at least one Justice wrote an opinion. A supplemental dataset backdates a subset of the data to the 1937 term.[40] The data include the Justices' votes in each of the cases, the identity of the case and the chro-

---

40. See note 8 above.

nology of the litigation, outcomes and issues, and whether the opinion was a majority, dissenting, or concurring opinion.

Because of concern with possible misclassifications in the Spaeth dataset, one of us (Posner) read a random sample of 110 cases drawn from it and—without being told how Spaeth had classified them—made his own classifications of liberal, conservative, and ideologically unclassifiable outcomes. His classifications agreed with the Spaeth classifications in 75 percent of the cases, and we have eliminated most of the remaining discrepancy by adjusting some of Spaeth's categorical determinations (for example, his classification of *every* decision in favor of the plaintiff in an intellectual property case as liberal, even though the plaintiff in such cases is often a large corporation suing a small one or an individual inventor) and by excluding most unanimous decisions from our analysis. These were the two sets of cases in which Posner's classifications of individual cases most often disagreed with Spaeth's, because Posner tended to find cases in these categories impossible to classify ideologically.

Besides changing all votes in intellectual property cases to other, we changed all votes to other from conservative or liberal in case type 30020, where every vote for the plaintiff in a commercial speech case had been coded as liberal, and in 30140, where likewise every vote in favor of requiring accountability in campaign spending had been coded as liberal (30140). We also changed to other the classification of votes in case types 70020, 70060, and 70120, because in antitrust cases against unions (70020) all pro-plaintiff votes had been coded as liberal, even though some liberal judges would put union interests ahead of the interests enforced by antitrust law; in disputes between a union and a union member (70060), all votes against the union member had been coded as liberal, though a liberal judge might well put the interests of the individual member ahead of those of the union; and in cases involving jurisdictional disputes (70120), which is to say disputes between unions, a pro-union vote (whatever exactly that could mean in such a case) had arbitrarily been coded as liberal.

On issues pertaining to federal judicial review of state court and federal administrative decisions, we changed all votes in favor of judicial power in case types 90060, 90090, 90150, 90190, 90200, 90360, 90370, 90430–90450, 90490, 90500, and 90520 from liberal to other. But in cases in these categories involving obscenity (90060), comity and civil procedure (90090), determinations that the writ of certiorari had been improvidently granted (90150), remanding a case to determine the basis of a state court decision (90190), miscellaneous nonmerits votes (90200), the jurisdiction or authority of the Court of Claims (90360), the Supreme Court's original jurisdiction (90370), certification of questions to a court (90430), resolution of intercircuit conflicts (90440), objections to denial of certiorari or appeal (90450), the Act of State doctrine (90490), miscellaneous judicial administration issues (90500), and other miscellaneous exercises of judicial power (90520), it would require a careful examination, which we have not undertaken, of individual cases to determine the ideological direction of a vote in favor of the exercise of judicial power.

CHAPTER 4

The Courts of Appeals

W E TURN NOW to the middle tier of the Article III judiciary, the federal courts of appeals. Their jurisdiction, unlike the Supreme Court's, is mandatory—a court of appeals cannot refuse to hear an appeal merely because it does not present an important or fraught issue—and therefore many of the cases they decide are unlikely to give rise to disagreement, ideological or otherwise. Also the exercise by their judges of rule discretion (changing legal doctrines) is constrained by the prospect of Supreme Court review, and the less discretion a judge has, the less scope he has to translate his ideological inclinations into law. Another difference is that court of appeals judges mostly hear cases in panels of three judges randomly selected from their court. All the courts of appeals have at least 6 authorized judgeships—the number ranges from 6 in the First Circuit to 29 in the Ninth, with five circuits having 11 or 12 judgeships and 5 having 13 to 17. (The mean is 14 and the median 12.5.) Each court therefore hears cases in many different panels, especially since the panels often include senior judges or visiting judges. The multiplicity of different panels gives rise to panel composition effects.

This is the book's longest chapter (in part because we test the same hypotheses on several ex post databases—that is, databases of judicial votes or decisions), so as with the preceding chapter we begin by sketching its organization.

After discussing the principal data that we'll be using (again supplemented at the end of the chapter, this time by two appendices), we apply the same methodology for determining ideological influence on judicial behavior that we used in the preceding chapter, and we tentatively find significantly less ideological influence in the courts of appeals than in the Supreme Court. We then supplement that methodology with a new one measuring the ideology of judges at the time of their appointment—a methodology that uses information available online rather than just in newspaper editorials—and comparing that to the ideology reflected in their judicial votes. This methodology yields substantial differences between ex ante and ex post ideology: some conservative judges, as one would assess on the basis of their careers and statements up to the time of their appointment, turn out to be liberal judicial voters, and vice versa. We argue that this is more plausibly explained by the force of legalist commitment at the court of appeals level than by ideological drift.

The last section of the chapter deals with group effects. We find a significant conformity effect (a tendency of judges in the minority to go along with judges in the majority) and significant panel composition effects, but no group polarization or political polarization.

Data

Most empirical studies of the courts of appeals have been based on the U.S. Courts of Appeals Database (the Songer database),[1] described in detail in Appendix A to this chapter. The database contains random samples of 15 decisions per year by each court of appeals from 1925 through 1960 and 30 per year from 1961 through 2002. The votes in these decisions were cast by a total of 538 judges[2]—almost 90 percent of the court

1. "Judicial Research Initiative," www.cas.sc.edu/poli/juri/appct.htm (visited Dec. 9, 2011).

2. We exclude two judges who cast no votes in the corrected dataset; 4483 votes of non-court of appeals judges (mainly district judges) sitting on the court of appeals as visiting judges; and 382 votes for which the subject matter and ideological direction could not be ascertained.

of appeals judges appointed between 1891, when these courts were created, and 2002. The database is limited to case information; judge attributes have to be added.[3] The average number of votes per judge is 78, but there are fewer votes for those judges appointed before 1925, the first sample year, and for those judges appointed not long before 2002, because both sets of judges cast relatively few votes in the period covered by the database. (Any time a sample has an end date, some individuals who enter the sample period near the end will have few observations.) All our court of appeals regressions are weighted and thus take account of the different number of votes per judge.

All decisions in the database were rendered in published opinions. Most court of appeals decisions are "unpublished" (nowadays they're actually published, but the word is still used, to denote opinions that are not considered precedents)—in fiscal year 2010, 84 percent of all case terminations on the merits, up from 76 percent in 1997.[4] Most are affirmances in uncontroversial cases. Figure 4.1 shows the distribution of votes in the database by the year in which the judge was nominated.

Many of the data that the coders collected about each case—such as the date, the main issue, and its disposition—are straightforward. But a critical datum is not—the classification of a judge's vote as "liberal," "conservative," "mixed," or "other." "Mixed" means that the judge cast a liberal vote on one issue and a conservative vote on another in the same case (for example, voting to affirm a criminal conviction but to reverse the sentence), or that the decision itself was mixed (both liberal and conservative). "Other" means that neither litigant's position could be classified as liberal or conservative; nor, therefore, could the outcome.

The coders had trouble classifying some outcomes, especially in the older cases, as liberal, conservative, or other. A spot check that we made

3. We rely for judges' attributes on data collected by the Federal Judicial Center and data published in Gary Zuk, Deborah J. Barrow, and Gerard S. Gryski, "The Attributes of Federal Court Judges Database," also archived at the Judicial Research Initiative, note 1 above, www .cas.sc.edu/poli/juri/attributes.htm (visited Dec. 9, 2011), and corrected by us. The attributes database is sometimes referred to as the Auburn database.

4. Calculated from U.S. Courts, "Judicial Business 2010," Table S-3, www.uscourts.gov/ uscourts/Statistics/JudicialBusiness/2010/tables/S03Sep10.pdf, /1997/tables/s03sep97.pdf (visited Dec. 16, 2011). The range is from 93 percent in the Fourth Circuit to 60 percent in the Seventh Circuit.

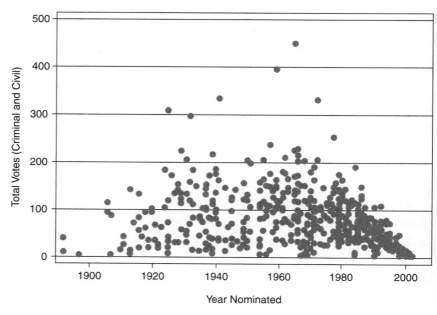

Figure 4.1   Total Judicial Votes by Court of Appeals Judges, by Year Appointed

of 40 cases—10 from each 20-year period in the database—revealed a high rate of erroneous classification (for example, a case that should have been classified as liberal being classified instead as other or conservative) in cases decided before 1960: 40 percent in cases decided between 1925 and 1940, 20 percent in cases decided between 1940 and 1959, but only 10 percent in cases decided between 1960 and 2002. The authors of the database also made category errors, as distinct from individual case errors, such as classifying all votes for plaintiffs in intellectual property cases as liberal—the same error as in the Spaeth database. Many plaintiffs in patent and other intellectual property cases are large firms suing small ones, and liberals tend to want to limit rather than expand patent, copyright, trademark, and other intellectual property rights.

We have reviewed and corrected the systematic classifications, as explained in Appendix A, but we have not reread enough of the actual decisions to be able to correct the misclassification of individual cases. One of us, however (Posner), read 110 of the cases in the database, selected at random, in an effort to determine the misclassification rate. He found that 26 (24 percent) had been misclassified. Seven votes that should have been classified as liberal were classified as conservative. Another 7 had been classified as liberal but should have been classified as conservative. The remaining 12 should have been classified as mixed or other but instead were classified as either liberal or conservative—the coders seem to have tried to shoehorn as many doubtful votes as possible into one or the other of the polar ideological classifications (liberal and conservative).

There are also a number of coding anomalies. For example, more than a thousand votes were associated with judge codes that unhelpfully denoted either a district judge sitting on the court of appeals as a visiting judge or a court of appeals judge who was not identified by name. We found instances in which the same judge code was assigned to different judges or multiple codes were assigned to the same judge. We even found instances in which the votes of two different judges in the same case were assigned to a single judge or in which the appeal was recorded as having been decided before the date on which the decision was issued. (These may, however, be cases in which a short decision is issued with the notation "opinion to follow.") We were able to correct some errors, but not all, because we didn't try to read all the cases in the databases.

Table 4.1 counts the number of votes in different subject-matter categories with and without our corrections (excluding Posner's corrections to the 110-case subsample). The total number of cases in the dataset, after our corrections, is 55,040. The principal effect of the corrections is to reclassify many votes classified as ideological by the Songer coders as other; after our corrections about 23 percent of the votes are in that category. The corresponding percentage in the uncorrected data is only 8 percent.

We also use a database originally created by Cass Sunstein and coauthors that contains all the published court of appeals opinions issued between 1995 (plus some from earlier years) and 2001 in fourteen subject-matter areas believed to have significant ideological stakes, such as abortion, capital punishment, and racial discrimination.[5] We updated the database through 2008 and added age discrimination cases, as explained in Appendix B. Our expanded Sunstein database contains 13,928 votes

5. Cass R. Sunstein et al., *Are Judges Political? An Empirical Analysis of the Federal Judiciary* (2006).

Table 4.1 Votes by Court of Appeals Judges, 1925–2002

	Criminal	Constitutional	Economics/Labor	Miscellaneous	All
Uncorrected					
Total minus	29%	15%	53%	3%	100%
Other	(16,938)	(8528)	(31,427)	(1889)	(58,782
Other	1%	2%	87%	10%	100%
	(54)	(103)	(4715)	(556)	(5428)
Total	26%	13%	56%	4%	99%
	(16,992)	(8631)	(36,142)	(2445)	(64,210
Corrected					
Total minus	22%	17%	59%	3%	101%
Other	(9333)	(6989)	(24,712)	(1106)	(42,140
Other	41%	3%	48%	7%	99%
	(5322)	(394)	(6226)	(958)	(12,900
Total	27%	13%	56%	4%	100%
	(14,655)	(7383)	(30,938)	(2064)	(55,040

Note: The database does not classify the ideological direction or subject matter of 4422 votes, so we exclude them from the analysis.

by court of appeals judges in 4948 cases (for the breakdown see Table 4.16). The reason the number of votes is fewer than three times the number of cases is that some votes were cast by visiting judges, whom we exclude from our analysis. The 4948 cases account for 6 percent of the approximately 80,000 published opinions of the courts of appeals in the period 1995–2008.[6]

And finally we use Corey Yung's data, described in chapter 2, on judicial votes cast in 2008 by more than 140 court of appeals judges.

Explaining the Judges' Votes (1)

We begin our statistical analysis with the data in the Songer database. Table 4.2 sorts the votes in that database into the three ideological categories (conservative, liberal, and mixed) and eight subject-matter categories (criminal, civil rights, First Amendment, due process, privacy, economic regulation, labor, and—a residual category—miscellaneous). Some of the subject-matter categories are Songer categories, others aggregates of

6. U.S. Courts, "Judicial Business 2009," tab. S–3, www.uscourts.gov/Statistics/Judicial Business/JudicialBusiness2009.aspx (visited Dec. 9, 2011).

Table 4.2 Votes, by Subject Matter and Ideology, of 538 Court of Appeals Judges, 1925–2002

	Conservative	Liberal	Mixed	Other	Total
Criminal	47%	13%	4%	36%	100%
	(6822)	(1876)	(635)	(5320)	(14,653)
Civil Rights	53%	34%	9%	4%	100%
	(2721)	(1766)	(460)	(210)	(5157)
First Amendment	46%	39%	7%	8%	100%
	(566)	(477)	(89)	(102)	(1234)
Due Process	58%	25%	6%	10%	99%
	(461)	(201)	(51)	(79)	(792)
Privacy	59%	34%	7%	2%	102%
	(117)	(67)	(13)	(3)	(200)
Economic Regulation	35%	37%	7%	22%	101%
	(9361)	(9883)	(1775)	(6036)	(27,055)
Labor	35%	50%	11%	5%	101%
	(1351)	(1922)	(420)	(179)	(3872)
Miscellaneous	25%	27%	1%	46%	99%
	(525)	(559)	(22)	(958)	(2064)
Total	40%	30%	6%	23%	99%
	(21,924)	(16,751)	(3465)	(12,887)	(55,027)

Songer categories. We reclassified habeas corpus cases (plus cases filed under section 2255 of the Judicial Code, the habeas corpus substitute for federal prisoners), which technically are civil, as criminal, since almost all involve efforts by criminal defendants to upset their conviction or sentence.

Table 4.3 correlates the ideological valence of votes in the different subject-matter categories with the party of the President who appointed the judge casting the vote. (The sum of the fractions of conservative and of liberal votes in the courts of appeals is less than one because of mixed votes, which account for between 8 and 9 percent of the total number.) We see that across all subject-matter areas the percentage of conservative votes by judges appointed by Republican Presidents is 55 percent, compared to 49 percent for judges appointed by Democratic Presidents. The respective percentages of liberal votes are 36 and 43. In civil cases the percentage of conservative votes is 49 for *R*s and 43 percent for *D*s, and of liberal votes 42 and 49. In criminal cases the respective conservative per-

Table 4.3 Fraction of Mixed *(M)*, Conservative *(C)*, and Liberal *(L)* Votes by 538 U.S. Court of Appeals Judges, Classified by Party of Appointing President at Time of Appointment, 1925–2002

	Appointed by Republican President			Appointed by Democratic President		
	M	C	L	M	C	L
All	.087	.550	.364	.078	.489	.433
Civil	.092	.486	.422	.081	.434	.486
Criminal	.069	.764	.167	.067	.694	.239
Constitutional	.092	.588	.320	.083	.514	.403
Economic and Labor	.095	.455	.450	.083	.412	.505

Note: Civil is all categories in Table 4.2 minus Criminal; Constitutional is Civil Rights, First Amendment, Due Process, and Privacy; and Economic and Labor is Economic Regulation and Labor.

centages are 76 and 69 (liberal 17 and 24), in constitutional cases 59 and 51 (liberal 32 and 40), and in economic and labor cases 46 and 41 (liberal 45 and 51).

The difference in the fraction of conservative votes between *R*s and *D*s, both when judges' voting is weighted by number of votes and when it is unweighted, is statistically significant in all subject-matter areas except the unweighted constitutional/civil liberties category. The table reports only the weighted averages. Some judges have very few votes in the Songer database, and it would be misleading to give a judge who had one vote in the database the same weight as one who had 100 votes. But we note later that the differences between the weighted and unweighted averages are generally small.

Table 4.4 breaks down the results in Table 4.3 by President. We see that the differences between *R*s and *D*s are greatest in a comparison between judges appointed by the most recent Republican Presidents to have appointed a substantial number of judges whose votes are sampled in the Songer database—Reagan and the first Bush—and judges appointed by Democratic Presidents. Only 7 judges in our sample were appointed by the second Bush—for remember that the period covered by the Songer database ends in 2002—and they account for only 10 votes in civil cases in the sample.

Although the first President Bush was less conservative than Reagan, their court of appeals appointments were ideologically similar. In a regression of the fraction of all conservative votes by Rs against dummy variables for court of appeals judges appointed by Reagan and the first President Bush, the coefficients are positive and highly significant but not significantly different from each other, though if we separate civil from criminal cases the dummy variables are significant in the civil regressions.

We tested for a positive trend by regressing the fraction of conservative votes on dummy variables for judges appointed by Carter, Reagan, the first Bush, and Clinton, plus a dummy variable for whether the judge was appointed by a Republican or a Democratic President. (The omitted variable is all judges appointed by Presidents before Carter.) All five dummy variables were positive, but the Carter dummy was not statistically significant, so we infer a trend beginning with Reagan toward more conservative court of appeals appointees.

Notice in Table 4.3 the high proportion of conservative votes in criminal cases by both Rs (76 percent) and Ds (69 percent).[7] The overwhelming majority of criminal appeals are by defendants whose appeals are financed by the government, and with the cost of appealing thus being zero to most criminal defendants there is a high percentage of groundless appeals. Votes affirming criminal convictions are classified as conservative, but liberals vote to affirm convictions when there is no colorable ground for an appeal. In contrast, when parties bear their own cost of appeal, as in most though by no means all civil cases (see next paragraph), the party who loses in the district court is unlikely to appeal unless the probability of reversal (which increases with the likelihood that the district court has committed a legal error), when multiplied by the likely monetary or other gain from reversal, exceeds the cost of appeal.

The last column in the bottom half of Table 4.4 indicates that the courts of appeals are more conservative than liberal in civil cases as well. But the margin is much smaller. And just as the courts' conservative cast in criminal cases may give a misleading impression of the influence of ideology, so may their conservative cast in civil cases. As we'll see in the next

---

7. In the unweighted sample these figures are 74 (versus 76) and 70 (versus 69) percent—confirming that the difference between the two methods of averaging judges' votes is indeed small.

Table 4.4 Fraction of Mixed (M), Conservative (C), and Liberal (L) Votes Cast by 538 U.S. Court of Appeals Judges, Classified by President at Time of Appointment, 1925–2002

Category	Harrison, McKinley, T. Roosevelt, and Taft			Wilson			Harding, Coolidge, and Hoover			FDR and Truman			Eisenhower			Kennedy and Johnson		
	M	C	L	M	C	L	M	C	L	M	C	L	M	C	L	M	C	L
All	.030	.489	.482	.049	.503	.448	.067	.482	.452	.052	.470	.478	.067	.543	.390	.078	.488	.434
Civil	.023	.449	.527	.051	.474	.474	.066	.454	.480	.054	.427	.519	.074	.473	.453	.086	.416	.498
Criminal	.073	.764	.164	.029	.757	.214	.070	.734	.196	.038	.738	.223	.045	.766	.189	.056	.686	.259
Constitutional	.000	.647	.353	.000	.800	.200	.000	.634	.366	.007	.654	.339	.046	.614	.340	.081	.483	.436
Economic and Labor	.026	.425	.549	.054	.450	.495	.070	.439	.491	.059	.408	.532	.083	.445	.472	.092	.398	.510
Number	11			16			38			76			44			59		
Tenure	26.2			17.9			15.3			14.0			12.5			15.1		

Category	Nixon and Ford			Carter			Reagan			Bush			Clinton			TOTAL		
	M	C	L	M	C	L	M	C	L	M	C	L	M	C	L	M	C	L
All	.093	.543	.364	.111	.503	.385	.111	.590	.299	.101	.619	.280	.096	.524	.380	.082	.520	.398
Civil	.102	.468	.430	.114	.447	.439	.120	.524	.356	.112	.557	.332	.103	.466	.431	.086	.460	.453
Criminal	.067	.764	.170	.103	.673	.224	.087	.766	.147	.075	.782	.143	.079	.679	.242	.068	.731	.201
Constitutional	.096	.556	.347	.104	.490	.406	.113	.591	.297	.101	.612	.287	.107	.513	.380	.088	.553	.359
Economic and Labor	.107	.434	.459	.124	.421	.455	.128	.489	.383	.124	.525	.351	.103	.436	.461	.089	.433	.478
Number	57			56			78			37			59			538		
Tenure	13.4			16.3			13.9			10.9			6.4			13.4		

Notes:

1. Republican Presidents appointed all judges in our sample before the Presidency of Woodrow Wilson.

2. Number denotes the number of judges who cast at least one vote in the sample.

3. Tenure denotes the mean years of active service of judges who cast at least one vote.

4. Fractions are weighted by the number of judge votes; for example, in the All category, the fraction of each judge's vote in the M, C, and L classes is weighted by the judge's total votes in the three classes.

5. The constitutional category includes civil rights, First Amendment, due process, and privacy cases.

6. Shaded areas are Republican Presidents; unshaded are Democratic Presidents.

7. The Total column includes seven judges appointed by the second President Bush.

chapter, most civil suits filed in federal courts lack even arguable merit. Many are filed by persons who do not have a lawyer. If these plaintiffs lose in the district court, then since they are not bearing any legal expense they may decide to appeal, and if their case is very weak they will lose in the court of appeals even if they draw a panel of liberal judges. Of the 41,491 appeals to federal courts of appeals in 2009, 13,292—32 percent—were by parties who had no lawyer.[8] The vast majority of those cases were losers, and most of the judges' votes in those cases are classified as conservative because in the Songer database most victories for defendants in civil cases are classified as conservative.

Table 4.5 substitutes the senatorial courtesy method of approximating a judge's ideology. The results are similar to the R/D measure. The average conservative judge (defined as a judge whose senatorial courtesy score is in the top quartile of the range between most liberal and most conservative) votes conservatively in 50 percent of civil cases, the average liberal judge (a judge in the bottom quartile) in 43 percent. The comparable figures from Table 4.3 are 49 and 43 percent. In criminal cases the respective percentages are 79 and 68 in Table 4.5, compared to 76 and 69 in Table 4.3.

We now subject the Songer data to regression analysis. Most of our independent variables are the same as in Table 3.10 in chapter 3. But some are new, as shown in Table 4.6, including dummy variables for the judge's circuit, sex, race, and prior experience as a district judge (denoted by *Former District Judge*). Although there have been too few black and female Supreme Court Justices (or for that matter ex–district court judges) to enable meaningful comparisons with other Justices, 8.3 percent of our court of appeals sample consists of female judges and 4.8 percent of black judges, along with a large percentage of judges promoted from the district court—42 percent, a percentage little changed since the earliest data in the database (1925).

Because our Songer data are limited to a small number of votes per

8. U.S. Courts, "Judicial Business 2009," tab. S–4, www.uscourts.gov/Statistics/Judicial-Business/JudicialBusiness2009.aspx (visited Dec. 9, 2011). We have adjusted the figures in the table to exclude "prisoner petitions" (i.e., habeas corpus and section 2255 cases, which we have reclassified from civil to criminal).

Table 4.5   Fraction of Conservative Votes by Subject Matter and by Judge's Ideology Based on Senatorial Courtesy Scores, 1925–2002

	Proportion of Conservative Votes			
	(1) Conservative Judges Ex Ante	(2) Moderate Judges Ex Ante	(3) Liberal Judges Ex Ante	Ratio of Column (1) to Column (3)
All Judges				
Civil	.497**	.456**	.434	1.15
Criminal	.791**	.730**	.680	1.16
Constitutional	.619**	.551**	.500	1.24
Economic and Labor	.463**	.428**	.415	1.12
All Categories	.557**	.521**	.486	1.15
Judges Appointed between 1925 and 1980				
Civil	.475**	.442**	.433	1.10
Criminal	.804**	.726**	.679	1.18
Constitutional	.624**	.544**	.502	1.24
Economic and Labor	.450**	.417**	.414	1.09
All Categories	.530**	.505**	.484	1.10
Judges Appointed between 1961 and 1980				
Civil	.504**	.442**	.421	1.20
Criminal	.814**	.705**	.667	1.22
Constitutional	.604**	.511**	.475	1.27
Economic and Labor	.469**	.412**	.402	1.17
All Categories	.589**	.511**	.482	1.22
Judges Appointed between 1981 and 2002				
Civil	.535**	.519**	.458	1.168
Criminal	.778**	.743**	.690	1.128
Constitutional	.616**	.566**	.487	1.265
Economic and Labor	.494	.490**	.444	1.113
All Categories	.597**	.585**	.516	1.157

Notes:

1. The level of statistical significance in the conservative column refers to the difference between conservative and moderate judges and in the moderate column to the difference between moderate and liberal judges.

2. Ideological classifications are based on the judges' senatorial courtesy scores, which range from −.684 (most liberal) to .756 (most conservative). Moderate judges (N = 267) fall in the interquartile range (−.337 to .353). Liberal judges (N = 137) have scores below below −.337. Conservative judges (N = 134) have scores above .353.

Table 4.6 Description of Variables in Regressions of Court of Appeals Votes, and Means

	Mean (Standard Deviation)
Dependent Variables	
Fraction Conservative in Civil Cases	0.470 (0.142)
Fraction Liberal in Civil Cases	0.441 (0.145)
Fraction Conservative in Criminal Cases	0.720 (0.186)
Fraction Liberal in Criminal Cases	0.205 (0.163)
Fraction Conservative in Civil Cases (Uncorrected Data)	0.474 (0.120)
Fraction Conservative in Civil Cases (Uncorrected Data)	0.714 (0.158)
Independent Variables	
President: Party of the appointing President (1 = Republican, 0 = Democratic)	0.505 (0.500)
Senate Republican: Fraction of Republican Senators at time of appointment	0.438 (0.094)
Year Appointed	1966.286 (24.252)
Sex: 1 = female judge	0.084 (0.277)
Race: 1 = black judge	0.048 (0.215)
Former District Judge: 1 = judge promoted from a U.S. district court	0.420 (0.494)
Fraction Economic: Fraction of judge's votes in economic and labor cases	0.723 (0.177)
Fraction Miscellaneous: Fraction of judge's votes in Miscellaneous category (civil)	0.033 (0.039)

Notes:
1. The mean and standard deviations for the dependent variables are unweighted averages across judges.
2. The equations include dummy variables for the judge's circuit (the omitted variable is the D.C. Circuit).

judge per year, we aggregate votes by judge over all years. In the Spaeth database an increase in the fraction of conservative votes translates into an identical decrease in the fraction of liberal votes because there is no mixed vote category in that database, but in the Songer database such an increase can reduce the fraction of mixed votes, liberal votes, or both. The biggest effect is on liberal votes, mixed votes being only 8.2 percent of all ideologically classifiable votes (that is, excluding "other" votes). Because of these differences we cannot make a direct comparison between judicial voting behavior in the Supreme Court and the courts of appeals.

Table 4.7 thus estimates separate regressions for the fractions of conservative and liberal votes. (We do not present the results of regressions on mixed votes, because the only variable that has a statistically signifi-

4.7   Regression Analysis of Court of Appeals Votes, 1925–2002

	Corrected Data				Uncorrected Data	
	Civil Cases		Criminal Cases		Civil Cases	Criminal Cases
	Fraction Conservative (1)	Fraction Liberal (2)	Fraction Conservative (3)	Fraction Liberal (4)	Fraction Conservative (5)	Fraction Conservative (6)
ent	0.031**	−0.034**	0.062**	−0.050**	0.035**	0.056**
	(3.27)	(3.75)	(3.88)	(3.41)	(3.88)	(4.20)
	0.144**	−0.158**	0.007	−0.128	0.072	−0.075
ublican	(3.25)	(3.56)	(0.08)	(1.59)	(1.66)	(1.06)
ppointed	−0.0002	−0.001*	−0.0003	−0.0003	0.0003	−0.001**
	(0.49)	(2.13)	(1.00)	(1.04)	(0.81)	(3.40)
	−0.005	0.003	−0.003	−0.004	−0.006	−0.014
	(0.24)	(0.14)	(0.15)	(0.20)	(0.27)	(0.70)
	−0.018	0.025	−0.072*	0.054	−0.028	−0.057*
	(0.69)	(1.06)	(2.28)	(1.50)	(1.16)	(2.05)
r District	−0.001	−0.004	0.005	−0.017	0.001	−0.001
ge	(0.17)	(0.53)	(0.45)	(1.56)	(0.10)	(0.13)
on	−0.131*	0.219**	—	—	−0.092	—
nomic	(2.20)	(4.09)			(1.68)	
on Misc.	−0.278	0.195	—	—	−0.058	—
	(1.67)	(1.28)			(0.42)	
t	**	**	**	**	**	**
mies						
ant	0.105	1.83**	1.322*	0.894	−0.020	2.420**
	(0.89)	(2.57)	(2.07)	(1.63)	(0.03)	(4.85)
	0.22	0.38	0.24	0.23	0.18	0.24
er of ervations	538	538	513	513	534	523

ꓱ regressions are weighted; the weights are equal either to the judge's total votes in civil cases (equations (1), (2),
ꓱ or to the judge's total votes in criminal cases (equations (3), (4), and (6)). Standard errors are robust.
ꓱ regressions include 11 dummy circuit variables, with the D.C. Circuit being the left-out variable.
ꓱe fraction of conservative votes is weighted by the number of cases in each category.

cant influence on them is the year in which the judge was appointed.)
Our civil-case regressions include independent variables for the fraction
of the judge's votes in economic and labor cases and in the "other" category, in order to account for differences in the mixture of civil cases across
circuits. We estimate separate regressions for criminal cases because, as
we know, conservative votes in this category (that is, votes against the defendant) are less likely to reflect the judge's ideological bent than conser-

vative votes in civil cases. We did not report a similar division for the Supreme Court because the Court's selectivity means that cases in all categories are likely to be difficult to decide on purely technical legal grounds. Indeed, the percentage of conservative votes in the Supreme Court's criminal cases is only moderately higher than in civil cases—54 percent versus 46 percent—whereas the corresponding percentages in the courts of appeals are 73 and 46 percent.

The table includes two regression equations that use the uncorrected Songer data. We did this to see whether our coding and ideological corrections, which eliminated 28 percent of the votes in the Songer database, would result in significantly different results. The main differences in the civil regressions on the uncorrected data are that the fraction of Republican Senators at the time of appointment is not a statistically significant predictor of judicial votes and that because there is more noise in the uncorrected data the regression has less explanatory power (a lower R^2). In criminal cases the regression coefficients and the R^2s are virtually identical in the two datasets. The effect on the R^2s of using the uncorrected data might, however, be greater for narrower classes of case with fewer data points.

Like Supreme Court Justices, court of appeals judges appointed by Republican Presidents are more likely, other things being equal, to vote for conservative than for liberal outcomes: 3 percent more likely in civil cases and 6 percent more likely in criminal cases. The larger difference in criminal than in civil cases is surprising for the reason presented earlier; we have no explanation. Substituting the senatorial courtesy measure of ideology does not alter our findings significantly.

Consistent with the simple correlations, the regression analysis indicates that ideological voting is less frequent in the courts of appeals than in the Supreme Court. The percentage of conservative votes in the Supreme Court by *R*s and *D*s is 57 percent and 40 percent respectively (see "All Categories" in Table 3.5 in chapter 3), a difference of 17 percent, compared to a difference in the courts of appeals of 4.5 percent. The difference is so small that one might wonder why any fuss is made in Senate confirmation hearings about the ideological leanings of nominees for court of appeals judgeships. A possible answer, explored later in this chapter using the Sunstein database because it focuses on subject-matter areas believed to involve significant ideological stakes, is that ideology plays a big role in decisions by courts of appeals in those cases that politicians and segments of the general public feel strongly about, as opposed to the routine and technical legal cases that dominate the dockets of those courts and hence are heavily represented in the Songer statistics.

In the court of appeals regressions as in the Supreme Court regressions, the larger the fraction of Republican Senators *(Senate Republican)* at the time of a judge's confirmation, the more likely the judge is to cast conservative judicial votes, though the correlation is statistically significant only in civil cases. This may reflect the Senate's greater interest in civil rights than in criminal justice in confirmation proceedings,[9] because most federal judges, regardless of the appointing President, are conservative in criminal cases. Also the judges tend to vote more conservatively in civil rights cases than in other civil cases, probably because a large fraction of the appeals brought by losing plaintiffs in those cases, which comprise about 70 percent of civil liberties cases (the category that includes civil rights, First Amendment, privacy, and due process), are completely meritless. Not only do many of the plaintiffs have no lawyer, but many are prisoners,[10] who besides not having lawyers have a lot of time on their hands; their opportunity costs of litigating are very low.

The judge-specific variables (*Sex, Black,* and *District Court*) are not significant except that black appellate judges are less likely than white ones to vote conservatively in criminal cases (regression (4)) even if the party of the appointing President is held constant. Findings regarding the influence of race and sex on judicial voting are important to assessing the role of ideology because both personal characteristics are irrelevant to a legalist decision. The absence of a significant sex effect, and of a race ef-

9. Lori A. Ringhand and Paul M. Collins, Jr., "May It Please the Senate: An Empirical Analysis of the Senate Judiciary Committee Hearings of Supreme Court Nominees, 1939–2009," http://papers.ssrn.com/sol3/papers.cfm?abstract_id=1630403 (visited Dec. 9, 2011), reports that 27 percent of the Senators' questions to Supreme Court nominees focused on civil rights and only 7.7 percent on criminal justice. We have found no similar studies of confirmation hearings for nominees to the courts of appeals.

10. We are referring here to prisoner civil rights cases, which are unequivocally civil, rather than to prisoner petitions (habeas corpus and section 2255 cases—see note 7 above), which we reclassified from civil to criminal.

fect in most civil cases,[11] thus suggests that legalist analysis is influential in the courts of appeals. It is not conclusive evidence, because other factors influence ideology besides race and sex; white men are not ideologically uniform.

Table 4.8 reestimates the regressions in Table 4.7, restricting them to votes by judges appointed since 1960. We do this to verify the results of the full sample because of the coders' difficulty in classifying judicial votes before 1960. We are indeed able to explain more of the variance in the later period. In the regression of the fraction of conservative votes in civil cases, the R^2 is .37 in the 1960–2002 period compared to .22 in the 1925–2002 period. The corresponding figures for criminal cases are .32 in 1960–2002 and .24 in 1925–2002. And the t-ratios for *President* (party of the appointing President) in the conservative and liberal regressions are typically about 25 percent higher, which jacks up their statistical significance.

Table 4.8 reveals that *R*s appointed before 1960 voted conservatively in 46 percent of civil cases and liberally in 47 percent; the corresponding figures for *R*s appointed since 1960 are 50 percent and 39 percent. For *D*s appointed before 1960 the percentages of conservative and liberal votes are 43 and 51; for *D*s appointed since 1960 they are 43 and 47. So in civil cases both *R*s and *D*s are becoming more conservative. In criminal cases there is little evidence of a trend, yet such as there is it is liberal and limited to Democratic judges. The percentage of conservative votes by *R*s in criminal cases is 76 before 1960 and 77 after, and of liberal votes by *R*s 19 percent before and 16 after. For *D*s the percentage of conservative votes in criminal cases is 74 before 1960 and 68 after, and of liberal votes 22 and 24, but only the decline in their conservative votes (from 74 to 68) is statistically significant.

The fraction of Republican Senators has no significant effect on conservative votes in the 1960–2002 regressions, but the coefficient of the

11. But Christina L. Boyd, Lee Epstein, and Andrew D. Martin, "Untangling the Causal Effects of Sex on Judging," 54 *American Journal of Political Science* 389 (2010), finds differences between male and female judges, though only in sex discrimination cases. And Adam B. Cox and Thomas J. Miles, "Judging the Voting Rights Act," 108 *Columbia Law Review* 1 (2008), finds that black judges are more likely to find liability under section 2 of the Voting Rights Act than white judges.

4.8 Regression Analysis of Court of Appeals Votes, 1960–2002

	Corrected Data				Uncorrected Data	
	Civil Cases		Criminal Cases		Civil	Criminal
	Fraction Conservative (1)	Fraction Liberal (2)	Fraction Conservative (3)	Fraction Liberal (4)	Fraction Conservative (5)	Fraction Conservative (6)
lent	0.054**	−0.064**	0.070**	−0.057**	0.048**	0.060**
	(4.15)	(4.97)	(4.12)	(3.73)	(3.84)	(4.06)
e	0.015	0.046	0.101	−0.230	0.011	−0.040
	(0.13)	(0.42)	(0.67)	(1.66)	(0.10)	(0.29)
publican Appointed	0.003**	−0.004**	0.00004	−0.001	0.003**	−0.001
	(3.25)	(4.36)	(0.04)	(0.59)	(3.43)	(0.83)
	−0.002	0.002	0.001	−0.007	−0.007	−0.005
	(0.11)	(0.11)	(0.05)	(0.32)	(0.35)	(0.27)
	−0.017	0.030	−0.067*	0.049	−0.022	−0.056
	(0.79)	(1.56)	(2.01)	(1.31)	(1.05)	(1.90)
er District	−0.004	−0.001	0.011	−0.019	0.003	0.009
ge	(0.40)	(0.12)	(0.87)	(1.51)	(0.27)	(0.79)
on	−0.048	0.143*	—	—	−0.019	—
onomic	(0.62)	(2.09)			(0.27)	
on Other	−0.096	0.088	—	—	−0.090	—
	(0.46)	(0.45)			(0.52)	
it Dummies	**	**	**	**	**	**
tant	−5.111**	7.354**	0.723	1.449	−4.973**	2.205
	(3.02)	(4.61)	(0.36)	(0.78)	−(3.17)	(1.23)
	0.37	0.43	0.32	0.31	0.35	0.31
er of servations	355	355	346	346	351	348

e: All regressions are weighted. The weights are equal either to the judge's total votes in civil cases (equations (1), d (5)) or to his total votes in criminal cases (equations (3),(4), and (6)). The asterisks in the circuit dummies row es that the circuit dummies are jointly significant; that is, taken together they have a statistically significant effect dependent variables.

year-of-appointment variable is highly significant. This may reflect the increase noted in chapter 3 in the number of dependably conservative court of appeals judges appointed by Republican Presidents beginning with Reagan.[12] He decided to give less weight to the preferences of home-state Senators, whose recommendations often reflect patronage rather than ideology. His Republican successors have tended to adhere to the pattern

12. See Sheldon Goldman, *Picking Federal Judges: Lower Court Selection from Roosevelt through Reagan,* ch. 8 (1997).

he set—and the Presidency was in Republican hands for 13 of the 22 years from Reagan's inauguration in 1981 through 2002, the last year of the Songer data.

Reagan was not the first President to try to change the ideological profile of the courts of appeals. The 56 court of appeals judges appointed by Franklin Delano Roosevelt were significantly more liberal in civil cases (but not less conservative in those cases—remember that there are three ideologically classifiable types of vote in the Songer database: conservative, liberal, and mixed), and significantly less conservative and more liberal in criminal cases, than Ds appointed since 1960. Although the Senate was Democratic throughout the Roosevelt Administration, the initiative for picking liberal judges came from Roosevelt rather than from Democratic Senators.[13]

If we separate the 1960–2002 sample into judges appointed by Republican Presidents (181 judges) and judges appointed by Democratic ones (174), the "more dependably conservative" hypothesis implies a larger effect of the appointment year in the R sample, as we find. But consistent with our earlier point that most criminal appeals are losers, the effect is confined to civil cases—and it disappears if we use senatorial courtesy scores to measure ideology. By that measure the ratio of conservative to liberal votes fell in all categories between 1981 and 2002—which is both a surprise and a commentary on the limitations of such scores as predictors of judicial voting.

The circuit dummy variables are jointly significant in all regressions in Tables 4.7 and 4.8, indicating significant unexplained differences among circuits in the fraction of conservative and liberal votes. As Table 4.9 shows, the differences are concentrated in the Seventh and Eighth Circuits, with smaller effects in the First and Fifth. All four circuits are more conservative than one would expect on the basis of the judges' ideology as proxied by the party of the President who appointed them and by the fraction of Republican Senators at the time of confirmation. So it's not that these are the four most conservative circuits; rather it's that they're more conservative than they "should be" on the basis of the presumed ideology of their judges. We offer an explanation later.

13. Id., ch. 2.

ble 4.9 Circuit Effects on Judges' Votes

Circuit	Civil Cases Fraction of Votes			Criminal Cases Fraction of Votes		
	Conservative	Liberal	Mixed	Conservative	Liberal	Mixed
t	+ +	−	−	+		
		−	+ +			+
				−	+	
h	+		−			
h	+ +		− −			
h	+			−	+	
h	+ +		− −	+ +	−	− −
h	+ +	−	− −	+ +	−	
h						
th			−			
th						
C.						

tes:

1. Shaded columns denote 1960–2002 regressions and unshaded columns 1925–2002 regressions.
2. The D.C. Circuit is again the excluded variable.
3. A positive (negative) sign denotes a significant positive (negative) effect compared to the D.C. Circuit.
4. The absence of a sign for a circuit indicates that there is no significant difference between that circuit and D.C. Circuit.

The next table conducts a similar though more limited analysis based on the data in the Sunstein dataset. We use senatorial courtesy scores as our proxy for court of appeals judges' ex ante ideology. On average, as expected, *R*s have higher scores than *D*s. The mean for the *R*s in our sample is .32 and the range is from −.21 to .57; the mean for the *D*s is −.33 and the range is −.65 to −.04.

To test the predictive accuracy of the scores, Table 4.10 divides both *R*s and *D*s into three groups: *R*s with senatorial courtesy scores in the top 25 percent (very conservative), between the 25th and 75th percentile (moderately conservative), and in the bottom 25 percent (weakly conservative), with mirror-image divisions for *D*s. A complication is that a judge's vote may be influenced by the voting of the other judges on the panel. We discuss these well-documented panel composition effects—an illustration of group influences on judicial behavior—in the final section of the chapter, but mention them here because they affect the determination of a judge's true ideology. (We couldn't consider them earlier because our corrected

Table 4.10   Court of Appeals Judges' Votes by Senatorial Courtesy Scores and Panel Composition, Sunstein Data, 1995–2008

Senatorial Courtesy Scores of R Judges	Conservative District Court Decision				Liberal District Court Decision			
	Panel Composition and Fraction of Conservative Votes on Appeal				Panel Composition and Fraction of Conservative Votes on Appeal			
	RRR	RRD	RDD	Votes	RRR	RRD	RDD	Votes
< .218	78%	73%	65%	1558	34%	30%	22%	658
.218–.502	78	74	66	3572	41	38	27	1580
> .502	74	64	61	784	38	36	31	480
Senatorial Courtesy Scores of D Judges	RRD	RDD	DDD	Votes	RRD	RDD	DDD	Votes
< −.422	72%	60%	59%	446	25%	21%	15%	241
−.422−−.267	68	56	46	2395	27	19	19	1084
> −.267	63	60	63	975	29	24	20	511

version of the Songer data doesn't enable us to determine panel composition.) A judge might be strongly conservative yet disinclined, perhaps because of fear of retaliation, to dissent from a liberal majority on his panel.

The table reveals strong panel composition effects: within each group of judges with similar senatorial courtesy scores, the fraction of conservative votes increases significantly as the panel changes from *DDR* to *DRR* to *RRR*, and this regardless of whether the decisions being affirmed or reversed are liberal or conservative. Moving down the columns we find no tendency for *R*s with higher senatorial courtesy scores to vote more conservatively than *R*s with low scores; and likewise *D*s, *mutatis mutandis*. In other words, the Senator's ideology doesn't seem to affect how the judge votes in cases. This should not be a surprise. Neither a Senator's electoral success nor his senatorial legacy is likely to be bound up with the ideology of the court of appeals judges whom he proposes to the President, or, if the judicial nominee is the President's choice, does not oppose. Until Reagan, court of appeals appointments were most often patronage appointments by a Senator or the Senators of the state to which a judgeship was allocated. From Reagan to the present, as we know, appointments have been much more heavily influenced by the President, but neither before nor after Reagan was Senators' ideology a dominant factor in court of appeals appointments.

Nevertheless, the table does confirm our earlier finding that in the courts of appeals as in the Supreme Court, *R*s tend to vote more conservatively than *D*s. This is most easily seen by comparing the percentage of conservative (or liberal) decisions by *RRR* and *DDD* panels. Notice also the tug that the ideological direction of the district court decision exerts on the court of appeals judges, so that *R*s, for example, are much less likely to vote to reverse a liberal decision than to vote to affirm a conservative one. This is another group influence that we discuss later.

Explaining the Judges' Votes (2)

The party of the appointing President, Segal-Cover scores, and other ex ante measures of judicial ideology are used not only to identify the ideology of a judge before he starts hearing cases, but also to explain judicial votes; *R*s, for example, are expected to be conservative judicial voters. In the case of Supreme Court Justices it is certainly plausible to suppose that their political ideology at the time of their appointment will influence their votes (though the influence may decline over time, and though a Justice's ex post as well as ex ante ideology may differ from the appointing President's ideology); the Supreme Court is to a considerable extent a political court. That cannot be assumed to be true of the lower federal courts, which do not decide which cases they will hear, have a less politically consequential docket, and are subject to review by a higher court.

We examine this issue further with the aid of a new measure of court of appeals judges' ideology at the time of appointment and a new database of their judicial votes. Our new measure of ex ante judicial ideology bears a family relationship to the Segal-Cover measure. That measure is not usable for court of appeals judges (or district judges, for that matter) because newspapers are rarely interested in nominees for such judgeships.[14]

---

14. However, Aspen Publishers Editorial Staff, *Almanac of the Federal Judiciary* (2 vols., looseleaf, updated semiannually), a massive tome, contains a great deal of information about court of appeals judges and district judges as well, though relatively little that bears directly on their ideology at the time of their appointment.

But we have created a parallel measure that makes use of even more information about each judge because it is based on an online search for information about court of appeals judges that illuminates their likely ideology when they were appointed. It has enabled us to classify individual judges in one of four ideological categories ex ante: strongly conservative, moderately conservative, moderately liberal, and strongly liberal.

We compare the validity of the Segal-Cover measure of ex ante ideology to the validity of our own measure by applying our measure to Supreme Court Justices. We divide the 37 Justices for whom we have Segal-Cover scores, ranked from most to least conservative, into four groups of equal size and call the top quartile strongly conservative, the second moderately conservative, the third moderately liberal, and the fourth strongly liberal; we need to make this division in order to enable comparison with our fourfold classification of court of appeals judges. The basis of our ranking is the secondary materials (corresponding roughly to the online research on which our classification of the court of appeals judges in this section of the present chapter is based) on which Table 3.6 in chapter 3 is based, but with the substitution of a fourfold classification for the threefold one (conservative, moderate, liberal) in that table in order to enable a more exact comparison between the ex ante ideology of Supreme Court Justices and that of court of appeals judges.

The two rank orders of Justices, Segal-Cover's and ours, are printed in Appendix C to this chapter. There is a good deal of convergence (the correlation between Segal-Cover and our measure is .8), and some of the differences reflect uncertainty in the data; an example is Segal-Cover's classification of Justice Whittaker as moderately conservative and our classification of him as moderately liberal. We do not think there are any anomalies in our list. But there are 7 anomalies in Segal-Cover's list of 37 (19 percent). They are the classification of Justices Powell and Stevens as strongly conservative rather than moderately conservative, Breyer as moderately conservative rather than moderately liberal, Frankfurter and Douglas as moderately liberal rather than strongly liberal, Stewart as moderately liberal rather than moderately conservative, and Harlan as strongly liberal rather than moderately conservative. Frankfurter's judicial votes, unlike Douglas's, were not consistently liberal, but ex ante he was strongly liberal; that was the source of liberals' great disappointment with his Supreme Court record.

Our judge sample consists of the 143 judges in Corey Yung's database, whom Yung ranked from most to least conservative on the basis of the judicial votes those judges cast in 2008. All the judges were appointed by Ford, Carter, Reagan, the first President Bush, Clinton, or the second President Bush (but very few by Ford or Carter). Republican Presidents appointed 85/143 = 59 percent of the judges.

We use this sample of judges because Yung has a more usable (for our present purposes) measure of ex post ideology than the fraction of conservative votes in the Songer database. Most of the judges in that database do not have enough votes for a meaningful comparison among judges; nor can the Songer data be used to control for panel composition effects, as Yung does. We would encounter a similar problem of vote scarcity if we used the Sunstein data to rank individual judges: 50 percent of the judges have fewer than 21 votes and 25 percent have fewer than 11. In contrast, each judge in Yung's sample has at least 100 votes. (The correlation between votes in the Sunstein database and in Yung's database is .66, weighting Sunstein's data by the number of votes cast by each judge.)

We now compare our ex ante measure with Yung's ex post measure to get a sense of how the judicial votes of court of appeals judges is likely to differ from the ideology they brought with them when they were appointed.

Application of our ex ante measure to Yung's sample of judges results in the following division:

Strongly conservative judges *(SC)*	47 (33%)
Moderately conservative *(MC)*	37 (26%)
Moderately liberal *(ML)*	45 (31%)
Strongly liberal *(SL)*	14 (10%)

Table 4.11 compares our ex ante ideological classifications with the judicial votes of the judges in each of the four classes. We divide judges into three groups on the basis of their votes. The top third we call conservative judicial voters (remember that Yung orders judges from the most conser-

Table 4.11   Yung's Ex Post Ideology Rankings Correlated with Epstein-Landes-Posner Ex Ante Ideology Rankings

	SC	MC	ML	SL
Conservative	54%	23%	23%	0%
Moderate	23%	35%	35%	6%
Liberal	21%	19%	36%	23%

	Conservative	Moderate	Liberal
SC	55%	23%	21%
MC	30%	46%	24%
ML	24%	38%	38%
SL	0%	21%	79%

Note: Conservative, Liberal, and Moderate are Yung's ex post ideology rankings; *SC, MC, ML,* and *SL* are our ex ante ideology rankings (strongly conservative, moderately conservative, moderately liberal, and strongly liberal).

vative judicial voter to the most liberal one), the middle third moderate, and the bottom third liberal. We experimented with dividing the judges into the three categories by identifying break points in ex post ideology scores. This gave us 44 conservatives, 54 moderates, and 45 liberals, but the ideological overlap between each of these groups and each of our ex post ideology groups of 48 conservatives, 48 moderates, and 47 liberals turned out to be almost complete. We also experimented with dividing the judges into four rather than three ex post ideology classes (strongly conservative, moderately conservative, moderately liberal, and strongly liberal), corresponding to our ex ante ideology classes. Surprisingly, the results were very similar, because there turned out to be few voting differences between moderately conservative and moderately liberal judicial voters.

The table reveals that 77 percent of the conservative-voting judges were either strongly or moderately conservative ex ante, while 59 percent of the liberal-voting judges were either strongly or moderately liberal ex ante. Interestingly, while 40 percent of the strongly and moderately conservative judges ex ante are liberal judicial voters, only 23 percent of the moderately liberal judges and zero percent of the strongly liberal judges, ex ante, are conservative judicial voters.

Another way to measure the divergences between ex ante and ex post ideology is to look at the distribution of judicial voting (conservative, moderate, and liberal) within each ex ante ideology category. The results are shown in the bottom part of the table. Notice that even strongly conservative judges ex ante are often moderate and even liberal judicial voters (21 percent are liberal voters), and that many moderately liberal judges ex ante are conservative judicial voters (23 percent), but that strongly liberal judges ex ante are overwhelmingly liberal judicial voters (79 percent)—they thus are more ideological judicial voters than strongly conservative judges are.

We now compare our ex ante and ex post ideology findings with the *R* and *D* ex ante ideology proxy that we use throughout the book. Because Republican Presidents appointed 59 percent of the judges in Yung's sample, we need to normalize the distribution of judges to analyze differences between Republican- and Democratic-appointed judges. We do this by multiplying the number of *D*s in each category by 1.466 (85/58), which weights each *D* so that it's as if there were 85 *D*s as well as 85 *R*s, rather than 58 and 85. The results are shown in Table 4.12.

The results are surprising. Although the correlation between the party of the appointing President and our fourfold ex ante ideology classification is high (.84), and although, also as expected, Republican Presidents appointed 75 percent of the judges who turned out to vote conservatively, when we normalize this falls to 65 percent and Republican Presidents are

Table 4.12 Yung's Ex Post Ideology Rankings and Epstein-Landes-Posner Ex Ante Ideology Rankings and Party of Appointing President

Type of Judge	Appointed by Republican Presidents	
	Normalized	Unadjusted
Ex Post		
Conservative	65%	75%
Moderate	51%	60%
Liberal	36%	45%
Ex Ante		
SC	100%	—
MC	86%	—
ML	8%	—
SL	0%	—

Note: "Normalized" means assuming that Republican and Democratic Presidents had appointed the same number of judges.

seen to have appointed more than one-third of the liberal voters. The figures are approximately reversed for judges appointed by Democratic Presidents.

In the bottom part of the table we see that all the strongly conservative judges ex ante were appointed by Republican Presidents, all the strongly liberal ones were appointed by Democratic Presidents, almost all the moderately conservative ones were appointed by Republican Presidents, and an even larger percentage of moderately liberal ones were appointed by Democratic Presidents. This shows, by the way, that at least in the modern era (for most of the judges in the sample were appointed after 1980), the party of the appointing President is a good proxy for the ex ante ideology of a court of appeals judge. But while modern Presidents try to appoint judges who will have an ideology as judicial voters that is consistent with the ideology of the President's party, they succeed only about two-thirds of the time. This is true for Republican as well as for Democratic Presidents—recall that more than a third of the *R*s are liberal judicial voters and more than a third of the *D*s are conservative judicial voters.

A possible explanation for these results is ideological drift (a change in the judge's ideology over time), but that seems unlikely given the symmetry of the change: why would a third of the *R*s become liberal and a third of the *D*s conservative? Furthermore, if drift were common we would expect *Year Appointed* in Table 4.15 (in the next section of this chapter) to be significant, and it is not. Panel composition is not a factor because Yung's rankings adjust for it.

An alternative explanation, which is consistent with the lesser ideological stakes at the court of appeals level, is that discrepancies between ex ante and ex post ideology—in other words, between a judge's ideology and his judicial votes—are likely if ideology doesn't play a strong role in decisions. For then a conservative judge might (for example) find himself frequently voting to reverse conservative district court decisions for non-ideological reasons. Those votes would be coded as liberal and move him down Yung's list, yet might be generated by conventional legal reasoning rather than by ideology.

Such judicial behavior is especially likely because of the greater weight of precedent in the courts of appeals than in the Supreme Court, which we document in chapter 6. Adherence to precedent is a prime example of legalist as distinct from ideological judicial voting.

In an attempt to get a better fix on the differences between ex ante and ex post ideology in the Supreme Court and the courts of appeals, we applied our ex ante ideology measure to the 44 Justices for whom we have Martin-Quinn (ex post) ideology scores (see chapter 3, Table 3.2). Table 4.13 presents the results and compares them with the results in Table 4.11 for the courts of appeals. The results are broadly similar, which gives us confidence in our ex ante measure.

Our measure of ex ante ideology likewise does a good job of predicting the fraction of conservative votes, our usual measure of ideological judicial voting, by court of appeals judges. As shown in Table 4.14, if within each of our four ideology classes we hold constant the ideological direction of the district court's decision that is being reviewed, the fraction of conservative votes declines in the Sunstein data as the other panel members

Table 4.13 Comparison of Ideological Voting in the Supreme Court and the Courts of Appeals

	SC	MC	ML	SL
Conservative Voters	67% / 54%	27% / 23%	7% / 23%	0% / 0%
Moderate Voters	13% / 23%	40% / 35%	20% / 35%	27% / 6%
Liberal Voters	0% / 21 %	21% / 19%	29% / 36%	50% / 23%

	Conservative Voters	Moderate Voters	Liberal Voters
SC	83% / 55%	17% / 23%	0% / 21%
MC	33% / 30%	42% / 46%	25% / 24%
ML	11% / 24%	44% / 38%	44% / 38%
SL	0% / 0%	37% / 21 %	64% / 79%

Notes:

1. The percentages to the left of the slash marks relate, for Supreme Court Justices, our ex ante ideology measure to the Martin-Quinn ex post ideology measure. (We use Martin-Quinn because, as mentioned in chapter 2, Yung's measure is a variant of it.) The percentages to the right of the slash marks relate, for the court of appeals judges in Yung's sample, our ex ante ideology measure to Yung's ex post ideology measure. So, for example, in the first cell in the table, 67 percent of the Justices who are conservative voters as measured by their Martin-Quinn scores we classify as strongly conservative ex ante and 54 percent of the court of appeals judges who are conservative judicial voters as measured by Yung we classify as strongly conservative ex ante. In the bottom part of the table we ask, for example, what percentage of Justices and judges whom we classify as strongly conservative ex ante are conservative voters ex post. The first cell in that part of the table indicates that these percentages are 83 for Supreme Court Justices and 55 for court of appeals judges.

2. The ex post classifications of Supreme Court Justices are derived from the Justices' Martin-Quinn scores: Conservative voters are the 15 highest-scoring Justices out of the 44 in the sample, Moderate Voters are the next highest 15, Liberal Voters are the lowest-scoring 14. The ex post classifications of the court of appeals judges are derived by dividing Yung's ex post scores into three parts, from most to least conservative voters.

Table 4.14 Votes Correlated with Our Ex Ante Rankings, Showing Reversal and Panel
Composition Effects for 142 Court of Appeals Judges, Sunstein Data,
1995–2008

Ex Ante Ranking	Liberal District Court Decision				Conservative District Court Decision			
	Fraction of Conservative Votes (i.e., reversals)				Fraction of Conservative Votes (i.e., affirmances)			
	RR	RD	DD	Votes	RR	RD	DD	Votes
SC	38.2	38.2	29.3	743	79.2	76.5	62.5	2030
MC	33.7	30.7	20.3	607	75.1	72.7	67.9	1562
ML	28.2	19.3	24.8	739	67.0	61.2	50.4	1782
SL	31.8	16.0	11.3	169	53.2	47.0	30.7	346

Note: Judicial votes of one judge in Yung's list of 143 judges are not in the Sunstein database.

shift from *RR* to *RD* to *DD*. Of the 16 comparisons, 14 move in the predicted direction. Also the fraction of conservative votes declines as we move from the most conservative judges *(SC)* to the most liberal ones *(SL)*, again holding both panel composition effects and the district court decision constant. Of the 18 comparisons, 15 change in the predicted direction.

Table 4.13 reveals that while conservative judicial voters in both the Supreme Court and the courts of appeals are never strongly liberal ex ante, conservative judicial voters in the courts of appeals are much less likely than their counterparts in the Supreme Court to be strongly conservative ex ante and much more likely to be moderately liberal ex ante. Similarly, while no liberal-voting Justices are strongly conservative ex ante, 21 percent of liberal-voting court of appeals judges are; while fully 50 percent of liberal-voting Justices are strongly liberal ex ante, only 23 percent of liberal-voting court of appeals judges are; while 83 percent of strongly conservative Justices ex ante are conservative judicial voters, only 55 percent of strongly conservative court of appeals judges ex ante are; and while 11 percent of ex ante moderately liberal Supreme Court Justices vote conservatively, 24 percent of ex ante moderately liberal court of appeals judges do.

The larger gap between ex ante and ex post ideology in the courts of appeals than in the Supreme Court supports the hypothesis that ideology plays a lesser role in the courts of appeals. The principal counterexample is that court of appeals judges who are strongly liberal ex ante are more consistent liberal voters than their Supreme Court counterparts (79 versus 64 percent). On the whole, however, court of appeals judges vote more often against the ideological grain than Supreme Court Justices do.

Group Influences in the Songer Data

As we noted in chapter 1, judges, like other workers, care about their working conditions, and one of those conditions is relations with coworkers. A judge who is constantly at odds with other judges of his court is likely to make himself and them unhappy, in part because disagreement implies criticism and in part because it makes for more work, to resolve the disagreement. (A vivid expression common in organizations—the "office asshole"—captures human beings' innate dislike for nonconformists.) Moreover, the more ideologically one-sided a circuit is, the likelier a decision by a panel dominated by the minority is to be reversed by the entire court, sitting en banc. Court of appeals judges also are more tethered to precedent than Supreme Court Justices are, and as a circuit shifts to the right (or left) the minority judges will find themselves bound to precedents increasingly being created by the majority because it is a larger majority and therefore dominates more panels; and panel decisions are the source of most circuit-level (as distinct from Supreme Court) precedents because en banc proceedings are rare. So we expect a judge who is in the ideological minority either in a three-judge panel or in the court as a whole to tend to soft-pedal any inclination to disagree with his colleagues.

We examine this and other group influences in this and the next section of this chapter. In this section we aggregate Songer data on judges' votes to the judge level, yielding a sample of 156 judges (see Table 4.15). The next section, based on Sunstein data, bases analysis on judges' votes in each case—a total of 8472 votes.

We can test for the presence in the courts of appeals of the three group effects that we tested for in the Supreme Court in chapter 3—conformity, group polarization, and political polarization—by examining the voting behavior of the court of appeals judges who were active in 2002, plus those who have taken senior status, retired, or resigned since 2000. This "current judge" sample enables a better test of the hypotheses than either the 1925–2002 or 1960–2002 samples would. Currently active court of appeals judges in a circuit, plus other judges appointed after 1960 who were active as of 2000 but not 2002, by definition interact with each other, whereas many of the judges in the same circuit in the 1925–2002 and 1960–2002 samples did not overlap, given the length of time covered by each sample, and so did not interact.

Our Songer-based current-judge sample consists, as we said, of 156 judges, of whom 141 were appointed after 1980. Eighty-two of the 156 were appointed by Republican Presidents and have an average tenure of 14.6 years, and 74 were appointed by Democratic Presidents and have an average tenure of 10.6 years.

Table 4.15 reestimates the regressions in Tables 4.7 and 4.8 for the Songer-based current-judge sample. Two of the independent variables relate to group effects: the fraction of the other judges in each circuit who were appointed by Republican Presidents *(Fraction Republican),* and that fraction weighted by the number of years of a judge's service through 2002 *(Fraction Republican Weighted).*

Because court of appeals judges almost always sit in panels of three randomly selected from the judges on the court,[15] an increase in *Fraction Republican* implies a higher probability that a panel will include two or more judges appointed by Republican Presidents. For example, of the 11 active judges on the court of appeals for the Seventh Circuit in 2002, Republican Presidents had appointed 8 and Democratic Presidents 3, making the probability that a judge appointed by a Republican President would sit with one or two *R*s 93 percent and the probability that he would sit with two *D*s only 7 percent, while the probability that a *D* would sit on a panel with one or two other *D*s was only 38 percent and the probability that he would sit with two *R*s was 16 percent.[16]

15. A complicating factor, which we ignore, is that many of the courts of appeals make extensive use of visiting judges from other circuits, both district judges, active and senior, and senior court of appeals judges.

16. The probabilities of various panel compositions for a given judge are calculated as follows. Let N be the number of judges in the circuit, R the number appointed by Republican Presidents, and D the number appointed by Democratic Presidents. Then:

Panel Composition	Judge Appointed by Republican President	Judge Appointed by Democratic President
All R	$(R - 1)(R - 2)/(N - 1)(N - 2)$	0
2R and 1D	$2(R - 1)D/(N - 1)(N - 2)$	$R(R - 1)/(N - 1)(N - 2)$
1R and 2D	$D(D - 1)/(N - 1)(N - 2)$	$2(D - 1)R]/(N - 1)(N - 2)$
All D	0	$(D - 1)(D - 2)/(N - 1)(N - 2)$

Table 4.15 Regression Analysis of Votes by Current Court of Appeals Judges
(t-statistics in parentheses)

	Civil Cases		Criminal Cases	
	Fraction Conservative (1)	Fraction Conservative (2)	Fraction Conservative (3)	Fraction Conservative (4)
President	0.103**	0.086**	0.110**	0.079**
	(3.96)	(3.02)	(3.88)	(2.50)
Senate Republican	−0.105	−0.090	0.374	0.347
	(0.52)	(0.44)	(1.73)	(1.52)
Year Appointed	−0.003	−0.0004	0.0003	0.001
	(0.18)	(0.25)	(0.17)	(0.32)
Sex	−0.024	−0.027	−0.014	−0.019
	(0.74)	(0.81)	(0.48)	(0.60)
Race	0.023	0.033	−0.006	0.010
	(0.63)	(0.96)	(0.16)	(0.19)
Former District Judge	−0.018	−0.020	0.019	0.018
	(0.81)	(0.87)	(0.80)	(0.66)
Fraction Economic	−0.226*	−0.246**	—	—
	(2.08)	(2.24)		
Fraction Other	−0.064	−0.108	—	—
	(0.16)	(0.26)		
Fraction Republican	0.256**	—	0.444**	—
	(3.38)		(5.50)	
Fraction Republican Weighted	—	0.183**	—	0.343**
		(2.66)		(4.76)
Constant	−0.145	−0.341	−0.325	−0.783
	(0.04)	(0.10)	(0.10)	(0.23)
R^2	0.23	0.19	0.36	0.31
Number of Observations	156	156	151	151

Note: All regressions are weighted by the judge's total votes in civil cases (equations (1)–(2)) or criminal cases (equations (3)–(4)).

The conformity hypothesis is that an increase in the proportion of judges appointed by Republican Presidents will increase the likelihood that any judge of the court will cast a conservative vote and a decrease in that proportion will increase the likelihood of a liberal vote. (And likewise, of course, with judges appointed by Democratic Presidents, but with the signs reversed.) The group polarization hypothesis is that judges appointed by Republican (Democratic) Presidents will vote more (less) conservatively in response to an increase in their number on the court. The political polarization hypothesis is that an increase in the size of one of the blocs relative to another will cause the second to vote more antagonistically to the first.

In Table 4.15 we test the first hypothesis by estimating a regression for all 156 judges in the sample and the second and third hypotheses by estimating separate regressions for R and D judges. The dependent variable in the first two regressions is the fraction of conservative votes in civil cases and in the third and fourth regressions it is the fraction of conservative votes in criminal cases. We omit regressions of the fraction of liberal votes, because the effects and significance levels of the independent variables are very similar to those of the conservative votes, except of course for the sign.

As with the Supreme Court, we do not find evidence of political polarization. We are not surprised, since political polarization is not implied by our labor theory of judicial behavior. We find support for the conformity effect: a judge, whether appointed by a Republican or a Democratic President, will vote conservatively more often in both civil and criminal cases when the fraction of other judges in the court who were appointed by Republican Presidents is greater. Remember that because the Songer database classifies votes in the courts of appeals as conservative, mixed, or liberal, an increase in conservative votes does not necessarily imply a decrease in liberal ones. But reestimating the regressions in Table 4.8 with fraction of liberal votes as the dependent variable, we find that the coefficients on *Fraction Republican* and *Fraction Republican Weighted* are indeed larger the lower the fraction of liberal votes.

The conformity effect may be greater in the case of judges appointed by Democratic Presidents, consistent with the proposition that R judges tend to be more committed ideologically than Ds. In separate civil-case regressions not reported in the table, the coefficients on *Fraction Republican* are .23 and .32 for Rs and Ds respectively, and in separate criminal regressions they are .38 and .52. All the regression coefficients are statistically significant, but the differences between the Rs and the Ds are not. The positive coefficients in the separate regressions are further evidence of the conformity effect, but contradict political polarization because Ds as well as Rs vote more conservatively as the fraction of Rs increases.

The fact that one of the blocs (say the conservative one) votes more conservatively as it grows larger is some evidence of group polarization. But it is not conclusive; it might just reflect the fact that the new addition to the majority votes more conservatively than its existing members—he might not have influenced *them* to vote more conservatively. So while we can exclude group polarization in the Supreme Court as explained in chapter 3, we can neither exclude nor confirm its existence in the courts of appeals.

It might seem that without knowing whether the new member of the majority was more or less conservative than the existing ones, we couldn't even predict an increase in conservative voting by the majority. But if he is less conservative, he might be influenced by his more conservative colleagues. If this is the common pattern, then on average an increase in the size of the conservative majority will cause an increase in conservative voting by the average member of the majority. But we haven't tried to test for this effect.

To estimate the overall ideological effect of changing the fraction of court of appeals judges appointed by Republican and Democratic Presidents, imagine a circuit of 6 judges appointed by (say) Republican Presidents and 6 by Democratic Presidents and that one of the *D*s is replaced by an *R*, so that *Fraction Republican* changes from .50 (6/12) to .5833 (7/12). The average percentage of conservative votes by the average judge will increase from 52 to 54 percent (.256 x [.5833 − .5]) in civil cases and from 74 to 78 percent in criminal cases (.444 x [.5833 − .5]). In a 10-year period, assuming an equal number of civil and criminal cases, the average judge will cast 20 more conservative votes in civil cases and 40 more in criminal cases.

If we set group polarization and political polarization to one side as unsubstantiated for the courts of appeals as for the Supreme Court, a change in the ideological complexion of a court of appeals that is brought about by replacement of a member of the court's minority bloc by a member of the majority bloc should have two effects: the majority is larger and therefore the court becomes more conservative (if it is a conservative majority), and the minority is more inclined to go along with the majority (conformity effect). There will be an equal and opposite effect if instead of the majority bloc growing at the expense of the minority, the minority bloc grows at the expense of the majority. Either way, judicial confirmation battles can be expected to be most intense in cases of nominees to a balanced circuit. This hypothesis is supported by a study that found that the odds of Senate confirmation decline for nominations to a balanced circuit, defined as a circuit in which 40 to 60 percent of the judges are either Rs or Ds.[17] For in a circuit that already has a large majority of Rs or Ds, the incremental effect on the ideological cast of the court's decisions of increasing the majority by one judge is unlikely to be great.

The effects of the other variables in Table 4.15—variables carried over from Tables 4.6 and 4.8—are similar to those in Table 4.6 for the 1960–2005 sample. In particular, judges appointed by Republican Presidents are significantly more likely to vote conservatively. None of the other carried-over variables is statistically significant.

Ideology, Conformity, and Panel Composition Effects in the Sunstein Data

We have made little use of the Sunstein database thus far in this chapter. We rectify the omission in this final section. We continue our discussion of group influences, but we also use the data for a further exploration of the role of ideology in court of appeals decisions. The Sunstein database is particularly suitable for this inquiry because, as shown in Table 4.16, it consists of published court of appeals opinions in subject-matter areas selected as being likely to involve significant ideological stakes. Discrimination cases preponderate. Disability discrimination cases alone comprise about 21 percent of the sample, and cases involving discrimination based on race, sex, age, or national origin account for another 50 percent.

Earlier, noting that the party of the appointing President had only a small effect on the voting behavior of court of appeals judges, we speculated that the reason Senate confirmations are nevertheless contentious is

---

17. Sarah A. Binder and Forrest Maltzman, *Advice and Dissent: The Struggle to Shape the Federal Judiciary* 91–94 (2009).

Table 4.16 Distribution of Votes and Cases by Subject-Matter Area, Sunstein Data, 1995–2008

Subject-Matter Area	Votes	Cases
Abortion	334	119
Americans with Disabilities Act	2960	1053
Affirmative Action	201	70
Age Discrimination	1828	650
Campaign Finance	184	66
Capital Punishment	929	315
Contract Clause	125	45
EPA	392	133
Federalism	1100	394
Piercing Corporate Veil	452	165
Sex Discrimination	1730	623
Sexual Harassment	1760	625
Takings	318	114
Title VII	1615	576
Total	13,928	4948

that the party-of-the-President effect is considerable in areas of federal law in which the ideological stakes are high. This conjecture is modestly supported by the Sunstein data. The fraction of conservative votes by *R*s and *D*s in civil cases is 61 percent and 47 percent respectively, compared to 52 and 44 percent of votes in the Songer database by judges appointed since 1960. The differences in the periods covered by and the types of error in the two databases, along with the fact that the Sunstein data are not just civil, preclude strong confidence in the comparison. Nevertheless it provides some reinforcement for our earlier finding that court of appeals judges are significantly less ideological in their judicial voting than Supreme Court Justices. Even though the cases in the Sunstein database resemble those in the Supreme Court more than the cases in the Songer database do, because they tend to be more ideologically charged, there is still a marked difference between the fraction of conservative and liberal votes by *R*s and *D*s in the courts of appeals and in the Supreme Court.

The Sunstein data enable us to assess group effects in the courts of appeals further, although we are unable to confirm or disconfirm the existence of group polarization or political polarization. However, Figure 4.2 shows that as the number of *R*s in a circuit increases relative to the num-

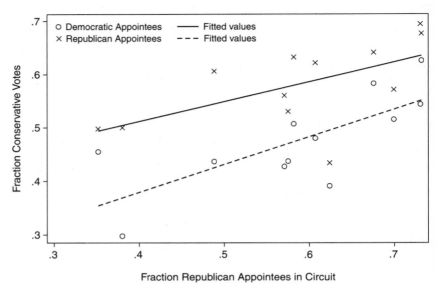

Figure 4.2   Fraction of Conservative Votes in Courts of Appeals, 1995–2008

ber of *D*s, both *R*s and *D*s tend to become more conservative.[18] This is the conformity effect.

We consider next panel composition effects. Panel composition is a function of the ideological balance within a court from which the three-judge panels that decide almost all the court's cases are drawn. The balance is uneven. As shown in Table 4.17, a majority of the judges in almost two-thirds of the panels were appointed by Republican Presidents. The highest percentages are found in the Seventh and Eighth Circuits (85 and 78 percent respectively). Only in the Second and Ninth Circuits (and barely the Sixth, with 51 percent) do a majority of panels have at least two *D*s.

A curiosity revealed by the table is that the Seventh and Eighth Circuits are greatly overrepresented in our sample. Although neither is above

18. In the regressions in Figure 4.2, Y_R and Y_D denote the fraction of conservative votes for *R*s and *D*s respectively:

$$Y_R = \quad .365 + .367 \ R/(R+D) \quad r^2 = .27$$
$$\quad (3.76) \quad (2.26)$$
$$Y_D = \quad .170 + .521 \ R/(R+D) \quad r^2 = .51$$
$$\quad (1.92) \quad (3.51)$$

Table 4.17   Distribution of Panels in Cases by Circuit, Sunstein Data, 1995–2008

Circuit	RRR	RRD	RDD	DDD	Total	Percent of Total That Is Either RRR or RRD
1st	69	159	73	8	309	74
2d	31	136	154	66	387	43
3rd	60	102	50	15	227	72
4th	43	112	75	13	243	64
5th	133	192	84	13	422	77
6th	48	160	153	63	424	49
7th	294	392	109	10	805	85
8th	249	340	157	13	759	78
9th	36	111	195	98	440	33
10th	66	143	112	31	352	59
11th	79	158	104	9	350	68
D.C.	45	103	72	10	230	64
All	1153	2108	1338	349	4948	66

average in size, together they account for 32 percent of the cases in the Sunstein database. We don't know why they're so overrepresented. They do have higher publication rates (remember that the database is limited to published opinions), but not so much higher as to explain the difference.

Table 4.18 reveals strong panel composition effects. A panel's ideological composition has a substantial impact both on a judge's vote (Part A) and on the panel's decision (Part B). Confirming the earlier empirical literature, we find that the presence on a panel of a judge appointed by a President of a different party from that of the President (or Presidents) who appointed the other judges on the panel tends to moderate the voting of those judges.

The first two columns in Part A indicate that the probability that a court of appeals judge appointed by a Republican President will vote conservatively is 66 percent if the other two judges are also *R*s but only 61 percent if the others are an *R* and a *D* and 52 percent if they are two *D*s, while the probability that a *D* will vote conservatively decreases from 55 percent when he sits with two *R*s to 45 percent if there is one other *D* and 37 percent if there are two other *D*s. The pattern is the same when the ideological direction of the district court decision is held constant (last four columns of Part A). With panel composition held constant instead, the likelihood of a conservative decision is significantly higher when the lower court decision is conservative than when it is liberal.

Table 4.18   Court of Appeals Judge Votes by Panel Composition and District Court
Decision, 1995–2008

Part A: Fraction of Conservative Votes of Judges Appointed by Republican
and Democratic Presidents

Other Panel Members	All District Court Decisions		Conservative District Court Decisions		Liberal District Court Decisions	
	R	D	R	D	R	D
RR	.657	.546	.774	.672	.388	.280
RD	.606	.452	.723	.577	.356	.207
DD	.521	.372	.650	.454	.270	.189
Number of Votes	8501	5418	5797	3645	2675	1753

Part B: Fraction of Conservative Decisions by Different Panel Compositions

	All District Court Decisions	Conservative District Court Decisions	Liberal District Court Decisions
RRR	.657	.774	.391
RRD	.589	.710	.338
RDD	.471	.599	.215
DDD	.364	.447	.173
Number of Cases	4948	3353	1578

Note: We start with a sample of 13,928 votes of court of appeals judges but exclude 49 votes where we have no information on the ideological direction of the district court decision and another 9 votes where we have no information on the ideological direction of the court of appeals judge's vote.

The fact that a judge of one ideological persuasion will tend to go along with the other judges on the panel even when they are of a different persuasion is unsurprising given dissent aversion; what is surprising is that a judge in the majority will also bend in the direction of the judge who has a different ideology. One possible explanation is that dissent aversion is not limited to judges who find themselves in the minority on a panel; the majority is averse to provoking a dissent. Another is what we'll call the "wobbler" effect. Suppose there were no dissent aversion; then if all *R*s, for example, were strongly conservative, an *RRD* panel and an *RRR* panel would produce equally conservative outcomes, though there would often be a dissent in the *RRD* panel. Yet we know that there are ideological differences among *R*s and among *D*s, as well as between the two groups. Suppose a particular *R* is a wobbler in the sense of not being strongly conservative in his judicial voting. If he is on a mixed panel with another *R* and a *D,* he may go along with the *D* (unless the latter is a wobbler too), and so the panel will render a liberal decision, as it would not have done if neither R had been a wobbler. But if he is on a panel with two other Rs, he is unlikely to dissent from a conservative decision. Thus panel composition effects could be produced without dissent aversion. But we haven't tried to test this alternative hypothesis, which would require analyzing a very large number of panels composed of different court of appeals judges.

In Part B of Table 4.18 we see the probability of a conservative decision increasing as the number of Rs increases, regardless of the ideological valence of the district court's decision. But we also find a tendency to affirm the district court that is independent of the ideological leanings of the judges—another group effect if we treat the trial judge and the appellate judges who decide an appeal from him as constituting a judicial group. Even though the Sunstein database is tilted toward cases that involve greater-than-average ideological stakes, a panel of 3 Ds will affirm a conservative district court decision 45 percent of the time, compared to 77 percent for a panel of 3 Rs, while a panel of 3 Rs will affirm a liberal district court decision 62 percent of the time, compared to 83 percent for a panel of 3 Ds. The decision of the district court exerts a pull on the appellate judges that weakens their ideological inclinations, although those inclinations continue to exert a significant influence. The results are similar for votes by individual judges (Panel A), as distinct from panel decisions.

These results could reflect just the fact that most appeals so lack merit in legalist terms that virtually any appellate judge would vote to affirm, regardless of the consonance between the district court's decision and the appellate court's ideology; judges are not indifferent to precedent and other orthodox legal materials. Yet one might think that, tugging in the opposite direction, a selection effect would produce a high reversal rate, because the expected benefit of appealing is higher the likelier the appellate court is to reverse. But this depends on the costliness of an appeal, the benefit to the appellant if the appeal is successful, and how accurately the probability of reversal can be estimated. The win rate in lotteries is a lot lower than the reversal rate in the federal courts of appeals, but more people buy lottery tickets than appeal federal district court decisions. Furthermore, effort aversion should predispose judges to affirm. It is easier to write an opinion affirming than one reversing, because when affirming a judge can rely heavily on the lower court's decision, whereas reversal requires refuting the grounds of that decision. In some circuits, many affirmances are announced in one-word orders: "affirmed." This is evidence of effort aversion.

A related factor is that standards of appellate review (discussed further in the next chapter) require deference (not complete, of course) to district court decisions, especially on issues of fact. These standards may be attributable in large part to effort aversion, as they reduce the amount of time that an appellate judge has to spend on most cases. But whatever their genesis, the standards are legally binding and even court of appeals judges who are not effort-averse can be expected to pay some heed to them; we'll come back to this point.

The ideological tension between trial and appellate court invites a comparison between two measures of circuit ideology depicted in Figure 4.3—the ratio of reversals of liberal district court decisions to reversals of conservative district court decisions (the higher the ratio, the more conservative the appellate court), and the fraction of judges appointed by Republican Presidents. The measures are positively correlated (.63), but the fit is not tight. So, for example, the Second and the Ninth Circuit have the lowest fraction of Rs among active judges and also the lowest ratios of reversals of liberal district court decisions to reversals of conservative decisions—that is, the lowest reversal ratios. The Second Circuit reverses 23 percent of liberal district court decisions and 42 percent of conservative ones, for a reversal ratio of .62. The corresponding percentages for the Ninth Circuit are 28 and 56 percent, a reversal ratio of .50. Among the circuits with the highest fraction of Rs, there is substantial variation in the reversal ratio. For example, the Seventh Circuit reverses about the same number of liberal and conservative district court decisions, while the Fifth Circuit reverses about 50 percent more of the former.

Regression analysis of the Sunstein data allows us to estimate panel and other group effects, including the effects of the "group" that consists of the trial court and the appellate court. Among other things it enables us to decompose the effect of an increase in the fraction of R judges into (1) a circuit ideology effect on both R and D judges, independent of changes in the relative frequency of R-dominated panels (the conformity effect,

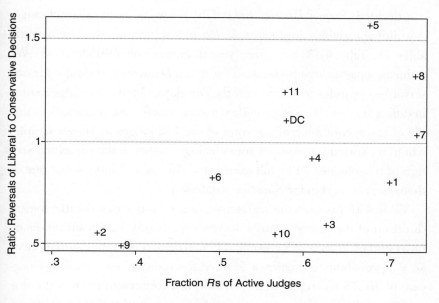

Figure 4.3   Fraction of Reversals of Liberal versus Conservative District Court Decisions, Correlated with Fraction of *R*s in Circuit, 1995–2008

in other words), and (2) a panel composition effect as the number of *R*-dominated panels increases.

Our regression equation is

$$V = f(DC, P, C, J, S, T, u).$$

V denotes the judge's vote (1 = conservative). *DC* is the ideological direction of the district court's decision (again 1 = conservative). *P* is a set of dummy panel variables for the party of the appointing President of the judge and the appointing President(s) of the other panel members. *C* is a proxy for circuit ideology and is equal to either the fraction of active court of appeals judges in the circuit appointed by Republican Presidents *(Fraction Republican)* or the ratio of the fraction of votes to reverse liberal district court decisions to the fraction of votes to reverse conservative district court decisions *(Reversal Ratio)*. *J* is a set of variables representing judges' characteristics: *Sex* if the judge is male; *Nonwhite* if the judge is black, Hispanic, or Asian; *Tenure* (number of years the judge has been on the court of appeals); *Senior* if the judge was a senior judge when the case was decided; *Former District Judge* if the judge had been a district judge. Additional variables are *Subject Matter* (14 subject-matter dummy variables; see Table 4.15) and *Time* (year dummies from 1995 to 2008). We estimate separate logit regressions for R and D judges and cluster the observations by judge to account for the correlation between a judge's votes in different cases. We also provide regression estimates for a smaller sample of cases, consisting of the votes of the 142 judges in Yung's sample, whom we sorted into four ex ante ideology classes in the preceding section of this chapter. (The full sample consists of 143 judges, but one of them had no votes in the Sunstein database.)

Table 4.19 presents the regression results. Notice that the ideological direction of the district court's decision is a highly significant influence on a court of appeals judge's vote. A liberal district court decision reduces an R's probability of casting a conservative judicial vote by .30 (41 percent of his .73 mean probability of casting a conservative vote if the district court decision is conservative), and a conservative district court decision reduces a D's probability of casting a liberal vote by .33 (43 percent of his .77 mean probability of casting a liberal vote if the district court decision is liberal). That the liberal district court decision tugs the conservative judge toward affirming (and thus casting a liberal vote) and the conservative district court decision tugs the liberal judge toward affirming (and thus casting a conservative vote) is evidence of legalistic decision-making—evidence that judges take seriously the standards of appellate review, which in most cases counsel deference to the district judge's rulings (again, see chapter 5). But the evidence is not conclusive; since less work is involved in affirming than in reversing, a tendency to affirm against the ideological grain may also or instead be due to effort aversion.

The coefficients of the RR and RD variables (DD is the left-out variable) measure panel composition effects. The probability that an R will vote conservatively is 52 percent if the other two panel members are Ds, 60 percent if one of the others is an R, and 66 percent if both of the others are Rs. In the D regression, the probability of a conservative vote is 37 percent when the other panel members are both Ds, 45 percent when one of the others is an R, and 52 percent when both of the others are Rs.

Changes in the fraction of R and D judges on the court as a whole amplify panel composition effects. In our regression, replacing two Ds with

Table 4.19 Logit Regression of Probability of Conservative Votes by Court of Appeals Judges, 1995–2008

	Appointed by Republican President		Appointed by Democratic President	
	(1)	(2)	(3)	(4)
Ideological Direction of District Court Decision	.298** (17.03)	.294** (16.48)	.334** (12.51)	.328** (12.12)
RR	.125** (6.19)	.128** (6.74)	—	—
RD	.071** (3.93)	.073** (4.05)	−.072** (4.06)	.071** (4.22)
DD	—	—	−.156** (7.03)	−.155** (6.61)
Reversal Ratio	.132** (5.57)	—	.206** (6.78)	—
Fraction Republican	—	.185** (3.26)	—	.355** (5.05)
District Court	.003 (0.19)	.001 (0.07)	.039 (1.69)	.048** (2.17)
Sex	−.077 (1.94)	−.079 (1.79)	−.016 (0.72)	−.29 (1.36)
Nonwhite	−.065* (2.04)	.067* (2.45)	−.015 (0.73)	−.002 (0.11)
Tenure	−.002 (1.44)	−.002 (1.57)	−.001 (0.82)	−.001 (0.41)
Senior Judge	−.0001 (0.01)	−.005 (0.23)	−.009 (0.20)	−.024 (0.59)
Subject-Matter Dummies	Yes**	Yes**	Yes**	Yes**
Time Dummies	Yes**	Yes**	Yes	Yes
Number of Observations	8472	8472	5398	5398

Notes:
1. Regression coefficients are marginal effects at mean values of all variables.
2. Standard errors are clustered by judge.
3. The data are for 317 judges.

two *R*s on a court of 5 *R*s and 7 *D*s increases the percentage of *RRR* panels from 5 to 16 percent and of *RRD* panels from 32 to 48 percent. These changes increase the likelihood of a conservative vote by both *R*s and *D*s irrespective of the overall change in circuit ideology. The changes increase the probability of a conservative vote by an *R* by 3 percent and by a *D* by 6 percent.

Circuit ideology has a highly significant effect on the probability of a conservative vote. This is the conformity effect. The reversal ratios in equations (1) and (3) range from .49 in the Ninth Circuit to 1.33 in the Eighth, implying that as one moves from the most liberal to the most conservative circuit the probability of a conservative vote increases by .11 for an R and .17 for a D. Regressions (2) and (4) proxy circuit ideology by the fraction of Rs among active judges in the circuit. If two Ds are replaced by Rs on a court previously consisting of 5 Rs and 7 Ds, panel composition effects are amplified because the percentage of RRR panels increases from 4.5 to 15.9 percent and of RRD panels from 31.8 to 47.7 percent, and the percentages of DDD and DDR panels decrease correspondingly. These changes increase the likelihood of a conservative vote by .024 for an R in equation (2) and by .028 for a D in equation (4).

An additional effect of replacing Ds by Rs is implied by the positive regression coefficient on *Fraction Republican*. An increase in Rs from 5 to 7 in a court of appeals of 12 judges is predicted to increase the probability of a conservative vote by .030 for an R and .058 for a D. The combined effect of replacing 2 Ds with 2 Rs is therefore to increase the fraction of conservative votes by .054 for an R ($= .024 + .030$) and .086 for a D ($= .028 + .058$), or by 10.5 and 22.6 percent, respectively, relative to the mean probabilities of a conservative vote for Rs and Ds when the court consists of 5 Rs and 7 Ds.

We reestimated the regressions in Table 4.19 for a sample limited to the 142 judges in Yung's sample who voted in cases in the Sunstein database. We combine Rs and Ds but add three ex ante ideology variables: strongly conservative, moderately conservative, and moderately liberal, the omitted category being strongly liberal. All three variables are positive and highly significant and properly ordered—the coefficient on strongly conservative exceeds that on moderately conservative (although the difference is not statistically significant), which in turn exceeds the coefficient on moderately liberal;[19] and all three coefficients exceed the coefficient on strongly liberal. These results, which hold constant the district court decision, panel effects, and the other variables included in the re-

19. The regression coefficients and t-values are as follows: .210 (6.67) strongly conservative; .164 (4.40) moderately conservative; .082 (2.94) moderately liberal. The regression contains 7978 observations, of which 4848 are votes by Rs and 3130 votes by Ds.

gressions in Table 4.19, are further evidence that our ex ante ideology method is a good predictor of judicial votes.

The results are shown in Table 4.20, which also decomposes the overall effect of a change in the composition of a court into its conformity and panel composition components. We assume a circuit of 6 *R*s and 6 *D*s and then vary the proportions while holding the total number of judges constant. Columns (1) through (3) test the conformity, panel composition, and total effects on the probability of a conservative vote by an *R* as the fraction of *R* judges on a court changes; columns (4) through (6) present the corresponding results for *D*s. The probability of a conservative vote is seen to increase by between 3 and 17 percent, depending on the increase in the proportion of *R*s. The conformity effect always dominates the panel composition effect, accounting for between 57 and 69 percent of the total. When, for example, in a 12-judge circuit consisting of an equal number of *R*s and *D*s, 2 *R*s replace 2 *D*s, thus changing the circuit composition to 8 *R*s and 4 *D*s, the probability of a conservative vote by an *R* increases by 54 percent. This is a substantial effect, which helps explain why Senate confirmation hearings for nominees to the courts of appeals often are controversial.

The upshot of our analysis in this chapter is to confirm the existence of a significant ideological influence on court of appeals decisions, though a significantly weaker influence than in the Supreme Court, and of strong group effects, which may mainly reflect effort aversion. Since the ideological stakes are greater in Supreme Court decisions than in court of appeals decisions, we expect effort aversion to play a bigger role in the courts of appeals (also because they have a heavier workload), which in turn should further reduce the influence of ideology in those courts.

Appendix A

The Original and Corrected Songer Database

The data in the Songer database include the history of a case, the participants, the issues involved, the resolution, the judges who decided the case, and each judge's vote on a maximum of two issues in the case. For

Table 4.20 Effects of Changes in the Number of *R*s and *D*s in a Court of Appeals of 12 Judges

Circuit Composition		Appointed by Republican President			Appointed by Democratic President		
		Direct Circuit Effect	Panel Composition Effect	Total	Direct Circuit Effect	Panel Composition Effect	Total
R	*D*	(1)	(2)	(3)	(4)	(5)	(6)
7	5	.015 (55.6%)	.012 (44.4 %)	.027	.029 (67.4%)	.014 (32.6%)	.04
8	4	.031 (57.4%)	.023 (42.6%)	.054	.059 (67.8%)	.028 (33.2%)	.08
9	3	.046 (57.5%)	.034 (42.5%)	.080	.089 (68.5%)	.041 (31.5%)	.13
10	2	.062 (57.9%)	.045 (42.1%)	.107	.119 (68.8%)	.054 (31.2%)	.17
5	7	−.015 (56.2%)	−.012 (43.8%)	.027	−.029 (67.4%)	−.014 (32.6%)	−.04
4	8	−.031 (56.0%)	−.024 (44.0%)	.055	−.059 (67.8%)	−.028 (32.2%)	−.08
3	9	−.046 (55.6%)	−.037 (44.4%)	.083	−.089 (67.4%)	−.043 (32.6%)	−.13
2	10	−.062 (55.2%)	−.050 (44.8%)	.112	−.119 (67.2%)	−.058 (32.8%)	−.17

Notes:

1. The direct circuit and panel composition effects assume that the court initially consists of 6 *R*s and 6 *D*s.

2. The percentages are percentage of total effect accounted for by the variable.

3. The *Direct* effect equals the marginal effect on *Fraction Republican* in equations (2) and (4) multiplied by the difference between the fraction of *R*s in the circuit and .5.

4. The *Panel Composition* effect equals the weighted sum of the marginal regression coefficients on *RR* and *RD* where the weights equal the change in the fraction of *RR*, *DD*, and *RD* panels as the fraction of *R* appointed increases or decreases from its initial value of .5.

the years 1925–1960 the database includes a random sample of 15 cases from each court each year, and for the years 1961–2002 it includes a random sample of 30 cases from each court each year.

We merged the Songer database with what is known as the Auburn dataset,[20] which contains attribute data for the judges in the Songer database; we refer to the combined databases as the Songer database. Although the two databases were intended to be used together, there are some inconsistencies in the judge identification codes. We made the cor-

20. See note 3 above.

rections suggested by the database's documentation and made further corrections as we discovered errors while working with the data. This appendix explains our corrections.

In Table 4.1 we distinguished between ideological misclassifications and other errors. But we corrected all the errors we found, and when we refer in the body of the chapter to the "corrected" Songer database, the reference is to the fully corrected database.

We used a computerized error-detection method to identify coding errors. The errors we found included duplication of case citation (92 cases with errors), two or more different judge codes in the same case (41), conflicting codes in the same case (51), and inconsistent indication of the presence of a federal district court in the procedural history of the case (37). We identified a total of 5818 errors in 3197 of the 20,355 cases in the database; thus some cases had multiple errors.

We removed as many errors as we could find that were relevant to our analytical work. For example, we removed cases involving errors in the coding of judges' votes, since such errors are germane to analyses of judicial ideology, but not cases involving errors in the designation of the bankruptcy status of the appellants, because such an error would be unlikely to affect our analyses. We removed a total of 1317 cases, which reduced the total number of judge votes in our sample from 64,212 to 59,974. Some errors we were able to correct, such as the assignment of the same judge code to both Otto Kerner Sr. and Otto Kerner Jr.—there was only one Judge Kerner—or of multiple judge codes to the same judge.

We eliminated the votes of judges whom we were unable to identify (frequently coded as 9999 or 99999) and votes by district judges sitting as visiting judges in the courts of appeals. These reduced the total number of votes in our sample from 59,947 to 55,041.

A complication arose from the fact that the unit of analysis in the database is the case rather than the judge—and some of our analysis requires judge data. The database permits only two type-of-case classifications per sampled case. We had to decide whether to treat the judge's votes on the two issue types as one vote or two. We compromised: if the case types were within the same general case category (the type of category we use in our analysis—for example, case type 1: federal murder (101); case type 2: state arson (123)), we tried to determine the overall ideological valence of the judge's vote. If in one of the narrow categories it was conservative and in the other liberal, his vote in the case was classified as ideologically mixed. But if the vote in one of the narrow categories was liberal or conservative and in the other mixed or other, his vote in the case was classified as either liberal or conservative, depending on his vote in the category in which he cast a liberal or a conservative vote. If the case types were in different general categories (for example, case type 1: federal murder (101), which is in category criminal; case type 2: mandatory sterilization (506), which is in category privacy), we treated the judge as voting in two separate cases.

We made corrections in the ideological classification of votes. All votes in case types 114–118, 134–138, and 154–158 were changed from liberal or conservative to other. All votes in criminal cases for the defendant had been coded as liberal, but we changed votes in cases involving morals charges (114, 134, and 154) to other because they could include child pornography, an issue on which neither liberal nor conservative judges are sympathetic to the defendant. And likewise with economic crimes (violations of government regulations of business, other white-collar crime, and other crimes), in which a liberal judge, as well as most conservative judges, would tend to favor the government rather than the defendant.

Votes for the plaintiff in sex discrimination cases unrelated to employment, brought by a man (235), classified by the original coders as liberal, we changed to other because the category could include cases in which a homosexual (or someone believed to be homosexual) had been harassed by another man; in such a case, and probably also in cases in which a man alleges harassment by a woman, a liberal judge might tend to favor the defendant. For the same reason we changed votes in suits charging race or sex discrimination in employment (239) from liberal to other, as it includes claims of discrimination by whites and men against blacks and women in cases of affirmative action.

Commercial speech cases (301) had been coded so that a vote for the broadest interpretation of First Amendment protection was liberal. We changed the classification of such votes to other because businesses are usually the plaintiffs in commercial speech cases. In obscenity cases

(307), where again a vote for the broadest interpretation of First Amendment protection had been coded as liberal, we changed the coding to other because some liberals (especially feminists) disapprove of obscenity.

In the original database, case type 412 was defined as a claim of "denial of due process under the 'taking' clause of the Fifth Amendment," and a vote for the plaintiff was coded as liberal. Yet in case type 771—eminent domain disputes—a vote for the government was coded as liberal. Due process is not mentioned in the takings clause and takings and eminent domains are virtual synonyms, so case type 412 is mysterious and we thought it better to shift the votes in it to other.

We changed votes for plaintiffs in labor cases from liberal to other if the party on one side of the case was the government and on the other side a union or an individual. This changed all the vote classifications in case types 600–699. We made the same change in categories 710–713, which cover cases involving copyrights, patents, trademarks, trade secrets, and other intellectual property. An intellectual property case often is brought by a large firm against a small firm or an individual, as when a giant pharmaceutical company sues the manufacturer of a generic drug or a large record company sues a file-sharing college student to make an example of him.

We made a similar reclassification of votes in case types 773–774, which involve the government's seizure of property either as an incident to the enforcement of criminal statutes (773) or in civil cases (774). All votes for the government in these categories had been coded liberal, but because the party whose property is seized could be either wealthy or poor the ideological classification was overbroad.

We likewise changed votes in all cases in type 903 from liberal to other. This case type is described only as "attorneys (disbarment, etc.)." There is no reason to expect a liberal judge to favor a lawyer in a disbarment proceeding. And we changed votes in all cases in types 905, 906, and 920 to other because the issues in these cases—challenges to the authority of a magistrate or bankruptcy judge, and international law—cannot be categorized ideologically.

We recoded the cases in type 921—government regulation of immigration—from liberal to conservative. A vote for government regulation had been coded as liberal, but a liberal judge would be likely to support the rights of the immigrant against the government rather than vice versa.

Appendix B

The Original and Expanded Sunstein Database

Sunstein and his coauthors compiled datasets on federal court of appeals decisions involving abortion, the Americans with Disabilities Act, affirmative action, campaign finance, capital punishment, the contracts clause, criminal appeals, environmental regulation, federalism, piercing the corporate veil, race discrimination, sex discrimination, sexual harassment, and takings. For each subject area they collected cases decided during particular years. All their datasets end in 2001, but their starting points differ. For example, their abortion dataset begins in 1982, affirmative action in 1979, and capital punishment in 1995.

For each case they recorded the judges who participated and whether the case was decided for or against the plaintiff. Following their coding rules, we updated their datasets through 2008 and added age discrimination cases and attribute variables (for example, the party of the President who appointed the judge and the judge's race and sex). The cases in the expanded dataset are broken down by subject-matter area in Table 4.9.

Appendix C

Measures of Ex Ante Ideology of Supreme Court Justices, 1937–2009

Segal-Cover Measure		Epstein-Landes-Posner Measure	
Scalia	1.000	Alito	*SC*
Rehnquist	0.955	Blackmun	*SC*
Alito	0.900	Burger	*SC*
Blackmun	0.885	Rehnquist	*SC*
Burger	0.885	Roberts	*SC*
Roberts	0.880	Scalia	*SC*
Thomas	0.840	Stone	*SC*
Powell	0.835	Thomas	*SC*
Stevens	0.750	Burton	*MC*
Burton	0.720	Clark	*MC*
Stone	0.700	Harlan	*MC*
Souter	0.675	Kennedy	*MC*
Byrnes	0.670	O'Connor	*MC*
Kennedy	0.635	Powell	*MC*
O'Connor	0.585	Souter	*MC*
Breyer	0.525	Stevens	*MC*
Clark	0.500	Stewart	*MC*
White	0.500	Vinson	*MC*
Whittaker	0.500	Warren	*MC*
Frankfurter	0.335	Brennan	*ML*
Ginsburg	0.320	Breyer	*ML*
Minton	0.280	Ginsburg	*ML*
Reed	0.275	Minton	*ML*
Douglas	0.270	Reed	*ML*
Goldberg	0.250	Sotomayor	*ML*
Stewart	0.250	White	*ML*
Vinson	0.250	Whittaker	*ML*
Warren	0.250	Black	*SL*
Sotomayor	0.220	Byrnes	*SL*
Black	0.125	Douglas	*SL*
Harlan	0.125	Fortas	*SL*
Brennan	0.000	Frankfurter	*SL*
Fortas	0.000	Goldberg	*SL*
Jackson	0.000	Jackson	*SL*
Marshall	0.000	Marshall	*SL*
Murphy	0.000	Murphy	*SL*
Rutledge	0.000	Rutledge	*SL*

Notes:

1. *SC* = strongly conservative, *MC* moderately conservative, *ML* moderately liberal, and *SL* strongly liberal.

2. Justices are listed in alphabetical order within each of the four classifications in the list on the right.

CHAPTER 5

The District Courts and the Selection Effect

F EDERAL DISTRICT JUDGES have received less attention in academic studies of judicial behavior than Supreme Court Justices and court of appeals judges.[1] There are several reasons. There are no datasets comparable to those that have been created for Supreme Court and court of appeals decisions (of course, this is a result of lack of academic interest as well as a cause). District court decisions do not create precedents, and precedents are a particular focus of legal training and scholarly interest; also, non-precedential decisions have less visible policy impact than decisions of higher courts. A substantial fraction of cases filed in the district courts (many by persons who do not have legal representation) have no possible merit and so really are just noise in the data. And information about district court decisions is hard to come by, because most are decided without written opinion, often on procedural grounds and rarely after a trial—in the 12-month period ending in March 2009, fewer than 2 percent of the 237,802 civil cases filed in district courts resulted in a judgment after trial.[2]

1. Not no attention, of course. See the list of studies of the district courts that is cited in the appendix to chapter 2.
2. U.S. Courts, "Federal Judicial Caseload Statistics 2009," www.uscourts.gov/Statistics/FederalJudicialCaseloadStatistics.aspx (visited Feb. 8, 2012).

Yet these courts are the largest component of the federal judiciary, deciding 6.9 times as many cases as the courts of appeal and about 3000 times as many cases as the Supreme Court.[3] There are 3.8 times as many authorized district judgeships as court of appeals judgeships (678/179). And district judges have a great deal of discretionary authority, the exercise of which is reviewed by the courts of appeals to only a limited extent—for example, authority to decide whether a witness at a bench trial, or at some other evidentiary hearing in which the judge is the trier of fact, is credible, authority to admit or exclude evidence at a trial or other proceeding, and authority to pick a criminal sentence within the sentencing limits set by Congress.

Our analysis makes use of five datasets. One is the Sunstein database that we used extensively in the preceding chapter. Its 4498 decisions are appeals from 962 district judges,[4] and for this chapter we have added information about the cases when they were at the district court level: whether a case was decided with or without a trial; whether if there was a trial it was a jury trial or a bench trial; whether if it was a jury trial the judge took the case from the jury before the jury began its deliberations and decided it himself; the ideological direction of the district court decision; whether the plaintiff or the defendant prevailed; who the district judge was and whether a Republican or a Democratic President had appointed him; the judge's own party affiliation if known; his senatorial courtesy score;[5] and his personal characteristics, such as race, sex, age, law school attended, professional experience, and date of appointment to the district court.

One use we make of these data, along with data from earlier chapters,

3. Calculated from id. and from John Roberts, "2009 Year-End Report on the Federal Judiciary," www.supremecourt.gov/publicinfo/year-end/2009year-endreport.pdf (visited Jan. 17, 2012).

4. Of the 962 judges, 443 were active in 2008 and 519 had either retired or taken senior status. We eliminated cases decided by an administrative agency, a magistrate judge, or a bankruptcy judge, rather than a district judge, and we eliminated 11 cases in which we could not identify the judge.

5. These other ideological proxies (judge's party affiliation and senatorial courtesy score) turn out not to alter significantly the results based on the cruder R/D classification, even though Presidents sometimes do appoint district judges who are of a different party or, more often, of no party. So we generally don't report the results of the other measures.

is to test the hypothesis that as cases move up the judicial hierarchy, ideology plays an increasingly important role in decision-making.[6] We discuss that selection effect in a later section of this chapter, along with a related issue, which we call the paradox of discretion: the more scrupulous a court of appeals is in adhering to standards of judicial review that command deference toward certain kinds of district court ruling, such as rulings on admission of evidence and on the credibility of witnesses, the more freedom district judges have to let their own ideological preferences influence their decisions. We test this proposition with the aid of a second dataset, compiled by Corey Yung (a variant of his dataset that we used in chapter 4), which ranks the courts of appeals by "activism," which he defines as the inverse of deference to district court decisions when the applicable standard of appellate review is deferential.

We also use the Sunstein dataset to explore reversals of district court decisions. A study of reversals in one circuit, the Eighth, found that the court of appeals for that circuit—a court dominated by judges appointed by Republican Presidents—reversed decisions by district judges appointed by Democratic Presidents at a significantly higher rate than those by district judges appointed by Republican Presidents.[7]

A third dataset that we use to explore the exercise of discretion by district judges consists of data compiled and published by the Sentencing Commission on federal criminal sentences. District judges traditionally were given almost unlimited discretion in picking the defendant's sentence within the normally broad range between the congressionally prescribed minimum and maximum sentences for a given crime. The federal sentencing guidelines promulgated by the Sentencing Commission pursuant to the Sentencing Reform Act of 1984 greatly curtailed district judges' sentencing discretion, but in 2005 the Supreme Court in the

6. For previous tests of this hypothesis, see Jeffrey A. Segal, Harold J. Spaeth, and Sara C. Benesh, *The Supreme Court in the American Legal System* 201 (2005); Daniel R. Pinello, "Linking Party to Judicial Ideology in American Courts: A Meta-Analysis," 20 *Justice System Journal* 219 (1999). As noted in chapter 2, Pinello's survey finds that the effect of ideology on judicial votes is about twice as strong in the Supreme Court as in the courts of appeals; we'll see that it's even weaker in the district courts than in the courts of appeals.

7. Robert Steinbuch, "An Empirical Analysis of Reversal Rates in the Eighth Circuit during 2008," 43 *Loyola of Los Angeles Law Review* 51 (2009).

Booker decision restored much of it in the name of the Constitution.[8] The exercise of sentencing discretion is an area in which ideology might be expected to influence the behavior of district judges, and in the final section of the chapter we use the Commission's post-*Booker* sentencing data to explore that possibility. We use still another dataset, of individual federal district judges' sentences, compiled by the Transactional Records Access Clearinghouse of Syracuse University (TRAC), to explore further the exercise of sentencing discretion by federal judges.

Our fifth dataset consists of 3893 cases in which motions were filed in district courts to dismiss a suit for failure to state a claim, pursuant to Rule 12(b)(6) of the Federal Rules of Civil Procedure.[9] The data cover the period from May 2006 to June 2010, a year before *Bell Atlantic Corp. v. Twombly*[10] and a year after *Ashcroft v. Iqbal*,[11] two Supreme Court decisions that made it easier for district courts to dismiss cases at the outset, before any pretrial discovery. We use these data to determine the impact of ideology, district court caseload, the prospect of reversal on appeal, and the changes in pleading standards brought about by *Twombly* and *Iqbal*, on the propensity of district judges to grant motions to dismiss.[12]

8. United States v. Booker, 543 U.S. 220 (2005).

9. We began with the data that Kendall W. Hannon used for his article "Much Ado about *Twombly?* A Study of the Impact of *Bell Atlantic Corp. v. Twombly* on 12(b)(6) Motions," 83 *Notre Dame Law Review* 1811 (2008). Being limited to cases decided between June 2006 and December 2007 that cited *Twombly* or the decision that it overruled, *Conley v. Gibson*, 355 U.S. 41 (1957), those data do not include decisions subsequent to the Supreme Court's decision in *Ashcroft v. Iqbal*, 129 S. Ct. 1937 (2009). We supplemented the data by searching Westlaw for all rulings, between May 2006 and June 2010 on Rule 12(b)(6) motions, which cited *Twombly, Conley,* or *Iqbal,* and drawing a random sample of 25 percent of these rulings. We excluded cases that were not decided by a district judge.

10. 550 U.S. 544 (2007).

11. See note 9 above.

12. Other empirical studies of the effect of these decisions include Hannon, note 9 above, finding little effect of *Twombly;* Patricia W. Hatamyar, "The Tao of Pleading: Do *Twombly* and *Iqbal* Matter Empirically?" 59 *American University Law Review* 553 (2010), finding that *Iqbal* but not *Twombly* affected dismissal rates (but her study is limited to rulings in the three months after *Iqbal*); and Andrea Kupperman, "Review of Case Law Applying *Bell Atlantic v. Twombly* and *Ashcroft v. Iqbal:* Memo to the Civil and Standing Rules Committees of the Judicial Conference Advisory Committee," www.uscourts.gov/uscourts/RulesAndPolicies/rules/ Iqbal_memo_072610.pdf (visited Dec. 9, 2011), finding, from a survey of a large number of cases, that *Iqbal* has not "dramatically changed the application" of pleading standards." Id.,

District Court Decisions Derived from the Sunstein Database

A limitation of the Sunstein database for analysis of the behavior of district judges is that we can derive from it only district court cases in which the appeal resulted in a published appellate opinion, and such cases are, as we know, an unrepresentative sample of all civil cases.[13] Most terminations of civil cases in district courts are not even appealable; the cases are either settled or simply abandoned. In 2008 nearly 80 percent of all civil cases in those courts—excluding prisoner petitions, which have on average even less merit than other civil cases and thus are even less likely, if dismissed and the dismissal is appealed, to be decided by the court of appeals in a published opinion—were resolved by dismissal (often as a consequence of settlement) or by summary judgment in favor of the defendant.[14] We estimate that fewer than 1 percent of cases terminated in the district court after some court action are appealed and the appeal decided in a published opinion, although our calculation of an appeal rate is rough because our district court and court of appeals cases are from 2008 even though many appeals decided in 2008 would have been from district court decisions in 2007 or even earlier.

Table 5.1 breaks down our Sunstein district court sample by type of disposition, ideology of the district judge as proxied by whether he was appointed by a Republican or a Democratic President, and the ideological direction of the decision. The table reveals that about a third of the cases went to trial (15 percent being jury trials, 14 percent bench trials, and 3 percent jury trials in which the judge took the case away from the jury and decided it himself), and the rest were disposed of by dismissal on the pleadings or by summary judgment. These figures support the un-

---

p. 2. A study of the effect of just *Twombly* finds, as do we, no effect of that decision on dismissals: William H. J. Hubbard, "The Problem of Measuring Legal Change, with Application to *Bell Atlantic v. Twombly*" (University of Chicago Law School, June 13, 2011).

13. The Sunstein database is not purely civil; it includes all criminal cases from three circuits (see chapter 8) plus capital punishment cases. In this chapter we omit all the criminal cases, except the capital cases because they involve such large ideological stakes.

14. U.S. Courts, "Federal Judicial Caseload Statistics 2008," www.uscourts.gov/uscourts/Statistics/FederalJudicialCaseloadStatistics/2008/tables/C04Mar08.pdf (visited Dec. 9, 2011).

Table 5.1 District Court Decisions by Type of Disposition, Party of Appointing President, and Ideological Direction of Decision, Sunstein Data, 1995–2008

Type of Disposition	Number of District Court Cases			Fraction of Conservative Decisions		
	All	R	D	All	R	D
Trial						
Jury	669	362	307	.230	.232	.228
Bench	608	342	266	.503	.500	.508
Judge Took Case from Jury	138	89	49	.725	.742	.694
Total Trial	1415	793	622	.396	.405	.384
Nontrial	3083	1847	1236	.835	.851**	.812
All	4498	2640	1858	.697	.717**	.669

representative character of district court decisions resolved by an appeal in the Sunstein database, limited as it is not only to published opinions but also to subject-matter areas that have higher-than-average ideological stakes.

While 77 percent of the jury trials in the sample resulted in a decision in the district court coded as liberal (generally a decision for the plaintiff), bench trials resulted in an equal number of liberal and conservative decisions. Of jury trials in which the judge took the case from the jury before verdict (as when the judge directs a verdict at the close of the plaintiff's case), 73 percent were decided conservatively. Thus the ratio of conservative nontrial outcomes to conservative jury decisions was 3.17.

Of decisions rendered at the pretrial stage (dismissals on the pleadings, mainly for failure to state a legally cognizable claim, and summary judgments), 84 percent were conservative, but this is not a reliable clue to the ideology of district judges. Not only is it inherently more difficult for the plaintiff to win at the pretrial stage (because he has the burden of proof) than the defendant, but that is the stage at which cases that virtually any judge of any ideological inclination would dismiss are filtered out, so most decisions at that stage favor the defendant irrespective of ideology. Yet most decisions in favor of the defendant in civil cases are, as we know, coded as conservative. The correlation between liberal and pro-plaintiff decisions is .64; and while 80 percent of the jury trials in the sample result in a judgment for the plaintiff, only 13 percent of non-trial decisions, which are much more numerous, do, consistent with the bur-

den of proof and filtering reasons for expecting plaintiffs to lose disproportionately when their cases are terminated before trial. It should also be
noted that the win rate of plaintiffs in jury trials exaggerates the winners'
actual success, since the damages award may be so small as to make the
plaintiff's victory Pyrrhic.

The table reveals that whether a Republican or a Democratic President appointed the district judge has no statistically significant effect on
the ideological direction of the decision except in cases in which there
was no trial, and even in those cases the difference between *R*s and *D*s is
only 4 percent (85 percent conservative decisions by *R*s, 81 percent by
*D*s). There is a statistically significant difference when cases decided in a
trial are included in the comparison, but again the difference is small: 5
percent (72 percent conservative decisions by *R*s, 67 percent by *D*s).

Table 5.2 compares the ideological differences between *R*s and *D*s in
the courts of appeals (derived from Table 4.13 in chapter 4). The *R* and
D columns present the fraction of conservative votes by an *R* and a *D*, respectively, assuming a mixed panel (that is, the other members are an *R*
and a *D*), while the last two columns assume that the other judges on the
panel were appointed by a President of the same party as the President
who appointed that judge. The ideological differences between *R*s and
*D*s are indeed greater in the courts of appeals than in the district courts:
there is a 15 percent average difference between *R*s and *D*s in a mixed
panel but a 20 to 30 percent average difference between *R*s on a panel of

Table 5.2 Votes of Court of Appeals Judges by Ideological Direction of District Court
Decision, Sunstein Data, 1995–2008

| | Fraction of Conservative Votes | | | |
| | Other Panel Members Are an *R* and a *D* | | Panel Consists of 3 *R*s or 3 *D*s | |
District Court Decision	*R*	*D*	*RRR*	*DDD*
Conservative	.725**	.578	.775**	.454
Liberal	.357**	.207	.388**	.189
All	.605**	.453	.657**	.371

Note: The reversal of a liberal district court decision, or the affirmance of a conservative one, is scored
as a conservative vote; the affirmance of a liberal district court decision, or the reversal of a conservative
district court decisions, is scored as a liberal vote.

just *R*s and *D*s on a panel of just *D*s. These results are independent of the ideological direction of the district court's decision, because, as we know, court of appeals judges tend to affirm district court decisions regardless of ideology.

Tables 5.1 and 5.2 reveal that district judges render conservative decisions in more cases in the Sunstein database than court of appeals judges do: 72 percent and 67 percent for *R* and *D* district judges (see columns labeled *R* and *D* in the last row in Table 5.1), compared to 61 percent and 45 percent for *R* and *D* court of appeals judges when there are no panel composition effects (see columns labeled *R* and *D* in the last row of Table 5.2). The higher conservative percentage in the district courts may seem surprising, for while a high percentage of suits are plainly meritless, district court cases in the Sunstein database have enough merit to have been decided on appeal in a published opinion. Effort aversion may be a factor; district judges have heavier caseloads than court of appeals judges, and dismissals—most of which are coded conservative—require less time and effort than judgments for the plaintiff. Dismissals usually come early in a litigation, which is a time-saver; and if a case is dismissed the judge will not have to spend any time calculating damages, or crafting an injunction that he might later be called on to enforce by contempt proceedings.[15]

The next two tables show the ideological direction of the district court and court of appeals decisions in each of the 14 subject areas (Table 5.3) and 12 circuits (Table 5.4) in the Sunstein database. Table 5.3 reveals significant differences between *R* and *D* district judges in only three circuits (the Fifth, Sixth, and Eighth) and three subject-matter areas: ADA (Americans with Disabilities Act), Title VII (employment discrimination), and abortion. Since all district judges within a circuit will be inclined to follow the same circuit precedents, as otherwise they would be at high risk of reversal, it's no surprise that the difference is not statistically significant in two-thirds of the circuits and is largely confined to a few Sunstein categories, even though all Sunstein categories are ones in which ideological

15. Other evidence of effort aversion by district judges is presented in Stephen J. Choi, Mitu Gulati, and Eric A. Posner, "What Do Federal District Judges Want? An Analysis of Publications, Citations, and Reversals," *Journal of Law, Economics, and Organization* (forthcoming); Ahmed E. Taha, "Publish or Paris? Evidence of How Judges Allocate Their Time," 6 *American Law and Economics Review* 1, 27 (2004).

Table 5.3 Fraction of Conservative Votes in Selected Subject-Matter Areas by *R* and *D* District and Court of Appeals Judges, Sunstein Data, 1995–2008

	District Court		Court of Appeals	
	R	D	R	D
Abortion	.42*	.22	.58**	.19
	(67)	(50)	(110)	(48)
Americans with Disabilities Act	.86**	.77	.66**	.51
	(562)	(399)	(840)	(569)
Affirmative Action	.39	.33	.53	.35
	(41)	(24)	(61)	(29)
Age Discrimination	.85	.82	.70**	.61
	(338)	(271)	(518)	(300)
Campaign Finance	.44	.48	.75*	.54
	(39)	(27)	(53)	(26)
Capital Punishment	.87	.80	.78**	.52
	(197)	(112)	(252)	(196)
Contract Clause	.37	.35	.24	.19
	(27)	(17)	(29)	(26)
EPA	.14	.17	.37	.36
	(7)	(6)	(109)	(84)
Federalism	.06	.04	.06	.09
	(222)	(157)	(277)	(226)
PCV (piercing the corporate veil)	.51	.61	.67	.68
	(91)	(54)	(124)	(75)
Sex Discrimination	.81	.74	.67**	.51
	(335)	(252)	(517)	(280)
Sexual Harassment	.79	.72	.58**	.39
	(344)	(217)	(502)	(308)
Takings Clause	.11	.24	.27*	.11
	(71)	(34)	(96)	(57)
Title VII	.89**	.80	.71**	.55
	(299)	(238)	(487)	(258)
All	.72**	.67	.61**	.45
	(2640)	(1858)	(3975)	(2482)

Note: Numbers in parentheses are decisions by district judges (district court column), or votes by court of appeals judges (court of appeals column) when the other panel members are an *R* and a *D*.

differences between judges are likely to influence their decisions. This suggests reversal aversion on the part of district judges. In contrast, *R* court of appeals judges vote significantly more conservatively than *D*s in the same 3 subject-matter categories and in 6 others as well (again holding panel effects constant by assuming the other members are an *R* and a *D*), and in 8 of the 12 regional circuits, including (of course) the 3 in which there are significant ideological differences among district judges.

Table 5.4 Fraction of Conservative Votes by District Judges and Court of Appeals Judges, by Circuit, Sunstein Data, 1995–2008

Circuits	District Court		Court of Appeals	
	R	D	R	D
1st	.64	.69	.57	.54
	(174)	(126)	(297)	(134)
2d	.66	.71	.47	.50
	(192)	(171)	(255)	(278)
3rd	.71	.69	.44	.40
	(141)	(71)	(186)	(92)
4th	.74	.66	.62*	.49
	(149)	(86)	(202)	(132)
5th	.70*	.60	.66*	.57
	(255)	(127)	(368)	(159)
6th	.71*	.60	.64**	.40
	(204)	(197)	(279)	(272)
7th	.80	.80	.69**	.54
	(457)	(285)	(784)	(218)
8th	.78**	.65	.67**	.49
	(393)	(290)	(631)	(280)
9th	.60	.60	.55**	.30
	(230)	(181)	(203)	(373)
10th	.69	.66	.53*	.44
	(214)	(116)	(283)	(213)
11th	.69	.64	.60*	.49
	(183)	(137)	(281)	(187)
D.C.	.67	.62	.48	.42
	(48)	(71)	(206)	(144)
All	.72**	.67	.61**	.45
	(2640)	(1858)	(3975)	(2482)

Note: See note to Table 5.3.

Ideological Influence on District Judges

We use regression analysis to relate the probability of a conservative district court decision to the type of disposition (nontrial, jury trial, bench trial, and judge removed case from jury and decided it himself), the party of the appointing President, and other factors that we think might influence the judge's decision. The dependent variable is a dummy variable that takes the value of 1 for a conservative decision and 0 for a liberal one. Table 5.5 lists the variables with their means.

Table 5.6 reports the marginal effects of the coefficients. The results

Table 5.5 Definitions and Means of Variables in District Judge Regression

Variable	Definition	Mean
District Court Decision	1 = conservative district court decision, 0 = liberal decision	.70
President	Party of the appointing President: 1 = Republican, 0 = Democratic	.59
Adjusted President	Party of the judge: 1 = Republican, 0 = Democrat or Independent	.57
Independent	Judge not affiliated with either party: 1 = Independent, 0 = Republican or Democrat	.05
Jury	1 = jury trial, 0 = all other dispositions	.15
Bench	1 = bench trial, 0 = all other dispositions	.14
Remove	1 = judge takes case away from jury, 0 = all other dispositions	.03
Nontrial	1 = case terminated before trial (dismissal or summary judgment), 0 = all other dispositions (jury, bench, or judge takes case away from jury)	.69
Nonwhite	1 = judge black, Hispanic, or Asian	.15
Sex	1 = female	.16
Fraction Republican	Fraction of active judges appointed by Republican Presidents	.60
Circuit Dummies	Dummy variable for each of the circuits	—
Subject-Matter Dummies	Dummy variables for each of the 14 subject-matter categories	—
Date Dummies	Dummy variables for each year of decision in the court of appeals (1995–2008)	—

are similar to those in Table 5.1. The predicted probability of a conservative nontrial outcome is more than 2.5 times greater than the predicted probability of a conservative jury outcome (.59, compared to the mean probability of .23 of a conservative vote in jury trials)—jury decisions being at the liberal extreme from decisions by judges in cases that do not go to trial. (In Table 5.1 the ratio was 3.17.) Even in cases that do go to trial, the probability of a conservative decision in bench trials and in cases in which the judge takes the case from the jury exceeds the probability of a conservative outcome in a jury trial (.28 and .37, compared to the .23 probability in jury decisions).

The probability of a conservative decision in a case decided without a trial is only .04 higher (see equation (2)) for R district judges than for Ds (4.6 percent higher, relative to the predicted mean of a conservative decision by a D). This is a small difference, and in cases that go to trial it's

Table 5.6 Logit Regressions of Probability of Conservative District Court Decisions, Sunstein Data, 1995–2008

	All (1)	Nontrial (2)	Jury, Bench, or Removed from Jury (3)	All (4)	Nontria (5)
			Probability of Conservative Vote		
President	.050*	.040**	.015	—	—
	(2.41)	(2.85)	(0.48)		
Adjusted President	—	—	—	.049*	.041*
				(2.33)	(2.93)
Independent	—	—	—	.097	.072
				(1.78)	(1.64)
Other	.587**	—	—	.587**	—
	(22.58)			(22.47)	
Jury	—	—	−.419**	—	—
			(7.67)		
Bench	.278**	—	−.203**	.279**	—
	(8.45)		(3.74)	(8.41)	
Remove	.373**	—	—	.371**	—
	(8.06)			(8.00)	
Nonwhite	−.043	−.0001	−.091*	−.047	−.002
	(1.46)	(0.00)	(2007)	(1.53)	(0.12)
Sex	−.053	−.022	−.053	−.060*	−.026
	(1.83	(1.03)	(1.25)	(2.21)	(1.31)
Fraction Republican	.127	.055	.141	.122*	.054
	(1.95)	(1.28)	(1.31)	(1.90)	(1.27)
Subject-Matter Dummies	Yes**	Yes**	Yes**	Yes**	Yes**
Year Dummies	Yes*	Yes	Yes	Yes	Yes
Number of Observations	4498	3083	1414	4498	3083

Notes:
1. Regression coefficients are marginal effects at mean values of all variables.
2. Standard errors are clustered by judge.

even smaller, and not statistically significant (compare equations (2) and (3)). This is not surprising. A judge will not allow a case to go to trial unless he thinks the plaintiff has a reasonably strong case. Conservative judges may allow fewer cases to go to trial because such judges are less friendly to plaintiffs in most civil cases, but those civil cases that they do allow to go to trial will be ones in which the plaintiff has a strong case. Liberal judges may have some inclination to decide cases for plaintiffs before trial, but as noted earlier that is difficult to do; the liberal judge may instead put pressure on defendants to settle.

Presidents occasionally appoint a district judge who is either of the other party or an independent. But fine-tuning our analysis to take account of these departures from the norm does not change our results (compare equations (4) and (5), second row, with equations (1) and (2), first row). Independents vote more conservatively than judges as a whole. Yet Democratic Presidents are slightly more inclined to appoint independents (7 percent of appointees of Democratic Presidents since 1980 were independent, compared to 5 percent of appointees of Republican Presidents), which is consistent with evidence presented in previous chapters that Democratic Presidents are somewhat less concerned with judicial ideology than Republican Presidents are. But the differences between Rs and independents and Ds and independents are not statistically significant.

In circuits that are conservative, as measured by the fraction of active appellate judges appointed by Republican Presidents *(Fraction Republican)*, district judges are more likely to render conservative decisions. But the difference is never statistically significant. The regression implies that even a large shift—from 4 to 8 Republican appointees in a court of appeals of 12 judges—would increase the fraction of conservative outcomes in the district court by only .04 (5.7 percent relative to the mean fraction of conservative decisions of .70). This suggests weak reversal aversion, but we revisit reversal aversion in the next section.

The subject-matter but not the year dummies (except in equation (1)) are jointly significant: employment and other discrimination cases tend to be decided more conservatively, and federalism and takings cases more liberally, than the cases in other categories. Female and nonwhite district judges are less likely to render conservative decisions than male or white ones, but this finding is statistically significant in only one of the five equations.

Reversals

Table 5.7 reports reversal rates by subject matter (and Table 5.8 by circuit) and by party of the appointing President. The overall rate of reversal of D district judges is 32 percent and of Rs 31 percent; these abnormally high rates reflect the skew of the Sunstein database in favor of controver-

Table 5.7   Reversal Rate for *R* and *D* District Judges by Subject-Matter Area,
Sunstein Data, 1995–2008

	Reversal Rate	
	R	*D*
Abortion	.37	.38
	(67)	(50)
Americans with Disabilities Act	.33	.34
	(562)	(399)
Affirmative Action	.39*	.67
	(41)	(24)
Age Discrimination	.28	.29
	(338)	(271)
Campaign Finance	.33	.41
	(39)	(27)
Capital Punishment	.32	.29
	(197)	(112)
Contract Clause	.30	.12
	(27)	(17)
EPA	.29	.33
	(7)	(6)
Federalism	.12	.08
	(222)	(157)
PCV	.41	.41
	(91)	(54)
Sex Discrimination	.32*	.41
	(335)	(252)
Sexual Harassment	.39	.40
	(344)	(217)
Takings Clause	.24	.21
	(71)	(34)
Title VII	.33	.32
	(299)	(238)
All Subject-Matter Areas	.31	.32
	(2640)	(1858)

sial subjects. In both tables reversal rates by subject matter and circuit are independent of whether the district judge is an *R* or a *D*, except in two instances: reversal rates of *D*s are higher than those of *R*s in both affirmative action cases (67 percent versus 39 percent in 65 cases) and sex discrimination cases (41 percent versus 32 percent in 587 cases).

Table 5.9 confirms the absence of significant differences in reversal rates between district judges appointed by Republican and Democratic Presidents (see the last two rows in the table). But it also reveals that

Table 5.8 Reversal Rates for District Court Judges Appointed by Republican and
Democratic Presidents, by Circuit

Circuit	Reversal Rate	
	R	D
1st	.22	.29
	(174)	(126)
2d	.34	.40
	(192)	(171)
3d	.44	.49
	(141)	(71)
4th	33	.29
	(149)	(86)
5th	34	.35
	(255)	(127)
6th	.32	.39
	(204)	(197)
7th	.23	.25
	(457)	(285)
8th	.24	.22
	(393)	(290)
9th	.43	.45
	(230)	(181)
10th	.31	.27
	(214)	(116)
11th	.40	.33
	(183)	(137)
D.C.	.44	.32
	(48)	(71)
All	.31	.32
	(2640)	(1858)

the ideological direction of the district court decision—as distinct from
the ideological leanings of the district judge—and the ideological composition of the appellate panel do have significant effects on the likelihood
of reversal. For example, a panel of three *R*s is less likely to reverse a
conservative than a liberal district court decision (23 percent compared
to 38 percent), while in a panel of three *D*s the percentages are 56 and
18. A mixed panel with a conservative majority is less likely to reverse
a conservative than a liberal decision (29 compared to 33 percent),
but if instead there is a liberal majority these percentages change to 41
and 20.

That the ideological direction of the district court decision but not the

Table 5.9   Reversal Rates by Ideological Direction of District Court Decision and Party of President Who Appointed District Judge, Sunstein Data, 1995–2008

	Composition of Appellate Panel				
	RRR	*RRD*	*DDR*	*DDD*	All Panels
Conservative District Court	.23**	.29	.41**	.56**	.33*
Decision	(741)	(1324)	(839)	(231)	(3135)
Liberal District Court	.38	.33	.20	.18	.29
Decision	(301)	(582)	(383)	(97)	(1363)
R District Judge	.26	.30	.36	.43	.31
	(611)	(1137)	(717)	(175)	(2640)
D District Judge	.29	.32	.32	.46	.32
	(431)	(769)	(505)	(153)	(1858)

ideological identity of the district judge influences the likelihood of a reversal makes sense. The ideologically motivated appellate judge cares about the ideological direction of the district court decision, but why should he care about the ideology of the district judge? It's not as if the district judge's ideology were a reliable signal of the ideological direction of his decision, for remember that the difference in the fraction of conservative decisions by *R* and *D* district judges is very small.

Table 5.10 presents the results of separate logit regressions of reversals of *R* and of *D* district judges. The panel composition variables turn out to be the most significant predictors of reversals. Not only are nearly all those variables statistically significant, but the difference between any two is significant; the only exception is that the fraction of reversals of a liberal district court decision in equations (2) and (4) by a *DDR* panel is not significantly greater than the fraction of reversals of such decisions by a *DDD* panel (the omitted variable). The coefficients in equation (1) imply that the probability of reversing a conservative district court decision is .49 if the panel consists of 3 *D*s, .38 if there are 1 *R* and 2 *D*s, .30 if there are 2 *R*s and 1 *D*, and .24 if there are 3 *R*s. Equation (2) indicates that the probability of reversing a liberal decision is .11 for a panel of 3 *D*s, .15 if there are 1 *R* and 2 *D*s, .27 for 2 *R*s and 1 *D*, and .35 for 3 *R*s. These probabilities are in the expected order. Equations (3) and (4), in which circuit dummies replace the two circuit-specific variables, exhibit the same pattern.

Equation (1) indicates that when the fraction of *R* court of appeals judges doubles, the probability of reversal of a conservative decision *ble 5.10*   Logit Regressions of Reversal of District Court Decisions, Sunstein Data, 1995–2008

	Probability of Reversal			
	Conservative District Court Decision (1)	Liberal District Court Decision (2)	Conservative District Court Decision (3)	Liberal District Court Decision (4)
?R	−.245**	.254**	−.250 **	.240**
	(5.58)	(4.21)	(5.84)	(3.97)
?D	−.182**	.185**	−.187**	.167**
	(4.37)	(3.20)	(4.49)	(2.87)
OR	−.103*	.051	−.106*	.035
	(2.43)	(0.88)	(2.58)	(0.59)
ry	−.041	−.054	−.054	−.051
	(0.82)	(1.53)	(1.05)	(1.53)
nch	.074*	−.034	.058	−.022
	(2.31)	(1.00)	(1.78)	(0.66)
move	.106*	−.029	.105*	−.015
	(2.52)	(0.45)	(2.55)	(0.23)
esident	.017	−.028	.012	−.019
	(0.74)	(1.09)	(0.49)	(0.75)
onwhite	−.002	.013	−.010	.015
	(0.09)	(0.35)	(0.36)	(0.47)
x	−.023	−.021	−.024	−.013
	(0.89)	(0.61)	(0.88)	(0.40)
action	−.358**	.019	—	—
publican	(4.92)	(0.18)		
umber of Judges	.007**	.089**	—	—
	(4.08)	(2.92)		
bject Dummies	Yes**	Yes**	Yes**	Yes**
ar Dummies	Yes	Yes	Yes	Yes
rcuit Dummies	—	—	Yes**	Yes**
umber of Observations	3133	1363	3133	1363

tes:
1. Regression coefficients are marginal effects at the mean values of all variables.
2. Standard errors are clustered by district court.

drops by .13 (39 percent, relative to the mean reversal rate of .32).[16] Yet
we find no significant effect of circuit ideology on reversals of liberal decisions; maybe as a court of appeals grows more conservative, the district
judges adapt by rendering liberal decisions in fewer borderline cases, to
minimize the likelihood of being reversed.

16. To calculate the change in the probability of reversal as we move from the most liberal
to the most conservative circuits, we multiply the coefficient on the fraction of *R*s in equation
(1) (−.358) by the difference between .73 and .365.

We also estimated regressions in which the average senatorial courtesy scores of ideology are substituted for the fraction of *R*s. The results regarding circuit ideology are similar and do not affect the coefficients on the other variables. This is not surprising; we saw in chapter 4 that substituting senatorial courtesy scores for the party of the appointing President did not improve our predictions of the voting behavior of court of appeals judges.

We expect higher reversal rates in circuits with more judges because of the greater likelihood of inconsistent circuit precedents; such inconsistency makes it harder for a district judge to decide a case in conformity with the law of the circuit. Equations (1) and (2) support this hypothesis. They imply that adding an additional judge to a circuit increases the probability of reversal by between 1 percent (equation (1)) and 1.5 percent (equation (2)). This is a small effect—but we added only one judge. If we compare the Seventh Circuit (11 active judges in 2008) and the Ninth Circuit (27 active judges in 2009), the coefficient on *Number of Judges* predicts that increasing the size of a circuit from 11 to 27 judges increases the reversal rate of conservative district court decisions by 15 percent and of liberal ones by 24 percent, relative to the mean reversal rate of 32 percent for all circuits. (In the 1995–2008 period, the average reversal rate was 23 percent in the Seventh Circuit cases in the Sunstein database and 44 percent in the Ninth Circuit cases.) Consistent with the size-of-circuit hypothesis, the reversal rate is significantly higher in the Ninth Circuit, when we include the circuit dummy variables in the regression (equations (3) and (4)), than in any other circuit; in no other circuit is the reversal rate significantly higher for both conservative and liberal district court decisions.

Reversals are significantly more likely if the judge takes the case from the jury and renders a conservative decision (compare equations (1) to (2) and (3) to (4)). Since juries tend to be liberal, the appellate court may think the district judge was acting out of hostility to trial by jury—but that doesn't explain why a conservative court of appeals would not applaud such hostility. Reversals are more likely for bench trials that end in conservative judgments (the coefficient on *Bench* is significant in equation (1) but only marginally so in equation (3)) than for bench trials that end in liberal judgments; we have no explanation.

The variables denoting characteristics of the district judge (*Nonwhite, Sex,* and *President*) have no significant effects on the likelihood of reversal in any of the regressions.

Dismissals

Our dismissal database consists of 3893 cases in which the defendant or defendants moved to dismiss the plaintiff's complaint. The motions were ruled on by 791 district judges scattered across all but one of the federal districts (Wyoming).

Normally such a motion is filed under Rule 12(b)(6) of the Federal Rules of Civil Procedure—dismissal for failure to state a claim upon which relief can be granted. We do not classify as dismissals cases in which the motion was granted in part, since in such cases what is dismissed is a claim or claims rather than the case itself.

We created the database from Westlaw data consisting of every decision, published or unpublished, that the authoring judge deemed a "written opinion,"[17] along with some decisions that the judge didn't so deem.[18] Westlaw excludes orders that it considers routine, doubtless including some dismissals. Some legal scholars have argued that relying on electronic databases rather than on courts' docket sheets can lead to biased results regarding summary judgments;[19] the same may be true for Rule 12(b)(6) motions, but we do not explore the issue. Complaints are sometimes dismissed under rules other than Rule 12(b)(6); our search method would not pick them up. Despite these qualifications, we have no reason to think our sample significantly skewed.

A motion to dismiss was granted in 1990 cases in our sample—51 percent. In the 971 decisions that we were unable to classify as liberal or conservative (169 nonideological and 802 mixed), the dismissal rate was

17. The Judicial Conference of the United States defines a written opinion as "any document issued by a judge . . . that sets forth a reasoned explanation for a court's decision." David A. Hoffman, Alan J. Izenman, and Jeffrey R. Lidicker, "Docketology, District Courts, and Doctrine," 85 *Washington University Law Review* 681 (2007).

18. Taha, note 15 above, at 4.

19. See, for example, Stephen B. Burbank, "Vanishing Trials and Summary Judgment in Federal Civil Cases," 1 *Journal of Empirical Legal Studies* 591 (2004).

only 9 percent, compared to 65 percent in the 2922 cases that we were able to classify ideologically. The reason for this disparity appears to be that most of the cases we were unable to classify ideologically were dismissed in part; and partial dismissals, as distinct from full grants and full denials, are mixed cases.

We test several hypotheses with this sample:

1. The grant of a motion to dismiss will confer utility on a district judge who has effort aversion, and since the utility conferred will be greater the heavier the judge's workload, workload should have a positive effect on dismissals. But the causation might run from dismissal motions to workload rather than the reverse: a reluctance to grant such motions might lead to an increase in workload by encouraging more suits to be filed. We have not tried to adjust for this possibility.

2. The reversal of a dismissal, if accompanied by a remand by the court of appeals for further proceedings (rather than ending the case), as it often is, will require the judge to do more work on the case. This will increase his overall workload, because a remand does not affect the number or difficulty of the judge's new case assignments (new case assignments are divided evenly among the district judges in a district). A further possible source of reversal aversion is that the judge's utility function is likely to include a desire for a good reputation with other judges, his staff, the lawyers who appear before him (maybe), and perhaps others. Since a dismissal is appealable but a refusal to dismiss rarely is (it is not final in the sense of ending the lawsuit, and in general only final orders are appealable in the federal judicial system), the prospect of a reversal and the potential damage it might do to the judge's reputation (a particularly important consideration if the judge is an aspirant for promotion to the court of appeals—see chapter 8) are an additional cost of dismissing.

For these reasons we predict that the greater the likelihood of reversal, the less likely a district judge is to dismiss a case.

3. A district judge's own ideology can be expected to influence some of his decisions, though probably only a small percentage because of the prospect of reversal if he deviates from the precedents established by and the known ideological propensities of the judges of the court of appeals for his circuit. In civil cases in which reversal risk is low we expect D district judges to favor plaintiffs and therefore to be less likely than Rs to

grant motions to dismiss.[20] So we analyze separately all 3893 cases in our sample and the 2922 of those cases in which we were able to pin an ideological label on the outcome.

4. The Supreme Court's decision in *Twombly* raised the pleading standards for plaintiffs, at least in complex cases. It might seem obvious that a Supreme Court decision that facilitated dismissals of civil cases would increase the dismissal rate; but it might not, because of a selection effect. (This selection effect is different from the one discussed later in this chapter.) Potential plaintiffs may adjust to a higher pleading standard by filing fewer cases that are unlikely to survive under the new standard, and defendants may adjust by filing Rule 12(b)(6) motions more frequently because they anticipate a higher probability that such motions will be granted. If plaintiffs and defendants adjust fully, the fraction of 12(b)(6) dismissals might well revert to its level under the old standard, although the new standard should still reduce the number of cases by reducing the incentive to file cases that fall below it.[21] But defendants are less likely to change their behavior than plaintiffs, as they will expect plaintiffs to adjust by refraining from filing complaints that fail to satisfy the new standard.

It might seem that defendants would file motions to dismiss as a matter of course, with little regard for the strength of the plaintiff's case, because such motions are cheap to prepare. But in fact motions to dismiss are filed in only about 5 to 15 percent of cases.[22] The percentage may rise as a result of *Iqbal;* it may not have risen yet because of adjustments described in the preceding paragraph or because lawyers are uncertain about how the new dispensation to dismiss is being or will be implemented. At first the scope of the higher pleading standard announced in *Twombly* was uncertain, and if limited to complex cases it would not have had a large impact, since most cases are not complex; that the new standard applied to all cases brought in federal district courts became clear only when the Supreme Court decided *Iqbal.*

Moreover, plaintiffs' lawyers may be able to overcome a new standard,

20. This correlation holds for the 86 percent of the cases that we were able to code as liberal or conservative.

21. These issues are analyzed more fully in Hubbard, note 12 above.

22. Joe S. Cecil et al., "Motions to Dismiss for Failure to State a Claim After *Iqbal*" (Federal Judicial Center, March 2011), www.fjc.gov/public/pdf.nsf/lookup/motioniqbal.pdf/$file/motioniqbal.pdf (visited Dec. 9, 2011).

if it is just a pleading standard, by conducting a fuller precomplaint investigation (unless the cost of the additional investigation required to satisfy the new standard would make the expected net benefit of suing negative), thus enabling them to resist a 12(b)(6) motion successfully. But by increasing prospective plaintiffs' litigation costs, this adjustment would cause a decline in the number of cases filed.

Selection effects to one side, the *Twombly* decision may merely have ratified a growing dissatisfaction in the lower federal courts with the extremely liberal pleading rule of *Conley v. Gibson*,[23] which enabled plaintiffs to extort settlements in weak cases by imposing heavy pretrial discovery costs on defendants. It appears that district judges, who may in any event for reasons of effort aversion favor dismissal, were already pushing the envelope by dismissing weak cases before the Supreme Court overruled *Conley* in *Twombly*. ("Pleading has always served as a preliminary gatekeeper to weed out potentially frivolous claims."[24]) For all these reasons there can be no confidence that *Twombly* caused an increase in the dismissal rate.

Table 5.11 reports the results of regressing the decision to dismiss on the following variables: *President; Ideologically Classifiable;* timing of decision (*Before Twombly, After Twombly Before Iqbal,* and *After Iqbal,* with *Before Twombly* the omitted category); *Workload* (the log of the weighted number of cases filed per judge in the district in the year the case was decided);[25] *Civil Rights* (civil rights or constitutional cases); *Reversal* (the fraction of cases reversed in the circuit in the year the case was decided);[26]

23. See note 9 above.

24. Colleen McNamara, "*Iqbal* as Judicial Rorschach Test: An Empirical Study of District Court Interpretations of *Ashcroft v. Iqbal*," 105 *Northwestern University Law Review* 401, 429 (2011).

25. These data are from "Federal Court Management Statistics," www.uscourts.gov/Statistics/FederalCourtManagementStatistics.aspx (visited Dec. 9, 2011), compiled annually by the Administrative Office of the U.S. Courts. Because we do not have weighted caseload data for the individual judges, we assign each judge in a district the average weighted caseload for the district in the year in which the motion to dismiss was ruled on.

26. These data are from Table B–5 of the annual reports of the Director of the Administrative Office of the U.S. Courts for the 12-month periods ending the last day of March in 2006 through 2008. See www.uscourts.gov/FederalCourts/UnderstandingtheFederalCourts/AdministrativeOffice/DirectorAnnualReport.aspx (visited Dec. 9, 2011). Again not having data for the individual judges, we assign each judge in a district the average reversal rate for the district in the year in which the motion to dismiss was ruled on.

Table 5.11   Logit Regressions of Decision by District Judges to Dismiss, May 2006–
June 2010

	All Cases		All Ideologically Classifiable Cases	
	(1)	(2)	(3)	(4)
President	.039*	.033	.046*	.040*
	(1.98)	(1.69)	(2.54)	(2.21)
Ideologically Classifiable	.790**	.790**	—	—
	(24.94)	(25.09)		
After *Twombly* Before *Iqbal*	.016	.079	.013	.016
	(0.73)	(0.78)	(0.67)	(.82)
After *Iqbal*	.238**	.236**	.210**	.210**
	(8.24)	(8.19)	(7.39)	(7.40)
Workload	.034	.032	.039	.028
	(0.66)	(0.75)	(0.80)	(0.70)
Civil Rights	.081**	.077**	.116**	.112**
	(3.92)	(3.80)	(5.80)	(5.66)
Fraction Republican	—	−.220**	—	−.212**
		(2.70)		(2.84)
Reversal	—	−.415	—	−.256
		(1.24)		(0.83)
Circuit Dummies	Yes*	No	Yes**	No
Eastern District of California	−.087	−.073	−.035	−0.19
	(1.18)	(1.04)	(0.46)	(0.26)
District of Columbia District	.177*	.201**	.202**	.212**
	(2.53)	(4.28)	(3.05)	(4.71)
Number of Observations	3893	3893	2922	2922

Notes:
1. The dependent variable is dismiss (= 1) or not (= 0).
2. Standard errors are clustered on district judges in all regressions.
3. The variable District Judge = 1 if the court of appeals judge had been a district judge.

Fraction Republican; Reversal; Circuit Dummies; and dummy variables for district judges in the Eastern District of California and in the District of Columbia, both district courts being outliers in the dataset. The Eastern District of California has the highest weighted judicial workload of any district court (1012 cases per judge on average, compared to 779 in the next busiest district and 470 in all districts other than the Eastern District of California) and yet a below-average dismissal rate (47 percent, compared to 51 percent for the other districts). The District of Columbia District has the third lowest average weighted caseload per judge (247) but a significantly higher dismissal rate (64 percent). We included circuit dummies (the omitted circuits are the Eleventh and the D.C. Circuits because we include a dummy variable for the D.C. District Court) in the two regressions that exclude the circuit-level *Fraction Republican* and *Reversal* dummies.

The regression coefficients on *President* are significant in three of the four equations, but the effect is small. The probability of dismissal by *R* district judges is only .03 to .05 higher than for *D*s, which is 6 percent of the 51 percent dismissal rate in the full sample and 7 percent of the 65 percent rate in the ideologically classifiable sample. The variable in which we have the greatest confidence in equations (1) and (2) on the basis of its t-ratio is *Ideologically Classifiable*. The probability of dismissal is .79 greater for cases that we were able to classify ideologically. *Workload,* although positive in all regressions (as we would predict), is never statistically significant.

None of the individual circuit dummies is significant either, although they are jointly significant. When we substitute *Fraction Republican* and *Reversal* for those dummies, *Reversal* has a negative effect but is never significant, probably because we measure an individual judge's reversal rate by the fraction of reversals of civil cases in the circuit; this assumes unrealistically that all the district judges in the circuit have the same reversal rate. In contrast, *Fraction Republican* has a significant but negative effect in the regressions. We expected the opposite—that district judges would be more rather than less likely to dismiss a case as the fraction of judges on the courts of appeals appointed by Republican Presidents increased. Since the vast majority of dismissals are classified as conservative (of the 2002 conservative outcomes, 89 percent were dismissals and 11 percent were refusals to dismiss, and of the 920 liberal outcomes 13 percents were dismissals and 87 percent refusals to dismiss), a greater fraction of *R*s in the circuit should reduce the likelihood of reversing a dismissal and so increase the fraction of dismissals.

When we estimate the regressions separately for *D* and *R* district judges, however, we find that only the former are less likely to dismiss a case as the fraction of *R*s on the court of appeals increases. *R* district judges are already prone to dismiss and so should not be affected by an increase in the court of appeals' conservatism. But why would *D* district judges react to an increase in the proportion of *R*s on the court of appeals by dismissing fewer cases? On the one hand, a case that is not dismissed may be won by the plaintiff as the litigation proceeds; and even though a decision for the plaintiff is more likely to be undone in the court of appeals the more conservative that court is, the tendency of courts of appeals to affirm regardless of ideology might outweigh the higher reversal rate of liberal decisions as the fraction of *R*s in the court of appeals increased. By reducing the rate at which he dismissed cases, a *D* district judge could somewhat offset the effect of the increased conservatism of the court of appeals. On the other hand, refusing to dismiss makes for more work by the district judge, and effort aversion should reduce ideological commitment; as the court of appeals grows more conservative, a liberal district judge may be less willing to incur the effort costs of taking a case to trial, only to see the liberal outcome (if that was the outcome) nullified on appeal.

We find no significant effect of *Twombly* on the dismissal rate but a large and highly significant effect of *Iqbal*. In the post-*Iqbal* period (June 2009 to June 2010 in Table 5.11), the predicted probability of dismissal increased by .24 in the full sample and .21 in the ideologically classifiable sample; these are increases of 49 and 35 percent relative to their levels pre-*Iqbal*. When we reestimated equation (1) for the 971 nonideological cases, the marginal coefficient on *Iqbal* was .053 (t-ratio = 2.45)—more than a 50 percent increase relative to the 9 percent dismissal rate of such cases pre-*Iqbal*. The decision's greater effect on cases that can't be classified ideologically than on those that can be is puzzling, but maybe before *Iqbal* ideology drove the decision whether to dismiss in many cases.

Civil rights cases are 17 to 19 percent more likely to be dismissed than civil cases as a whole (calculated by dividing the coefficient on *Civil Rights* by the fraction of dismissals in other cases), doubtless because such cases, many filed by prisoners, are disproportionately lacking in merit. Finally, the outlier status of the D.C. District and the Eastern District of California is supported, though only the coefficient on the D.C. District variable is significant.

Another Selection Effect

We expect ideology to play an increasingly important role in decision-making as cases move up the judicial hierarchy from the district court level to the Supreme Court. Even at the first level we expect to find many cases that cannot be resolved by the standard legalistic methods, because most of the cases that can be so resolved will be settled or abandoned. Nevertheless, because so many cases are filed by pro se or emotional litigants and by litigants represented by inept or inexperienced lawyers, only a minority of cases cannot be readily resolved legalistically at the district court level by dismissal, which is encouraged by effort aversion as well as by a commitment to legalist decision-making.

The appeal process provides a further filter. A losing party in a civil case, at least if he is rational and his lawyer competent, is unlikely to appeal unless he has a nontrivial chance of prevailing and the parties cannot agree on what that chance is (for if they could agree, they would be likely to settle at the appellate level, since settlement is cheaper than litigation, even appellate litigation). These conditions are unlikely to be satisfied unless there is uncertainty about how the court of appeals will decide, and uncertainty is likely to be greater when a case cannot be resolved by a legalist methodology. For then the luck of the draw (the randomly selected appellate panel's ideological composition) is likelier to determine the outcome.

Nevertheless many civil appeals have no arguable merit and are easily affirmed. Many lawyers are not very good and therefore fail to estimate the likely outcome of an appeal accurately; appeals are cheap compared to the cost of a trial, so settlement at the appeal stage may not yield substantial cost savings; there are sometimes strategic or financial reasons for filing a hopeless appeal; and some appeals are driven by a client's emotion or a lawyer's desire for a fee. All this is apart from pro se prisoner appeals, which very often are frivolous. Because the jurisdiction of the courts of appeals is mandatory rather than discretionary, they cannot refuse to hear and decide an appeal just because it should not have been filed. So they decide a great many one-sided cases, in which an appellate judge's ideology plays no role in the decision.

What we are describing is a selection effect as cases move up the judicial hierarchy. The term "selection effect" is usually used in empirical analyses of litigation to denote the tendency of potential litigants to adjust their behavior to changes in the likely outcome of particular types of lawsuit. We used the term in that sense in discussing the possible effects of the *Twombly* and *Iqbal* decisions. But a selection effect can also operate directly on judges—and we gave an example of that too when we noted that judges select cases for trial by filtering out the weak ones (deciding them without a trial). We hypothesize that a similar filtering effect operates throughout the federal judicial hierarchy.

We test this hypothesis indirectly in Table 5.12 by comparing the difference between the fraction of conservative votes by *R*s and *D*s in mixed panels in the courts of appeals and conservative decisions by *R* and *D* district judges. We hold panel composition effects constant by restricting our court of appeals sample to votes of *R* and *D* judges who sit on identical mixed panels. The other independent variables are the same as in equations (2) and (4) in Table 4.19 except that we've added dummy variables for the court of appeals judge's circuit, type of case, and year of decision. To test directly whether the ideological makeup of the circuit influences an individual court of appeals judge's vote, we substitute the fraction of *R*s in the circuit for the circuit dummy variables.

Table 5.12   Logit Regressions of a Conservative Vote by Court of Appeals Judges on Mixed Panels Only

	(1)	(2)
President	.144**	.143**
	(8.85)	(8.85)
Ideological Direction of District Court Decision	.322**	.319**
	(18.41)	(18.31)
Former District Judge	.020	.021
	(1.27)	(1.42)
Nonwhite	−.018	−.015
	(078)	(0.64)
Sex	−.004	−.009
	(0.19)	(0.45)
Tenure	−.002	−.002
	(1.83)	(1.55)
Senior Judge	.002	−.010
	(0.07)	(0.45)
Fraction Republican	—	.298**
		(5.66)
Subject Dummies	Yes**	Yes**
Circuit Dummies	Yes**	No
Decision Year Dummies	Yes**	Yes**
Number of Observations	6430	6430

Notes:
   1. Regression coefficients are marginal effects at mean values of all variables.
   2. Robust standard errors were used in all the regressions.

Both regressions indicate that Rs are indeed significantly more likely to vote conservatively if they are court of appeals judges than if they are district judges: the .14 higher probability (a 32 percent increase relative to the mean probability of .45 for Ds on mixed panels) is 3.5 times the difference we found between R and D district judges in cases decided without a trial (equation (2) in Table 5.6). We also find that both R and D appellate judges vote significantly more conservatively in circuits that have a higher fraction of Rs (holding panel effects and the other variables in equation (2) constant). For example, the coefficient on *Fraction Republican* implies an increase of .10 in the probability of a conservative vote (18 percent relative to the mean probability of a conservative vote, which is .55) if the number of Rs on a court of appeals of 12 judges increases from 4 to 8. The circuit, subject-matter, and year-of-decision dummy variables are all jointly significant, indicating unexplained differences across circuits and subject matter and over time in the probability of a conservative vote. None of the personal-characteristics variables is statistically significant, which is similar to the result in Table 4.15.

The Supreme Court decides cases that are more evenly balanced than those in the court of appeals (and *a fortiori* in the district courts). One-sided cases tend not to present significant issues, and the Court's decisional capacity is highly limited in relation to the many thousands of federal court of appeals and state supreme court decisions rendered each year.[27] The difference in selectivity between the courts of appeals and the Supreme Court is especially pronounced in criminal cases. Most of them are subsidized and lack merit, so that even liberal judges usually vote to affirm; that is why, as we have seen, the study of ideological influences in the federal courts of appeals is better focused on civil appeals than on all appeals. But the Supreme Court reviews only a tiny, atypical fraction of criminal cases, selected by the Court for their importance, implying at least arguable merit. As a result, the ratio of conservative to liberal votes in the Court's criminal cases is only 1.17 to 1, compared to 1.59 to 1 in the courts of appeals (computed from text preceding Table 4.7).

What we observe in the structure of the federal judiciary is a counter-

---

27. Some decisions by intermediate state appellate courts are also reviewable by the U.S. Supreme Court. But only state court decisions that raise a federal-law question can be reviewed by the Court.

part to "management by exception" in a business or government bureaucracy. The easy, recurrent matters (commonplace complaints by customers, for example) are resolved at the lowest rung of the employment ladder. More difficult questions are referred to the first supervisory level, and questions that are even more difficult are relayed for decision to the next level in the management hierarchy, and so on up. At each level there are fewer decisions made and therefore fewer—and, because of the increasing difficulty of the cases, abler, or at least more experienced—decision-makers.

Management by exception works differently in the federal courts. Federal judges are selected by politicians. Merit is not irrelevant but is rarely the only factor in the selection. More often than not the higher judges are not promoted from the ranks of the lower ones but instead are lateral entrants (we present statistics on promotion in chapter 8), and rarely are the higher judges more experienced than the lower ones. Maybe on average court of appeals judges are abler than district judges and Supreme Court Justices abler than court of appeals judges, but there are many exceptions and the average differences are not great. The way the system copes with the increasing difficulty of the cases as they rise through the judicial hierarchy is to increase the size of staff relative to the number of cases. Number of cases declines from the bottom to the top of the judicial hierarchy but staff increases, so staff per case increases dramatically. Quality of staff also increases, because the prestige and positive effect on future job opportunities of a judicial clerkship increase with the rank of the judge.

The novel cases that dominate the docket of the Supreme Court cannot be decided by application of existing rules; if they could be, they would not be novel. They require instead the creation of a new (or modification of an existing) rule, which is a legislative rather than a conventionally adjudicative act. When a judge or Justice has to make a legislative decision rather than decide the case just by following clear statutory or constitutional text or clearly applicable precedent, ideology may determine the outcome.

The effect of filtering on the incidence of ideological decision-making is further seen in a comparison of judicial votes in the civil liberties category, which we used for the Supreme Court in chapter 3, to votes in the constitutional category (civil rights, First Amendment, due process, and privacy), which we used in analyzing the courts of appeals in chapter 4. The fraction of conservative votes by Rs and Ds is .59 and .51, respectively, in the courts of appeals, compared to .57 and .43 in the Supreme Court. The ratio of conservative votes by Rs to conservative votes by Ds is thus 1.14 to 1 in the courts of appeals (.588/.514) and 1.33 to 1 in the Supreme Court (.570/.428), indicating that there is more ideological voting in the Supreme Court. Limiting the comparison to decisions by court of appeals judges appointed since 1981, when President Reagan largely ended the tradition of senatorial appointments of court of appeals judges, increases the ratio in the court of appeals, though only very slightly, from 1.14 to 1 to 1.16 to 1.

As shown in the preceding paragraph, the fraction of conservative votes, as distinct from the ratio of conservative to liberal votes by Rs and by Ds respectively, is higher in the courts of appeals than in the Supreme Court. The selection effect explains this. The liberal side of a civil case is generally the plaintiff's side. Yet most cases are losers—for example, most employment discrimination cases (a major category of civil rights cases) are dismissed and the dismissal affirmed. The affirmance of a civil rights case that has been dismissed, as of most civil cases in which the defendant won in the district court, is classified as a conservative vote. So, since most dismissals of civil rights cases would be affirmed by any judge who was not ultra-liberal, even liberal court of appeals judges vote conservatively in a large fraction of civil cases. The appeals that the Supreme Court accepts for review, including civil rights appeals, are on average more meritorious than appeals to the courts of appeals, as indicated by the fact that the Court reverses about two-thirds of the cases it decides. (The Court doesn't have time to waste on losers.) Being more meritorious on average than plaintiff civil rights appeals in the courts of appeals, plaintiff civil rights appeals decided by the Supreme Court attract a higher fraction of liberal votes. This is the same phenomenon as the lower ratio of conservative to liberal votes in criminal cases in the Supreme Court than in the courts of appeals.

Comparing the difference in the fraction of conservative (or liberal) votes of Rs and Ds at all three levels of the Article III federal judiciary is difficult because the composition of the caseload is different at each level. But we can make the comparison for a small sample of cases—the 73 cases in the expanded Sunstein dataset that were heard at all three levels. The

Table 5.13   Voting by *R*s and *D*s in the Same Cases, Sunstein Data, 1995–2008

	Fraction of Conservative Votes		
	R	D	R to D Ratio
Supreme Court Justices	.527	.217**	2.429
	(499)	(143)	
Court of Appeals Judges	.574	.299**	1.920
	(122)	(97)	
District Judges	.587	.519	1.131
	(46)	(27)	

Note: N = 73 cases for the courts of appeals and the district courts; N = 72 for the Supreme Court because the Court consolidated 2 of the 73 cases. Numbers in parentheses are votes.

sample includes votes of 16 Justices and cases decided in all 12 regional circuits and in 41 district courts. The results are shown in Table 5.13. In the last column the ratio of Republican to Democratic conservative votes is seen to increase as cases move up the judicial ladder, consistent with ideology playing an increasing role at each level because the constraints on judicial discretion lessen as one moves up.

The Paradox of Discretion

The selection effect just discussed, and this chapter as a whole, indicate that ideological decision-making is a consequence of the structure of the judiciary and not just of the personal preferences of judges. As cases rise in the judicial hierarchy, the possibility of deciding them on legalistic grounds declines, because increased selectivity inevitably results in selecting for further review cases not readily decidable on those grounds. The diminished role of ideology as one moves down the ladder reflects the competing effect on ideology of effort aversion and the commitment (albeit incomplete) of judges to legalistic methods of decision-making where usable.

But there's a complication: we noted at the outset that in part because the standard for appellate review of many district court rulings (for example, findings of fact, rulings on whether to admit or exclude evidence, and sentence length within the statutory limits) is deferential, district judges exercise a good deal of discretionary authority which they could use to influence and in many cases determine the outcome. Exercising discretion is the opposite of applying rules. Rules cabin ideological voting by limiting discretion; discretion gives free play to the subjective and idiosyncratic, including ideological, preferences of the officials who are vested with the discretion.

This leads to a paradox: because the appellate judges who are most scrupulous in applying the deferential standards of review encourage ideological decision-making by district judges, the more rule-abiding the appellate judges are, the less rule-abiding the district judges are free to be. As Corey Yung has shown systematically, court of appeals judges vary in the degree to which they defer to district judges' rulings—some review those decisions more searchingly than others do even when the standard of review is deferential, thus curtailing the district judges' exercise of discretion.[28] This variance across court of appeals judges may reflect the fuzziness of the deferential standards ("clear error," "substantial evidence," "abuse of discretion," and so forth), differences in appellate judges' confidence in their own ability relative to the ability of the district judges they review, differences in the amount of care or effort invested in reviewing district judges' rulings, differences in knowledge and self-confidence, a stronger desire of some judges for particular outcomes, or some combination of these factors. But whatever the cause or causes, the fact that court of appeals judges vary in the deference they give to rulings by district judges suggests the possibility of an empirical answer to the question whether the latter take advantage of the leeway given them by some court of appeals judges to decide cases on ideological grounds.[29]

We use regression analysis to test the hypothesis of a positive correlation between appellate adherence to deferential standards of review and ideological decision-making at the district court level. We modify Table 5.6, which reports the role of ideology in district courts, by adding data from Yung's paper that quantify what he calls "activism," defined as the difference between the rate at which a court of appeals judge votes to re-

28. Corey Rayburn Yung, "Flexing Judicial Muscle: An Empirical Study of Judicial Activism in the Federal Courts," 105 *Northwestern University Law Review* 1 (2011).

29. The Supreme Court tends not to apply deferential standards of review in the cases that it takes, because usually it is taking a case to decide a pure issue of law. It is because it reviews such a tiny fraction of court of appeals decisions that it perforce allows court of appeal judges to exercise a great deal of discretionary authority.

verse a district court decision when the standard of appellate review is deferential and the rate at which he votes to reverse when the standard is non-deferential (what is called "plenary" or "de novo" review). The reason for subtracting the latter rate is that giving no deference to the district judge when the appellate judge isn't supposed to give any deference to him is not activist; it is consistent with his deferring to district judges' ruling when he's supposed to. (Typically this subtraction produces a negative number, because a judge is more likely to reverse under a de novo standard than under a deferential one.)

Yung adjusts the raw difference for each judge by differences in the judge's mixture of criminal and civil cases, and after further adjustments ranks the judges in his dataset (the same dataset, with one correction made by him, that we used in chapter 4) from 100 (most activist) to 0 (most deferential).[30] To avoid confusion we substitute "non-deferential" for "activist."

We break the sample of 4498 district court decisions that we used in Table 5.6 into three groups on the basis of Yung's average non-deferential score per circuit of the judges in his sample.[31] The low-deference circuits are the First, Third, Eighth, and Ninth (all ≥ 57.0 on Yung's scale); the moderate-deference circuits are the Second, Sixth, Seventh, Tenth, and Eleventh (43.8–52.4); and the high-deference circuits are the Fourth and Fifth (22.4–34.9).[32] Next we reestimate the logit regression in equation (1) of Table 5.6 for each of the three groups. The

---

30. The most deferential judge in his list, Judge Wilkinson of the Fourth Circuit, has an "activist" score of 3.7 rather than 0. The reason is that although Yung computed deference scores for 177 court of appeals judges, he reported the results only for the 142 judges who had voted in at least 100 cases in his sample period (2008).

31. Yung, note 28 above, at 32 (Fig. 7). Yung's circuit rankings are more reliable than his individual judge rankings because they are based on a much larger number of observations. Indeed, the differences in rank of individual judges may not be statistically significant, because small changes in the number of reversals for a judge in another year (remember that his data are limited to 2008) could lead to large changes in the judge's rank. Still, Yung's gross differences in judge rankings are plausible—for example, no one familiar with the federal courts of appeals will question Judge Wilkinson's very high deference score.

32. Remember that Yung excluded judges of the D.C. and Federal Circuits from his judge sample.

dependent variable is the probability of a conservative vote and the independent variables are the same ones we used in that equation.

The larger and more significant the coefficient on *President* (party of the appointing President), the greater the predicted difference in the probability of a conservative decision between an *R* and a *D* district judge (holding constant the other independent variables), and therefore the greater the presumed influence of ideology on decisions. The first row of Table 5.14 reports the marginal effects of *President* in each of the three groups of circuits. (We do not report the coefficients on the other independent variables because they differ only slightly from their values in Table 5.6.) The regressions do not support the hypothesis that district judges decide cases on ideological grounds more frequently when the court of appeals for their circuit is more deferential to district judges' rulings (column (3))—in fact the district judges are significantly *more* ideological in the low-deference circuits.

But we must consider the possibility that this result is attributable to differences in overall reversal rates across circuits. Suppose that in circuit A the court of appeals reverses 20 percent of district court decisions both when the standard of appellate review is deferential and when it is non-deferential; in circuit B the court reverses 10 percent of both types of case. Although Yung's deference score would be the same in the two courts, the threat of reversal is twice as high in A as in B, and this can be expected to curb the district judges' incentive to indulge their own ideo-

Table 5.14 Regression of Probability of Conservative Decision by an *R* versus a *D* District Judge on Levels of Appellate Court Deference to District Court Rulings

| Measure of Non-deference | Extent to Which Appellate Court Is Not Deferential | | |
	High	Moderate	Low
Yung Score	.075*	.030	.054
	(2.05)	(1.04)	(0.98)
Yung Adjusted Reversal Rate	.042	.015	.082*
	(0.83)	(0.50)	(2.46)
Sunstein Reversal Rate	.091	.078*	.028
	(1.49)	(2.22)	(1.02)

Note: Sunstein reversal rates are the mean reversal rates per circuit of the cases in the Sunstein dataset.

logical preferences in deciding cases, assuming—realistically—reversal aversion.

We test this hypothesis by first dividing Yung's table of adjusted circuit reversal rates[33] into high-, moderate-, and low-reversal-rate circuits. High is between .23 and .27 (First, Sixth, and Ninth Circuits), moderate between .19 and .21 (Second, Fourth, Seventh, and Tenth Circuits), and low between .16 and .18 (Third, Fifth, Eighth, and Eleventh Circuits). We then reestimate equation (1) in Table 5.6 for each of the three groups. The results, shown in the second and third rows of Table 5.14, are mixed. In the second row we see that in low-reversal-rate circuits, R district judges are significantly more likely to render conservative decisions than Ds, implying, consistently with the hypothesis, that judges are more likely to indulge their ideological preferences in such circuits. But the coefficient on *President* is insignificant in the other circuits, implying that in those circuits R and D district judges are equally likely to decide cases conservatively.

The third row in the table substitutes circuit reversal rates calculated from the Sunstein database. Contrary to our hypothesis, the regression coefficients indicate that ideological differences among R and D district judges are smaller when the court of appeals for the district judges' circuit is more deferential.

We conclude that the selection effect discussed in the preceding section of this chapter holds even when intercircuit differences in deferential appellate review and in reversal rates are taken into account as possible influences on ideological decision-making by district judges. Courts of appeals apparently exert sufficient control over district judges, even when the appellate judges are adhering scrupulously to a deferential standard of review, to dissuade the district judges from allowing ideology to determine their decisions.

Ideology in Sentencing

Pursuing the theme of the preceding section, we conclude with empirical analyses of whether district judges use the discretion granted to them by

33. Yung, note 28 above, at 32 (Fig. 6).

the *Booker* decision[34] to inject ideology into the sentencing of criminal defendants.[35]

As shown in the top half of Table 5.15, even before *Booker* there were sentences outside the applicable guidelines range; these were called "departures," and the Sentencing Commission had established a list of authorized departures—for example, when the defendant's criminal record understated his history of involvement in crime (thus justifying an upward departure) or when it overstated that history (justifying a downward departure). But demoting the guidelines from mandatory to advisory status enabled judges to give a much higher percentage of sentences outside the applicable guidelines ranges, since the Sentencing Commission's list of permissible departures was no longer exhaustive.

An initial question is how soon *Booker*, decided in 2005, could have been expected to change the behavior of district judges. Like other people, judges are creatures of habit. Handed greater discretion in sentencing, they might be expected to take a while to exploit this new authority. But the data in Table 5.15 suggest otherwise. District judges changed their sentencing behavior almost immediately after *Booker*. The case was decided on January 11, 2005, and in the eight succeeding months of the 2005 fiscal year the percentage of below-guideline sentences rose from an average of 32.1 percent in the 2000–2005 pre-*Booker* period to 36.8 percent, while the percentage of above-guideline sentences more than doubled (though from a low level) from 0.7 to 1.6 percent.[36] Notice how steep the jump in fiscal 2005 was—in below-guideline sentences from 28.4 percent to 36.8 percent (a 33 percent increase over the pre-*Booker* 2005 percentage) and in above-guideline sentences from 0.7 percent to 1.6 percent (a 129 percent increase).

34. See note 8 above and accompanying text.

35. The source of our data is U.S. Sentencing Commission, "Federal Sentencing Data by State, District & Circuit," various years, www.ussc.gov/Data_and_Statistics/Federal_Sen tencing_Statistics/State_District_Circuit/index.cfm (visited Dec. 9, 2011).

36. Because the data in Table 5.15 are for fiscal years that run from October 1 to September 30, the Sentencing Commission split the data for fiscal 2005 between a pre-*Booker* period (October 1, 2004, to January 11, 2005) and a post-*Booker* period (January 12, 2005, to September 30, 2005).

Table 5.15 Percentage of Below-Guideline and Above-Guideline Sentences, Fiscal Years 2000–2010

Year	Percent Below	Percent Above
2000	34.9	0.7
2001	35.4	0.6
2002	34.2	0.8
2003	29.7	0.8
2004	27.0	0.8
2005 Pre-*Booker*	28.4	0.7
2005 Post-*Booker*	36.8	1.6
2006	36.7	1.6
2007	37.7	1.5
2008	39.0	1.6
2009	41.3	1.9
2010	43.2	1.8
2000–2005 Pre-*Booker*	32.1	0.7
2005–2010 Post-*Booker*	39.4	1.7

Note: Yearly averages weight the district percentages by the number of persons sentenced in the district.

The table also suggests that sentencing has not changed a great deal since the first post-*Booker* year, though there has been a small (though, as we'll see, a statistically significant) increase, mainly in the 2009–2010 period, in the percentage of both below-guideline and above-guideline sentences.

The disparity in both the pre- and post-*Booker* periods between the percentage of below- and above-guideline sentences is startling but is consistent with the widespread view that the sentencing guidelines were unduly severe, particularly with regard to drug crimes, which are a large fraction of all federal criminal convictions. Thirty percent of defendants sentenced under the guidelines in 2010 were sentenced for such crimes, down from 40 percent in 2000 and 2001. (Currently, immigration offenses account for the highest percentage of federal sentences—34 percent in 2010 compared to 20 percent in the 2000–2001 period.) The size of the disparity suggests that this sense must have been quite widespread among district judges, crossing conventional ideological lines, since throughout this period there were more R than D district judges: 53.6 percent of the active district judges who served at some point during the period 2000–2010 were *R*s, as were 56.4 percent in the post-*Booker* period, 2005–2010.[37]

Table 5.16 presents the results of regressing below- and above-guideline sentences on the presumed ideological priors of district judges and on other variables. Each regression contains 1092 observations—11 years of sentencing data in the 2000–2010 period for each of 91 district courts, plus the pre- and post-*Booker* months of 2005, which we treat as two separate periods. The dependent variable is the fraction of sentences per district that were below the guidelines range (equations (1) and (2)) and the fraction above (equations (3) and (4)). We weight each observation by the number of defendants sentenced in each district to adjust for the large differences across districts (from 65 defendants sentenced in the Eastern District of Oklahoma in 2000 to 8479 in the Southern District of Texas in 2010). We would have preferred to use as our dependent variable the sentencing behavior of the individual judges rather than of the district, but the Sentencing Commission, perhaps for security reasons (such as reducing the likelihood of threats against heavy sentencers), would not release sentencing data for individual judges. In March 2012, however, after our analysis was completed, the Transactional Records Access Clearinghouse of Syracuse University (TRAC)[38] was able to obtain, and make available to us, data on individual sentences by federal district judges; we present a limited study of those data at the end of this chapter.

In this part, where we use district rather than judge sentencing data, the main hypothesis we test is that *R* district judges are tougher than *D*s on criminal defendants. We use the percentage of *R*s in a district *(Fraction Republican District)* as a proxy for the conservatism of a district's judges and thus predict that the higher that percentage, the lower the percentage of below-guideline sentences and the higher the percentage of above-guideline sentences. (The average number of judges in a district was 7.24.)

37. On average there were 658 district judges in each year during the 2000–2010 period, of whom 305 were *D*s and 353 *R*s. Federal Judicial Center, "Biographical Dictionary of Federal Judges," www.fjc.gov/history/home.nsf/page/export.html) (visited Dec. 9, 2011).

38. See http://trac.syr.edu/ (visited Apr. 8, 2012).

Fraction Republican Circuit in Table 5.16 denotes the fraction of active court of appeals judges appointed by Republican Presidents. We have used this variable frequently in our regressions under the name *Fraction Republican,* but that name would be misleading here because we are also interested in the fraction of *R*s per district. We predict a negative coefficient in the below-guideline regressions because *D* as well as *R* district judges should react to a more conservative appellate court by reducing the fraction of below-guideline sentences, and a positive coefficient in the above-guideline regressions.

Table 5.16 Regression Analysis of Fraction of Criminal Sentences Below and Above Federal Sentencing Guidelines, 2000–2010

	Fraction of Sentences Below Guidelines		Fraction of Sentences Above Guidelines	
	(1)	(2)	(3)	(4)
Fraction Republican District	−.040	−.045	.0001	−.0000
	(1.02)	(1.12)	(0.02)	(0.01)
Fraction Republican Circuit	−.503**	−.506**	.009	.009
	(4.27)	(4.26)	(1.42)	(1.41)
Caseload	.0000	.0000	−.0000	−.0000
	(0.44)	(0.21)	(1.50)	(1.76)
Fraud	.010	.010	.003	.003
	(0.14)	(0.14)	(0.40)	(0.42)
D.C. District	.108**	.106**	−.002	−.002
	(6.03)	(5.67)	(1.28)	(1.42)
Booker	.115**	.085**	.009**	.008**
	(8.14)	(7.77)	(9.35)	(9.04)
Year 2006	—	−.004	—	−.0001
		(0.48)		(0.08)
Year 2007	—	0.12	—	−.001
		(0.98)		(1.02)
Year 2008	—	.037**	—	−001
		(2.77)		(0.45)
Year 2009	—	.063**	—	.003*
		(4.15)		(2.14)
Year 2010	—	.060**	—	.003*
		(2.84)		(2.09)
Constant	.588**	.598**	.004	.005
	(648)	(6.52)	(0.85)	(0.96)
R^2	.36	.38	.19	.20
Number of Observations	1092	1092	1092	1092

Note: Standard errors are clustered by district court.

Caseload equals the number of civil plus criminal cases filed per district divided by the number of active judges in the district. We predict that the heavier the caseload, the less likely the judge is to impose an above- or below-guideline sentence, because when a judge does so he has to spend more time justifying the sentence.

D.C. District is a dummy variable that takes the value 1 for the District of Columbia District and 0 otherwise. We include it to account for the unusually low criminal caseload per judge in that district (28.3 cases compared to the average of 102 for the other districts). Another dummy variable, *Booker*, takes the value 1 for post-*Booker* periods and 0 for pre-*Booker* ones. We add dummy variables in equations (2) and (4) for five post-*Booker* years (the omitted variable is the years prior to *Booker* plus the year 2005) to test the hypothesis that district judges took several years to adjust their sentencing fully to the greater latitude allowed them by the Supreme Court's decision.

Fraud is the fraction of defendants sentenced for fraud. We include this variable in an attempt to test the hypothesis that conservative judges are more sympathetic than liberal ones to that class of defendants because it includes businessmen. The weighted average of defendants sentenced for fraud, across districts, is 9.4 percent.

Although the coefficient on *Fraction Republican District* is negative in equations (1) and (2), indicating that Rs are less likely than Ds to sentence defendants below the applicable guideline range, it is not statistically significant; and likewise in the above-guideline regressions (equations (3) and (4)). But *Fraction Republican Circuit* is highly significant in equations (1) and (2), and the effect is large; the coefficients on that variable imply that doubling the percentage of Rs on a court of appeals from 40 percent (the Ninth Circuit) to 80 percent (the Eighth Circuit) would lead to a .20 decrease (56 percent relative to the weighted mean of .36) in the fraction of below-guideline sentences. But in equations (3) and (4), where the dependent variable is the fraction of above-guideline sentences, the coefficients on *Fraction Republican Circuit* are positive but not significant—further evidence that even conservative judges believe that guideline sentences are very severe.

Fraud is insignificant in all the regressions, probably because very few fraud prosecutions are of "respectable" businessmen, though such cases receive attention from the media.

The negative coefficients on *Caseload* in equations (3) and (4) are as expected—the heavier the caseload, the less likely judges are to impose an above-guideline sentence—but are not statistically significant. (We also estimated *Caseload* using the number of cases terminated instead of commenced. This substitution had no effect on the regression results.) We expected the coefficients to be negative in the below-guideline equations ((1) and (2)); in fact they are positive, but again not significant. What makes these results surprising is effort aversion, since the judge bears an extra burden of justification when he imposes a sentence outside the applicable guideline range. The results are especially surprising with regard to above-guideline sentences. A defendant is much more likely to appeal an above-guideline sentence than the government is to appeal a below-guideline one—and if the defendant's appeal is successful, the case will be returned to the district judge for resentencing, thus increasing his caseload. The judge can avoid this extra work by never imposing an above-guideline sentence.

The coefficient on the *Booker* dummy is highly significant in all equations, and in the predicted direction. For example, equation (1) indicates that the fraction of below-guideline sentences increased by .12 in the years after *Booker* (38 percent relative to the mean pre-*Booker* value), and equation (3) that the fraction of above-guideline sentences increased by .009 (128 percent relative to the pre-*Booker* mean).

Equations (2) and (4) add a dummy variable for each post-*Booker* year. This enables us to test the hypothesis that judges took several years to adjust fully to the decision. Since the effect of *Booker* for a given year equals the sum of the regression coefficients on the *Booker* dummy and on the year dummy, the greater the initial response to *Booker* the larger will be the coefficient on the *Booker* dummy compared to the coefficients on the individual post-*Booker* year variables. The regressions indicate that district judges responded immediately to *Booker* but that their adjustment was not complete until 2008 or 2009. For example, in equation (2) we find a .085 increase in below-guideline sentences in fiscal 2005, 2006, and 2007, but we also find a significant additional increase of .037 in 2008, .063 in 2009, and .060 in 2010. In percentage terms, the initial increase accounted for 60 percent of the total increase in below-guideline sentences. Above-guideline sentences had a similar effect (equation (4)).

The year dummies are significant only for 2009 and 2010. This implies an initial increase in above-guideline sentences of .008 in the year following *Booker*, which continued through 2008, followed by an additional increase of .003 in 2009 and 2010. The initial increase accounted for 67 percent of the total increase in above-guideline sentences.

We've been using percentages of sentences below and above the applicable guidelines ranges as our measure of sentencing severity, rather than sentence lengths, because sentence lengths are highly sensitive to differences in the composition of offenses across districts. We experimented by picking one offense category—firearms—for a comparison of actual sentence lengths, thinking that firearms offenses would be numerous in all districts and relatively homogeneous, so that differences in sentencing severity could be attributed to differences in judges' sentencing proclivities rather than in the gravity of offenses. Firearms offenses are indeed numerous; they are the third largest federal offense category, after immigration and drugs, accounting for 7986 offenders in 2010. But they are not homogeneous. The mean sentence for a firearms offense was 90 months in 2010, but the standard deviation was 38 months and mean sentences per district ranged from 36 months in the District of Idaho to 303 months in the Eastern District of California. These differences are too great to be the result of different sentencing proclivities of different district judges.

We turn now to the TRAC data—and here we use sentence lengths rather than percentages of below- and above-guideline sentences. TRAC provided us with a dataset consisting of sentences imposed in 581,193 federal cases between 2003 and 2011. The cases are sorted into 108 Department of Justice program categories. We limited our analysis to the post-*Booker* cases (2006–2011) in the four largest categories: Drugs–Organized Crime Task Force (that is, organized-crime drug offenses), Drugs–Drug Trafficking (other drug offenses), Weapons–Operation Triggerlock Major (weapons offenses), and Immigration offenses. Because of random assignment to the judges in each district, there should be no systematic differences between the cases assigned to *R*s and *D*s in the same category of cases in the same district.

Table 5.17 reports the mean prison and probation sentences by *R*s and

Table 5.17   Prison and Probation Sentences Imposed by District Judges Appointed by
Republican and Democratic Presidents, Fiscal Years 2006–2011

Type of Offense	Mean Prison Sentence in Months			
	All	R	D	R/D
Organized-Crime Drugs	100.76	104.19	95.69	1.09**
	(32,457)	(19,361)	(13,096)	
Other Drug Offenses	73.40	73.39	73.42	1.00
	(86,028)	(55,277)	(30,751)	
Weapons Offenses	81.97	84.12	78.37	1.07**
	(39,925)	(25,028)	(14,897)	
Immigration Offenses	18.96	18.61	19.68	0.95**
	(123,079)	(82,863)	(40,216)	
	Mean Probation Sentence in Months			
Organized-Crime Drugs	39.73	38.99	40.83	0.96
	(2084)	(1243)	(841)	
Other Drug Offenses	43.35	43.78	42.53	1.03
	(4482)	(2932)	(1550)	
Weapons Offenses	40.91	41.15	40.47	1.02
	(3002)	(1885)	(1117)	
Immigration Offenses	41.06	43.06	36.06	1.19**
	(4847)	(3461)	(1386)	

Note: The number of cases is in parentheses.

*D*s in our four categories. In two of them—organized-crime drug offenses
and weapons offenses—the *R*s imposed significantly longer prison sentences on average; in one category, immigration, the *D*s imposed significantly longer sentences; and in the remaining category, other drug offenses, the average sentences were the same. These results are surprising.
We would have expected little difference between *R*s and *D*s in organized-crime offenses, because no federal judges, to our knowledge, are
soft on organized criminals. And we would have expected *D*s to be harder
than *R*s on weapons offenders, because *R*s are more sympathetic to private ownership of guns.

Where there are statistically significant differences between *R* and *D*
sentencers, they aren't large. Even in the organized-crime drug category,
where the *R/D* ratio is highest, sentences imposed by *R*s are on average
only 8.5 months (8.9 percent) longer than those imposed by *D*s.

To assess the robustness of the results in Table 5.17, we ran three
checks. We separately examined cases that went to trial and cases that did

Table 5.18 Prison Sentences Imposed by District Judges Appointed by Republican and Democratic Presidents in Cases That Went to Trial, Fiscal Years 2006–2011

Type of Offense	Mean Prison Sentences (Months)			
	All	R	D	R/D
Organized-Crime Drugs	313.82	330.53	290.93	1.13*
	(1678)	(970)	(708)	
Other Drug Offenses	242.53	250.00	229.91	1.09
	(3001)	(1885)	(1116)	
Weapons Offenses	209.62	219.03	193.99	1.13*
	(2727)	(1702)	(1025)	
Immigration Offenses	53.85	53.20	54.93	0.97
	(996)	(604)	(362)	

Note: The number of cases is in parentheses.

not. (Table 5.17 includes both types of case.) Trials are only 2.97 percent of the cases in our four offense categories in which a prison sentence was imposed, but it is a nontrivial number—8372.[39] On average, judges impose much longer prison sentences when there is a trial (see Table 5.18): in organized-crime drug cases, 314 months versus 89 months; in other drug cases, 243 months versus 67; in weapons cases, 210 months versus 73; and in immigration cases, 54 months versus 19. Notice that in all four categories prison sentences are more than twice as long in cases that are tried than in cases in which the defendant pleads guilty.

The findings for the *R*s and *D*s are broadly similar to those in Table 5.17 but also and interestingly different. In organized-crime drug cases and weapons cases that go to trial, the *R/D* ratios are higher—1.13 (for both) versus 1.09 (organized-crime drug cases) and 1.07 (weapons cases) if the defendant pleads guilty rather than going to trial. In other drug cases there is, as before, no difference, but in immigration cases, in contrast to the data in Table 5.17, *R*s and *D*s are now statistically indistinguishable. These findings are noteworthy because judges have, as a practical matter, greater sentencing latitude when a case goes to trial than when it is plea-bargained, where the tendency is to defer to the negotiated

39. The fraction of trials in cases resulting in a sentence of probation is, as one would expect, even smaller—1.1 percent of the 12,649 cases in the four offense categories in which the sentence was probation.

Table 5.19 Prison and Probation Sentences Imposed by Northern and Southern District Judges Appointed by Republican and Democratic Presidents, Fiscal Years 2006–2011

	Judges in Northern Districts			Judges in Southern Districts		
	R	D	R/D	R	D	R/D
Mean Prison Sentence in Months						
Organized-Crime	92.58	87.35	1.06**	118.77	110.49	1.07**
Drugs	(10,871)	(874)		(8580)	(4722)	
Other Drug Offenses	68.40	69.45	0.98	78.96	79.90	0.99
	(29,163)	(19,055)		(26,114)	(11,696)	
Weapons Offenses	73.37	69.43	1.05**	94.38	90.89	1.04
	(13,143)	(9359)		(11,885)	(5538)	
Immigration Offenses	18.23	21.57	0.84**	19.02	17.52	1.09**
	(42,690)	(21,425)		(39,903)	(18,791)	
Mean Probation Sentence in Months						
Organized-Crime	34.79	41.92	0.83**	45.88	38.01	1.21*
Drugs	(772)	(606)		(471)	(235)	
Other Drug Offenses	42.30	42.58	0.99	45.82	42.44	1.08**
	(1698)	(975)		(1234)	(575)	
Weapons Offenses	40.32	38.57	1.05	41.84	43.97	0.97
	(1108)	(765)		(777)	(352)	
Immigration Offenses	40.76	37.43	1.09**	42.83	35.31	1.21**
	(1393)	(707)		(2434)	(903)	

recommendation of the parties. Hence the trial ratios are better evidence of the relative severity of *R*s and *D*s as sentencers than the entire set of cases, which is dominated by nontrial cases.

We also subdivided the data by whether the judge's district was in the North or in the South.[40] We did this because federal judges in the South have historically been heavier sentencers than federal judges in the North. The results are shown in Table 5.19. As expected, prison sentences are longer in the southern districts for both *R*s and *D*s. And as before the *R/D* ratios exceed 1 in both regions, with the exception that in northern districts *D*s are heavier sentencers in immigration cases than *R*s. But this is due entirely to a single district—the District of New Mexico, in which,

40. We define the South as districts in the former Confederate states: Alabama, Arkansas, Florida, Georgia, Louisiana, Mississippi, North Carolina, South Carolina, Tennessee, Texas, and Virginia.

Table 5.20 Regressions of Prison and Probation Sentences, Fiscal Years 2006–2011
            (t-statistics in parentheses)

	Organized-Crime Drugs	Other Drug Offenses	Weapons Offenses	Immigratio⬛ Offense
Prison Sentences				
Party of Appointing President	5.20**	4.63**	3.68**	1.00*⬛
(1 = R; 0 = D)	(3.45)	(6.81)	(3.34)	(7.08)
Trial	220.80**	162.55**	130.01**	34.20*⬛
(1 = Trial; 0 = No Trial)	(72.09)	(97.13)	(66.19)	(47.64)
Fraction R in Court of Appeals	58.70**	44.39**	20.18*	10.24*
	(4.00)	(6.19)	(2.00)	(6.16)
District Dummies	Yes	Yes	Yes	Yes
Constant	66.43**	63.94**	45.07**	1.54
	(6.10)	(9.76)	(5.34)	(0.99)
Probation Sentences				
Party of Appointing President	−1.33	1.16	0.45	5.96
(1 = R; 0 = D)	(0.52)	(1.37)	(.33)	(1.91)
Trial	—	—	—	—
(1 = Trial; 0 = No Trial)				
Fraction R in Court of Appeals	29.95**	−5.96	−28.79*	−7.83
	(3.06)	(.70)	(2.25)	(.43)
District Dummies	No	Yes	Yes	No
Constant	23.11**	35.17**	49.14**	41.09*⬛
	(3.82)	(3.11)	(4.33)	(3.71)

Note: All regressions include dummies for each district except organized-crime drugs and immigration
probation sentences. Owing to collinearity we could not include all 90 dummies. We estimated these models b⬛
clustering on districts.

for reasons that we have not tried to plumb, the *D*s give much longer sentences than the *R*s.

As a final check, we estimated regressions in which the dependent variable is either the length of the prison sentence or the length of probation,
and the independent variables are whether there was a trial (= 1) or not
(= 0), the party of the appointing President, and 90 dummy variables (1
for each district, with Wyoming being the excluded district). We include
the district dummies in order to hold constant differences across district
courts in the gravity of the crime, the policies of prosecutors, and other
factors that might, apart from ideology, influence the severity of sentences.
A final independent variable, which we also included in our analysis of
the effect of the *Booker* decision on sentencing, is the fraction of active
court of appeals judges appointed by Republican Presidents. Table 5.20
presents the regression results.

The results are consistent with our previous findings. In three of the four categories, the fraction of *R*s in the court of appeals significantly lengthens prison sentences. In organized-crime drug cases, we predict that a district judge in the Eighth Circuit, where more than 80 percent of the judges were *R*s in the relevant period, would sentence a defendant to 25 more months (a 26 percent increase) than a district judge in the Ninth Circuit, where only 40 percent of the judges were *R*s. The difference in other drug cases is 19 months (a 22 percent increase), in weapons offenses 8 months (15 percent), and in immigration cases 4 months (65 percent).

Differences between *R*s and *D*s persist when district effects and the other independent variables are held constant, although the differences are small. On average *R*s can be expected to sentence defendants to 6.5 more months in prison than *D*s in organized-crime drug cases (a 6.6 percent increase), 4.4 months in other drug cases (4.8 percent), 3.5 months in weapons cases (6.4 percent), and 1.1 months in immigration cases (17.7 percent).

To summarize our analysis of sentencing, there is evidence of ideological influence, with judges appointed by Republican Presidents generally imposing heavier sentences when other influences on sentencing are corrected for. The ideological influence is modest, however, consistent with the overall result of the analysis in this chapter that ideology plays only a small role at the district court level, even though district judges have considerable discretionary authority. This conclusion provides further support for the selection effect discussed earlier in the chapter, and more generally for the proposition that legalistic as distinguished from ideological decision-making characterizes much of the behavior of federal judges. We have also found evidence of reversal aversion, and more broadly of effort aversion, among district judges as among appellate judges.

CHAPTER 6

Dissents and Dissent Aversion

THIS CHAPTER USES our model of judicial behavior to explore dissent in the Supreme Court and the courts of appeals, emphasizing what we have referred to in earlier chapters as "dissent aversion,"[1] which sometimes causes a judge not to dissent even when he disagrees with the decision. Our data for the Supreme Court are all the Court's opinions in the 1963, 1980, and 1990 terms, with the exception of 5 cases decided by an equally divided vote and 11 cases in which there was no majority opinion. We chose those years to give us opinions in three different Chief Justiceships, those of Warren, Burger, and Rehnquist.

Our court of appeals data consist primarily of a random sample of 1025 published opinions (about 30 per circuit) in the 1989–1991 period, drawn from the Songer database. We selected that period so that we could obtain a nearly complete history of citations to each majority and dissenting opinion, since court of appeals opinions are rarely cited more than 20 years after they were decided.[2] (The citation data are from Lexis and

---

1. Richard A. Posner, *How Judges Think* 31–34 (2008), introduced the term and presented an informal model.

2. A recent study shows that judges are about 75 percent less likely to cite a 20-year-old Supreme Court or court of appeals precedent than a recent one. Ryan C. Black and James F. Spriggs II, "The Depreciation of U.S. Supreme Court Precedent" (Jan. 3, 2011), http://polisci.wustl.edu/files/polisci/black_spriggs_depreciation.pdf (visited Dec. 9, 2011).

Westlaw searches.) We excluded 58 opinions because of the coding errors in the Songer database discussed in chapter 4, and 7 en banc decisions, which, however, we discuss separately. Our Songer sample unfortunately includes only 80 dissenting opinions, fewer than 8 percent of the decisions in the database. But we also draw on the Sunstein database, and that gives us another 422 such opinions.

Costs and Benefits of Dissenting

Judges are assigned majority opinions to write and must do so in order to remain in good standing with their colleagues, but dissenting is optional. Since writing a dissenting opinion requires effort, a judge will not dissent unless he anticipates a benefit that offsets that cost. One benefit is to undermine the influence of the majority opinion, with which by assumption he disagrees, although possible offsets are that a dissent will draw attention to the majority opinion and may even magnify its significance by exaggerating its potential scope in order to emphasize the harm that it will do. And undermining a majority opinion with which one disagrees is not an end in itself; the aim is to promote one's own legal views.

The main benefits of dissenting thus derive from the influence of the dissenting opinion, and, a closely related point, the enhanced reputation of the judge who writes the dissent. In our empirical analysis we proxy this benefit by the number of citations to the dissenting opinion.[3] If dissenting opinions are rarely cited, this suggests that the benefits from dissenting are small. Another possible benefit of a dissenting opinion in a court of appeals, however, is that the Supreme Court is more likely to grant certiorari in a case in which there is a dissent.[4] Dissents can also

3. On the use of citation counts to measure the influence of judicial opinions and judges, see, for example, James H. Fowler et al., "Network Analysis and the Law: Measuring the Legal Importance of Precedents at the U.S. Supreme Court," 15 *Political Analysis* 324 (2007). See also Richard A. Posner, "An Economic Analysis of the Use of Citations Analysis in the Law," 2 *American Law and Economics Review* 381 (2000); William M. Landes, Lawrence Lessig, and Michael E. Solimine, "Judicial Influence: A Citation Analysis of Federal Court of Appeals Judges," 27 *Journal of Legal Studies* 271 (1998); Richard A. Posner, *Cardozo: A Study in Reputation* 80–91 (1990).

4. Gregory A. Caldeira, John R. Wright, and Christopher J. W. Zorn, "Sophisticated Voting and Gate-Keeping in the Supreme Court," 15 *Journal of Law, Economics, and Organiza-*

trigger congressional scrutiny and even congressional overruling of the rule or principle announced in the decision.[5]

Dissent aversion is bound to vary in intensity among judges. A judicial opinion has a self-expressive character, as well as its instrumental effect in resolving the case at hand and influencing the course of the law. A judge who derives great utility from expressing his views may, especially if he finds himself on a court in which those views are shared by few of the other judges, derive a benefit from frequent dissenting that exceeds the cost he incurs in effort and in impairment of collegiality. Dissents can burnish a judge's reputation. Holmes's judicial reputation rests to a considerable extent on his dissents, as does that of the second Justice Harlan—a lonely dissenter on the Warren Court; his dissent rate was 27 percent, versus the average Justice's dissent rate of 18 percent.

To explain dissents we must first explain why judges are unable to resolve disagreements when they confer to decide the case, whether by compromise or by surrender, and avoid a public spat. Personality is doubtless a factor. But personality to one side, the more heterogeneous a panel—which is to say, the greater the difference among judges along such dimensions as education, religion, race, gender, social class, and career before judging—the less likely the judges are to think alike, to understand and trust each other, to have similar priors, and in short to be predisposed to agree.[6] This implies that disagreements over technical points of law, where the judges are reasoning from shared premises and there is therefore apt to be a right and a wrong answer, are less likely to result in dissents than ideological disagreements are; the latter are more difficult to resolve by discussion or compromise, being rooted more in values, expe-

---

tion 549 (1999); Ryan C. Black and Ryan J. Owens, "Agenda Setting in the Supreme Court: The Collision of Policy and Jurisprudence," 71 *Journal of Politics* 1062 (2009); Adam Hallowell, "Colleagues and Contexts: Dissent Rates on the United States Courts of Appeals" (Harvard College, Dept. of Economics, March 19, 2009, on file with the authors).

5. William N. Eskridge, Jr., "Overriding Supreme Court Statutory Interpretation Decisions," 101 *Yale Law Journal* 331 (1991).

6. For evidence supporting these points but based on dissents in state rather than federal courts, see Joanna Shepherd Bailey, "Diversity, Tenure, and Dissent," *2010 Judicial Workshop Symposium, Duke Law Journal Legal Workshop* (March 2, 2010), http://legalworkshop. org/2010/03/02/diversity-tenure-and-dissent (visited Dec. 9, 2011).

rience, personal-identity characteristics, and temperament than in beliefs based on verifiable facts, and, for most judges, being more important. Some evidence for this conjecture is presented, for the Supreme Court and the courts of appeals respectively, in Tables 6.1 and 6.2.

In Table 6.1 we see how in civil liberties cases, and to a lesser extent in economic ones, as the number of dissenting votes increases, the ratio of conservative votes by conservative Justices to liberal votes by them changes. When a decision is unanimous (the first row), by definition of unanimity conservatives and liberals agree. (The ratio in the table is more than one only because over the period covered by the data there were more conservative than liberal Justices.) When unanimity is lost, the ratio rises in proportion to the number of dissenting votes. Thus, 5–4 decisions in civil liberties cases draw 11 times as many conservative as liberal votes by conservative Justices, while liberal Justices like Warren, Ginsburg, and Breyer vote conservatively 8 percent of the time in such cases and conservative Justices like Rehnquist and Scalia more than 90 percent. As the table also shows, the lopsided ratio persists regardless of whether the lower court decision is liberal or conservative. That is in contrast to the courts of appeals, whose judges as we know from chapter 4 are influenced by the district court's decision even if that decision has an ideological slant different from that of the appellate judges.

We infer that closely divided decisions in the Supreme Court tend to be ones in which the ideological stakes are high, for if the division were based on technical or legalistic considerations, we would not expect it to be correlated with the Justices' ideology. But while a high rate of dissent correlated with ideological differences (presumed from the party of the appointing President) is indicative of ideological decision-making, a low rate need not indicate the opposite (legalist decision-making). Apart from dissent aversion, an ideologically motivated court may exhibit a low dissent rate simply because all the judges share the same ideology.

Turning to the courts of appeals in Table 6.2, we need first to make a clarifying distinction between a per-panel dissent rate and a per-judge dissent rate, the latter being our main interest. The odds of a dissent on a panel of three judges are roughly three times the odds of a dissent by a particular judge if all the judges have the same propensity to dissent and the probability of a dissent by a particular judge is low. Thus, the per-

Table 6.1   Dissenting Votes of Liberal *(L)*, Moderate *(M)*, and Conservative *(C)* Justices, 1953–2008

	Civil Liberties Cases				Economic Cases			
	Percentage of Conservative Votes			Ratio	Percentage of Conservative Votes			Ratio
Dissenting Votes	L	M	C	C/L	L	M	C	C/L
0	.364	.373	.418	1.15	.307	.315	.331	1.08
1	.336	.464	.628	1.87	.406	.464	.504	1.24
2	.270	.661	.794	2.94	.287	.599	.603	2.10
3	.169	.670	.846	5.01	.268	.620	.640	2.39
4	.083	.653	.908	10.94	.202	.642	.749	3.71

Conservative Lower Court Decision

	Percentage of Conservative Votes			Ratio	Percentage of Conservative Votes			Ratio
Dissenting Votes	L	M	C	C/L	L	M	C	C/L
0	.211	.217	.253	1.20	.200	.216	.216	1.08
1	.259	.341	.529	2.04	.282	.296	.358	1.27
2	.235	.550	.731	3.11	.186	.533	.583	3.13
3	.177	.604	.803	4.54	.255	.597	.581	2.28
4	.097	.670	.896	9.24	.202	.618	.747	3.70

Liberal Lower Court Decision

	Percentage of Conservative Votes			Ratio	Percentage of Conservative Votes			Ratio
Dissenting Votes	L	M	C	C/L	L	M	C	C/L
0	.620	.597	.657	1.06	.427	.416	.444	1.04
1	.477	.647	.776	1.63	.554	.633	.634	1.14
2	.316	.756	.868	2.75	.412	.659	.628	1.52
3	.160	.723	.889	5.56	.284	.641	.702	2.47
4	.064	.635	.924	14.44	.205	.675	.746	3.64

Note: The conservatives are Minton, Burton, Clark, Reed, Harlan, Burger, Rehnquist, Scalia, Kennedy, Thomas, Roberts, and Alito; the moderates are Jackson, Whittaker, Frankfurter, Stewart, Powell, White, Blackmun, and O'Connor; and the liberals are Goldberg, Warren, Fortas, Black, Douglas, Brennan, Marshall, Ginsburg, Stevens, Breyer, and Souter. These classifications are explained in chapter 3.

panel probability of a dissent if each judge has a 2 percent probability of dissenting is $1 - (1 - .02)^3 = 5.9$ percent. If each has a 15 percent probability of dissenting, the per-panel probability of a dissent is $1 - (1 - .15)^3 = 38.6$ percent, which is less than three times 15 percent. Since the per-judge dissent rate is closer to 2 percent than to 15 percent, we'll as-

Table 6.2   Dissents and Panel Effects, Sunstein Data, 1995–2008

R and D Composition of Other Panel Members	Percentage of Dissents					
	Total Votes		Votes to Reverse District Court		Votes to Affirm District Court	
	R	D	R	D	R	D
RR	1.89	5.94	3.65	8.04	1.22	5.07
	(3287)	(1986)	(905)	(597)	(2376)	(1380)
RD	1.73	2.74	3.01	2.50	1.19	2.88
	(3980)	(2483)	(1197)	(841)	(2764)	(1634)
DD	6.45	2.63	11.75	2.91	3.79	2.43
	(1240)	(952)	(417)	(413)	(819)	(536)
All Panels	2.48	3.89	4.68	4.38	1.56	3.66
	(8507)	(5421)	(2519)	(1851)	(5959)	(3550)

Notes:

1. The sum of the votes in the reversed plus affirmed columns is smaller than the sum of all votes because we lack information on whether the appellate court affirmed or reversed the district court in cases in which there were 49 votes in the database.

2. The number of votes is in parentheses.

sume for the sake of simplicity that the probability of a dissent in a three-judge panel is three times the probability that any particular member of the panel will dissent.

By aggregating the Sunstein data on dissenting votes in Table 6.2 to the panel level, we derive a per-panel dissent rate of 9.1 percent.[7] This exceeds the dissent rate (7.8 percent) in our Songer sample. Since the Sunstein sample, unlike the Songer sample, is limited to cases expected to have above-average ideological stakes, the difference in dissent rates is evidence that dissents are indeed more likely in ideologically charged cases. Because both databases exclude unpublished opinions, they greatly exaggerate the overall average dissent rate per court of appeals judge, as we'll see.

The dissent rate of *R* judges in panels composed entirely of *R*s is only 1.9 percent, but it rises to 6.5 percent if the panel has two *D*s. It is also higher when the panel is reversing rather than affirming the district court decision. For example, in a panel of all *R*s the dissent rate is 1.2 percent if the panel is affirming but 2.7 percent if it's reversing. Dissenting is more

7. We do this by multiplying the average of the percentage of dissenting votes for *R*s and *D*s weighted by their respective number of votes (= $(2.48\% \times 8507 + 3.89\% \times 5421) / 13928$) = 3.03 percent) by 3 (the panel size).

inviting when the panel is reversing because the dissenter then has an ally in the district court—the judge voting the same way as he—upon whose reasoning he can draw, as well as invoking the deference that appellate courts are supposed to accord to most rulings by district judges, as we noted in chapter 5. This effect is not found in Table 6.1 for the Supreme Court, but the difference is consistent with greater dissent aversion in the courts of appeals as a result of these courts' heavier workload, and, as we'll see, the lesser influence of dissents in those courts.

Dissenting imposes an effort cost on the majority too, and sometimes a reputation cost as well if the dissenting opinion criticizes the majority forcefully. To minimize the dissenter's criticisms and retain the votes of the other judge in the majority, the author of the majority opinion often will revise his opinion to meet the points made by the dissent. The effort involved in these revisions, and resentment at criticism by the dissenting judge, may impose a collegiality cost on him by making him less well liked by his colleagues, which may make it harder for him to persuade other judges to join his majority opinions in future cases.[8] This assumes that judges refuse to treat such costs as bygones to be ignored in future inter-actions with the dissenter. But such refusal is rational, for by withholding or reducing collegiality in the future the judges in the majority punish the dissenter, and this may deter him from dissenting as frequently. We there-fore predict that dissents will be less frequent in smaller courts of appeals, because any two of its judges will sit together more frequently and thus have a greater incentive to invest in collegiality.[9]

The effort cost of writing a dissent will tend to be greater as the court's caseload grows heavier;[10] likewise the ill will generated by a dissent. We therefore expect that, other things being equal, the number of dissents

---

8. See, for example, Collins J. Seitz, "Collegiality and the Court of Appeals," 75 *Judicature* 26, 27 (1991).

9. Stefanie A. Lindquist, "Bureaucratization and Balkanization: The Origins and Effects of Decision-Making Norms in the Federal Appellate Courts," 41 *University of Richmond Law Review* 659, 695–696 and tab. 5 (2007).

10. Virginia A. Hettinger, Stefanie A. Lindquist, and Wendy L. Martinek, *Judging on a Collegial Court* 61 (2006), advance a similar hypothesis. By a court's "caseload" we mean caseload per judge, a measure of each judge's workload, rather than the absolute number of the court's cases.

will be inverse to a court's caseload. The Supreme Court's caseload is lighter than that of the courts of appeals, especially relative to its staff. A court of appeals judge has 3 or 4 law clerks and issues 54 opinions a year,[11] making the ratio of opinions to law clerks between 18 to 1 and 13.5 to 1. In the 2009 term (the last term that we have studied), the average Justice issued 8 majority and 13 separate (dissenting plus concurring) opinions, for a ratio of opinions to law clerks of only 5 to 1 (each Justice has 4 law clerks). It's true that Supreme Court law clerks are burdened with screening thousands of petitions for certiorari each year. But court of appeals law clerks work on their judges' unpublished as well as published opinions, and on average the former are more numerous. Supreme Court law clerks are generally more experienced and more carefully selected than court of appeals clerks, moreover, and work even harder, in conformity to the Court's current institutional culture; so the quality-adjusted and time-adjusted ratio of Supreme Court opinions to law clerks is even lower than 5 to 1.

The Justices' lighter adjusted caseload reduces the opportunity cost of dissenting—and this apart from the fact that the Supreme Court tends to limit its consideration to one or two issues presented in the cases that it hears, and it has the aid of an appellate court's opinion and more thorough and careful briefing and argument than are common in lower courts; the Court is inundated nowadays with amicus curiae opinions, many of high quality. Because concurring and dissenting opinions are optional, the fact that so high a proportion of Supreme Court opinions—62 percent—are concurring or dissenting rather than majority opinions (and even at the Supreme Court level most concurring and dissenting opinions are pretty ephemeral, as we'll see, with the exception of dissents by such famous dissenters as Holmes, Brandeis, and the second Harlan) is evidence that the Court's workload is indeed light.

And although the average Supreme Court case is more difficult than the average court of appeals case, often the difficulty is not analytical complexity but indeterminacy, either because the case presents ideological is-

---

11. The average number of signed opinions per active court of appeals judge in 2008. See U.S. Courts, "Federal Court Management Statistics, 2008, Courts of Appeals," www.uscourts. gov/cgi-bin/cmsa2008.pl (visited Dec. 9, 2011).

sues on which the Justices are irreconcilably at odds or because the orthodox materials of legalist analysis are missing or hopelessly ambiguous or contradictory. Indeterminacy may not increase workload, but it is an independent reason for expecting a higher dissent rate in the Supreme Court than in the courts of appeals. This is an implication of the selection effect discussed in chapter 5; the more difficult a case is to decide, the more likely it is to rise to the top of the judicial hierarchy.

Caseload affects the benefits of dissenting as well as the costs. The heavier a court's caseload, the less likely the court is to reexamine its precedents. Deciding a case on the basis of precedent reduces the effort cost of judicial decision-making and also reduces caseload by making the law more predictable. The less likely a court is to reexamine its precedents, the less effect a dissenting opinion is likely to have, because the majority opinion will be a precedent and will therefore be unlikely to be reexamined in a future case. The Supreme Court's lighter caseload should make the Court more willing to reexamine its precedents, and this should increase the benefit to Supreme Court Justices of dissenting. Moreover, when the Court unsettles the law by overruling or narrowing a precedent, the caseload consequences are felt mainly by the lower courts.

The political nature of so many of the Court's cases and the fact that no higher court can discipline the Supreme Court's decision-making make the Justices chafe at having to follow precedents created by their predecessors. (Justice Thomas has made clear that he does not follow precedent.) There is also more room for disagreement in a court of nine judges than in one of three, so we can expect more dissents as more judges hear a case. And the larger the panel and therefore the greater the likelihood that several judges, not just one, will be dissenting, the lower the cost of dissent, because a dissenting judge may be making another judge or judges (his fellow dissenter or dissenters) happy. A single dissenting judge has no allies.

Against all this it might be argued that the collegiality costs of dissenting are greater in the Supreme Court because the Justices sit with each other in every case, whereas court of appeals judges, especially in the larger circuits, sit with a given colleague infrequently. One might think that the very high dissent rate in the Supreme Court would make life unbearable, driving up dissent aversion. Indeed there have been periods when the Justices have had poor relations with each other (the 1940s, for example, and the Burger Court years in the 1970s and early 1980s), and other times when they have had good relations, such as the present. But these fluctuations in collegiality do not appear to be related to the frequency of dissents, and animosities having sources other than frequent dissenting might of course stimulate dissents.

Moreover, when a court's workload is light, as the Supreme Court's is nowadays (as further evidenced by the heavy extracurricular activities of the current Justices, noted in chapter 1), so that the incremental cost of a dissent to a judge in the majority is slight, the judge is unlikely to be greatly irritated by the dissent; the dissent will be imposing only a slight cost on him. And beyond some point a high dissent rate may actually reduce dissent aversion: judges in the majority will have less cause for irritation if everyone dissents a lot, while judges who don't dissent will feel like wallflowers.

The preceding analysis leads us to expect a higher dissent rate in the Supreme Court than in the courts of appeals—and so we find. As shown in Table 6.3, the dissent rate is 57.4 percent in the Supreme Court and only 2.7 percent in the courts of appeals, though the rate varies widely across circuits and also over time (see minimum and maximum columns). These are "all opinion" dissent rates; that is, all dissents divided by terminations on the merits, though there is slight understatement because Lexis and Westlaw, the sources of "all opinion" dissents, do not actually report all unpublished court of appeals opinions (that is, opinions that the issuing court does not deem important enough to warrant publication in the *Federal Reporter*—and publication there is a signal that the court regards its decision as having the weight of precedent). The understatement is slight, however, because dissents are extremely rare in such cases.

The last column in the table changes the denominator for calculating the court of appeals dissent rate from terminations on the merits to terminations on the merits plus procedural terminations. These are terminations, mainly of prisoner civil rights suits, because of some procedural defect, such as failure to invoke federal jurisdiction or to file a timely appeal. They are mainly unpublished, summary orders, without full briefing or oral argument, and very rarely generate a dissent, which is why the

Table 6.3 All-Opinion Dissent Rates in the Courts of Appeals and the Supreme Court, 1990–2007

Court	Average	Minimum	Maximum	Average with Procedural Terminations Included
Circuits				
1st	1.7%	0.8%	3.1%	1.4%
2d	1.7	0.6	3.8	1.3
3d	2.4	1.5	3.2	1.8
4th	2.5	1.8	3.4	1.8
5th	1.2	0.5	1.7	0.8
6th	4.8	3.5	6.2	3.5
7th	3.0	1.6	4.4	2.2
8th	4.1	2.6	6.1	3.2
9th	4.1	3.1	4.8	3.0
10th	2.3	1.6	3.3	1.9
11th	1.0	0.6	2.4	0.7
D.C.	4.6	2.4	6.6	3.6
All	2.7	—	—	2.0
Supreme Court	57.4%	45.6%	68.7%	

Notes:

1. Court of Appeals Dissent Rates: We tabulated the number of opinions with dissents in each circuit (both published and unpublished opinions) in each year from 1990 through 2007 from Lexis searches and divided by the number of cases terminated on the merits in each circuit each year. See U.S. Courts, "Judicial Caseload Statistics," tab. B, various years, www.uscourts.gov/Statistics/FederalJudicialCaseloadStatistics/FederalJudicialCaseloadStatistics.aspx (visited Dec. 9, 2011). The "average" for each circuit is the percentage of dissents in each year weighted by the number of cases terminated on the merits in the circuit that year. "Minimum" denotes the lowest and "maximum" the highest annual dissent rates in the 1990–2007 period. The average for all circuits is the average of the individual circuits weighted by the number of cases terminated on the merits in each circuit.

2. The column labeled With Procedural Terminations Included computes the average dissent rate in a circuit as the number of dissents divided by the sum of terminations on the merits and procedural terminations.

3. The Supreme Court Dissent Rate is the percentage of orally argued opinions with at least one dissenting vote (from the Spaeth database for the terms 1990–2007). The minimum and maximum rates are the lowest and highest annual rates, as in the case of the courts of appeals.

4. We also collected Westlaw data on court of appeals opinions with dissents. The number of dissents recorded by Westlaw (12,909) was very close to the number reported by Lexis (13,288); the difference is too small to affect our analysis.

court of appeals dissent rate falls (to 2 percent from 2.7 percent) when they are included in terminations. The much higher dissent rates in the Songer and Sunstein samples provide a more meaningful basis for comparison with the Supreme Court than the all-opinions or all-terminations figures; judges rarely bother to dissent publicly from an unpublished de-

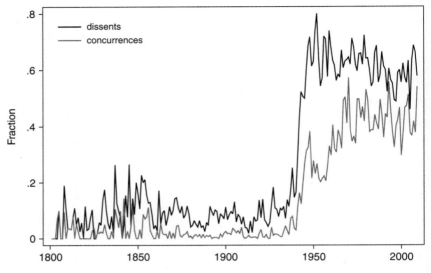

Figure 6.1   Dissenting and Concurring Opinions in Supreme Court, 1950–2010
Terms

cision, because in most courts such a decision cannot be cited as a precedent and is therefore of little consequence.

The high rate of dissenting opinions in the Supreme Court is a recent
phenomenon. As shown in Figure 6.1, the rate was low until the early
1940s, when it jumped suddenly and very steeply, even though almost all
the Justices by then had been appointed by the same President, Franklin
Roosevelt. We conjecture that the surge was attributable to the Justices'
having observed that many dissents by Holmes, Brandeis, Stone, and
Cardozo had become law, whereas previously dissents had rarely become
law. Holmes became the most prominent Supreme Court Justice since
John Marshall primarily on the strength of his dissents. The perceived
value of dissenting shot up.

A more common explanation for the surge in dissents is poor management of disagreement among the Justices by Stone, who became Chief
Justice in 1941.[12] Stone was indeed a notable flop as Chief Justice, but we
would expect that to have led his successors back to the consensus model
of Chief Justices like Taft and Hughes. Some less transitory development

12. See note 6 in chapter 2.

(or developments) would be a better candidate for the cause of a permanent increase in the dissent rate; the increased prestige of Supreme Court dissents may have been that cause.

Concurring opinions, like dissents, are much more frequent in the Supreme Court than in the courts of appeals. There were one or more concurring opinions in 40.3 percent of Supreme Court cases in 1953–2008, compared to only 0.6 percent in our court of appeals sample.[13] Many concurring opinions express disagreement with the majority opinion, albeit disagreement about grounds or reasoning or implications for future cases rather than about outcome. It is therefore no surprise that, as shown in Figure 6.1, the number of concurring opinions surged in the early 1940s along with dissents and are now almost as common as the latter.

We need to consider the possibility that because the likelihood of disagreement among judges grows with the size of the panel, the higher dissent rate in the Supreme Court is an artifact of the difference between a panel of nine judges and one of three.

Assume that all judges on a panel of size n have identical and independent probabilities of voting in favor of the appellant, A (with probability p), and the appellee, B (with probability $(1 - p)$). Let δ (< 1) denote the willingness of a judge to dissent when he disagrees with a majority of the judges on the panel; in a case of extreme dissent aversion, δ will be close to zero. We assume for the moment that δ is the same for all judges, as we are trying to determine the pure effect of panel size on the propensity to dissent.

Since the probability of a unanimous decision is $p^n + (1 - p)^n$, the probability of at least one dissent in a panel of size n is $Pd = \delta[1 - p^n - (1 - p)^n]$. Pd increases both with δ and with panel size, because $\partial Pd/\partial \delta > 0$ and $\partial Pd/\partial n = - \delta p^n \ln p - \delta (1 - p)^n \ln (1 - p) > 0$, provided that $p < 1$. Pd is maximized when $p = .5$ and decreases symmetrically as p deviates from .5 (holding panel size constant). That is, $\partial Pd/\partial p = -np^{n-1} + n(1 - p)^{n-1} = 0$ when $p = .5$. The intuition behind this result is that there is a greater probability of dissent if the judges think the case is close—and a p of .5 implies that the case is a toss-up.

13. Lee Epstein, William M. Landes, and Richard A. Posner, "When and Why Judges Dissent: A Theoretical and Empirical Analysis," 3 *Journal of Legal Analysis* 101, 107 (2011).

Table 6.4 shows how the probability of at least one dissent depends on panel size, the judges' probability of voting for the appellant (p), and dissent aversion (or its converse, δ). For example, increasing panel size from three to nine increases the likelihood of a least one dissent by 25 to 50 percent if dissent aversion is held constant, while a reduction from 90 percent dissent aversion ($\delta = .10$) to zero ($\delta = 1$) increases the probability of at least one dissent tenfold if panel size is held constant. That probability also increases as the probability of the court's siding with the appellant decreases from .90 to .50. If p were 1 or 0, there would be no dissents, because all the judges would vote for either the appellant ($p = 1$) or the appellee ($p = 0$).

Table 6.5 extends the analysis to ideologically divided judges and shows that such a division increases the likelihood of a dissent. For constant dissent aversion (that is, reading across the rows of the table), the probability of dissent in a nine-judge panel is roughly twice that in a three-judge one. This is the pure panel-size effect. But we know that the actual dissent rate in the Supreme Court is closer to 10 times the rate in the courts of appeals—and more than 20 times if unpublished court of appeals decisions are included. These ratios are powerful evidence that dissent aversion is indeed greater in the courts of appeals than in the Supreme Court.

One reason is that the Supreme Court "panel" in the period covered by our data was always mixed—that is, always contained Justices ap-

Table 6.4   Probability of at Least One Dissent in a Panel of Size n

		Panel Size (n)	
p	δ	3	9
.90	.10	.027	.061
.90	.25	.068	.153
.90	1.00	.270	.613
.70	.10	.063	.096
.70	.25	.158	.240
.70	1.00	.630	.960
.50	.10	.075	.100
.50	.25	.188	.249
.50	1.00	.750	.996

Table 6.5   Probability of at Least One Dissent in a Panel of Size n with Ideologically Divided Judges

			Panel Size and Composition			
pR	*pD*	δ	2*R*s & 1*D*	2*D*s & 1*R*	5*R*s & 4*D*s	4*R*s & 5*D*s
.90	.70	.10	.043	.055	.086	.089
.90	.70	.25	.108	.138	.215	.222
.90	.70	.70	.301	.399	.601	.623
.90	.70	1.00	.430	.550	.858	.890

Note: pR and *pD* are the probabilities of dissent by an *R* and a *D* respectively.

pointed by Presidents of different political parties; there were never nine *R*s or nine *D*s. The dissent rate in mixed rather than in all court of appeals panels provides the proper comparison to the Supreme Court, and indeed we find a higher dissent rate in the mixed panels in our sample of 1025 published court of appeals opinions: 8.6 percent (54 dissents out of 626 opinions) versus 6.5 percent in the other panels (26 out of 399). But the difference is not statistically significant, and the higher percentage is still far lower than the dissent rate in the Supreme Court.

En banc decisions are the closest counterpart in the courts of appeals to Supreme Court decisions in point of panel size, ideological diversity, difficulty or importance, and, related to difficulty and especially importance, the fact that the court is selecting a case for decision rather than being forced to decide it. So it's no surprise that only in the seven en banc decisions in the Songer sample is the dissent rate in the courts of appeals comparable to that in the Supreme Court. There were dissents in three of those decisions—43 percent.

But a sample of seven is too small to enable a statistically significant inference to be drawn. We have therefore searched Westlaw for all en banc decisions in the five-year period 2005–2010. The results are presented in Table 6.6. The dissent rate—77 percent—turns out to be much higher than the dissent rate in our sample of seven (illustrating the pitfalls of inference from small samples) and substantially higher than in the Supreme Court as well. But this does not refute the claim that dissent aversion is greater in the courts of appeals than in the Supreme Court. For one

Table 6.6 Dissents in En Banc Cases in Federal Courts of Appeals, 2005–2010

Circuit	Number of Authorized Active Judgeships	Number of Decisions on the Merits	Number of En Banc Decisions 2005–2010 Found in Our Westlaw Search	En Banc Decisions as Percentage of Decisions on the Merits	Number of En Banc Decisions with Dissent	En B⟩ Dissen⟩
1st	6	5157	10	0.19	8	.8⟩
2d	13	16,072	6	0.04	5	.8⟩
3rd	14	11,672	15	0.12	9	.6⟩
4th	15	14,348	8	0.06	7	.8⟩
5th	17	21,148	22	0.10	18	.8⟩
6th	16	12,888	29	0.23	27	.9⟩
7th	11	7679	12	0.16	7	.5⟩
8th	11	10,431	33	0.32	28	.8⟩
9th	29	30,523	88	0.26	70	.8⟩
10th	12	7584	15	0.20	9	.6⟩
11th	12	16,714	19	0.11	10	.5⟩
D.C.	12	2763	7	0.22	5	.7
Total	179	156,979	264	0.17	203	.7⟩

thing, the average number of judges who participate in en banc hearings is roughly 12.5.[14]

More important is the fact that, as shown in the table, cases are heard en banc in fewer than one quarter of 1 percent of all cases decided by the courts of appeals, which is evidence of strong dissent aversion. Apart from the extra work involved (with very few exceptions, the en banc hearing is a rehearing—the case had already been heard and decided by a three-judge panel), judges are highly sensitive to the rejection of their decisions by their colleagues, as distinct from strangers, such as the Justices of the Supreme Court (who are not colleagues even if the judge is personally acquainted with some or all of the Justices). As a result, frequent en bancs take a heavy toll on collegiality, and so a case is very unlikely to be heard en banc unless members of the court disagree strongly with the panel decision; and with strong disagreement virtually a precondition to

14. Computed from Table 6.5, except that in the Ninth Circuit, though there are 29 authorized judgeships, only 11 of the judges (the chief judge, plus 10 other judges chosen at random) constitute a panel to hear cases en banc. We say "roughly 12.5" because judgeships may be vacant and also because a senior judge who was on the panel the decision of which is being reheard en banc is authorized to participate in the rehearing.

a case being decided en banc, the dissent rate is bound to be very high. In the Supreme Court, in contrast, the decision to hear a case, while likely to reflect disagreement with the lower court (as suggested by the two-thirds reversal rate), need not reflect a disagreement among the Justices about the merits, though of course it often does.

Our analysis might seem to imply that dissent aversion is nonexistent in the Supreme Court. But we know that this is not true, not only from the Court's determination to present a united front in the segregation cases of the 1950s and 1960s but also from our analysis in chapter 3 of unanimous Supreme Court decisions, where we found evidence of at least faint dissent aversion. We must also consider the bearing of what has been called vote "fluidity"—a Justice's changing his vote between the post-argument conference and the issuance of the decision. In the 1969–1985 terms, at least one Justice changed his vote in 36.6 percent of the cases,[15] though an individual Justice switched, on average, in just 7.5 percent of the cases.[16] The switchers usually joined the majority. For example, when Justice White initially voted with the majority, he ultimately joined the dissenters only 3.3 percent of the time, but when he initially voted with the minority he ultimately joined the majority 22.5 percent of the time.[17]

Although vote fluidity could be the result of the persuasiveness of the majority opinion rather than of dissent aversion, it could also result from institutional pressure to decide a substantial fraction of cases unanimously in order to make the Supreme Court seem more lawlike and less political than it is. Such institutional dissent aversion has been a conspicuous feature of continental European judiciaries, which traditionally forbade public dissents.

We cannot even be certain that there is less dissent aversion in the Supreme Court than in the courts of appeals. Recall that the overall dissent rate in the courts of appeals is less than 3 percent, the dissent rate in the Songer sample of published court of appeals decisions is 7.8 percent, the dissent rate in the Sunstein sample of published court of appeals cases

---

15. Forrest Maltzman and Paul J. Wahlbeck, "Strategic Policy Considerations and Voting Fluidity on the Burger Court," 90 *American Political Science Review* 581, 587 (1996).

16. Id. at 588 (tab. 1).

17. Id.

drawn from ideologically charged subject-matter categories is 9.1 percent, and the dissent rate in en banc cases is 77 percent. This ladder of
dissent rates suggests that case characteristics dominate the decision to
dissent (though in the case of en banc dissents, panel size is almost certainly a factor also), and this in turn opens up the possibility that the
higher dissent rate in the Supreme Court reflects primarily the characteristics of the cases that the Court decides to hear.

The Effect of Panel Composition

To examine the effect of panel composition on the frequency of dissents
we need to consider more carefully why a majority of the judges on a
panel would ever yield to the wishes of the minority member (we assume
a three-judge panel). One possibility is that the odd man out acts as a
whistleblower.[18] Another is that he may bring to the panel's deliberations
insights that the other judges, having different priors, overlooked.[19]

This of course presupposes deliberation. There is less deliberation
among judges, at least in the common understanding of the word, than
outsiders assume (a point we come back to in the next chapter). Henry
Friendly, the ablest and most influential court of appeals judge since
Learned Hand, was a frequent dissenter. "During his nearly twenty-seven
years on the bench—from September 1959 to March 1986—Judge
Friendly wrote not only 800 or so published majority opinions for his
own court but also 103 dissents and 88 opinions that were either concurrences or partial dissents. All of these separate opinions may be fairly
treated as dissents to some degree. Even when an opinion began with the
phrase 'Friendly, J., concurring' and even when Judge Friendly joined in
the panel's judgment, his rationale usually differed from the majority's. A
different rationale matters, of course, because it often points to a different

18. Frank B. Cross and Emerson H. Tiller, "Judicial Partisanship and Obedience to Legal
Doctrine: Whistleblowing on the Federal Courts of Appeals," 107 *Yale Law Journal* 2155,
2175–2176 (1998).

19. See Matthew Spitzer and Eric Talley, "Left, Right, and Center: Strategic Information
Acquisition and Diversity in Judicial Panels," *Journal of Law, Economics, and Organization*
(forthcoming).

result on somewhat different facts."[20] Why was Friendly unsuccessful in persuading his colleagues in so many cases? Ideological tensions seem not to have been a major factor. The reason (or a reason) may have been that the Second Circuit, on which Friendly sat, did not deliberate in the usual manner during his tenure on the court. The judges did not routinely confer after hearing oral argument, although often they exchanged post-argument memos in advance of assignment of the majority opinion to one of the judges on the panel.[21] This meant that a judge was likely to commit himself in writing before hearing from the other judges, and once a judge had done that, he would be reluctant to change his vote—he would lose face.

Obviously a key factor influencing the likelihood of a dissent is differences among panel members in intensity of preference for a particular outcome, as proxied by the ideological distance between the dissenting judge and his majority colleagues with respect to the particular case—the greater the distance, the likelier a dissent.[22] If one judge feels strongly that the case should be decided one way rather than another, while the other two judges, though inclined to vote the other way, do not feel strongly, one of them may decide to go along with the third to avoid creating ill will, perhaps hoping for reciprocal consideration in some future case in which he has strong feelings and the other judges do not. Once one judge swings over to the view of the dissentient judge, the remaining judge is likely to do so as well, for the same reason or because of dissent aversion.

Ideological disagreement is unlike a disagreement over the best means to a shared end, because ideological disputants rarely argue from shared premises. A liberal on a panel with two conservatives is unlikely to produce facts or arguments that will alter the ideology of his colleagues, or

20. Michael Boudin, "Friendly, J., Dissenting," 61 *Duke Law Journal* 881, 882 (2012). His writing 800 published opinions implies that he heard approximately 2400 cases, and if we follow Boudin in treating his 88 concurrences or partial dissents as dissents, so that the total of his dissenting opinions was 191, this translates to a dissent rate of 8 percent.
21. See David M. Dorsen, *Henry Friendly: Greatest Judge of His Era* 87 (2012).
22. Virginia A. Hettinger, Stefanie A. Lindquist, and Wendy L. Martinek, "Separate Opinion Writing on the United States Courts of Appeals," 31 *American Politics Research* 215 (2003).

vice versa. But if he feels more strongly about how the case should be decided than the other judges do, this implies that he would derive greater benefits than they from a decision of the case his way and therefore that he would be willing to incur greater costs to get his way—as by writing a dissent. His threat to dissent is thus a credible threat to impose effort and maybe humiliation costs on his colleagues. If his colleagues' costs of deciding the case his preferred way are less than the benefits to him, because they do not feel strongly about the outcome, one or both of them will give way to him.

There is a parallel to jury holdouts. A juror who feels very strongly about what the verdict in the case he's hearing should be will be willing to incur costs by protracting the jury's deliberations. By thus imposing costs on the majority he may induce the jurors in the majority to yield to him, or at least to compromise with him. The usual requirement that a jury verdict be unanimous strengthens the holdout's hand relative to that of the dissentient judge on a three-judge panel. And the normal pressures to conform to prevailing views in social settings, including jury deliberations, are weaker in appellate panels because of the long and honorable tradition of dissent. But they are not nonexistent, as we know from our findings in chapter 4 concerning the conformity effect in the courts of appeals.

A Formal Model of Deciding Whether to Dissent

We can learn more about likely dissent behavior with the help of a formal model in which a judge's vote depends on his view of the applicable law and precedents, his ideological leanings, panel composition, and how dissent-averse he is.

Let C_R and C_D be the respective probabilities that a judge appointed by a Republican President and a judge appointed by a Democratic one will favor a conservative outcome in a case in which $1 > C_R > C_D > 0$. (We ignore case outcomes in which there are no or mixed ideological stakes.) Let V_R and V_D be the respective probabilities that judges will actually vote for a conservative outcome. These probabilities depend not only on C_R and C_D but also on panel composition, the likelihood that the judge will disagree with the majority, and his willingness to dissent if he disagrees. Thus,

$$V_R = \mu_R(C_R) + (1 - \mu_R)[C_D(1 - \delta) + C_R\delta] \tag{1}$$

$$V_D = \mu_D(C_D) + (1 - \mu_D)[C_R(1 - \delta) + C_D\delta] \tag{2}$$

where μ_R and $(1 - \mu_R)$ are the fractions of panels with a majority of Rs and Ds, respectively, when the judge in question is an R, and μ_D and $1 - \mu_D$ are those fractions when the judge in question is a D. As before, δ is the willingness of a judge to dissent. Another way to think of δ is as the percentage of cases in which a judge disagrees with the majority and actually dissents.

We model δ as

$$\delta = f(N, X/N, z) \tag{3}$$

where N is the number of judges in a circuit, X/N is the circuit's average caseload, and z are other factors influencing δ. We expect that the greater N is, the smaller the benefits of collegiality will be and the greater, therefore, the willingness of a judge to dissent. We also expect that the greater X/N is, the greater the marginal effort and collegiality cost of a dissent will be and hence the lower the incentive to dissent.

Because there are no panel composition effects in the Supreme Court, equations (1) and (2) simplify to $V_R = C_R$ and $V_D = C_R(1 - \delta) + C_D\delta$ for that Court, assuming that Rs are in the majority and therefore $\mu_R = 1$ and $\mu_D = 0$. If δ is close to one in the Supreme Court, as we believe it probably is for reasons noted earlier, then Justices almost always vote according to their true ideological preferences, C_R and C_D.

Although δ denotes willingness to dissent, the fraction of dissenting votes will be lower than that willingness might lead one to expect, especially in the three-judge panels of the courts of appeals. Consider an R whose δ is 25 percent if he finds himself in disagreement with the other two judges on the panel when they are both Ds. Assume that four other judges of his court are Rs and seven are Ds. On average he will be the only

R on the panel in 38 percent of his cases, so that the probability that he will sit with one or two other Rs will be .62. Assume further that there is a wide ideological gap between Rs and Ds—for example that C_R and C_D are .7 and .3. Then an R and a D will disagree 40 percent of the time. And since δ is 25 percent, an R will dissent in 10 percent of the cases (25 percent of 40 percent) in which he is the minority member of a panel. But the overall dissent rate will be lower than that because he also sits on panels in which he is in the majority. In our example an R will dissent only 3.8 percent of the time, because he sits on a panel with two Ds only 38 percent of the time and dissents in only 10 percent of the cases decided by that panel. In contrast, a D will have a dissent rate of 1.8 percent, because he sits with two Rs in only 18.1 percent of the cases.

The average dissent rate for all the judges in our example is the weighted average of the dissent rates of the five Rs and the seven Ds and is therefore 2.6 percent, which is much lower than the δ of 25 percent that we started with. But the number of dissents as a fraction of decided cases is (approximately) three times 2.6 percent, because there are three votes in each case. So if each judge hears 100 cases a year, making 1200 cases in a 12-judge circuit, there will be 3600 total votes, 94 of them dissenting, or 7.8 dissents per 100 decided cases.

Table 6.7 shows how the dissent rate can be expected to change as panel composition, dissent aversion, and the ideological gap between Rs and Ds changes in a hypothetical 12-judge circuit. We assume for the sake of simplicity (an assumption to be relaxed shortly) that a judge dissents only when he is sitting with two judges appointed by a President of the opposite party from the one who appointed him. So if there are 10 Rs and 2 Ds, an R will sit with 2 Ds only 1.8 percent of the time, while a D will sit with 2 Rs 81.8 percent of the time. As we see in columns (5) and (6), assuming that a judge in the minority disagrees with the majority 40 percent of the time and dissents in 25 percent of those cases, the Rs will dissent in only .2 percent of the cases and the Ds in 8 percent. In contrast, in the shaded row in the table, in which the number of Rs and Ds is equal, the dissent rate of both Rs and Ds will be 2.7 percent.

If the ideological gap between Rs and Ds declines, so will the fraction of potential disagreements and therefore the dissent rate. For example, if the ideological variables C_R and C_D are .6 and .4 rather than .7 and .3,

Table 6.7 Dissent as a Function of Willingness to Dissent, Ideological Differences, and Court Composition

Court Composition		Fraction of Opportunities to Dissent in Circuit		Fraction of Dissenting Votes		Fraction of Cases with a Dissenting Vote			
				$C_R = .7$ $C_D = .3$		$C_R = .7$ $C_D = .3$		$C_R = .6$ $C_D = .4$	
R	D	R	D	$\delta = .25$	$\delta = .25$	$\delta = .25$	$\delta = .10$	$\delta = .25$	$\delta = 1$
(1)	(2)	(3)	(4)	R (5)	D (6)	All (7)	All (8)	All (9)	All (10)
10	2	.018	.818	.002	.082	.045	.009	.023	.091
9	3	.055	.655	.006	.066	.062	.012	.031	.123
8	4	.109	.509	.011	.051	.073	.015	.034	.145
7	5	.181	.382	.018	.038	.079	.016	.040	.159
6	6	.272	.272	.027	.027	.082	.016	.041	.163
5	7	.382	.181	.038	.018	.079	.016	.040	.159
4	8	.509	.109	.051	.011	.073	.015	.034	.145
3	9	.655	.055	.066	.006	.062	.012	.031	.123
2	10	.818	.018	.082	.002	.045	.009	.023	.091

Notes:

1. C_R = fraction of conservative votes of judges appointed by a Republican President; C_D = fraction of conservative votes by judges appointed by a Democratic President; δ = fraction of times a judge will dissent when the other two judges on the panel were appointed by a President of the opposite party.

2. No span of time is indicated for this table because the table is based on our formal model rather than on data.

making the ideological gap .2 rather than .4, so that an R and a D will disagree in 20 percent rather than 40 percent of the cases in which they are on the same panel, the dissent rate will fall by a half (compare columns (7) and (9)). But the per-judge dissent rate will be low even if dissent aversion vanishes ($\delta = 1$), as in column (10), and the circuit is evenly balanced between Rs and Ds, which maximizes the fraction of mixed panels and hence the occasions on which, on our assumptions, a judge would consider dissenting. An individual judge will dissent in only 5.4 percent of the cases ($.2 \times .272$), though there will be a dissent in 16.2 percent (3×5.4) of them.

The assumption in equations (1) to (3) that a judge will dissent only if he is an R or a D on a panel in which the two other judges were appointed by a President of a different party is unrealistic, as is the assumption that all Ds are liberal in all cases and all Rs conservative in all cases. There will be cases in which (1) a judge will dissent even if the panel consists of all Rs or all Ds, or (2) one or two members of the panel will switch and support the potential dissenter if the latter feels more strongly about the case than either of the other judges. And (3), sometimes the majority will narrow the grounds of the decision, or soften the language of the opinion, to accommodate the concerns of the third judge and thereby head off a dissent.[23] (1) will increase the dissent rate, (2) will leave it unchanged if one judge switches his vote and reduce it if both do, and (3) will reduce it.

The combined effect of dissent aversion and ideological diversity is to make a judge's voting behavior less ideological, implying that $V_R < C_R$ and $V_D > C_D$—that is, that the difference between the actual votes of Rs and Ds will be smaller than would be predicted on the basis of the party of the appointing President. We therefore rewrite the equations for the judge's voting behavior (equations (1) and (2)) as a weighted average of his ideology and the ideology of the judges in his circuit who were appointed by a President of the opposite party, with the weights dependent

---

23. Cass R. Sunstein et al., *Are Judges Political? An Empirical Analysis of the Federal Judiciary* 20–21 (2006) (tab. 2-1), presents evidence of ideological "moderation of the majority position when a panel contains two rather than three judges appointed by a president of the same party."

on both the ideological composition of panels and dissent aversion. Hence

$$V_R = C_R(\mu_R + (1 - \mu_R)\delta) + C_D(1\text{-}\mu_R)(1 - \delta) \tag{4}$$

$$V_D = C_D(\mu_D + (1 - \mu_D)\delta) + C_R(1\text{-}\mu_D)(1 - \delta) \tag{5}$$

Ideological moderation will be observed in (4) and (5) if a judge gives a positive weight to the ideology of judges of the opposite ideology, provided that the judge has at least some dissent aversion.

In Table 6.8 we see that as the ratio of Rs to Ds falls, all the judges vote less conservatively when both δ and a judge's own ideology are held constant (provided that $\delta < 1$). Comparing the voting behavior of judges in courts that have different ratios of Rs to Ds can therefore yield misleading inferences concerning a judge's ideology. For example, an R in a court with 3 Rs and 9 Ds will appear to be less conservative than a D in a court of 10 Rs and 2 Ds if δ is less than or equal to .25.

This suggests that a judge's overall voting record in the court of appeals may be a poor predictor of how he will vote if appointed to the Supreme Court, where dissent aversion is weak. So consider the current Supreme Court Justices (plus the recently retired Justice Stevens) who had served on a court of appeals for a substantial period of time before their appointment to the Court. The fraction of conservative votes in our Songer sample by court of appeals judges later appointed to the Supreme Court is (number of votes in parentheses) Stevens .372 (43), Scalia .571 (35), Kennedy .421 (19), Ginsburg .371 (97), Breyer .592 (103), and Alito .386 (44).[24] Except in the case of Stevens, these numbers are only weakly related to the fraction of the judges' conservative votes (from the

---

24. We exclude Roberts, Sotomayor, Souter, and Thomas because they have very few votes in our Songer sample. Thomas has 15, Souter 3, Roberts and Sotomayor zero. We estimated the fraction of active Rs in a circuit by averaging the yearly fractions for the periods in which the judge served. Since circuit composition changes over a judge's tenure, we do not know how closely the sampled votes match the average circuit composition. Nor can we match the panel composition to the judge's votes, because the panel composition of the cases in our sample in which a judge voted may differ from the average panel composition in the circuit.

Table 6.8 Ideological Voting

| Court Composition | | Fraction of Conservative Votes by Judges Appointed by President of Same or Different Party Assuming True Ideological Preferences Are C_R = .7 and C_D = .3 | | | | | | | |
| | | $\delta = 0$ | | $\delta = .25$ | | $\delta = .50$ | | $\delta = 1$ | |
R (1)	D (2)	V_R (3)	V_D (4)	V_R (5)	V_D (6)	V_R (7)	V_D (8)	V_R (9)	V_D (10)
10	2	.693	.627	.694	.545	.696	.464	.7	.3
9	3	.678	.562	.684	.497	.689	.431	.7	.3
8	4	.656	.503	.667	.453	.678	.402	.7	.3
7	5	.628	.453	.646	.414	.664	.376	.7	.3
6	6	.591	.408	.618	.382	.646	.354	.7	.3
5	7	.547	.372	.585	.354	.624	.336	.7	.3
4	8	.496	.344	.547	.333	.598	.322	.7	.3
3	9	.438	.322	.503	.317	.569	.311	.7	.3
2	10	.372	.307	.455	.305	.536	.304	.7	.3

Notes:

1. V_R = fraction of conservative votes by judges appointed by Republican Presidents; V_D = fraction of conservative votes by judges appointed by Democratic Presidents.

2. See note 2 to Table 6.7.

Spaeth database) in the Supreme Court: Stevens .313, Scalia .774, Kennedy .655, Ginsburg .274, Breyer .327, and Alito .756. Scalia and Kennedy, sitting with a majority of judges appointed by Democratic Presidents, voted more liberally than they do in the Supreme Court. Stevens and Ginsburg also sat with a majority of judges appointed by Democratic Presidents in their courts of appeals and voted liberally in both the court of appeals and the Supreme Court. Breyer sat with a majority of judges appointed by Republican Presidents in his court of appeals and voted more conservatively in that court than in the Supreme Court, while Alito also sat with a majority of judges appointed by Republican Presidents in the court of appeals but votes more conservatively in the Supreme Court than he did in that court.

Empirical Analysis

We expect a decline in judicial workload to lower the opportunity cost of dissenting and thus increase the frequency of dissents, and we also expect that the greater the judges' ideological heterogeneity, the likelier they are to disagree and so the higher the dissent rate will be. We expect similar effects for concurring opinions. To test these hypotheses we estimate in Table 6.9 regressions from annual data on the Supreme Court for the 1953–2008 terms.

The dependent variables are the number of dissenting opinions divided by the number of decisions (equation (1)), and the number of concurring opinions also divided by the number of decisions (equation (2)).[25] If the Court decides 100 cases and in 40 there is one dissenting opinion, in 20 two, and in 5 three, that makes 95 dissenting opinions in all (40 × 1 + 20 × 2 + 5 × 3), which is an average of .95 dissenting opinion per case. The independent variables are *Caseload* (the number of decisions in orally argued cases); *Other Cases* (decisions in nonargued cases plus a small number of decisions in original as distinct from appealed cases and

---

25. We also estimated regressions using alternative dependent variables, such as the fraction of cases with at least one dissenting opinion (which does not distinguish between a case with one dissenting opinion and a case with two or more such opinions), the average number of dissenting votes per opinions, and the fraction of cases with one or more concurring opinions. The results were similar to those reported here.

Table 6.9 Regression Analysis of Log of Dissent and Concurrence Rates in the Supreme Court, 1953–2008

	Log (Total Number of Dissenting Opinions/Number of Opinions) (1)	Log (Total Number of Concurring Opinions/Number of Opinions) (2)
Log Caseload	−.330*	−.059
	(2.52)	(0.29)
Log Other Cases	−.015	.211**
	(0.45)	(3.10)
Standard Deviation of Segal-Cover Scores	.596**	.307
	(3.95)	(0.93)
Time	−.004	.017**
	(1.94)	(3.18)
Dummy 1953–1955	−.351**	−.360
	(3.63)	(1.64)
Constant	8.867*	−33.912**
	(2.02)	(2.99)
R^2	.34	.70
Number of Observations	56	56

Note: All regressions have 56 observations and use robust standard errors.

a few cases decided by a tie vote); the standard deviation of Justices' Segal-Cover scores; a time-trend variable that accounts for the combined effect on dissents of other factors such as the rise in the number of opinions dissenting from denial of certiorari, increased use of word processing and electronic research, and increased number of law clerks; and a dummy variable for the 1953–1955 terms because of the unusually small number of opinions (50 percent below 1956 and subsequent years) issued in those terms, both in cases that were and in cases that were not orally argued.[26]

26. The number of opinions after oral argument was 84 (1953), 93 (1954), and 98 (1955), compared to 121 (1956), 127 (1957), and between 101 and 153 over the next 15 years. The number of other decisions was 4 (1953), 5 (1954), and 6 (1955), followed by 6 (1956), 28 (1957), and between 11 and 75 over the next 15 years. Several factors in conjunction may explain the low number of opinions in the 1953 through 1955 terms. On September 8, 1953, right before the start of the 1953 term, Chief Justice Vinson died suddenly; Warren took the oath of office on the first day of the term. The Court probably wasn't up to speed on certiorari grants. Moreover, *Brown v. Board of Education,* reargued on December 9, 1953, took a great deal of the Court's time. And in 1954 Justice Jackson died at the start of the term, and he wasn't replaced until March 1955.

Since both the dissent and the caseload variables are in logarithms, the regression coefficient indicates that a 10 percent decrease in caseload increases the dissent rate by 3.3 percent. Also, the greater the ideological heterogeneity of the Justices, the greater the number of dissenting opinions. Of the remaining variables, only the 1953–1955 dummy variable is significant. It has a large negative effect—a 35 percent drop in the dissent rate. But the effect is offset by the negative coefficient on the caseload variable, making the net effect on the dissent rate close to zero.

The time variable in equation (2) reveals a 1.7 percent annual increase in the frequency of concurring opinions. *Caseload* has no significant effect on the number of concurring opinions, but *Other Cases* has a significant positive effect; we have no explanation.

If we are right that a dissent imposes an effort cost on the majority because the author of the majority opinion is likely to revise his opinion to address the objections raised by the dissent, this implies that majority opinions will usually be longer when there is a dissent. To test that hypothesis we collected data on the number of words in our Supreme Court sample and in a sample of court of appeals opinions.

Our Supreme Court sample (446 cases) includes 202 cases with one dissenting opinion (45.3 percent), 60 with two or more dissenting opinions (13.5 percent), and 147 with one or more concurring opinions (33 percent). Table 6.10 reveals that a Supreme Court majority opinion tends to be longer if there is one dissenting opinion and longer still if there is more than one. The differences are statistically significant for both the full sample and the 335 orally argued signed opinions when we combine all three years, and significant in most of the individual years as well.

A problem in interpreting these data is that the difficulty or importance of a case is likely to influence both the length of the majority opinion and the presence and number of dissents. To isolate the effect of dissent on length we regress length on dissent, the importance of the case, and other factors that might be expected to influence length:

$$W_{sc} = f(\text{Oral, Dissent1, Dissent2, Mention, Concur, Term, Subject Matter, Importance, u})$$

W_{sc} is the number of words (including words in footnotes) in the Supreme Court's majority opinion. *Oral* means there was both an oral argument

Table 6.10 Average Number of Words in Majority Opinions in Supreme Court Cases in 1963, 1980, and 1990 Terms *(number of cases in parentheses)*

	All Cases			Signed Opinions in Orally Argued Cases		
	Number of Dissents			Number of Dissents		
Year	0	1	2 or More	0	1	2 or More
1963	2337	2399	4206*	3432	4059	5624*
(179)	(72)	(84)	(23)	(44)	(48)	(17)
1980	4530	5527	5570	5307	6082	6910
(143)	(54)	(71)	(18)	(41)	(62)	(14)
1990	3564	4536*	5884*	4376	4687	6130*
(124)	(54)	(51)	(19)	(42)	(49)	(18)
All	3362	4006*	5146*	4308	5041*	6177*
(446)	(180)	(206)	(60)	(127)	(159)	(49)

and a signed opinion, *Dissent1* that there is one dissenting opinion and *Dissent2* more than one, *Mention* that the majority opinion mentions the dissent, *Concur* that there is a concurring opinion. *Term* consists of dummy variables denoting the term of the Court (1963, 1980, or 1990) and *Subject* consists of dummy variables denoting subject matter. *Importance* indicates the importance of the case, proxied by the average number of Supreme Court plus court of appeals citations to the Supreme Court majority opinion; the average number in an orally argued case is 172.

The results of the regression analysis are shown in Table 6.11. *Oral* is a significant variable in equation (1), indicating that opinions in orally argued cases are on average nearly 3000 words longer than other opinions. In equation (2), which restricts the sample to the 335 orally argued cases decided in a signed opinion, a dissenting opinion increases the length of the majority opinion by more than 1000 words if the majority mentions the dissent. If not, the effect, though still positive (277 words), is much smaller and statistically insignificant, except that *Dissent1* and *Mention* are jointly significant in both equations. When there are two or more dissenting opinions, not only is the majority opinion more than 1000 words longer but the difference is statistically significant whether or not the majority mentions the dissent, although a mention adds between 700 and 900 words to the opinion, depending on the equation.

In both equations the importance of the case as proxied by the combined number of citations to the majority opinion by the Supreme Court

Table 6.11   Regression Analysis of Words in Supreme Court Majority Opinions in 1963, 1980, and 1990 Terms

	(1)	(2)
Oral	2924**	—
	(10.17)	
Dissent1	141	277
	(0.58)	(0.87)
Dissent2	913*	1357**
	(2.51)	(2.93)
Mention	867*	725
	(2.63)	(1.86)
S. Ct. Citations	91.6**	93.8**
	(7.63)	(6.88)
Ct. App. Citations	−0.721	−0.823
	(1.51)	(1.52)
Concurrences	75.6	76.1
	(0.32)	(0.26)
1980 Term	1751**	2056**
	(6.52)	(5.87)
1990 Term	957**	1202**
	(3.29)	(3.29)
Subject Matter	Yes	Yes
Constant	308	2673**
	(0.72)	(4.66)
R^2	.49	.23
Number of Observations	446	335

Note: S. Ct. Citations denotes citations in subsequent Supreme Court cases to the Supreme Court's majority opinion, and Ct. App. Citations denotes citations in subsequent court of appeals opinions to the Supreme Court's majority opinion.

and the courts of appeals is positively and significantly correlated with the length of the majority opinion. But citations by the courts of appeals alone are not significantly correlated with the length of the Supreme Court's majority opinion; we have no explanation.

Neither *Concur* nor *Subject Matter* is significant in any regression. The fact that concurring opinions do not elicit longer majority opinions is anomalous, since such opinions often reflect disagreement with the majority's reasoning. Not always, of course; they may address a point that the majority opinion omitted because it did not command a majority of the Justices; or they may criticize a dissent—"riding shotgun," as it were, for the author of the majority opinion.

The time dummy variables are highly significant, indicating that majority opinions were longer in both the 1980 and 1990 terms. As the number of decisions declined, from 179 in 1963 to 143 in 1980 to 124 in 1990, Supreme Court Justices wrote (or had their law clerks write) longer majority opinions. This may be attributable to the growth in the ratio of staff to number of cases. In 1963 the Justices had only two law clerks apiece; by 1990 they had four even though the number of majority opinions had declined significantly.

We turn now to dissents in the courts of appeals. We started with 500 cases randomly selected from volumes 888 to 921 of the *Federal Reporter,* second series. Most of the opinions in these volumes were published in 1990. We excluded 67 cases not published in that year, 21 duplicate cases, and 8 cases not decided in a published opinion. These adjustments left us with a sample of 404 cases, which we later expanded to 1025, covering 1989–1991.

Table 6.12 reveals that the majority opinions in our sample are on average 41 percent longer when there is a dissent.[27] (The comparable figure for the Supreme Court, calculated from Table 6.9, is 23 percent.) To correct for differences in importance between cases that do and do not draw a dissent, we divide our court of appeals sample into reversals and affirmances. Since the former are more likely to involve difficult issues, we expect them to induce longer majority opinions and more dissents. The table shows that opinions reversing are indeed typically longer than opinions affirming and also more likely to draw a dissent (9.6 percent versus 6.5 percent), although only the difference in length is statistically significant. Opinions that reverse are even longer if there is a dissent: 26 percent longer. Yet opinions that affirm are 54 percent longer if there is a dissent. This result may reflect increasing marginal effort cost, since opinions reversing are already longer than opinions affirming even when there is no dissent.

To determine more rigorously the impact of dissents on the length of majority opinions in the courts of appeals, we estimate the following regression equation:

$$W_{CA} = f(Dissent, Reverse, First, Caseload, Circuit, Civil, Subject\ Matter, u)$$

The principal independent variables are *Dissent, Reverse, First* (meaning the case was decided for the first time rather than after rehearing or re-

27. Frank B. Cross, *Decision Making in the U.S. Courts of Appeals* 174 (2007), using a different dataset, also finds that majority opinions in cases in which there is a dissent are longer.

Table 6.12 Words in Majority Opinions in Court of Appeals Cases, 1989–1991
(*number of cases in parentheses*)

Dissent	All	Reversed	Affirmed
No	3354	3799	3046
	(945)	(387)	(558)
Yes	4733*	4774*	4690*
	(80)	(41)	(39)
All	3462	3893	3153
	(1025)	(428)	(597)

Note: Reversals include reversed, reversed in part, and vacated.

mand[28]), and *Caseload* (number of appellate cases decided on the merits in each circuit per year divided by the sum of active and senior judges weighted by the number of votes by a senior judge relative to an active one). We expect positive coefficients on *Dissent, Reverse,* and *First* (there are likely to be more issues to discuss when a case is heard the first time) and a negative coefficient on *Caseload.* We add circuit dummies *(Circuit)* to account for circuit-specific factors that might affect the length of published opinions, such as different circuit rules or norms on publication of opinions. And we add subject-matter variables (either *Civil* = 1 for a civil case and 0 for a criminal one, or *Subject Matter,* which consists of dummy variables for respectively a criminal, civil rights, labor, economic, due process, privacy, or First Amendment case), to allow for the possibility that the type of case influences the length of a majority opinion.

Table 6.13 presents the regression results. We see that *Dissent, Reverse,* and *First* have positive and highly significant effects on the length of majority opinions. A dissent causes the length of the majority opinion to increase by roughly the same number of words (1380) as the combined effect of a decision's being a reversal (654 words) and being the first decision in the litigation (820 words). The circuit's caseload has, as effort aversion implies, a significant negative effect on the length of the majority opinion; an increase in the caseload from a low of 66.8 cases per judge (the average for the D.C. Circuit) to 130.1 (the mean of all circuits) re-

28. In our sample of 1025 court of appeals cases, 949 cases were decided for the first time, 9 on rehearing, 20 after remand to the district court, and 9 on remand from the Supreme Court; 34 could not be classified. We assigned the value 1 only to the 949 cases decided for the first time.

Table 6.13 Regression Analysis of Words in Majority Opinions in U.S. Court of Appeals
Cases, 1989–1991

	(1)	(2)
Dissent	1384**	1382**
	(4.65)	(4.54)
Reversal	654**	654**
	(4.44)	(4.33)
First	819**	822**
	(2.73)	(2.70)
Civil	139	—
	(0.99)	
Caseload	−7.34**	−7.45**
	(2.49)	(2.46)
Circuit Dummies	Yes**	Yes**
Subject-Matter Dummies	No	Yes
Constant	3829**	3812**
	(6.71)	(6.52)
R^2	.11	.12

Note: All regressions have 1025 observations and use robust standard errors.

duces the average number of words in a majority opinion by 468. Raw
caseload figures do not reflect differences in the average difficulty of cases
across circuits, however, and we have not tried to adjust for that difference. The circuit dummy variables are jointly significant in both equations; but with circuit caseload, subject matter, and other variables held
constant, only the Second and Eighth Circuits produce shorter, and the
Third Circuit longer, opinions than the other circuits. We find no significant effects of case type.

Our focus thus far has been on the costs of dissenting. We can estimate
the benefits by comparing the number of judicial citations to majority and
dissenting opinions. Table 6.14 compares the number of citations in Supreme Court and court of appeals opinions to majority and dissenting
opinions of the Supreme Court.

The average Supreme Court dissent is not heavily cited. A dissenting
opinion in cases decided by the Court during the 1963, 1980, and 1990
terms was cited on average only .24 times by the Supreme Court and 1.54
times by the courts of appeals. There are, of course, many more court of
appeals decisions than Supreme Court decisions; yet when the difference
is corrected for, court of appeals judges are found to be even less likely to
cite Supreme Court dissents than Supreme Court Justices are, maybe because lower courts are more tightly bound to follow majority rulings by

Table 6.14 Citations in Majority and Dissenting Opinions to 266 Supreme Court Opinions with Dissents, 1963, 1980, and 1990 Terms

	Supreme Court Citations		Court of Appeals Citations	
	Mean	Median	Mean	Median
One Dissenting Opinion				
Majority	7.81	5	144.96	60
One Dissent	0.24	0	1.54	0
Ratio	32.1	—	94.2	—
Two or More Dissenting Opinions				
Majority	9.93	6	146.97	87
Two or More Dissents	0.53	0	3.00	1.5
Ratio	18.6	—	49.0	—

Note: There were 206 cases with one dissenting opinion and 60 with two or more such opinions, for a total of 266. In the group of 206, 175 dissenting opinions were never cited by the Supreme Court and 108 were never cited by courts of appeals. In 38 of the 60 cases in which there were two or more dissents, the dissenting opinions were never cited by the Supreme Court and in 17 were never cited by courts of appeals. In contrast, of the 266 majority opinions, only 34 were never cited by the Supreme Court and only 19 were never cited by courts of appeals.

the Supreme Court than Supreme Court Justices are. Not only are the Justices less tethered to precedent, but because of this a number of dissenting opinions in the Supreme Court later became law—some, indeed, landmarks of the law (such as the dissents in *Plessy v. Ferguson, Lochner v. New York, Abrams v. United States, Olmstead v. United States, Minersville School District v. Gobitis,* and *Betts v. Brady*) and thus de facto majority opinions.

The ratio of citations to a Supreme Court majority opinion to citations to the dissent in cases in which there is one dissenting opinion is on average 32 to 1 in the Supreme Court but 94 to 1 in the courts of appeals. When there are two or more dissenting opinions, dissents are cited more frequently, but still rarely; the ratio falls to 19 to 1 in the Supreme Court and 49 to 1 in the courts of appeals.

The regression analysis in Table 6.15 shows that the more frequently the majority opinion is cited, the more frequently the dissent is cited, and also that there are more citations in the courts of appeals to Supreme Court dissents when the Supreme Court's majority opinion mentions the dissent and when the number of dissenting Justices is greater. But this effect is not found in citations by the Supreme Court to dissenting opinions.

Table 6.15 Regression Analysis of Citations in Supreme Court Majority Opinions to
Dissenting Opinions in 1963, 1980, and 1990

	Supreme Court Citations	Court of Appeals Citations
Supreme Court Citations to Majority Opinion	.012**	—
	(2.77)	
Court of Appeals Citations to Majority Opinion	—	.002**
		(2.90)
Signed Opinions in Orally Argued Cases	.077	.640
	(0.64)	(1.32)
Two or More Dissenting Opinions	.228*	.837
	(2.05)	(1.75)
Mention	−.025	.968*
	(0.23)	(2.06)
Number of Dissenting Votes	.038	.415*
	(0.83)	(2.09)
1980 Term	.266*	.536
	(2.42)	(1.14)
1990 Term	.149	.646
	(1.19)	(1.21)
Constant	−.120	−.803
	(0.93)	(1.45)
R^2	.08	.15
Number of Observations	266	266

Note: We also estimated regressions of citations to majority opinions. Signed opinions in orally argued cases had a positive and significant effect on both Supreme Court and court of appeals citations. The only other significant variables were the 1980 and 1990 year variables, which had positive and significant effects in at least one regression.

As shown in Table 6.16, dissents in the courts of appeals are almost never cited by those courts. The mean and median number of citations to a dissent are .138 and 0 both within and outside the circuit, whereas majority opinions in cases in which there is a dissent are cited an average of 13.2 times inside the circuit and 5.3 times outside, the medians being 7 and 3.5.[29] Of the 82 dissenting opinions in our court of appeals sample, 72 were never cited inside the circuit and 75 never outside. There thus appears to be little payoff to a court of appeals judge from writing a dissent—the influence of his dissent, at least as proxied by citations to it, is likely to be zero. This helps to explain the low dissent rate in the courts of

29. There is a positive correlation between citations to dissenting and majority opinions, but it is weak and not statistically significant.

Table 6.16   Citations to 82 Court of Appeals Opinions with Dissents, 1990

Opinion	Inside Circuit		Outside Circuit	
	Mean	Median	Mean	Median
Majority	13.188	7	5.338	3.5
Dissent	0.138	0	0.1375	0
Ratio	95.9	—	38.8	—

Table 6.17   Certiorari Petitions Denied and Granted in the 1986–1994 Terms Seeking Review of Federal Court of Appeals Decisions

	Court of Appeals Decision	
	No Dissent	Dissent
Random Sample of Cases in Which Cert. Was Denied	90.6%	9.4%
(N = 683)	(619)	(64)
All Cases in Which Cert. Was Granted (N = 693)	67.7%	32.3%
	(469)	(224)
Number of Cases	1088	288

Notes:

1. The numbers in parentheses denote the number of cases.

2. The source of these data is the Epstein-Segal dataset mentioned in chapter 3, note 32.

appeals relative to any plausible estimate of the amount of actual disagreement among court of appeals judges.

Another possible benefit of dissenting is that the Supreme Court is more likely to grant certiorari when there is a dissent in the court of appeals. Comparing the 693 petitions for certiorari that were granted in the 1986 through 1994 terms (excluding petitions to review en banc decisions) with a random sample of 683 petitions to review court of appeals decisions that were denied in the same terms, we see in Table 6.17 that there was a dissenting opinion in almost 33 percent of the court of appeals decisions in which certiorari was granted but in fewer than 10 percent of decisions in which certiorari was denied.

But the probability that the Supreme Court will review a court of appeals decision in which there was a dissent, and having decided to review it reverse, is too low to create a strong incentive for court of appeals judges to dissent, given dissent aversion, unless a judge would derive very great self-expressive utility from dissenting. There were 89,942 decisions in orally argued cases in the courts of appeals in the 1986–1994 terms;[30] this would be the pool from which almost all court of appeals cases decided by the Supreme Court would come. Suppose the dissent rate in this pool of cases was 7.8 percent (the rate in our Songer sample); then in 7015 decisions there was a dissent. Yet we know from the table that only 224 petitions for certiorari were granted during that period in cases in which there had been dissents in the courts of appeals. Suppose two-thirds resulted in a reversal; then there would be 149 cases in which a dissent in the court of appeals had resulted in a reversal by the Supreme Court. That is only 2 percent of our estimate of the number of court of appeals cases in which there was a dissent, which suggests that the expected payoff from dissenting for a judge deciding whether to dissent in the hope of obtaining a reversal by the Supreme Court is small. Furthermore, there is a danger of a double defeat: if a judge dissents and the decision from which he dissents is affirmed by the Supreme Court, his position has been rejected not only by his colleagues but also by his judicial superiors.

We expect the dissent rate in a circuit to be higher when there are more judges in the circuit, their workload is lighter, and their ideological differences are greater. A larger number of judges lowers the collegiality cost of dissenting; a lighter workload lowers the opportunity cost of dissenting; and greater ideological differences increase the occasions on which a judge would be inclined to dissent.

To test these hypotheses, we regress in Table 6.18 court of appeals dissent rates on possible explanatory factors. We compute dissent rates by dividing number of dissents by number of cases terminated on the merits; the number of judges by the number of active judges plus the number of senior judges adjusted downward by the ratio of the average number of cases in which a senior judge participates to the number in which an active judge participates; workload by cases terminated on the merits divided by number of judges;[31] and judges' ideological differences by the standard deviation of their ideologies as measured by the senatorial cour-

30. Calculated from Richard A. Posner, *The Federal Courts: Challenge and Reform* 72 (tab. 3–6) (1996).

31. Caseload is an imperfect measure of workload because cases are not uniform with respect to the time and effort required to decide them. The Administrative Office of the U.S. Courts calculates weighted caseload statistics for the district courts but not for the courts of appeals. Posner, note 30 above, at 227–236, calculates weighted caseload statistics for the

Table 6.18   Regression Analysis of Log of Dissent Rates in Courts of Appeals, 1990–2006

	(1)	(2)
Judges (adjusted)	.634**	.676**
	(3.88)	(3.65)
Caseload (adjusted)	−.685**	−.714**
	(2.98)	(3.06)
Standard Deviation of Ideology	.584*	.689*
	(2.09)	(2.51)
Year Dummies	No	Yes**
Year	−.037**	—
	(4.52)	
Constant	72.34**	−1.168
	(4.44)	(1.14)
R²	.47	.49
Number of Observations	204	204

Note: Data for 2007, included in Table 6.4, are omitted from this table because we have no 2007 data for Standard Deviation of Ideology.

tesy method. We include dummy year variables and cluster the observations by circuit. All variables are in logarithms except for the year variables.

The table reveals that the dissent rate is positively related to the number of judges and the ideological difference among judges in the circuit and negatively to the circuit's caseload. The correlations are high. For example, a 10 percent increase in the number of judges in a circuit increases the dissent rate by about 6.5 percent, and a 10 percent increase in caseload per judge decreases the dissent rate by about 7 percent. The dissent rate in the court of appeals declined between 1990–1992 and 2005–2007 from 3.4 to 2.4 percent, a 23 percent decline ((3.1 − 2.4) / 3.1 = .23). This decline was broadly consistent with the 33 percent increase in caseload during this period from an unweighted mean across circuits of 155 cases per active judge to 204 cases per active judge. But we hesitate to draw a causal inference because that growth and the consequent reduction in the dissent rate may both have been due to an increase in the proportion of meritless cases.

We need to consider another bit of evidence potentially relevant to the effect of circuit size and caseload on dissent rates. In 1982 the Fifth Cir-

courts of appeals for 1993, and that year falls within our sample period, but we have not calculated weighted caseloads for the other years in the sample.

cuit was divided into the Fifth Circuit and the newly created Eleventh Circuit. Before the split, the Fifth Circuit had 25 judges; after, it had 13 judges and the Eleventh Circuit had 12. Since the cost in impaired collegiality of dissenting is greater the smaller the circuit, the sharp drop in the number of judges in the Fifth Circuit could be expected to have led to a reduction in the frequency of dissents. And because the collegiality cost would be roughly the same in the newly created Eleventh Circuit, the combined Fifth and Eleventh Circuits should have a lower overall dissent rate than the Fifth before it was divided. That is what we find, as shown in Figure 6.2. The average dissent rate in the Fifth Circuit was 3.6 percent from 1971 to 1982 and 1.7 percent from 1983 to 2007, and also 1.7 percent in both the Eleventh Circuit and the combined Fifth and Eleventh Circuits.

A closer look at the data, however, suggests that the decline in the dissent rate after 1982 was caused not by a reduction in circuit size but instead by a caseload surge (see Figure 6.3), which would have increased the cost of dissenting. Although there were 25 judges in the Fifth Circuit before the split, 10 had been appointed in 1980, so for most of the presplit era the number of judges (15) had been only slightly greater than the number (13) after. It is implausible to attribute the large drop in the dissent rate in 1982–2007 to the small decrease in the number of judges. Regression analysis confirms this, revealing a significant decrease in the dissent rate because of an increase in the caseload but no significant effect of changes in the number of judges.[32]

Effects of Senior Status and Age on Dissent Rates

We have emphasized personal motives, such as dissent aversion, as factors in a judge's decision to dissent when he disagrees with the majority. Two correlated factors that we have not yet discussed may affect the

---

32. The regression is

$$D = \quad .062^{**} - .0002\,(C/\mathcal{J})^{**} - .0003\,\mathcal{J} \quad R^2 = .74$$
$$(7.67)\quad\quad (10.07)\quad\quad\;\; (0.80)$$

where D = dissent rate, $C/\mathcal{J}$ = caseload, and $\mathcal{J}$ = number of judges.

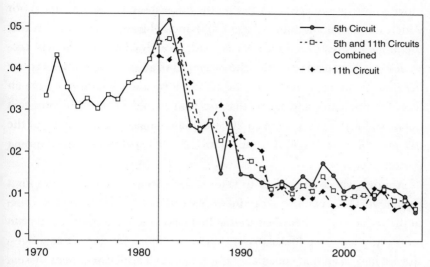

Figure 6.2   Ratio of Dissents to Cases Terminated on the Merits in the Fifth and Eleventh Circuits, 1971–2007

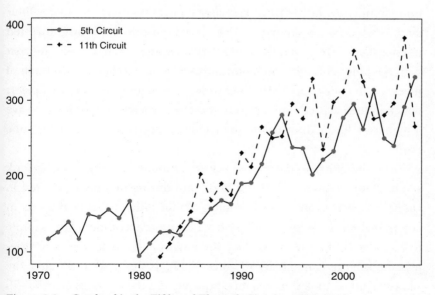

Figure 6.3   Caseload in the Fifth and Eleventh Circuits, 1971–2007

Note: Caseload = terminations on the merits/number of judges.

judge's motivation: age and whether the judge has taken senior status (for which minimum eligibility is age 65), which almost always implies that the judge desires to reduce his caseload, though sometimes he will take senior status instead to reduce the caseloads of all the judges on his court, because by taking senior status he creates a vacancy. We examine the effect of senior status and age on dissents using two databases: the Sunstein database for the years 1995 to 2008 and a database created by us of the careers of judges who took senior status in a different though overlapping period.

A judge who by deciding to take senior status signifies a desire for a lighter workload can further reduce his workload by dissenting less often in the reduced number of cases that he hears as a senior judge. This factor should lead to a lower dissent rate for senior than for active judges. But we have seen that collegiality is a reason that appellate judges dissent as infrequently as they do, and the benefits of collegiality are smaller for senior judges because they interact with their colleagues less frequently. A related factor is that judges on senior status occasionally and sometimes frequently (but active judges almost never) sit on cases outside their circuit, which is to say with judges in whom they have little invested in collegiality. Moreover, the more they visit, the less frequently they sit with the judges of their own court, further reducing the gains to them of investing in collegiality with those judges. We cannot be certain a priori which influence predominates, and therefore whether senior judges have a higher or lower dissent rate than active judges (or perhaps the same rate).

From the Sunstein database we drew a sample of all judges who took senior status between 1996 and 2007 and during that interval voted in cases both before and after becoming senior judges; this enables us to compare their behavior in each status, but our criteria limited the sample to 72 judges out of the more than 300 judges in the database. Nevertheless the sample contains 3756 votes—2571 before and 1185 after the sampled judges took senior status. Equivalently, these judges heard 3756 cases, since each judge cast one vote per case.

Table 6.19 presents the results separately for judges appointed by Republican and by Democratic Presidents, in order to control for the effects of panel composition. We find as expected that *R*s and *D*s are more likely

Table 6.19 Dissents and Panel Effects for 72 Judges Who Took Senior Status between 1996 and 2007

R and D Identity of Other Panel Members	Votes of Judges When on Active Status		Votes of the Same Judges When on Senior Status	
	R	D	R	D
RR	1.26% (712)	3.28% (183)	1.85% (324)	3.74% (107)
RD	1.42 (986)	1.10 (272)	1.78 (393)	3.01 (133)
DD	5.45 (312)	2.83 (106)	9.72 (144)	2.48 (84)
All Panels	1.99 (2010)	2.14 (561)	3.14 (861)	3.09 (324)

Note: In this and the succeeding tables in this chapter the number of cases is in parentheses.

to dissent when a President of the opposite party appointed the other panel members. We also find that senior status does not reduce and may actually increase the dissent rate. In five of the six possible comparisons between Rs and Ds before and after the judge took senior status (holding the ideological identity of the other panel members constant), the dissent rate is higher in senior than in active status, though in none of the comparisons is the difference statistically significant.

We also estimated logit regressions on the probability of dissent (1 if the judge dissented, 0 if not) for Rs and Ds separately. The independent variables include a dummy variable for whether the judge's vote was cast before or after he took senior status (0 if before and 1 if after); panel composition dummy variables (the omitted category is DD); a dummy variable indicating whether the court reversed or affirmed the district court (we include this variable because we found earlier in the chapter that if the court reverses, the dissent rate is significantly higher); and dummy variables for the judge's sex, race, and whether he had been promoted from the district court, the 14 subject-matter areas in the Sunstein database, the individual circuits, and the date of the decision. We clustered the regressions by judges to take account of the possibility that some judges may dissent more or less often than others even after we have controlled for all the variables in the regression. In both the R and D regressions the coefficient of senior status is positive but not statistically significant. When we combine Rs and Ds in a single regression, holding panel effects constant by including only votes of judges on mixed R/D panels, we also find a positive but now a statistically significant effect of senior status on the frequency of dissent.

We can also use the Sunstein data to test whether the dissent rate of senior judges depends on whether they sit in their home circuit or in another circuit. The judges in the sample cast 125 of their 1185 votes (10.5 percent) after they took senior status in other circuits, compared to only 3 of 2570 votes when they were active judges. Table 6.20 reveals that the dissent rates of senior judges are higher in their home circuit than in other circuits in all panels and also in just mixed panels, but the difference is not statistically significant. We added a dummy variable for dissenting votes in other circuits to the regressions described in the preceding paragraph; again the coefficients were not significant.

To examine the effect of age on dissents without confounding the effects of age and of senior status, we limit our analysis of age to the votes of active judges. We expect a decline in effort beyond some age, which should lower the dissent rate. But the discounted benefits in future collegiality also decline with age, and the net effect of age on dissents is therefore uncertain. We distinguish among five age groups, as shown in Table 6.21. The first column includes the votes (cases heard: a total of 10,928) of all the judges; the second includes only the votes of judges on mixed

Table 6.20   Dissents in Home and Other Circuits of 72 Judges Who Took Senior Status between 1996 and 2007

	Dissent Rate of Senior Judges on All Panels	Dissent Rate of Senior Judges on Mixed *(RD)* Panels
Home Circuit	3.4% (1058)	2.4% (526)
Another Circuit or Circuits	1.6% (127)	0% (60)
Both Types of Circuit	3.12 (1185)	2.1% (526)

Table 6.21   Dissents and Age

	Dissent Rates of Active Judges	
Age Group	All Panels (1)	Mixed *(RD)* Panels (2)
< 65	3.10% (7941)	2.23% (3721)
66–69	2.24 (1918)	1.33 (901)
70–74	3.14 (636)	2.81 (285)
75–79	4.46 (269)	1.65 (121)
≥ 80	1.22 (184)	2.50 (80)

panels, thus holding panel effects constant. The dissent rates are sometimes lower and sometimes higher above age 65 in both columns (1) and
(2), but the differences among age groups are not statistically significant.
We estimated separate logit regressions for Rs and Ds, adding four age
dummies (the omitted age category is < 65) to the independent variables
in the senior status regressions; again we find no significant effect of age.

A shortcoming of using the Sunstein database for these purposes is
that its limited time period (1995 to 2008) eliminates many votes of
judges before they took senior status or before they reached the age of 65.
A possibly offsetting benefit, though, is that the before and after periods
(either before and after taking senior status or before and after reaching
65) are close in time, and therefore the votes are less likely to be influenced by the declining dissent rate in the court of appeals over the last 20
years (see Table 6.18) and by changes over time in the ideological composition of the different circuits.

To compensate for the compressed time period in the Sunstein sample, we created a sample of votes cast by two court of appeals judges from
each circuit (except the Federal Circuit, which we consistently omit from
our analysis in this book), chosen randomly from the limited pool of
judges who had at least 20 years of service on their court by the end of the
sample period (2011), of which at least 5 years had been spent as a senior
judge. Table 6.22 presents the results.

The table reveals that the dissent rate of active judges tends to decline
between the first and second half of their active service. Although the difference is small (see the averages at the bottom of columns (6) and (7)), it
is statistically significant because the sample size is so large (> 90,000
votes). We find significantly lower dissent rates in the second half than in
the first half of active service for 14 judges, a significantly higher rate in
the second half for only 1 judge, and insignificant differences for the remaining 9 judges. Senior judges dissent only slightly less often than active judges who are in the second half of their active service, and the difference is statistically significant. Of the 24 judges, 10 had significantly
higher dissent rates as active judges, 3 significantly lower, and for 11 there
were no significant differences.

Table 6.22 also shows that, on average, senior judges have significantly
higher dissent rates when they visit other circuits, although this shows up

Table 6.22 Dissent Rate Statistics for 24 Court of Appeals Judges

	Circuit (1)	Year Judge Was Appointed (2)	Year Judge Took Senior Status (3)	Years as Active Judge (4)	Years as Senior Judge (5)	Dissent Rate in First Half of Active Service (6)	Dissent Rate in Second Half of Active Service (7)	Senior Dissent Rate (8)	Senior Dissent Rate in Home Circuit (9)	Senior Dissent Rate as Visitor (10)	Age When Took Senior Status (11)
Selya	1st	1986	2006	20	6	0.7% (2373)	0.5% (1884)	0.5% (828)	0.5% (827)	0% (1)	72
Stahl	1st	1992	2001	9	11	0.8% (1028)	0.9% (909)	1.1% (926)	1.0% (881)	2.2% (45)	70
Kearse	2d	1979	2002	23	10	3.4%** (1117)	1.8% (2167)	1.0% (1274)	1.0% (1274)	NA	65
Newman	2d	1979	1997	18	15	2.2% (920)	2.5%** (1092)	0.3% (2837)	0.3% (2820)	0% (17)	65
Nygaard	3d	1988	2005	17	7	5.0%* (641)	2.9%** (1259)	1.1% (1238)	1.1% (1238)	NA	65
Aldisert	3d	1968	1986	18	26	4.4%* (911)	7.3%** (600)	1.6% (2229)	1.5% (1476)	1.9% (753)	67
Hamilton	4th	1991	1999	8	13	0.7% (2307)	0.6%* (3178)	0.3% (10,080)	0.3%** (10,025)	3.6% (55)	65
Phillips	4th	1978	1994	16	18	2.3%** (1017)	0.8% (4581)	0.6% (3226)	0.6% (3166)	0% (60)	72
Higginbotham	5th	1982	2006	24	6	1.1%** (3195)	0.1% (7627)	0.2% (3240)	0.2% (3226)	NA	68
Reavley	5th	1979	1990	11	22	2.4% (889)	2.0%** (1041)	0.6% (6308)	0.6% (5418)	0.6% (890)	69
Merritt	6th	1977	2001	24	11	3.9%** (2828)	2.4%** (3033)	5.8% (1113)	5.8% (1080)	3.0% (33)	65
Keith	6th	1977	1995	18	17	1.6%	2.1%	2.3%	2.3%	1.7%	73

Judge	Circuit										
Bauer	7th	1974	1994	20	18	2.5%** (925)	1.2%** (2031)	0.5% (2406)	0.5% (1819)	NA (587)	68
Bowman	8th	1983	2003	20	9	2.5%** (1091)	0.4% (2614)	0.4% (5429)	0.4% (5429)	0% (0)	70
Bright	8th	1968	1985	17	17	2.4% (2249)	2.8%** (3682)	6.7% (1457)	8.5%** (1358)	2.6% (99)	66
Wallace	9th	1972	1996	24	16	5.5%** (1054)	1.9% (1828)	1.4% (2821)	1.4% (1937)	1.3% (884)	68
Hug	9th	1977	2002	25	10	1.6%** (1371)	0.5% (3074)	0.6% (5287)	0.5%* (4824)	4.8% (463)	71
Holloway	10th	1968	1992	24	20	3.9%* (1276)	2.0%* (4526)	3.5% (1690)	3.5% (1669)	NA (21)	69
Seymour	10th	1979	2005	26	7	2.1%** (845)	1.1% (1021)	0.5% (1419)	0.4%* (1419)	5.6% (18)	65
Cox	11th	1988	2000	12	12	2.7% (1836)	3.6%* (3407)	1.3% (917)	1.2% (899)	4.8% (21)	65
Kravitch	11th	1981	1996	15	16	3.2% (744)	2.7%* (568)	1.5% (1104)	1.5% (1083)	1.3% (21)	76
Edwards	DC	1980	2001	21	11	2.8%* (1298)	1.7%** (1039)	0.7% (2187)	0.7% (2110)	NA	65
Silberman	DC	1985	2000	15	12	3.0%** (1042)	0.9% (2636)	0.9% (1360)	0.9% (1360)	0% (0)	65
Average of All Judges		1980	1998	18	14	2.5%** (936)	1.4%** (2083)	1.2% (339)	1.3%* (338)	1.8% (1)	68
						(34,486)	(57,949)	(60,954)	(42,923)	(4085)	

Notes:

1. "NA" means that judge did not visit any other circuit.

2. The total number of votes cast by senior judges (60,954) exceeds the sum of votes cast by senior judges in their home circuit (42,923) and other circuits (4085) because the total includes all 24 judges but the latter two sums include only the 18 judges who visited.

3. The asterisks in column (6) denote the levels of significance (* at the .05 level and ** at the .01 level) between the first and second half of active service. In column (7) the levels of significance are between the second half of active service and senior status and in column (9) between senior status in the home and in visiting circuits.

4. The average of all judges is a weighted average, the weight for each judge being the number of votes he cast.

only weakly in the statistics for the individual judges. In this group of 18 judges, 3 had significantly higher dissent rates as visitors and 1 a significantly lower dissent rate as a visitor; for 14 there was no significant difference.

Turning now to the effect of age on dissent rate, we see that 9 judges took senior status at age 65 and 15 later and that the former group had had a significantly higher dissent rate when they were active judges than judges taking senior status after age 65—2 percent compared to 1.7 percent. But they had a significantly lower dissent rate after taking senior status—.8 percent compared to 1.4 percent. We have no explanation for this pattern.

The results in Table 6.22 are suggestive but not definitive, because we have not collected data on the individual cases and therefore have not been able to adjust for other possible influences on dissent rates, including panel effects and other variables included in the Sunstein regressions. Nor have we tried to adjust for the declining dissent rate in the courts of appeals in the 1990 to 2007 period. The decline was from 3.1 percent in 1900–1993 to 2.5 percent in 2004–2007, and the coefficient on the time trend variable in the dissent regressions in Table 6.18 is negative and highly significant. Adjusting the dissent rates for that trend would eliminate many of the differences associated with age and senior status in Table 6.22. Furthermore, for some of the judges, particularly Bauer, Hamilton, and Higginbotham, the number of cases that our Westlaw search records them as having heard per year of senior status is too high. We do not understand this anomaly (it seems to be a Westlaw problem), but eliminating these judges from our sample would not alter the results significantly.

Our reasons for presenting results for each judge rather than just the aggregate results (the last two rows) are twofold. First, with such a small sample of judges (24, although they cast a total of 153,389 votes), and with the votes distributed unevenly among the judges, as shown in the table, an outlier judge can skew the aggregate results. Second, we wanted to show the striking variance in dissent rates across judges. That variance underscores the important question—not explored in this book except with reference to Supreme Court Justices, mainly in chapters 3 and 7, and court of appeals judges only in chapter 8—of differences among individual judges. Those differences invite further analysis—for example, of the existence noted briefly at the beginning of this chapter of dissent preference, as distinct from the more common dissent aversion. A further extension of the analysis in this section would consider the full careers of appellate judges. Neither the Sunstein nor the Songer data allow us to do this, so it would require a substantial investment in data collection.

CHAPTER 7

The Questioning of Lawyers at Oral Argument

C HIEF JUSTICE JOHN ROBERTS and others have noticed that the lawyer at an oral argument in the Supreme Court who is asked more questions than his opponent is likely to lose. Roberts examined 28 cases—14 each from the 1980 and 2003 terms. In 24 of the cases the Justices posed more questions to the losing party, leading Roberts to conclude that "the secret to successful advocacy is simply to get the Court to ask your opponent more questions."[1] (This probably is true in the federal courts of appeals as well, but our analysis is limited to the Supreme Court; oral arguments in the courts of appeals are not transcribed, so it is infeasible to count questions digitally, let alone to associate particular questions with particular judges.)

Three other studies reach similar conclusions. Two, like Roberts's, involve very small samples.[2] In contrast, Timothy Johnson and his coau-

---

1. John G. Roberts, Jr., "Oral Advocacy and Re-emergence of a Supreme Court Bar," 30 *Journal of Supreme Court History* 68 (2005).

2. Sarah Shullman, "The Illusion of Devil's Advocacy: How the Justices of the Supreme Court Foreshadow Their Decisions during Oral Argument," 6 *Journal of Appellate Practice and Process* 271 (2004); Lawrence S. Wrightsman, *Oral Arguments before the Supreme Court* 138–141 (2008).

thors analyzed all oral arguments in cases decided in the 1979 through 1995 terms, and after controlling for other factors that might affect outcome found that the Court indeed tended to rule against the party asked more questions.[3] We use their data but update the data through the 2009 term.

There are two competing explanations for the phenomenon revealed by these studies. The first is legalistic. Suppose a judge asks a question of one of the lawyers and gets an unsatisfactory answer. So he asks a follow-up question, and suppose he again gets an unsatisfactory answer. The longer the string of such answers, the likelier the judge will be to believe that the lawyer has a weak case, and so the likelier the judge will be to rule against the lawyer's client. Moreover, a judge who coming into the argument is (as is quite likely) leaning against one party on the basis of a reading of the briefs and his other preargument study may direct most of his questions to the lawyer for that party in order to test whether the party's case is indeed as weak as the judge's preparatory study had indicated.[4]

The competing explanation, the realist one, is that strategic reasons, rooted in the limitations of formal judicial deliberation, cause judges to concentrate their questioning on the party whom they want to lose the appeal. Although appellate judges like to say they deliberate carefully before deciding a case, deliberation in most appellate courts is limited in duration, artificial in structure, stilted in content,[5] and, in general, overrated as an effective means of exchanging ideas, sharpening arguments, and forging consensus. Judicial deliberation usually is limited to a brief conference shortly after the court has heard oral argument in several cases; it is rare for judges to discuss a case with each other before their post-argument conference. At the conference judges speak their piece, usually culminating quickly in a statement of the vote they're casting. They speak either in order of seniority, as in the Supreme Court, or in reverse order of seniority, as in many of the federal courts of appeals. Often

3. Timothy R. Johnson et al., "Inquiring Minds Want to Know: Do Justices Tip Their Hands with Questions at Oral Argument in the U.S. Supreme Court?" 29 *Journal of Law and Policy* 241 (2009).

4. We thank Chris Nosko for suggesting the first explanation. The second was suggested by Justice Ginsburg to Linda Greenhouse.

5. See Richard A. Posner, *How Judges Think* 2–3, 302–304 (2008).

there is no discussion at all but merely statements of the judges' votes. It is a serious breach of etiquette to interrupt a judge when he has the floor at the post-argument conference, and this too discourages free give-and-take.

The elaborate structuring of the deliberative process reflects the potential awkwardness of a discussion among persons who may not be comfortable arguing with each other. (It is also designed to economize on time.) Judges do not select their colleagues or successors, though Supreme Court Justices have occasionally weighed in on the choice of future colleagues.[6] Nor are all the judges of a court selected for the same reasons or on the basis of the same criteria. In short, the judges of a federal appellate court, including the Supreme Court, are not picked to form an effective committee. Even when they've been appointed by the same President, their appointment will have been influenced by considerations unrelated to the likelihood that the appointees would form with the other judges a coherent deliberating body—considerations such as friendship with a Senator, past political services, an appealing life story, a desired ideological profile, or personal-identity characteristics such as race, sex, and ethnicity that may give rise to sensitivities that inhibit discussion at conference of legal issues involving race, sex, religion, criminal rights, immigrants' rights, and other subjects that arouse strong emotions. The situation both of courts of appeals judges and of Supreme Court Justices resembles that of married couples in a society of arranged marriage and no divorce.

Judicial deliberation can nevertheless be productive when the issues discussed are technical in character rather than entangled with moral or political questions the frank discussion of which is likely to produce animosity. But many cases that reach the appellate level are indeterminate to legalist analysis; and when the outcome of a case cannot be determined by an objective method of inquiry, often because the judges do not share common premises, deliberation may have little influence on the judges'

---

6. In the 1850s the entire Supreme Court asked President Pierce to appoint John Campbell to the bench. See Henry J. Abraham, *Justices, Presidents, and Senators* 84 (1999). A century later Chief Justice Burger "constantly supplied the [Nixon Administration] with names" for "his" Court. John W. Dean, *The Rehnquist Choice* 52 (2001).

votes. As Aristotle put it, "We deliberate not about ends, but about means."[7]

Then too, a strong norm of equality within a court, and the limited power that even a chief judge has over his colleagues, promote a norm of collegiality, one aspect of which is treating colleagues with kid gloves and so avoiding sharp debate, especially on sensitive issues. A notable exception was Justice Frankfurter's efforts to dazzle his colleagues with his intelligence and erudition, which indeed exceeded theirs—but the result was to reduce his influence. Most judges, whatever their actual quality, consider themselves to be deservedly important people and expect to be treated respectfully by their colleagues, as well as by lawyers and staff.

Judicial deliberation, in short, is overrated. English judges until recently (when caseload pressures forced them to change their traditional methods) did not deliberate at all. They were committed to the principle of "orality"—that everything a judge does must be done in public, to facilitate public monitoring of judicial behavior. They actually were *forbidden* to deliberate; instead, at the end of the lawyers' appellate arguments each judge would state his view of the case. Yet the English judiciary was highly regarded. And as we noted in chapter 6, panels of the highly regarded Second Circuit did not routinely deliberate during the era in which Judge Henry Friendly was its dominant figure; instead they exchanged memos after oral argument.

Questioning at oral argument provides a supplement to or even substitute for judicial deliberation.[8] The opportunity cost is zero because judges have to attend oral argument. Although the post-argument conference must also be attended, it does not have a fixed length, so judges in-

7. *Nicomachean Ethics*, bk. 3, ch. 2, p. 11, in *Aristotle*, vol. 19, p. 137 (Loeb Classical Library, H. Rackham trans., 2d ed. 1934).

8. Several Justices have made this point. See, for example, William H. Rehnquist, *The Supreme Court* 244 (1999), noting that "judges' questions, although nominally directed to the attorney arguing the case, may in fact be for the benefit of their colleagues," and Ruth Bader Ginsburg, "Remarks on Appellate Advocacy," 50 *South Carolina Law Review* 567, 569 (1999), saying that "sometimes we ask questions with persuasion of our colleagues in mind." See also Joseph T. Thai and Andrew M. Coats, "The Case for Oral Argument in the Supreme Court of Oklahoma," 61 *Oklahoma Law Review* 695 (2008); Timothy R. Johnson, *Oral Arguments and Decision Making on the United States Supreme Court* (2004).

cur a cost if they spend a lot of time at the conference wrangling with each other. Concern with sharp-edged confrontational debate among judges is alleviated at oral argument because the judges are talking directly to the lawyers and only indirectly to their colleagues. One can imply in one's questioning that a lawyer's argument is ridiculous, but one cannot call the same argument ridiculous when it is made by a colleague at the post-argument conference. So oral argument, which precedes the conference, gives a judge a shot at trying to persuade a colleague nonconfrontationally before the colleague decides how to vote.

Questioning at oral argument also gives a judge an opportunity to signal colleagues who respect his superior expertise regarding a particular type of case. Without that signal the colleague might vote the "wrong" way at conference—before the more knowledgeable judge had a chance to speak, if the colleague spoke before him in the prescribed order of discussion. The vote would be tentative, but once a judge casts even a tentative vote he may fear loss of face if he allows his mind to be changed by another judge at the conference. We know from the discussion of voting "fluidity" in chapter 3 that Supreme Court Justices sometimes change their vote between the post-argument conference and the decision. But that is rare unless the switchers join the majority rather than the dissenters and so can be credited with giving up their personal views in deference to the majority and for the sake of consensus. And there is less loss of face when the switch occurs after the conference rather than in the presence of the other Justices.

The realist theory of questioning at oral argument that we have just been expounding is especially applicable to the Supreme Court. Because of the indeterminacy of so many of its cases to lawyerly arguments, Justices often make up their mind before oral argument, that is, before the lawyers have completed presenting their case. Indeed, since Justices choose which cases they will hear, their minds will often be made up when they decide, long before the argument, whether to vote to hear the case. But as long as not all the Justices have already made up their minds, those who have can use questioning at argument to try to persuade the undecided. This implies asking more questions of the lawyer for the party whom they plan to vote against, in order to punch holes in that lawyer's case and perhaps prevent him from articulating his best arguments (a form of filibustering). Hostile questions to a lawyer resemble cross-examination at trial and are more effective than softball questions pitched to the side the Justice favors, though Justices do ask questions of a party they are leaning in favor of, presumably questions designed to elicit information or argument that will advance the party's cause. And not all questioning at oral argument is tendentious; some questions are neutral quests for information to help an undecided Justice make up his or her mind.

If all the Justices have made up their minds before oral argument, there is no point in asking questions intended to sway their colleagues. But what we are calling making up one's mind before oral argument is more realistically understood as forming a probability, prior to hearing oral argument, that one will vote for a particular side. That is consistent with being persuadable by facts or reasons elicited at oral argument, perhaps in answer to a Justice's questions rather than as part of a lawyer's prepared remarks.

We said that a judge might be recognized by his colleagues as expert in the relevant field of law, so that questioning that conveys his view of the case will influence them before they vote. But this is more likely to be a factor in a court of appeals, with its heavier caseload, larger range of cases, and higher proportion of cases in which the judges do not have an emotional or ideological stake, than in the Supreme Court. In addition, the Court's light caseload, high ratio of law clerks to cases, quasi-specialization (a heavy concentration in constitutional law), and the tendency of prominent people to be self-important can be expected to make a Justice unlikely to defer to any supposed superior expertise possessed by another Justice.

And just as students of free speech distinguish between instrumental and expressive functions of speech, so questioning that signals a judge's view of the merits of the case being argued can provide expressive utility to a judge quite apart from its effect on other judges. This is especially likely in the Supreme Court because the views expressed by Justices in open court are newsworthy. Tendentious questioning enables a Justice to express himself to a potentially large audience, other than just in a judicial opinion, speech, or interview—settings in which judicial ethics forbid a judge to express himself about a pending or impending case. The secular increase in Justices' questioning may be connected to their growing immersion in a celebrity culture. The frequency with which a Justice's questions or comments from the bench invite and elicit laughter in the courtroom[9] may be evidence of this.

Although our emphasis is on strategic questioning, there is evidence that some questions that Justices ask are indeed innocently intended to elicit information. A content analysis of oral argument transcripts in 57 cases in the 2005–2008 terms found that information-seeking questioning was inverse to the number of words spoken by Justices at oral argument. Excluding Thomas, who asks virtually no questions, Alito was the least talkative and most inquisitive Justice, and Breyer, Scalia, and Souter the most talkative and least inquisitive.[10]

Empirical Analysis

Timothy Johnson and his colleagues, in the study we mentioned at the beginning of the chapter, downloaded all available transcripts of Supreme Court oral arguments and then used a computer program to count the number of questions asked by the Justices and the number of words in their questions.[11] We updated the data through the 2009 term using similar procedures. The earliest data that we (like them) used are for the 1979 term, because data for earlier terms were not in an analyzable form. But the data for the 1979–2003 terms are incomplete, because the transcripts for those terms don't reveal the names of Justices asking particular questions. For case characteristics we rely on the Spaeth database.

In 1970 the Court formally reduced the time allotted to each side from

---

9. See Adam Liptak, "A Taxonomy of Supreme Court Humor," *New York Times,* Jan. 24, 2011, p. A16; Adam Liptak, "So, Guy Walks Up to the Bar, and Scalia Says. . . ," *New York Times,* Dec. 31, 2005, p. A1.

10. James C. Phillips and Edward L. Carter, "Oral Argument in the Early Roberts Court: A Qualitative and Quantitative Analysis of Individual Justice Behavior," 11 *Journal of Appellate Practice and Process* 325 (2010).

11. See Johnson et al., note 3 above. We did a reliability analysis of a randomly drawn 10 percent sample of the data and found the counts by Johnson and his colleagues to be accurate.

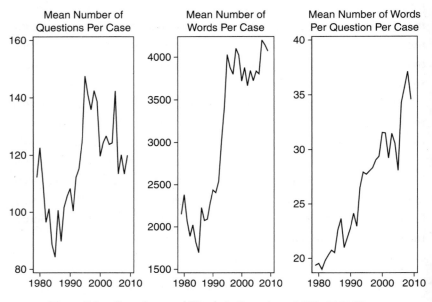

Figure 7.1   Questions and Words in Questions, 1979–2009 Terms

one hour to one-half hour.[12] (There are exceptions, but they are rare.) One might expect that with less time per case for questioning, there would be less questioning per case. We cannot determine this directly because we lack data for the period before the change in the time allotment, and indeed for a number of terms after it. But an indirect answer is suggested by Figure 7.1, which reveals that the average number of questions per case increased by 7 percent (from 112 to 120) from 1979 to 2009, while the total number of words in questions per case increased by 90 percent (from 2154 to 4075). The increase in the number of questions is not great, and we're about to see it disappear when we correct for other variables that influence that number. But the increase in the amount of speaking at oral argument by the Justices, relative to speaking by the lawyers, is great because of the increase in the length of questions.

To get a better fix on these trends, and on what might explain them, we regressed the log of the mean number of questions per case per term

12. This rule change formalized what had become the normal time allotment. See Eugene Gressman et al., *Supreme Court Practice* 672–673 (2007).

(lnQ), and the log of the mean number of total words in questions per case per term *(lnW),* on both a time (term) variable and a variable for number of cases per term. Each regression contains 31 observations, covering the 1979–2009 terms.

The regression results are

$$lnQ = 19.41 - .569lnCases - .006\,Term \qquad R^2 = .66$$

$$\quad (2.67) \qquad\quad (5.18) \qquad\quad (1.76)$$

$$lnW = -12.16 - .704lnCases + .012\,Term \qquad R^2 = .92$$

$$\quad (1.59) \qquad\quad (6.08) \qquad\quad (3.24)$$

In both regressions number of cases has a significant negative effect. For example, a 10 percent decline in that number leads to a 5.7 percent increase in questions and a 7 percent increase in words. Maybe as caseload shrinks, Justices have (and spend) more time to prepare for each oral argument and, being thus better prepared, engage the lawyers more by asking more and longer questions. But while there is a significant positive time trend (about a 1.2 percent growth rate per year) in total number of words (holding constant the number of cases), there is no significant time trend in number of questions.

A possible interpretation of the increase in wordiness that is independent of the decline in the number of cases is a "law professor" effect stemming from the appointment of Ginsburg, who replaced White in 1993, and of Breyer, who replaced Blackmun the following term. Until then Scalia was the only member of the Court who had been a professor—and we conjecture that until Breyer's appointment Scalia was the most voluble questioner. It is conjecture because we don't have question data by individual Justice until the 2004 term, but it is supported by the fact that over the period for which we do have data, Scalia ranked second only to Breyer in number of words uttered at oral argument. Ginsburg, however, the other former professor (there is now a fourth, Kagan, but she was appointed too recently to be included in our study), ranks only sixth.

Scalia and Roberts ask the most questions, followed closely by Breyer; Ginsburg again ranks sixth. We do not have individual data for White and Blackmun, but if their numbers were merely average (about 450), Breyer's appointment would be sufficient to explain the time trend (see Figure 7.1, middle panel) in number of words since the early 1990s. To test this hypothesis we added a 1994 dummy variable (Breyer's first term) to the regressions; the variable is indeed positive.[13]

With the replacement of Souter by Sotomayor and Stevens by Kagan the Justices' volubility has become remarkable: the lawyers have trouble getting a word in edgewise. Roberts has noted that the Justices have become more active at oral arguments—and sometimes get a little too "carried away."[14] The Justices joke and clown, interrupt each other,[15] give the impression of playing to the crowd—and certainly seem to be having a good time. Justice Thomas does not ask questions, but he chats and chuckles with Breyer, who sits beside him on the bench.

One explanation for the Justices' increased volubility may be a wallflower effect. Once several Justices emerge as active questioners, observers begin to wonder whether those who do not ask many questions are reticent because they can't keep up with the fast question-and-answer pace set by the active ones; thus Thomas's nearly complete silence at oral argument (he hasn't asked a question in years) has raised questions about his capacity. So there is pressure to conform to an emerging volubility norm. Another way to state this point is that a Court in which some Justices are talkative and some taciturn may not be an equilibrium, whereas all talkative or all taciturn may be one. Volubility is the current equilibrium, with Thomas an unexplained exception.

13. The regression results are:

$$lnQ = 28.06 - .393\ln \text{Cases} - .011 \text{ Term} + .196 \text{ Dummy94} \qquad R^2 = .74$$
$$(3.98) \qquad (3.46) \qquad (-3.16) \qquad (2.98)$$

$$lnW = -.820 - .473 \ln \text{Cases} + .005 \text{ Term} + .257 \text{ Dummy94} \qquad R^2 = .95$$
$$(0.12) \qquad (4.36) \qquad (1.66) \qquad (4.09)$$

With the 1994 dummy variable added to the regressions the time trend is significant in the question regression but not in the word regression.

14. Remarks by Chief Justice John Roberts at the Fourth Circuit Court of Appeals' Judicial Conference (White Sulphur Springs, West Virginia, June 27, 2009).

15. See Timothy R. Johnson, Ryan Black, and Justin Wedeking, "Pardon the Interruption: An Empirical Analysis of Supreme Court Justices' Behavior during Oral Argument," 55 *Loyola Law Review* 331 (2009); Adam Liptak, "Nice Argument, Counselor, But Let's Hear Mine," *New York Times*, Apr. 5, 2011, p. A12.

The existence of the volubility equilibrium—and at a very high level of volubility—may be, to return to an earlier point, a result of the Justices' immersion in a celebrity culture (see chapter 1), resisted only in recent years by Justice Souter, who is now retired. The existence of this equilibrium illustrates the weakness of hierarchy in the federal judiciary. The most effective public relations strategy for a court might well be dignified silence (and no dissents!), projecting a mystique of detachment, disinterested wisdom, consensus, and esoteric technical knowledge. Many institutions want to be opaque, and most want to control information about themselves. But opacity is not necessarily the optimal strategy for an individual Justice to pursue. He trades off institutional prestige (and perhaps efficacy) against his personal prestige, which may be served by his becoming a celebrity—a hero to the masses, or at least the highly educated masses, of one political persuasion or another.

The unprecedented range of the Justices' public activities—during the first 80 years of the twentieth century, the only Justice who had sought, and achieved, celebrity status was William O. Douglas[16]—makes their continued refusal to permit the televising of Supreme Court oral arguments puzzling. One explanation may be that for reasons of security they don't want be recognized by members of the public other than in venues of their choice. Another (suggested by Emily Bazelon) is that they lack confidence that they can fully control their "performance" in the rough-and-tumble of oral argument.

Number of Questions or Number of Words?

Returning to the issue with which we began—inferring the likely outcome of a case from the pattern of questions asked at oral argument—we consider whether number of questions or number of words in questions provides the stronger signal. Both measures are subject to the idiosyncrasies of particular Justices. Suppose Justice A is wordy and ponderous whereas

16. Hughes achieved celebrity status by resigning from the Supreme Court to run for President in 1916, but apparently had not sought it. Taft was a celebrity by virtue of having been President, but did not seek to enhance his celebrity status as Chief Justice; nor did Hughes, when he succeeded Taft as Chief Justice in 1930.

Justice B is precise and efficient. Then A might consume more of one party's time even though he asked fewer questions. But actually there is a strong positive correlation (.76) between number of questions and number of words.

Figures 7.2 and 7.3 present frequency distributions of the number of questions asked petitioner and respondent (actually, of course, asked the petitioner's lawyer and the respondent's lawyer, but we omit that refinement for the sake of brevity) in the 1979–2009 terms, and the number of words in those questions. The mean number of questions and of words (not shown in the figures) to both sides combined is 113 and 2838; the average number of words per question is therefore 25. The means for questions to petitioner and respondent are 56 and 57 for questions and 1391 and 1448 for words. The difference is statistically significant for words but not for questions. The standard deviations are large—23 (petitioner) and 223 (respondent) for questions and 630 (petitioner) and 669 (respondent) for words.

In Figures 7.4 and 7.5 we see that the losing party is indeed asked more questions (and with more words) than the winning one: specifically

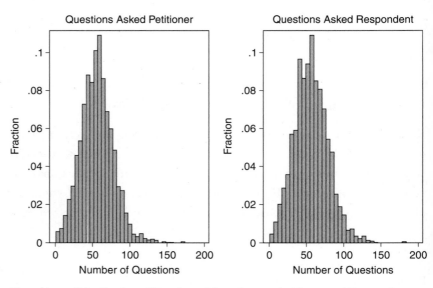

Figure 7.2   Distribution of Number of Questions to Petitioner and Respondent, 1979–2009 Terms

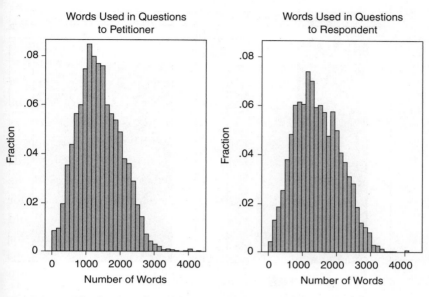

Figure 7.3   Distribution of Total Words in Questions to Petitioner and Respondent, 1979–2009 Terms

(again not shown in the figures) 6.3 more questions and 157 more words on average to the petitioner when the respondent wins and 4.4 more questions and 185 more words to the respondent when the petitioner wins.

Petitioners won 62 percent of the 3110 cases in our sample. But when the petitioner is asked fewer questions than the respondent, the petitioner's win rate increases to 72 percent, while when the respondent is asked fewer questions his rate of winning increases from 38 percent (100 percent minus 62 percent) to 46 percent. The results are similar if we substitute words for questions: for example, if there are fewer total words in the questions asked the respondent, this raises his rate of winning to 50 percent. In the small number of cases (55) in which the parties are asked the same number of questions, the petitioner and respondent success rates are not significantly different from their overall success rates.[17] Of course

17. Because the Justices' questions to each party contained the same number of words in only one case in the sample, we cannot study win rates for such cases.

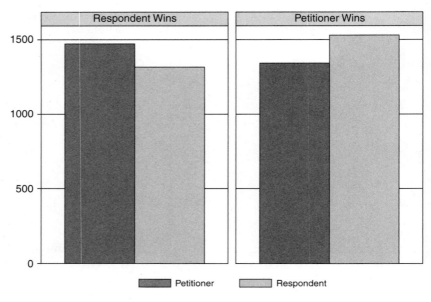

Figure 7.4   Mean Number of Words in Questions Asked Each Party, According to Which Party Wins, 1979–2009 Terms

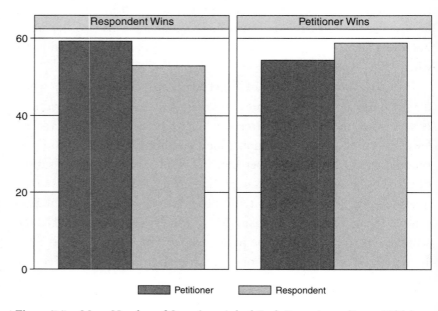

Figure 7.5   Mean Number of Questions Asked Each Party, According to Which Party Wins, 1979–2009 Terms

factors besides the ratio of the number of questions asked each side also influence which side wins, but we try to account for those later.

We expect that the smaller the difference in number of questions, or in words in questions, asked each side, the closer the votes are likely to be. Table 7.1 supports this hypothesis. The table omits cases in which not all nine Justices participated—about 12 percent of the cases in our sample— because the number of questions is likely to depend on the number of participating Justices. Later we test this proposition and find it supported.

We use regression analysis to deepen our analysis. The regression equations take the form

$$Win = f(Q, T, US, S, A, u).$$

The dependent variable is whether the petitioner wins. The independent variables are as follows: Q is a set of question variables—number of questions to each party, total number of words, and average number of words per question; the results are unaffected by which of these specifications is used. T is a set of dummy variables denoting the Court's terms, US a set identifying the federal government as a petitioner or respondent, S a set denoting four subject-matter areas (civil liberties, economics, judicial power, and federalism), and A a set relating to amicus curiae participation, including the number of briefs filed in support of the respective parties and whether the Solicitor General filed an amicus brief and if so on whose side.[18] The government and amicus (particularly the government amicus) variables are especially large and highly significant.

Table 7.2 lists the variables and their means and other information about them, and Table 7.3 presents the regression results. The question variables are the ones we're interested in; the others are control variables, that is, other factors that affect the dependent variable but do not test our hypotheses. Nevertheless, the regression results for two of the control variables are worth mentioning. First, the government as petitioner wins

---

18. We used a dataset created by Paul Collins of amicus curiae participation through the 2001 term. See www.psci.unt.edu/~pmcollins/data.htm (visited Dec. 9, 2011). We updated his dataset through the 2009 term.

Table 7.1 Number of Questions Asked Petitioner and Respondent and Closeness of the Outcome, 1979–2009 Terms

	Number of Cases (1)	Petitioner Wins			Respondent Wins		
		Questions to Petitioner (2)	Questions to Respondent (3)	Ratio (4)	Questions to Petitioner (5)	Questions to Respondent (6)	Ratio (7)
5–4	618	58.2	58.2	1.000	60.5	59.9	1.010
6–3	461	58.8	58.5	1.005	60.3	55.8	1.081
7–2	358	58.4	63.1	.926	63.2	54.5	1.160
8–1	253	54.5	59.9	.910	60.2	52.4	1.149
9–0	1076	51.2	58.9	.869	58.9	49.1	1.200
All Votes	2746	55.2	59.4	.929	60.2	54.0	1.115

Note: Cases in which fewer than nine Justices voted are excluded.

Table 7.2   Summary of Variables in Regression Analysis of Petitioner Win Rate, 1979–2009 Terms

	Mean	Standard Deviation	Minimum	Maximum
Petitioner Win Rate	0.62	0.48	0	1
Questions to Petitioner	56.2	21.8	1	174
Questions to Respondent	56.5	22.7	1	184
Words to Petitioner	1390.5	630.3	1	4375
Words to Respondent	1447.8	669.4	1	4123
Words/Questions to Petitioner	24.9	7.5	1	61.9
Words/Questions to Respondent	25.8	7.9	1	67.5
U.S. Petitioner	0.17	0.38	0	1
U.S. Respondent	0.14	0.35	0	1
Civil Liberties	0.56	0.50	0	1
Economics	0.24	0.43	0	1
Judicial Power	0.14	0.34	0	1
Federalism	0.05	0.23	0	1
Amicus Briefs Supporting Petitioner	2.29	3.50	0	44
Amicus Briefs Supporting Respondent	2.26	4.00	0	83
Solicitor General Amicus Briefs Supporting Petitioner	0.19	0.40	0	1
Solicitor General Amicus Briefs Supporting Respondent	0.11	0.31	0	1

Note: The number of observations is 3110.

about 76 percent of the time compared to the overall petitioner win rate of 62 percent, while as respondent the government wins 56 percent of the time compared to the overall respondent win rate of 38 percent. The government is a repeat player in the Supreme Court and seeks to maximize its win rate by persuading the Justices that it is a particularly scrupulous litigator (the Solicitor General is sometimes referred to as the "Tenth Justice"). Second, an amicus curiae brief in support of a party's position has a positive effect on the likelihood of that party's winning. There is a cost to preparing a brief and so a party can be expected to prepare one only if it expects the brief to influence the outcome. An alternative motive is to express solidarity with a party that belongs to the organization filing the amicus brief, or to draw attention to oneself or express a view publicly. But we expect, and our regression confirms, that the government, presumably because of its status as a repeat player, is reluctant to file an amicus brief in support of a party likely to lose.

Table 7.3　Logit Regression of Probability of a Win for Petitioner, 1979–2009 Terms

	(1)	(2)	(3)
Questions to Petitioner	−0.020**	—	−0.025**
	(9.34)		(10.80)
Questions to Respondent	0.020**	—	0.025**
	(9.31)		(11.10)
Words to Petitioner	—	−0.001**	—
		(11.62)	
Words to Respondent	—	0.001**	—
		(12.20)	
Words/Questions to Petitioner	—	—	−0.055**
			(6.86)
Words/Questions to Respondent	—	—	0.061**
			(7.80)
U.S. Petitioner	0.711**	0.739**	0.742**
	(5.68)	(5.82)	(5.84)
U.S. Respondent	−0.897**	−0.948**	−0.954**
	(7.37)	(7.61)	(7.68)
Amicus Briefs Supporting Petitioner	0.052**	0.053**	0.052**
	(3.00)	(3.07)	(3.04)
Amicus Briefs Supporting Respondent	−0.069**	−0.071**	−0.069**
	(4.66)	(4.46)	(4.47)
Solicitor General Amicus Briefs	0.759**	0.711**	0.695**
Supporting Petitioner	(6.10)	(5.63)	(5.52)
Solicitor General Amicus Briefs	−1.20**	−1.090**	−1.086**
Supporting Respondent	(8.05)	(7.67)	(7.67)
Subject-Matter Dummies	Yes	Yes	Yes
Term Dummies	Yes	Yes	Yes
Constant	0.514	0.458	0.515
	(1.40)	(1.40)	(1.17)

Note: The number of observations is again 3110.

As expected, the fewer the questions (or number of words in the questions) that the Justices ask a party's lawyer, holding constant the number asked the opponent, the higher the probability that the party will win. It makes no difference whether the winner is the petitioner or the respondent. So we could substitute for our separate variables for questions to petitioner and questions to respondent a single variable—the ratio of questions asked the petitioner to questions asked the respondent. We have estimated several regressions using that specification, but the results do not differ materially from those in Table 7.3.

When the Justices ask the same number of questions to each side, the petitioner prevails in about 63 percent of the cases. But his ad-

Table 7.4   Logit Regression of Probability of a Win for Petitioner Given U.S. Government's Participation in Case, 1979–2009 Terms

	U.S. Petitioner (1)	U.S. Respondent (2)	U.S. Not a Party (3)
Questions to Petitioner	−0.033**	−0.018**	−0.019**
	(5.21)	(2.97)	(7.45)
Questions to Respondent	0.017**	0.042**	0.017**
	(3.03)	(6.48)	(6.71)
Amicus Briefs Supporting	0.062	0.144**	0.080**
Petitioner	(1.18)	(2.66)	(4.10)
Amicus Briefs Supporting	−0.115**	−0.094*	−0.101**
Respondent	(2.64)	(1.98)	(5.49)
Civil Liberties	0.486	−0.764	0.017
	(0.75)	(1.21)	(0.08)
Economics	0.106	−1.016	−0.218
	(0.16)	(1.57)	(1.03)
Judicial Power	−0.166	0.746	−0.391
	(0.23)	(1.07)	(1.73)
Term Dummies	Yes	Yes	Yes
Constant	1.741*	−1.086	0.609
	(1.97)	(−1.12)	(1.61)
Number of Observations	537	436	2137

vantage quickly dissipates as the Justices ask him more and more questions relative to the respondent. For example, holding the number of questions to the respondent constant at 57 (the mean number of questions asked a respondent), if the petitioner is asked 25 more questions his probability of prevailing drops to 51 percent.[19] Were the Justices to be especially inquisitive and ask the petitioner 125 questions, our regression analysis predicts that the probability of his winning would fall to 32 percent, and if they asked the petitioner 57 questions and the respondent only about half as many to 48 percent. All these figures are within the sample range; that is, we are not trying to predict what the probabilities would be were the ratio of questions to the two sides higher or lower than anything found in our sample of actual questioning by Justices.

19. We calculated these predicted probabilities for an abbreviated version of equation (3): instead of adding dummy variables for each term, we clustered on term. The results for the variables of interest are virtually identical.

We experimented with adding three more variables to equations (1) through (3) in Table 7.3: the ideology of the median Justice as measured by Martin-Quinn scores, whether the lower court decision was liberal or conservative, and an interaction term between ideology and that decision. The question and word variables remain statistically significant and have the expected sign.

Table 7.4 presents separate regressions for the government as petitioner, as respondent, and as neither. The coefficients indicate that the proportionate change in the petitioner win rate for a given percentage change in the number of questions is greater for the federal government. The explanation may be that the Justices respect the Solicitor General's competence and probity, so that if the government's lawyer cannot dispel the doubts reflected in the Justices' questions this indicates its case is weak, while if its case seems strong the Justices ask few questions rather than thinking it necessary to probe for possible weaknesses.

Explaining Variations in the Number of Questions and the Total Number of Words in Questions

We offer several hypotheses regarding such variations:

The more Justices who attend the oral argument, the greater will be both the number of questions (N) and the total number of words in each question (W). Although we don't know the number of Justices present at any given oral argument, the number voting will approximate the number present. In 2746 cases in our sample of 3110, nine Justices voted, in 323 cases eight, in 35 cases seven, and in 6 cases six.

The closer the case, the more questions the Justices will ask. We proxy distance/closeness as follow: *Unanimous* if the vote is unanimous (9–0, 8–0, 7–0 or 6–0, though 98 percent of the 1251 unanimous decisions in our sample are either 9–0 or 8–0), and *Close* if the vote is 5–4, 4–3, or 4–2 (698 decisions, of which 618 were 5–4). The left-out variable is cases that are neither unanimous nor close. We predict a negative coefficient on *Unanimous* and a positive one on *Close*.

The more important the case, the more (or longer) questions the Justices will ask. We use two measures of importance: Epstein and Segal's

Table 7.5 Summary of Variables in Regression Analysis of Questions, 1979–2009 Terms

	Mean	Standard Deviation	Minimum	Maximum
Questions	112.7	37.22	16	322
Words in Questions	2838.4	1161.53	175	8134
Number of Judges Voting	8.87	0.39	6	9
Close Vote	0.22	0.42	0	1
Unanimous Vote	0.40	0.49	0	1
Neither Close Nor Unanimous	0.37	0.48	0	1
U.S. a Party	0.31	0.46	0	1
N.Y. Times Coverage	0.13	0.34	0	1
Number of Amicus Briefs	4.55	6.63	0	102

Note: The number of observations is again 3110.

measure of front-page coverage in the *New York Times*[20] and the number of amicus curiae briefs.[21] The two variables are highly correlated.[22]

Table 7.5 lists the variables we use to test the foregoing hypotheses and Table 7.6 presents the regression results. We cluster the observations by term to account for any correlation between questions and words in a given term.

The regression analysis reveals that the more Justices voting (and hence, with rare exceptions, the more who attended oral argument), the greater the number of questions and words. One additional Justice produces an 8 percent increase in the number of questions or words. But

20. See Lee Epstein and Jeffrey A. Segal, "Measuring Issue Salience," 44 *American Journal of Political Science* 66 (2000).

21. See Forest Maltzman and Paul J. Wahlbeck, "May It Please the Chief? Opinion Assignments in the Rehnquist Court," 40 *American Journal of Political Science* 421 (1996).

22. We estimated the following regression (t-statistics in parentheses):

$$AC = -512.67 + 5.86\,NYT + .259\,\text{Term} - .004\,\text{Cases} \quad R^2 = .19 \; N = 3110$$
$$\quad\;\; (11.86) \quad\; (10.74) \qquad (12.01) \qquad\quad (1.01)$$

where AC is the number of amicus briefs filed in a case, NYT a dummy variable indicating front-page coverage in the *Times*, Term the term of the court (which is associated with the increase in the number of lawyers and lobbyists), and Cases the number of cases per term. There are strong positive effects of both the *Times* variable (front-page coverage is associated with 5.9 more amicus briefs) and the term of the Court (in each term there is an average of .26 more amicus briefs per case than in the preceding term), whereas the number of cases per term has no observable effect on the number of amicus briefs.

Table 7.6   Regression Analysis of Questions, 1979–2009 Terms

	Ln (Question) (1)	Ln (Words) (2)
U.S. a Party	−0.047**	−0.031*
	(−3.55)	(−2.39)
Civil Liberties	0.104**	0.130**
	(3.82)	(4.76)
Economics	0.058*	0.040
	(2.03)	(1.38)
Judicial Power	0.086**	0.105**
	(2.78)	(3.39)
Unanimous Vote	−0.077**	−0.078**
	(−5.52)	(−5.58)
Close Vote	−0.012	−0.000
	(−0.72)	(−0.02)
Number of Justices Voting	0.084**	0.078**
	(5.32)	(4.91)
1994 Term Dummy	0.312**	0.406**
	(12.59)	(16.06)
Term	−0.004**	0.014**
	(0.86)	(10.70)
N.Y. Times Coverage	0.084**	0.070***
	(4.36)	(3.63)
Number of Amicus Briefs	0.002	0.002
	(1.47)	(1.60)
Constant	11.46**	−20.25**
	(4.02)	(7.12)
Adjusted R^2	.17	.48
Number of Observations	3110	3110

there is no significant increase in either questions or words if the case is close, even when there are more Justices voting (and so, presumably, attending the argument). This is consistent with the fact that the Justices ask more questions in close cases. The Justices' demand for answers is greater in such cases, and so the smaller the panel and therefore the more time each Justice has to ask questions, the more questions he asks.

Unanimous has, as expected, a negative effect on questions and words in questions; these are the least controversial cases, and hence the value (whether expressive, tendentious, or information-seeking) to the individual Justices of asking questions is least.

The Justices ask more questions in civil liberties and judicial power cases than in economics and federalism (the left-out issue) cases. This is surprising, because both our measures of importance are positively correlated with number of questions and total words (although only the *Times* variable is statistically significant), so we would expect the two importance variables to account for any greater importance of civil liberties and judicial power cases.

The dummy variable for the 1994 term (Justice Breyer's first term) is correlated with large (31 to 41 percent) and statistically highly significant increases in question and words. The regressions reveal no time trend in the number of questions but a positive and significant trend in the number of words, and fewer questions and words when the federal government is a party.

Individual Justices

We now examine how an individual Justice's vote relates to his questioning and that of the other Justices. We exclude O'Connor and Rehnquist, who participated in only 41 and 22 cases, respectively, in our dataset, which for questions by individual Justices is limited to the 2004 through 2009 terms. We exclude Sotomayor in Table 7.11 because she participated in too few cases (68) for the analysis reported in that table. (Kagan wasn't a member of the Court during the relevant period.)

We estimate multiple regressions for each Justice of the form

$$Win_i = f(Q, T, US, S, LC, u).$$

We include the *LC* variable (the ideological valence of the lower court decision) to account for the tendency of liberal Justices to vote to reverse conservative decisions and conservative Justices to vote to reverse liberal ones.

Table 7.7 presents the regression results for the question variables; the results for the other variables are similar to the results in the earlier regressions. The more questions the Court as a whole asks the petitioner, the less likely a particular Justice is to vote for the petitioner (or the respondent, if the Court asks more questions of the latter). Thus Ginsburg, if we set the numbers of questions to respondent and petitioner at their means (65 to respondent and 63 to petitioner during her years on the

Table 7.7 Logistic Regressions of Votes of Each Justice on Number of Questions Asked by All Justices

Justice	All Cases		Non-unanimous Cases Only	
	Questions to Petitioner (1)	Questions to Respondent (2)	Questions to Petitioner (3)	Questions to Respondent (4)
Alito	−0.020**	0.015*	—	—
(N = 315)	(2.52)	(1.94)		
Breyer	−0.022**	0.020**	−0.015**	0.014**
(N = 1186/677)	(5.80)	(5.58)	(2.82)	(2.99)
Ginsburg	−0.02**	0.015**	−0.011*	0.008**
(N = 1287/736)	(6.00)	(4.42)	(2.20)	(2.25)
Kennedy	−0.019**	−0.018**	−0.005	0.008*
(N = 1927/1115)	(6.60)	(6.49)	(1.45)	(9.444)
O'Connor	−0.016**	0.017**	−0.006*	0.006*
(N = 2505/1468)	(6.72)	(7.36)	(1.94)	(2.00)
Rehnquist	−0.016**	0.018**	−0.005	0.006
(N = 2700/1616)	(6.56)	(7.76)	(1.45)	(1.86)
Roberts	−0.024**	0.016*	−0.016	0.005
(N = 348/206)	(3.30)	(2.26)	(1.46)	(1.34)
Scalia	−0.019**	0.016**	−0.007	0.005
(N = 2143/1259)	(7.07)	(6.09)	(1.89)	(1.34)
Sotomayor	−0.051**	−0.006	—	—
(N = 68)	(2.52)	(.41)		
Souter	−0.024**	0.017**	−0.054**	0.010**
(N = 1516/868)	(7.38)	(5.49)	(3.52)	(2.38)
Stevens	−0.024**	0.023**	−0.019**	−0.022**
(N = 3056/1831)	(11.13)	(11.12)	(6.41)	(8.00)
Thomas	−0.019**	0.009**	−0.001	−0.004
(N = 1473/843)	(5.58)	(2.78)	(0.23)	(0.85)

Notes:

1. N = number of observations. The first number is for all cases, the second for non-unanimous cases.

2. All regressions include dummy variables indicating whether the U.S. is a respondent or a petitioner, dummies for each term the Justice served (excluding his or her first term), the ideological direction of the lower court's decision (liberal or conservative), and dummies for civil liberties, economics, and judicial power cases.

3. The data are from the 1979–2009 terms. To maintain consistency with our other analyses of the individual Justices, we estimated regression models only for those Justices serving at some time during the 2004–2009 terms.

4. Because of collinearity, we cannot estimate a non-unanimous model for Alito. We do not estimate a non-unanimous model for Sotomayor either, because she participated in only 37 non-unanimous cases.

Court), has a .72 probability of voting to reverse a conservative decision. But if the Justices as a whole ask the petitioner 25 more questions than they ask the respondent, the probability of Ginsburg's voting for the petitioner falls to .60—and to below .50 if they ask 50 more questions of the petitioner. Scalia's probability of voting to reverse a liberal decision is .75, but if the Justices as a whole ask the petitioner 25 more questions than the respondent that probability falls to .66.

The reason the voting of the individual Justices is a function of the balance of questions by the Court as a whole is that the Court decides a substantial fraction of its cases unanimously. Aggregated-question variables are less significant predictors of a Justice's vote if the sample is limited to non-unanimous cases (see equations (3) and (4) in Table 7.7), since if the balance of questions correctly predicts the majority decision it must incorrectly predict the votes of the dissenters.

In non-unanimous cases the balance of questions by the Court as a whole is a statistically significant predictor of the votes of Breyer, Ginsburg, O'Connor, Souter, and Stevens, but, with the partial exception of Kennedy, not of the conservative Justices, though the signs of the variable are as expected and the number of questions asked the respondent but not the petitioner is a statistically significant predictor of Kennedy's vote. So for the conservative Justices the unanimous cases are driving the overall result that the questions asked by the Court as a whole predict the votes of the individual Justices. This suggests that those Justices are less easily swayed by the give-and-take of oral argument than the liberals.

As Table 7.8 shows, the Justices vary considerably in the amount of questioning they do. Ginsburg and Sotomayor are the only Justices who ask at least one question in every case, but measured by number of questions Scalia is the most inquisitive, and in only four cases in our sample did he fail to ask a question. On average he asks 22 questions per case, though his standard deviation is high (12.8). Roberts asks 21.54 questions and Breyer 17.45 (Breyer's standard deviation, 11, is second highest to Scalia's). Breyer, as noted earlier, is the wordiest Justice and Scalia the second wordiest, with Roberts in third place. If we exclude Sotomayor because of the fewness of the arguments she heard during the sample period, Ginsburg is in the middle of the Court in both number

Table 7.8   Number of Questions and Total Words in Questions by Individual Justices, 2004–2009 Terms

	Cases	Questions per Case		Words per Case	
		Mean	Standard Deviation	Mean	Standard Deviation
Scalia	436	22.43	12.80	664.47	315.34
Roberts	354	21.54	9.18	630.88	280.74
Breyer	430	17.45	11.00	862.08	472.20
Sotomayor	68	15.97	8.77	532.81	231.08
Souter	362	14.22	8.98	605.15	348.14
Ginsburg	436	13.56	7.35	526.41	266.36
Kennedy	435	11.43	7.74	344.00	222.42
Stevens	435	11.05	8.59	294.17	205.75
Alito	321	5.53	4.27	213.98	185.09
Thomas	433	0.02	0.30	0.64	8.30

of questions and number of words, but her maximum words in an individual case of 1846 place her behind only Breyer's 2550 and Souter's 1997.

Regarding number of questions, the Justices can be divided into three groups: Scalia, Roberts, Breyer, and Sotomayor significantly above average; Souter and Ginsburg about average; and Stevens, Kennedy, Alito, and of course Thomas significantly below average. With respect to number of words, the Justices can be divided into two groups: Breyer, Scalia, Roberts, Souter, Ginsburg, and Sotomayor significantly above average, and Stevens, Kennedy, Alito, and of course Thomas significantly below.

The fact that Alito's means are second lowest may reflect his having been a recent appointee to the Court in the period covered by our dataset and therefore still feeling his way. Sotomayor exhibited no similar shyness. During her first term she asked more questions than five of the other Justices. The difference between the two Justices may reflect a personality difference—introvert versus extrovert. The introverted Souter asked few questions his first term. The biggest questioners—Scalia and Breyer—are extroverts.

Since a celebrity culture selects for, rewards, and encourages extroverts, we are led to wonder whether there mightn't be a correlation between the number of questions a Justice asks (and the number of words in the questions) and the Justice's extrajudicial activities. We have sufficient *e 7.9*   Mean Number of Questions and Words to Petitioner and Respondent, 2004–2009 Terms

	Mean Number of Questions Asked to			Mean Number of Words in Questions Asked to		
	Petitioner	Respondent	Difference	Petitioner	Respondent	Difference
erts (354)	10.27	11.27	−1.00	291.08	339.80	−48.72
a (436)	11.23	11.20	0.03	328.01	336.46	−8.45
mayor (68)	9.26	6.71	2.55*	313.44	219.37	94.07*
er (430)	7.26	10.19	−2.93*	351.38	510.70	−159.32*
er (362)	7.16	7.06	−0.10	305.29	299.86	5.42
burg (436)	7.54	6.02	1.52*	287.86	238.55	49.31*
ens (435)	5.34	5.71	−0.37	134.46	157.71	−25.26*
nedy (435)	6.19	5.24	0.94*	191.24	152.75	38.49*
(321)	2.88	2.64	0.24	111.15	102.82	8.33
mas (433)	0.00	0.02	−0.02	0.09	0.55	−0.47

Number of cases in parentheses.
We exclude cases in which the Justice did not participate.

data for all the Justices except Sotomayor to be able to correlate the average number of public events in which they participated between 2004 and 2009 (see Table 1.1 in chapter 1) with the average number of questions (and words) they asked at oral argument during the same period. Contrary to our expectation, the correlation is only .45 for questions and .40 for words. (The rank correlation—the correlation between how the Justices rank in public event activity and how in questioning—is .42 for questions and .47 for words.) Scalia and Breyer rank high on both questions and public events, Alito and Stevens relatively low on both. Thomas and Souter are anomalies: Thomas ranks fifth in public events but last in questions. Souter was the reverse—fourth in questions, last in public events. Since Souter is an introvert, the fact that he nevertheless asked a lot of questions suggests that he was deeply engaged in the work of the Court.

Table 7.9 explores differences in Justices' questioning of lawyers for petitioners and for respondents. Sotomayor, Ginsburg, and Kennedy ask significantly more questions (and wordier questions) to petitioners. Breyer asks more questions to respondents and both he and Stevens ask wordier questions to them. Roberts, Scalia, and Alito ask roughly the same number of questions (with roughly the same words) to both sides. We do not have an explanation for these results.

We expect, and in Table 7.10 we find, that the pattern of questioning by individual Justices reflects the Justices' ideological propensities. The five liberals in the period covered by our study asked fewer questions of liberal petitioners than of conservative respondents (for three of the five the difference is statistically significant), and four of the five asked significantly more questions of conservative petitioners than of liberal respondents (Breyer is the exception; he always asks more questions of the respondent). Three of the four conservatives (Thomas, who asked only one petitioner a question and four respondents questions in the 433 cases in our sample in which he voted, is excluded) are significantly less likely to question a conservative party, whether petitioner or respondent. Kennedy is the exception; he is significantly less likely to question conservative parties only when they are respondents; when they are petitioners he is

Table 7.10   Number of Questions by Ideology of Parties, 2004–2009 Terms

Justice (Number of Cases for Scenario 1, Number of Cases for Scenario 2)	Scenario 1: Liberal Petitioner v. Conservative Respondent		Scenario 2: Conservative Petitioner v. Liberal Respondent	
	Mean Number of Questions	Difference	Mean Number of Questions	Difference
Stevens (231, 197)	3.38 v. 7.62	−4.24**	7.09 v. 3.99	+3.10**
Souter (192, 164)	5.69 v. 8.18	−2.49**	8.411 v. 6.06	+2.35**
Ginsburg (232, 197)	6.95 v. 6.91	−0.04	8.01 v. 5.29	+2.79**
Breyer (69, 92)	6.86 v. 10.21	−3.35**	7.67 v. 10.20	−2.53**
Sotomayor (37, 30)	7.33 v. 7.67	−0.33	10.84 v. 6.11	+4.73**
Kennedy (231, 197)	6.14 v. 5.10	+1.04**	6.21 v. 5.38	+0.83*
Roberts (191, 157)	12.10 v. 8.41	+3.69**	8.59 v. 13.65	−5.07**
Alito (165, 150)	4.26 v. 1.53	+2.73**	1.61 v. 3.72	−2.11**
Scalia (232, 197)	12.27 v. 9.39	+2.89**	10.16 v. 12.76	−2.60**

Note: We order the Justices from most liberal (Stevens) to most conservative (Scalia) based on the mean of their Martin-Quinn scores in the 2004–2009 terms.

more likely to question them than to question liberal respondents. In other words, he questions petitioners more, suggesting that affirmance (that is, victory for the respondent) is his default position. This suggests a degree of neutrality or ambivalence between conservative and liberal extremes, consistent with Kennedy's role as the swing Justice. The same results hold for number of words in questions.

Figure 7.6 reveals the mean number of questions asked each party when the Justice votes for the respondent and when he votes for the petitioner. As expected, asking more questions of a party's lawyer predicts that the Justice will vote against the party. Chief Justice Roberts, when he votes for the respondent, asks an average of three more questions to the petitioner and when he votes for the petitioner asks an average of three more questions to the respondent. A similar pattern holds for most of the other Justices, although the difference is not statistically significant when Breyer and Kennedy vote for the respondent; in number of words, however, the difference is significant for Kennedy. Kennedy and Sotomayor ask the petitioner more questions when they vote for the petitioner, but in the case of Sotomayor the difference is not statistically significant. The divergence of Kennedy from the other Justices is further evidence of his swing status. The results are virtually identical for number of words rather than number of questions.

We expect the behavior of individual Justices to be less predictable than that of the Court as a whole. Suppose Justice A asks the respondent 20 questions and the petitioner none and as a result the remaining Justices fully appreciate the weaknesses in the respondent's position and have little interest in asking the respondent additional questions; so instead each of them asks the petitioner three questions and the respondent one. Adding the questions asked the two parties, we would find that the petitioner has been asked 24 questions and the respondent 28, yet eight of the nine Justices asked the petitioner more questions than the respondent. This might appear to contradict our finding that questions predict outcomes, but it doesn't, because in the example the pattern of questioning by the other Justices is shaped by the questioning of the Justice who has the strongest views about the case.

To explore the questioning by individual Justices more deeply, we estimate multiple regressions for each Justice (except Thomas, and also

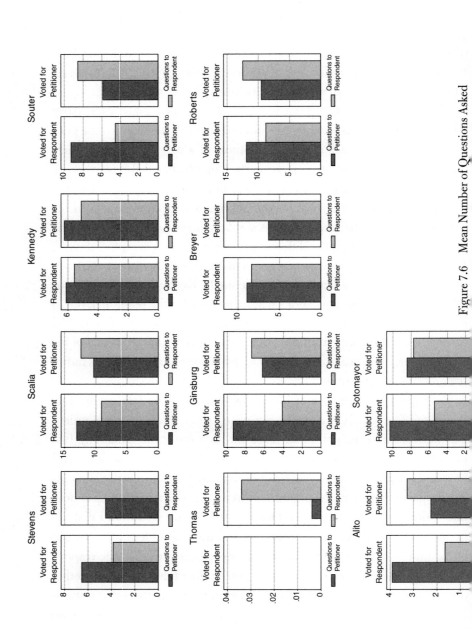

Figure 7.6   Mean Number of Questions Asked

Table 7.11 Logistic Regressions of the Votes of Each Justice on the Number of Questions and Words, 2004–2009 Terms

	Number of Questions		Ideological Direction of Lower Court's Decision	Number of Words		Ideological Direction of Lower Court's Decision
	Petitioner	Respondent		Petitioner	Respondent	
Alito (315)	−0.049	0.170**	−0.488	−0.001	0.002#	−0.647*
	(1.11)	(2.85)	(1.52)	(1.11)	(1.73)	(2.08)
Breyer (423)	−0.053**	0.063**	1.358**	−0.002**	0.003**	1.364**
	(3.23)	(3.77)	(5.05)	(3.83)	(4.87)	(4.96)
Ginsburg (429)	−0.159**	0.200**	1.571**	−0.005**	0.007**	1.533**
	(5.77)	(6.21)	(−3.31)	(6.52)	(7.07)	(2.77)
Kennedy (428)	−0.002	−0.030	−0.261	−0.001	0.000	−0.260
	(0.06)	(1.08)	(1.04)	(1.21)	(0.14)	(1.04)
Roberts (348)	−0.046*	0.065**	−0.280	−0.002**	0.002**	−0.203
	(2.22)	(3.27)	(0.92)	(3.28)	(2.84)	(0.65)
Scalia (429)	−0.043**	0.065**	−0.727**	−0.003**	0.003**	−0.511*
	(2.90)	(4.01)	(2.89)	(5.13)	(4.73)	(1.94)
Souter (356)	−0.082**	0.096**	1.683**	−0.002**	0.002**	1.617**
	(4.03)	(3.94)	(5.43)	(4.35)	(4.16)	(5.18)
Stevens (428)	−0.063**	0.116**	1.294**	−0.002**	0.004**	1.331**
	(3.00)	(4.60)	(4.88)	(2.21)	(3.396)	(5.01)

Note: All regressions include dummy variables indicating whether the U.S. is respondent or petitioner, whether the Solicitor General filed an amicus curiae brief for respondent or for petitioner, and the ideological direction of the lower court's decision (0 = liberal; 1 = conservative).

Sotomayor because she participated in too few cases for meaningful analysis), using the same specification as before except that we substitute questions asked by the particular Justice for all questions asked by the Court. We cluster the observations by term.

The regression results are shown in Table 7.11. Even with the ideological direction of the lower court decision and the participation of the United States held constant, the number of questions and the total words in questions are good predictors of most Justices' votes, though in the case of Alito the number of questions (and words in questions) that he asks the respondent is more predictive of his vote than the number of questions he asks the petitioner.

The principal exception is Kennedy. None of his question variables produces a statistically significant coefficient. This is additional evidence of his status as the swing Justice.

CHAPTER 8

The Auditioners

D ESIRE FOR PROMOTION is a significant motivating factor in many workplaces, and we expect it to operate in the Article III federal judiciary as well, though both the system of appointment and the age of appointment limit the opportunities for promotion. Promotion from within is common in many institutions and the rule in some, but in the case of the federal judiciary lateral entry is not only permitted but is the dominant route of appointment. In recent years, it is true, almost all Supreme Court Justices have been promoted from within, namely from court of appeals judgeships; only Justice Kagan is a lateral entrant. But the ratio of court of appeals judges to Supreme Court Justices is so high that the promotion rate is very low. As shown in Table 8.1, since 1933 only 3 percent of court of appeals judges have been appointed to the Supreme Court.

As shown in Table 8.2, 10 percent of district judges have been promoted to a court of appeals or the Supreme Court since 1933. Although the ratio of court of appeals judges to district court judges (2216 / 588 = 3.77) is lower than the ratio of Supreme Court Justices to court of appeals judges (588 / 39 = 15.1), there is much more lateral entry in the courts of appeals. That is why, although the percentage of district judges promoted to a court of appeals is more than twice as high as the percentage of court of appeals judges promoted to the Supreme Court (11. / .041 = 2.68), it is a lower than a comparison of the ratios of court of appeals judges to

Table 8.1   Promotions from Courts of Appeals to Supreme Court, by President

President (Years)	Number of Active Court of Appeals Judges	Number of Appointments to the Supreme Court	Fraction of Supreme Court Appointments of Court of Appeals Judges	Fraction Court of A Judge Appoint Supreme
Roosevelt/Truman	119	13	0.15	0.02
(1933–1952)			(2/13)	(2/11
Eisenhower	108	5	0.60	0.03
(1953–1960)			(3/5)	(3/10
Kennedy/Johnson	127	4	0.0	0.0
(1961–1968)			(0/4)	(0/12
Nixon/Ford	144	5	0.60	0.02
(1968–1976)			(3/5)	(3/14
Carter	148	0	—	—
(1977–1980)				
Reagan	205	4	0.5	0.01
(1981–1988)			(2/4)	(2/20
Bush I	186	2	1.0	0.01
(1988–1992)			(2/2)	(2/18
Clinton	211	2	1.0	0.01
(1993–2000)			(2/2)	(2/21
Bush II	201	2	1.0	0.01
(2001–2008)			(2/2)	(2/20
Obama	169	2	0.5	0.01
(2008–2010)			(1/2)	(1/16
All Years	588	39	0.44	0.03
(1933–2010)			(17/39)	(17/58

Notes:

1. Number of Active Judges: Judges who were confirmed before the last year in the President's term and who di take senior status or otherwise depart before the President's first year. For example, for the Truman and Roosevelt the number of active court of appeals judges equals those confirmed in or before 1952 who departed after 1932.

2. The number of promoted judges excludes appointments of former judges.

Supreme Court Justices and of court of appeals judges to district judges —15.1 / 3.77 = 4.01—would predict. If all court of appeals judges were promoted from the ranks of the district judges and all Supreme Court Justices from the ranks of court of appeals judges, there would be a 4.01 times, rather than a 2.68 times, greater probability of being promoted to the court of appeals than from the court of appeals to the Supreme Court.

The age of appointment of federal judges further limits the opportunities for promotion. Almost 50 percent of American lawyers are under the age of 45, and more than 75 percent are under 55.[1] In contrast, the me-

1. The median age is 45. The age distribution of practicing lawyers in the United States in 2000, as shown in American Bar Association, "Lawyer Demographics," http://new.abanet

dian age of the 163 active (that is, not senior-status) judges serving on the federal courts of appeals in 2010 was 62 and the average age 62.2, and none of the judges was younger than 40. The median age of the 632 active district judges was 60 (and the mean 59.9), and of the nine Supreme Court Justices 62 (with a mean of 64). These high ages, especially of district judges (court of appeals judges and Supreme Court Justices often have been promoted from lower ranks of the federal judiciary), reflect the later entry of lawyers into judging than into other legal careers.

If only because the number of district judges has risen faster than the number of court of appeals judges, and the number of court of appeals judges faster than the number of Supreme Court Justices (the number of Justices has been unchanged at nine since 1869), promotion rates have declined. Of court of appeals judges confirmed before 1960, 6.6 percent were promoted to the Supreme Court, compared to 2.6 percent since then. The drop would have been even more precipitous had not the percentage of Supreme Court appointments from the court of appeals increased. In 1960 only three Justices were former court of appeals judges; today only one is not.

The comparable percentages for district judges promoted to the courts of appeals are 17 before 1960 and 8.5 since. But these numbers, and likewise the corresponding numbers for court of appeals judges promoted to the Supreme Court, overstate the decline because some judges appointed since 1960 may yet be promoted to the Supreme Court and some district judges appointed since then will certainly be promoted to courts of appeals.

We are interested in how the desire for promotion affects judicial behavior.[2] That of course is a different question from whether promotion

---

.org/marketresearch/PublicDocuments/Lawyer_Demographics.pdf (visited Jan. 5, 2012), was as follows:

29 years or less	7%
30–34	12
35–39	14
40–44	15
45–54	28
55–64	13
65+	12
Median	45

2. For previous studies, see Erin Kaheny, Susan Haire, and Sara C. Benesh, "Change over Tenure: Voting, Variance, and Decision Making on The U.S. Courts of Appeals," 52 *Ameri-*

Table 8.2 Promotions from the District Courts to the Courts of Appeals, by President

President (Years)	(1) Number of Active District Judges	(2) Number of Appointments to the Courts of Appeals	(3) Fraction of Court of Appeals Appointments That Were of District Judges	(4) Fraction of District Judges Who Were Appointed Courts of App
Roosevelt/Truman (1933–1952)	380	76	0.36 (27/76)	0.07 (27/380)
Eisenhower (1953–1960)	331	45	0.40 (18/45)	0.05 (18/331)
Kennedy/Johnson (1961–1968)	458	61	0.44 (27/61)	0.06 (27/458)
Nixon/Ford (1968–1976)	559	57	0.54 (31/57)	0.05 (31/559)
Carter (1977–1980)	576	56	0.27 (15/56)	0.03 (15/576)
Reagan (1981–1988)	772	78	0.42 (33/78)	0.04 (33/772)
Bush I (1988–1992)	696	37	0.59 (22/37)	0.03 (22/696)
Clinton (1993–2000)	857	61	0.31 (19/61)	0.02 (19/857)
Bush II (2001–2008)	867	60	0.23 (14/60)	0.02 (14/867)
Obama (2008–2010)	681	15	0.53 (8/15)	0.01 (8/681)
All Years (1933–2010)	2216	546	.39 (214/546)	0.10 (214/2216

Note: See notes to Table 8.1.

should be a feature of a judicial system. It has been argued both that a norm against promotion encourages judicial independence and that it diminishes incentives to excel.[3] We do not take sides. As throughout this book, our analysis is positive rather than normative.

can Journal of Political Science 490 (2008); Gregory C. Sisk, Michael Heise, and Andrew P. Morriss, "Charting the Influences on the Judicial Mind: An Empirical Study of Judicial Reasoning," 73 *New York University Law Review* 1377 (1998); Mark A. Cohen, "The Motives of Judges: Empirical Evidence from Antitrust Sentencing," 12 *International Review of Law and Economics* 13 (1992), and Cohen, "Explaining Judicial Behavior or What's 'Unconstitutional' about the Sentencing Commission," 7 *Journal of Law, Economics, and Organization* 183 (1991).

3. See, for example, Eli Salzberger and Paul Fenn, "Judicial Independence: Some Evidence

We study both court of appeals judges who have a realistic prospect of promotion to the Supreme Court and district judges who have a realistic prospect of promotion to a court of appeals. We ask whether any of these potential "auditioners" alter their behavior in order to improve their promotion prospects. This would be consistent with our realistic model of judges.

Appointment and Promotion in the Federal Judiciary

Table 8.3 presents historical data on age and other characteristics of federal judges at appointment.[4] The span covered is 1789 to 2010 for Supreme Court Justices and district judges and 1869 to 2010 for circuit judges. Circuit judgeships were first created in 1869, although the modern system of federal courts of appeals, whose judges are officially termed "circuit judges," dates from 1891.

Appointment to the district court is the first judicial appointment of two-thirds of district judges. Six percent, however, held another federal judicial appointment (usually as a magistrate judge or bankruptcy judge, occasionally as an administrative law judge) and another 28 percent were state court judges. Surprisingly, the mean age of appointment to the district court of lawyers with prior judicial experience is the same as the mean age of those without such experience—50, compared to 50.8 for former state judges and 49 for former non–Article III federal judicial officers—even though the former state judges had already served on average 9.5 years in state courts before being appointed to the district court.

Judges of the courts of appeals are generally older at the time of their appointment than district judges, the average being 53. A majority are appointed from other judicial positions: 41 percent had been district judges, 1 percent other federal judicial officers, and 14 percent state judges. District judges are appointed to courts of appeals at an older age on average than nonjudicial appointees (55 versus 51), as are former state judges

---

from the English Court of Appeal," 42 *Journal of Law and Economics* 831 (1999); Daniel Klerman, "Nonpromotion and Judicial Independence," 72 *Southern California Law Review* 455 (1999).

4. Our information on judges comes from biographical sources, including a database on the federal judiciary created by us and described in the conclusion of this book.

Table 8.3 Appointments to Federal Courts

	Supreme Court (N = 116)	Courts of Appeals (N = 682)	District C (N = 2
Mean Age at Appointment	53.4	52.9	50.(
Mean Age at Departure (N)	69.3	68.2	66.
	(107)	(504)	(178
Employment at Time of Nomination			
Judge (All)	.47	.56	.34
	(55/116)	(379/682)	(898/2(
Federal Judge	.62	.75	.17
	(34/55)	(284/379)	(157/8
State Judge	.38	.25	.83
	(21/55)	(95/379)	(741/8
Private Practice	.21	.26	.45
	(24/116)	(175/682)	(1190/2
Government Attorney	.10	.07	.12
	(12/116)	(48/682)	(313/2(
Elected Office	.11	.03	.05
	(13/116)	(18/682)	(142/2(
Other Government Position	.09	.03	.03
	(10/116)	(22/682)	(87/26
Law Professor	.02	.06	.01
	(2/116)	(40/682)	(38/26
Fraction Promoted	—	.04	.11
		(28/682)	(292/2(
Fraction Republican	.65	.56	.57
	(54/83)	(382/682)	(1435/2
Fraction of Cross-Party Appointments	.16	.08	.09
	(13/83)	(57/682)	(230/2.
Fraction Nonwhite (1980–2010)	.17	.16	.18
	(2/12)	(41/260)	(199/1
Fraction Female (1980–2010)	.33	.20	.21
	(4/12)	(52/260)	(229/1

Notes:

1. The Supreme Court column includes all Justices appointed between 1789 and 2010. Of the 160 nomination transmitted to the Senate (not double-counting recess appointees—for example, we count Stewart once, not twice) failed of confirmation and some failed initially but ultimately succeeded. A total of 116 were confirmed, of whom 4 served both as an Associate Justice and as a Chief Justice—White, Hughes, Stone, and Rehnquist—and so appear t in the data.

2. The court of appeals column includes all circuit judges appointed since 1869. We exclude two recess appoint who were not confirmed: Wallace McCamant and Charles Pickering.

3. The district court column includes all district judges appointed between 1789 and 2010, with the exception 21 recess appointments that were never confirmed.

4. Age at Time of Appointment: We are missing the year of birth for one judge (Philip Kissick Lawrence).

5. Age at Departure: For district and court of appeals judges, departure is the age at which the judge took senior or died or resigned. The court of appeals column excludes judges elevated to the Supreme Court, and the district column excludes judges elevated to the Supreme Court or to a court of appeals.

8.3 (continued)

───

b at Time of Appointment: "Elected position" includes members of Congress, state legislators, governors, and s. We are missing the preappointment job of three district court judges.

omotion to the Supreme Court from the Court of Appeals: Includes four former court of appeals judges who had bench for other jobs before being appointed to the Supreme Court: McKenna (U.S. Attorney General), Taft sor), Vinson (U.S. Treasury Secretary), and Marshall (U.S. Solicitor General).

omotion from the District Court: We include one failed promotion attempt (Pickering to the court of appeals) and motions to the Supreme Court. We include two former district judges who had left the bench for other positions their appointment to the court of appeals: Walter Gresham (Postmaster General) and Louis McComas (U.S. r).

arty and Cross-Party Appointments: 1857–2010 for the Supreme Court and district courts and 1868–2010 for rts of appeals. We begin in 1857 because this was when the current two-party system became entrenched. party appointments mean (1) a Republican President appoints a Democrat or an Independent or (2) a Democratic nt appoints a Republican or an Independent.

───

(52 versus 51), though only the first difference is statistically significant. Judges appointed to courts of appeals from other judgeships have usually spent a considerable period in those judgeships: 9 years is the average for former district judges and 12 for former state judges.

The mean age of appointment of Supreme Court Justices is roughly the same as that of court of appeals judges—53.4. Almost half came directly from federal or state judgeships, though for those promoted from another federal court the mean is slightly higher (55). They had served 7 years on average in a federal court of appeals if promoted from that court and 9 years in a federal district court if promoted from that court.

Age at time of appointment has not varied a great deal at any of the three levels of the Article III judiciary (see Figures 8.1 and 8.2). The mean age of appointment of Supreme Court Justices and court of appeals judges peaked in the 1920s at 58 in the Supreme Court and 56 in the courts of appeals. In the district courts the mean increased steadily from about 44 in the 1790s to 52 in the 1950s. A regression of years on age shows that the average age of appointment of Supreme Court Justices increased by about 4 years every 100 years. But if we limit the analysis to 1900–2010, + 4 becomes − 3, leading us to predict a mean age (holding other factors constant) of 55.6 in 1900, 54.2 in 1950, and 52.7 in 2000.

Table 8.4 reveals only slight correlation between age at appointment and party of the appointing President. If we go back to 1857 (the first year in which the Democratic and Republican parties between them controlled a majority of seats in both houses of Congress), the mean age of Supreme Court Justices appointed by Republican Presidents was higher (55.5) than that of Justices appointed by Democratic Presidents (54.7), but the difference is not statistically significant. In the twentieth century Republican Presidents appointed slightly older Justices than Democratic Presidents (55.7 versus 54.5), but again the difference is not statistically significant. Since 1950, Justices appointed by Democratic Presidents have been older (54.1 versus 53.9), but again not significantly. The average age at appointment of court of appeals judges appointed by Republican Presidents is 52.8 and by Democratic Presidents 53.2, and again the difference is not statistically significant. But as we saw in chapter 3, beginning with Reagan the average age of court of appeals judges appointed by

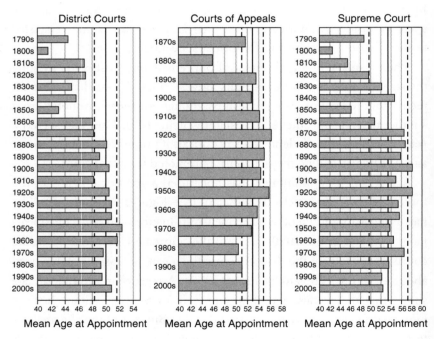

Figure 8.1   Mean Age of Federal Judges at Appointment, by Decade

Notes:

    1. The solid vertical line is the mean of the means, weighted by the number of confirmations in each decade; the dashed lines are one standard deviation from the mean of the means.

    2. The decade of the 1790s includes 1789; the 2000s include 2010. For the courts of appeal the decade of the 1870s includes 1869.

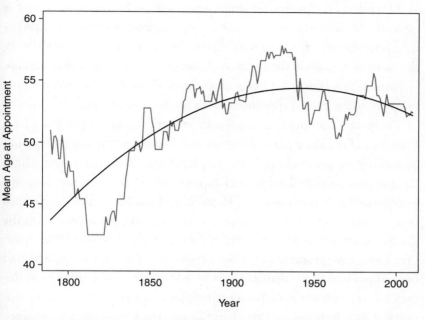

Figure 8.2   Mean Age of Supreme Court Justices at Appointment, 1788–2010

Republican Presidents (50.4) has been significantly lower than that of the Democratic Presidents' appointees (52.8)—and 23.4 percent of Republican Presidents' appointees have been 45 or younger compared to only 13.2 percent of Democratic Presidents' appointees.

We noted in chapter 3 the tradeoff between the legacy effect of an appointment, which is greater the younger the appointee, and the ideological drift and ideological divergence effects, which are smaller the older the appointee. Both are particular concerns in the case of the Supreme Court. Although the youngest Justice ever appointed, Joseph Story, was only 32 and the oldest, Horace Lurton, was 65 (Harlan Fiske Stone was 68 when promoted to Chief Justice, but he had been an Associate Justice for many years), such extremes have become rare. None of the 10 Justices appointed since 1986 has been younger than 43 (Thomas) or older than 60 (Ginsburg). The standard deviation in the ages of these 10 Justices has been a relatively low 4.5, and the mean (52) has remained close to the overall mean for Supreme Court Justices of 53.

The lesson for judges seeking promotion to the Supreme Court is clear: the likelihood of such a promotion will drop in the late 50s and to near zero after 60. The lesson for district judges aspiring to promotion to the court of appeals is similar, though not quite so extreme; although appointment to a court of appeals of someone 60 or older is rare, it is less rare than in the case of appointments to the Supreme Court.

The promotion pools normally are limited to judges appointed by a President of the same party as the current President (the one who would be making the promotion). For example, of the 33 district judges whom Reagan promoted to the courts of appeals, 32 (97 percent) had been appointed to the district court by a Republican President.[5] All 8 of Obama's promotions to courts of appeals at this writing had been appointed to the district court by Democratic Presidents, though generally Democratic Presidents have promoted a smaller percentage of district judges who had been appointed to the district court by a Democratic President than Republican Presidents have promoted district judges who had been appointed by a Republican President (79 percent versus 92 percent since 1933). The overall percentage of same-party promotions to courts of appeals since 1933 has been 86 percent. A notable exception is Sotomayor,

5. The statistics in this paragraph are based on the following table:

	Appointment of District Judges to Courts of Appeals		
	Total Number	Same Party	Percent Same Party
Roosevelt/Truman (1933–1952)	23	17	74
Eisenhower (1953–1960)	18	14	78
Kennedy/Johnson (1961–1968)	27	24	89
Nixon/Ford (1969–1976)	31	28	90
Carter (1977–1980)	15	10	67
Reagan (1981–1988)	33	32	97
Bush I (1989–1992)	23	22	96
Clinton (1993–2000)	19	14	74
Bush II (2001–2008)	13	12	92
Obama (2009–2010)	8	8	100

Note: The source for these data is U.S. Courts, "Biographical Directory of Federal Judges," www.uscourts.gov/JudgesAndJudgeships/BiographicalDirectoryOfJudges.aspx (visited Dec. 9, 2011). We include Independents in the denominator but not in the numerator; since the Nixon administration the percentage of Independents has varied from 2 to 6 percent.

Table 8.4 Average Age of Appointment to Court of Appeals, by Appointing President

President	Number of Appointees	Mean Age of Appointees	Median Age
Harrison	11	52.5	53
Cleveland (2)	9	53.3	53
McKinley	6	54.5	53
T. Roosevelt	18	51.1	51
Taft	13	57.8	58
Wilson	20	52.7	56
Harding	6	59.8	60
Coolidge	16	55.9	57
Hoover	16	57.1	59
F. Roosevelt	50	53.4	52
Truman	26	55.6	56
Eisenhower	45	56.6	56
Kennedy	20	54.7	55
Johnson	41	52.4	52
Nixon	45	54	53
Ford	12	52.6	53
Carter	56	52.3	53
Reagan	78	50.5	51
Bush I	37	49.5	49
Clinton	61	52.3	51
Bush II	59	51.0	51
Obama (through 2010)	15	55.0	56
Democrats	293	53.2	53
Republicans	362	52.8	53
Total	655	53.0	53

appointed to the district court by the first President Bush and to the court of appeals and then the Supreme Court by Democratic Presidents.

The probability of a same-party district judge being promoted depends not only on how strongly the President favors same-party appointments but also on the number of vacancies and the number of eligible district judges to fill those vacancies. Since roughly 57 percent of the active-service district judges during Reagan's Presidency had been appointed by a Republican President, the probability of promotion was 7 percent for district judges who had been appointed by a Republican President (32/440) and close to zero for district judges appointed by a Democratic one (1/332). Clinton appointed 61 judges to the courts of appeals, of whom 19 had been district judges, 14 appointed by Democratic

Presidents. Since roughly 368 district judges had been appointed by Democratic Presidents, the probability of promotion by Clinton was 4 percent for those district judges (14/368) and 1 percent for district judges appointed by Republican Presidents (5/489).

But the limitations we've imposed on the likely promotion of district judges who had been appointed to the district court by a President of the opposite party to the current President are too stringent. Such judges would have a realistic possibility of being appointed to the court of appeals by a future President of the same party as the Presidents who had appointed them to the district court.

Auditioning for the Supreme Court

Given the slight probability that a court of appeals judge will be appointed to the Supreme Court, one might expect promotion-seeking behavior by court of appeals judges to be rare. Why would a judge alter his behavior to advance his career ambitions when the chance of success was so small?

One possibility is that just being considered for an appointment to the Supreme Court, or indeed just being thought by the media, other judges, etc., to be under consideration, may confer utility because it increases the judge's visibility and prestige (and can even lead to book deals, as in the case of Robert Bork). If the appointment, or just being known to be under consideration (or to have been under consideration though the appointment went to someone else), confers utility on the judge, it would be rational for him to expend resources on increasing the probability of that happy event, even if the maximum feasible expenditure would increase the probability only slightly. That is an implication of simple cost-benefit analysis: if an increase in cost will produce a greater increase in pb, where b is the benefit and p the probability of obtaining the benefit, then an additional expenditure on c is likely to be worthwhile if b is high relative to c, even if p is low and the increase in p brought about by the change in c is small.

By "expending resources" on improving the probability of obtaining a judicial promotion we don't mean spending money; we have in mind such things as judicial voting against one's convictions in order to be a more attractive candidate for promotion and taking time to ingratiate one-self with officials or other opinion makers likely to have influence on a future Supreme Court appointment. Voting against one's convictions is disreputable behavior, but that doesn't mean it's nonexistent; it may, however, be largely unconscious.

The odds of appointment to the Supreme Court are of course not constant across court of appeals judges as winners are across purchasers of tickets to a lottery. The actual promotion pool is much smaller and the probabilities of promotion for members of the pool are therefore higher.[6] They are the judges who have an incentive to take steps to improve their chances of appointment to the Supreme Court. We call these judges "auditioners," though actually they are potential auditioners, because many of them would not lift a finger to increase the likelihood of such an appointment, either because they're not interested or because they have ethical objections to auditioning for promotion.

To identify the auditioners (in the broad sense in which we're using the word—that is, as including potential auditioners), we have examined presidential short lists, available for Supreme Court Justices since 1930,[7] plus newspaper and scholarly accounts covering the same period.[8] These sources, which reveal that more than 20 percent of active court of appeals judges since 1930 have been considered for appointment to the Supreme Court, or at least have been believed to be under consideration or worthy of consideration, enable us to compile a promotion pool; the names of these 122 auditioners are listed in the appendix to this chapter.

Table 8.5 provides summary statistics for them and for the 475 other active court of appeals judges in service at some time between 1930 and 2009, who constitute therefore a control group. A word of caution is necessary. Some judges may have been placed in the promotion pool to appeal to interest groups and were never serious contenders. Such *faux* au-

6. See Klerman, note 2 above.

7. Christine L. Nemacheck, *Strategic Selection: Presidential Nomination of Supreme Court Justices from Herbert Hoover through George W. Bush* (2007).

8. The sources are three newspapers (the *New York Times,* the *Washington Post,* and the *Wall Street Journal*); David Alistair Yalof, *Pursuit of Justices: Presidential Politics and the Selection of Supreme Court Nominees* (1999), and Henry J. Abraham, *Justices, Presidents, and Senators* (5th ed. 2007).

Table 8.5 Auditioners and Non-Auditioners among Active Court of Appeals Judges, 1930–2009

| | Number | | |
	Auditioners	Non-Auditioners	Percent of Auditioners
All Judges	122	463	20.9
Circuits			
2d	15	40	27.3
5th	18	56	24.3
D.C.	23	28	45.1
Other	66	339	16.3
Attributes			
Mean Age at Appointment	48.6	53.8	
Mean Year Confirmed	1970	1971	—
Republican President	74	243	23.3
Democratic President	48	220	17.9
Female	23	36	39.0
Male	99	427	18.8
White	104	431	19.4
Nonwhite	18	32	36.0
Harvard or Yale Law School	41	94	30.3
All Other Law Schools	81	369	18.0
Mean Absolute Senatorial Courtesy Score	0.39	0.35	—
Prior Employment			
Federal or State Judge	56	264	17.5
Federal Government	19	31	38.0
State Government	3	16	15.8
Law Professor	14	24	36.8
Private Sector	30	128	19.0

Note: See notes to Tables 8.1 and 8.3.

ditioners are likely to be similar to non-auditioners; so the differences we find between auditioners, using a list that doubtless includes some of the *faux* auditioners, and non-auditioners probably understate the actual differences between judges who do and do not have an incentive to audition.

The table reveals a number of differences between auditioners and non-auditioners:

1. Auditioners are concentrated in the Second, Fifth, and D.C. Circuits, even though these are not the largest circuits and a larger circuit might be expected to contain more auditioners. Auditioners constituted

31 percent of the judges of those circuits, compared to 16 percent of the judges of the other circuits. The D.C. Circuit is especially overrepresented—45.1 percent of its members were auditioners at some point during the period of our study. But that isn't surprising. The D.C. Circuit has a disproportionate percentage of major cases; the judges, being located in Washington, are in a better position to "network" with high government officials likely to be influential in choosing a Supreme Court nominee; and, perhaps most important, because the District of Columbia has no Senators, a President has greater latitude in picking judges for the D.C. Circuit, and it is natural for him to exploit that latitude by picking auditioners in order to increase the promotion pool from which he will pick Supreme Court nominees if there are vacancies during his term or terms.

2. Younger appointees to the courts of appeals are significantly more likely to be in the promotion pool than those appointed at older ages; the average appointment age of an auditioner is 48.6, compared to 53.8 for non-auditioners. The Reagan administration, as we noted in chapter 3, was explicit about this, deeming youth "a very important" factor in the selection process, in order to ensure Justices' and judges' "lasting impact" on the law.[9]

3. Judges appointed by Republican Presidents are proportionately more likely to be in the promotion pool; 23.3 percent of the members of the pool were such appointees, and only 17.9 percent were appointees of Democratic Presidents—a ratio of 1.3 to 1—though the ratio of Supreme Court Justices appointed by Republican Presidents to those appointed by Democratic Presidents between 1930 and 2009 was only 1.05 to 1. This is further evidence of the greater ideological ambition of modern Republican Presidents.

4. Members of the promotion pool are disproportionately nonwhite and female. Of the 50 Hispanic, black, and Asian court of appeals judges appointed since 1930, 36 percent were in the promotion pool, compared to only 19.4 percent of white judges. The corresponding percentages of female and male judges are 39 and 18.8 percent.

9. Statement of Edward C. Schmults, Deputy Attorney General of the United States, in Arnold H. Lubasch, "3 Reported Picked for Appeals Court," *New York Times,* July 26, 1981, §1, p. 1. See also Sheldon Goldman, *Picking Federal Judges* 337 (1997).

5. The American Bar Association evaluates the qualifications of candidates for court of appeals judgeships. No members of our promotion pool received a "not qualified" rating—but only 1 percent of the non-auditioners received it. We find no statistically significant difference between the percentages of judges in and outside the promotion pool who received "qualified" versus "well qualified" ABA ratings.[10]

6. The quality (or reputed quality) of the law school attended by the auditioner—another possible proxy for competence—makes a difference. Of judges who had graduated from either the Harvard or Yale law school, 30.3 percent were in the promotion pool, compared to 18 percent who had gone elsewhere. We single out these two law schools (with a reservation noted later) because all the current Justices of the Supreme Court attended one of them, although Ginsburg for only one year (Harvard, before transferring to Columbia). More refined tests for determining which court of appeals judges would be the best candidates for the Supreme Court on pure competence grounds[11] have been proposed but, unsurprisingly, have had no influence on appointments.

7. Auditioners are slightly more ideological as measured by the absolute value of their senatorial courtesy score of .39, compared to .35 for non-auditioners. Remember that the senatorial courtesy score runs from a high positive number to a low negative one, so that the absolute score (that is, eliminating the minus sign) is a measure of how ideological the judge is in either a liberal or a conservative direction. The less ideological the judge, the less opposition he's likely to encounter in the Senate confirmation process, but also the smaller the President's legacy gain from appointing him.

8. Auditioners are more likely to be former federal lawyers or members

10. We have American Bar Association ratings for 485 court of appeals judges (97 auditioners and 388 non-auditioners). The ABA rated 36 percent of the auditioners as qualified and 64 percent as well qualified, and thus none unqualified. For non-auditioners the percentages were 31 percent qualified and 68 percent well qualified, besides the 1 percent unqualified.

11. See, for example, Stephen Choi and Mitu Gulati, "Choosing the Next Supreme Court Justice: An Empirical Ranking of Judicial Performance," 78 *Southern California Law Review* 23 (2004), and the comprehensive literature review by Frank B. Cross and Stefanie Lindquist, "Judging the Judges," 58 *Duke Law Journal* 1383 (2009).

of Congress than non-auditioners, although the numbers are small. Of the 31 court of appeals judges who had federal legal jobs when appointed, 12 (39 percent) were in the promotion pool, as were 4 of the 6 former members of Congress. These figures may seem to belie claims that the United States is moving toward a European-style professional judiciary.[12] But this ignores the facts that 8 of the 9 Supreme Court Justices today are former federal court of appeals judges and that 40 percent of court of appeals judges are former district judges and a number of others are former state judges, as are a number of district judges. Some district judges are former federal magistrate or bankruptcy judges.

9. Judges appointed to a court of appeals from another court are rarely found in the Supreme Court promotion pool. Of the 19 court of appeals judges appointed to the Supreme Court between 1930 and 2009, only Sotomayor and Whittaker had moved from the district court to the court of appeals. A judge who has served in two courts is likely to be too old to be considered for appointment to a third (the Supreme Court), though one of the 19 (Souter) started his judicial career in a state court and had served as a federal court of appeals judge, but only briefly (a matter of months), before his appointment to the Supreme Court.

Results of regressing the probability of being an auditioner on the variables in Table 8.5 are shown in Table 8.6. The only difference between the table's two regression equations is that the second has dummy variables for the Second, Fifth, and D.C. Circuits.[13] Unsurprisingly, we find that *Age at Appointment* has a significant negative coefficient; each additional year reduces by .015 the probability of the judge's being an auditioner. A judge appointed to the court of appeals at age 53 (the average

12. See William H. Rehnquist, "2001 Year-End Report on the Federal Judiciary," www .supremecourt.gov/publicinfo/year-end/2001year-endreport.aspx (visited Dec. 9, 2011); Teddy Davis, "Justice Scalia Praises Elena Kagan's Lack of Judicial Experience," *ABC News,* May 26, 2010. http://blogs.abcnews.com/politicalpunch/2010/05/justice-scalia-praises-elena-kagans-lack-of-judicial-experience.html (visited Dec. 9, 2011); Stephen Breyer, "Federal Judicial Compensation," Testimony before the House Committee on the Judiciary, Apr. 19, 2007, http://judiciary.house.gov/hearings/printers/110th/34757.PDF (visited Dec. 9, 2011).

13. We use regression (2) in Table 8.6 to calculate the probability estimates reported in the text. Regression (1) yields essentially the same estimates.

Table 8.6 Logit Regressions on Probability of Being an Auditioner, 1930–2009

Independent Variables	(1)	(2)
Age at Appointment	−.014**	−.015**
	(4.91)	(4.56)
Year Confirmed	−.012**	−.011**
	(5.60)	(4.77)
President (1 = Republican)	.109**	.106**
	(3.97)	(3.63)
Law School (1 = Harvard or Yale)	.076**	.067**
	(2.84)	(2.92)
Senatorial Courtesy Score	.200	.174
	(1.91)	(1.87)
Sex (1 = Female)	.208*	.203**
	(4.17)	(3.44)
Nonwhite (1 = Black, Hispanic,	.198**	.188**
or Asian)	(4.15)	(3.87)
Former District or State Judge	.002	.013
	(0.04)	(0.26)
Federal Government	.125*	.107
	(2.47)	(1.72)
State Government	−.049	−.032
	(0.43)	(0.28)
Law Professor	.082	.079
	(1.40)	(1.09)
D.C. Circuit	—	.128**
		(5.59)
Second Circuit	—	.087**
		(6.25)
Fifth Circuit	—	.095**
		(6.62)
Number of Observations	582	582

Notes:

1. All regression coefficients have been converted to marginal effects.

2. The number of observations is 582 rather than 585 because we do not have ideology scores for three judges.

3. Standard errors in eq. 1 are clustered by circuit.

age of appointment of the judges in our sample) has a 16 percent probability of being in the promotion pool, all else being equal, rising to 28 percent for a judge appointed at age 46 (one standard deviation below the mean age of appointment) and falling to 7 percent for a 60-year-old (one standard deviation above the mean age).

We find a negative and significant coefficient on *Year Confirmed:* a judge appointed earlier tends to have more years of service and hence a greater opportunity to be in the promotion pool and a longer time to remain there. Of course, eventually *Year Confirmed* loses all explanatory power; 30 years (say) after confirmation, the judge will have aged out of the promotion pool. To account for the aging-out effect, we make 1979 the *Year Confirmed* for judges confirmed in or before that year and use the actual year of confirmation for judges confirmed after 1979. Thus in regression (2) a judge confirmed before 1980 (57.6 percent of the judges in our sample) has a 23 percent probability of being in the pool, falling to 10 percent for a judge confirmed in 1990 and 5 percent for one confirmed in 2000. A judge confirmed in 1971 (the mean confirmation year for judges in our sample) had a 16 percent probability of being in the pool, and this increased to 22 percent for a judge confirmed in 1947 (one standard deviation below the mean) but fell to 11 percent for a judge confirmed in 1995 (one standard deviation above).

Judges appointed by Republican Presidents have a significantly higher probability of being in the pool: 21 percent, compared to 12 percent for judges appointed by Democratic Presidents. This partly reflects the greater number of Supreme Court Justices appointed from courts of appeals by Republican than by Democratic Presidents in the 1933–2009 period: 12 of 17 of the court of appeals judges promoted to the Supreme Court in that period (71 percent). But the *number* of Justices appointed by Democratic Presidents during this period was greater—21 out of the 39 appointed (54 percent)—which suggests that the incentive to audition might be greater among D than R court of appeals judges.

Diversity concerns have significantly influenced the makeup of the promotion pool. In 1980 only 8 percent of active court of appeals judges were female and 11 percent nonwhite; by 2010 these figures had grown to 30 percent and 20.5 percent. With other variables held constant, a white male has a 12 percent chance, a nonwhite male a 37 percent chance, and a white female a 39 percent chance of being in the pool. Because diversity concerns are recent, we reestimated the regressions for court of appeals judges active since 1970 rather than 1930 (429 versus 582 judges). But the results were very similar because there were so few female and nonwhite judges before 1970.

Graduates of the Harvard or Yale law school have a significantly higher probability of being in the pool than graduates of other law schools (21 versus 14 percent). This is a poor test of the effect of elite education, because there are other elite law schools, but it's a good test of the effect of attending Harvard or Yale. Because of the historical primacy of those schools in American legal education, the lay public and perhaps many members of Congress as well regard a degree from either of them as a qualification for the Supreme Court, though of course not the only qualification. In addition, the large pool of influential alumni (both inside and outside the Beltway) of these schools offers superior networking opportunities for judges seeking promotion.

Three of the four previous-employment variables (the omitted category is the private sector) are insignificant predictors of becoming an auditioner. But in equation (1) we see that a court of appeals judge who had worked for the federal government in a nonjudicial position is significantly more likely to be in the pool. In equation (2), the dummy variable for the D.C. Circuit captures the previous-employment effect; its judges are significantly more likely to be in the pool than judges in other circuits (27 percent versus 14 percent)—and 31 percent of its judges, but only 6 percent of judges of other courts of appeals, had worked for the federal government in nonjudicial positions. Second and Fifth Circuit judges also have a significantly higher probability of being in the auditioner pool—21 percent and 23 percent respectively, compared to 12 percent for circuits other than those two circuits plus the D.C. Circuit.

We find no significant difference in likelihood of being an auditioner between court of appeals judges without prior judicial experience and those who had been state judges or federal district judges. The absolute value of the senatorial courtesy score also has no significant effect on the probability of being an auditioner, and neither does prior experience as a state judge or federal district judge.

The regression analysis does a reasonable job of identifying the characteristics that distinguish auditioners from non-auditioners. The average judge on our list of 122 auditioners has a .38 predicted probability of being in the promotion pool, compared to .16 for the 460 other judges in the sample, only 9 percent of whom had a predicted probability of being an auditioner that was as high as the mean predicted probability of judges on our list of auditioners.

Our model also does well in predicting that judges who have a higher probability of being in the promotion pool are also more likely to be promoted to the Supreme Court. Nineteen judges in our sample were promoted, 17 directly from courts of appeals and 2 others—Vinson and Marshall—after they had resigned from those courts. The mean predicted probability that one of the 19 would be an auditioner is .50, compared to .36 for auditioners who were not promoted. And a 10 percent increase in the predicted probability of being an auditioner increases the probability of promotion to the Supreme Court by 5.8 percent.[14]

Of the 13 judges appointed to a court of appeals after 1950 who had the highest predicted probabilities (ranging from 77 to 94 percent, with a mean of 84 percent) of being in the promotion pool, five became Justices (Ginsburg, Kennedy, Scalia, Sotomayor, and Thomas). One was nominated but forced to withdraw (Douglas Ginsburg). Another (Kenneth Starr) resigned from the court of appeals in 1989 when passed over for appointment to the Court but until then had been a leading candidate. Three others (Edith Jones, Amalya Kearse, and Patricia Wald) were in the pool at one time but are now too old. None of the remaining judges (Harry Edwards, Carolyn King, and Deanell Tacha) were ever in the promotion pool and are unlikely to be so in the future because of their age.

Seven of the 19 court of appeals judges appointed to the Supreme Court during the period covered by our study had predicted probabilities of being appointed of between 12.7 percent (Whittaker) and 26.1 percent (Minton), with a mean of 19.1 percent, the others being Blackmun, Harlan, Roberts, Souter, and Stevens. How to explain the appointment of these seven to the Court? It is well known that personal connections played a critical role in the appointment of Minton, Blackmun, Stevens, and Souter: Minton had served in the Senate with Truman (who appointed him) and was a close friend—and Truman was notorious for appointing cronies to high office. Blackmun was a friend of Chief Justice

14. This is calculated from a logit regression in which the dependent variable equals 1 if the court of appeals judge is promoted to the Supreme Court and 0 if he is not and the independent variable is the estimated probability of being an auditioner, derived from equation (2) in Table 8.6. The 5.8 percent increase in the probability of promotion (or the elasticity of .58) is the marginal regression coefficient of .09 multiplied by the ratio of the mean probability of being an auditioner to the probability of promotion to the Supreme Court (2096 /.0325 = 6.449).

Burger, who pressed Nixon to appoint him. Stevens was a former college roommate of Senator Percy, a highly influential Republican Senator (Stevens was appointed to the Supreme Court by President Ford), and Souter was a protégé of Senator Rudman of New Hampshire, who persuaded his friend John Sununu, chief of staff to the first President Bush, to persuade Bush to appoint Souter.

Less well known are the connections that played a significant role in the appointments of Harlan and Whittaker. Harlan was close to Eisenhower's attorney general, Herbert Brownell, Jr., and his appointment to the Supreme Court has been called "an abdication [by Eisenhower] to the personal preference of [Eisenhower's] attorney general."[15] Whittaker had "a sponsor, someone with enough influence and connections to the right people in power to get him appointed"[16]—namely Roy Roberts, who, being close to Eisenhower before, during, and after his election, was one of his trusted political advisers. Notice too that the pool from which Eisenhower picked Supreme Court Justices (after his first appointment, that of Warren to be Chief Justice) was smaller than usual because he limited it to sitting judges, which Harlan and Whittaker happened to be. Harlan turned out to be an outstanding Supreme Court Justice, Whittaker a dreadful one who resigned after five years in the wake of a nervous breakdown brought about by inability, apparently of psychiatric origin, to cope with the Court's workload.

The current Chief Justice, John Roberts, doesn't fit this mold. His relatively low predicted probability of being an auditioner (.23) is attributable to how recently he had been appointed to the court of appeals (2003) given the highly significant negative effect of *Year Confirmed* in the regressions in Table 8.6. He probably owed his appointment to factors that, unlike his having attended Harvard Law School and served in the executive branch and as a judge of the D.C. Circuit, we have not attempted to quantify: his sterling academic record, his enormous success as a Supreme Court advocate, his unimpeachable conservative credentials, and his personal charm.

15. Craig Alan Smith, *Failing Justice: Charles Evans Whittaker on the Supreme Court* 86 (2005). See also id. at 78.

16. Id. at 44–45.

Voting Behavior of Auditioners for the Supreme Court

If we assume, plausibly, that most judges in the promotion pool desire elevation to the Supreme Court, do they audition—that is, do they (or some of them) do things intended to increase the probability of their being appointed to the Court? One of the things an auditioner might try to do would be to vote in cases in a way designed to ingratiate himself with the present or a future President, or with other present or future officials or opinion makers who might influence a Supreme Court appointment. It's difficult for judges to assess the impact of any particular decision on their promotion chances. But since the 1960s, a period that saw a sharp rise in crime rates and a series of notorious Supreme Court decisions favoring criminal defendants, the rights of such defendants have been widely unpopular.[17] Efforts by the courts and Congress to cut back on the rights the Warren Court bestowed on criminal defendants and prison inmates have been supported by Republicans and Democrats (notably President Clinton) alike. No President since Carter has called for the abolition of capital punishment; and though support for capital punishment has declined in recent years, 64 percent of Americans continue to support it,[18] while 82 percent believe that judges are "not harsh enough" on criminals.[19]

Being tagged as "soft on crime" would be sure to lengthen the odds of a judge's being promoted to the Supreme Court, and knowing this, some judges in the promotion pool might change their judicial voting behavior in criminal cases. We test this hypothesis on data from the updated Sunstein database,[20] which though primarily civil contains two categories of criminal cases (like all cases in the database, decided in published court

---

17. See, for example, William J. Stuntz, *The Collapse of American Criminal Justice*, ch. 8 (2011).

18. See Frank Newport, "In U.S. 64% Support Death Penalty in Cases of Murder: Half Say Death Penalty Not Imposed Often Enough," Nov. 8, 2010, www.gallup.com/poll/144284/Support-Death-Penalty-Cases-Murder.aspx (visited Jan. 5, 2012).

19. James A. Davis, Tom W. Smith, and Peter V. Marsden, *GSS (General Social Survey) Update 1972–2010*, www.norc.uchicago.edu/GSS+Website/ (visited Jan. 5, 2012). The relevant variable is "COURTS" in the mnemonic index.

20. See chapter 4. We exclude votes cast by district judges sitting in a court of appeals by designation.

of appeals opinions between 1995 and 2008)—death penalty appeals, and all criminal appeals in the Third, Fourth, and D.C. Circuits. We divide the latter group into ordinary ("street crime") and white-collar appeals, thus producing a threefold division:

> *Death penalty appeals.* This subset covers 11 of the 12 circuits (there were no capital cases in the D.C. Circuit) and includes 314 cases, or 942 votes. Eliminating votes cast by district court judges and others sitting by designation (that is, visiting judges) left 926 votes.
> *Ordinary ("street crime") criminal appeals.* This subset includes 1274 criminal appeals in cases primarily involving drug possession and distribution, robbery, and illegal possession of guns but is limited to judges in the three circuits. Excluding votes cast by judges sitting by designation, we are left with 3542 such votes.
> *"White-collar" criminal appeals.* This subset, also limited to the three circuits, consists of 468 cases of white-collar crime (fraud, bribery, money laundering, tax evasion, embezzlement, etc.),[21] which yield a total of 1298 votes cast by court of appeals judges (again we exclude visiting judges).

Americans have been said to believe "that street crime is our worst social problem and that corporate crime is not as dangerous or costly."[22] Consistent with this suggestion, a national public opinion poll in 2005 reported that a majority of Americans believe that "violent criminals should be punished more severely than white-collar criminals."[23] This leads us to suspect that auditioner effects, if they exist, will be smaller in category (3) than in (1) or (2). True, the poll predated the Madoff, insider-trading, and other recent corporate scandals, which may have changed the public's view of the relative gravity of the two sorts of criminal; but our data (which end in 2008) also precede those scandals.

---

21. For a list of white-collar crimes, see Cornell University Law School, Legal Information Institute, "White-Collar Crime: An Overview," http://topics.law.cornell.edu/wex/White -collar_crime (visited Dec. 9, 2011).

22. David M. Newman, *Sociology: Exploring the Architecture of Everyday Life* 113 (2010).

23. Kristy Holtfreter et al., "Public Perceptions of White-Collar Crime and Punishment," 36 *Journal of Criminal Justice* 50 (2008).

We trimmed the auditioner list by excluding votes by judges older than 60 unless they had been appointed by a President of the same party as the current President, in which event we extended the eligibility age to 62. Only one of the 29 Justices appointed since 1945 was older than 62—Powell, who was 64 (and not a judge, so he wouldn't be on our list of auditioners regardless of his age). Four others, however—Warren, Burger, Blackmun, and Ginsburg—were between 60 and 62.

This trimming gives us a set of ex-auditioners—judges who were once auditioners but were too old when they cast some of the judicial votes in the database to be included in the auditioner pool. For example, Judge Wilkinson of the Fourth Circuit cast 113 votes in the Sunstein database as an auditioner and 24 as an ex-auditioner, and Judge Wilkins (also of the Fourth Circuit) cast 98 judicial votes as an auditioner and 26 as an ex-auditioner. The ex-auditioner sample enables us to test the alternative hypothesis that judges who are less likely to favor criminal defendants are more likely to be selected as auditioners in the first place; for if that hypothesis is correct we would find no difference in voting behavior between auditioners and ex-auditioners.

Table 8.7 reveals that auditioners are significantly less likely to vote for defendants in capital punishment and street-crime cases than either non- or ex-auditioners are. There are no significant differences in the white-collar category, where the emotions of the public are less likely to be aroused by the reversal of a conviction or sentence.

Regression analysis allows us to test whether these results hold when we control for other variables. We expect the judge's ideology (proxied

Table 8.7 Fraction of Votes against Defendant in Criminal Appeals, Sunstein Data, 1995–2008 *(number of votes in parentheses)*

Judge Type	Capital Punishment	Street Crime	White-Collar Crime
Non-auditioners	.662**	.634**	.605
	(678)	(2562)	(979)
Auditioners	.796	.714	.592
	(157)	(685)	(223)
Ex-auditioners	.659*	.667	.573
	(91)	(295)	(96)

Note: The asterisks indicate statistically significant differences between auditioners and non-auditioners or between auditioners and ex-auditioners.

by the party of the appointing President), the ideology of the panel (prox-ied by whether a majority of the judges on the panel were appointed by Democratic or Republican Presidents), and the ideology of his circuit (as proxied by the fraction of active judges appointed by Republican Presidents) to influence the judge's vote. In the capital-punishment regression we need to determine whether the lower court decision was for or against the defendant, in order to control for the appellate courts' propensity to affirm; this adjustment is unnecessary in the other two categories, in which almost all appeals are by defendants. Since the street-crime and white-collar categories include only votes of judges in three circuits, we control for ideological and other differences among these circuits by in-cluding dummy circuit variables (with the D.C. Circuit the omitted cate-gory). We include sex and race variables and a variable for whether the judge had worked as a government lawyer before being appointed to the court of appeals.

Table 8.8 presents our regressions, which are logit regressions because the dependent variable (whether the judge voted for or against the crimi-nal defendant) is dichotomous. In the death penalty and street-crime re-gressions, auditioners are significantly more likely to vote against defen-dants than either non-auditioners or ex-auditioners (who vote almost identically). The regression coefficients imply that, other things being equal, the probability of voting against the defendant in death penalty cases is 81 percent for auditioners and 71 percent for non-auditioners and ex-auditioners when the defendant is appealing his conviction. If the government is appealing, the probability of reversal and thus of a decision in the government's favor is 65 percent for auditioners compared to 51 percent for ex-auditioners and 52 percent for non-auditioners. Audition-ers are also more likely to vote to affirm convictions of street crimes—the predicted probability is 64 percent, compared to 51 percent for ex-auditioners and 50 percent for non-auditioners. But we find no statistically significant differences among auditioners, non-auditioners, and ex-auditioners in the white-collar regression.

The only significant circuit variable is *Fourth Circuit* in the street-crime regression. Fourth Circuit judges are more likely to favor the gov-ernment in criminal appeals than judges in the Third and D.C. Circuits; the respective predicted probabilities are .69, .62, and .64. These results

Table 8.8 Regression Analysis of Votes for Government in Criminal Appeals, Sunstein Data, 1995–2008

	Death Penalty (1)	Street Crime (2)	White-Collar Crime (3)
Auditioner	.122*	.054**	−.058
	(2.06)	(2.40)	(1.48)
Ex-Auditioner	.004	.009	−.078
	(0.05)	(0.27)	(1.38)
Lower Court Decision	.185**	—	—
(1 = for defendant)	(4.01)		
President (1 = Republican)	.108*	.021	.068
	(2.23)	(1.01)	(1.89)
Panel Majority (1 = Democratic)	−.055	−.078**	−.023
	(0.82)	(3.89)	(0.67)
Former Government Attorney	−.019	−.007	.032
	(0.65)	(0.38)	(1.11)
Nonwhite	−.013	−.035	−.051
	(0.23)	(1.31)	(1.09)
Sex (1 = female)	−.081	.029	.078*
	(1.39)	(1.43)	(2.25)
Fraction Republican	.457*	—	—
	(1.52)		
Third Circuit		−.024	−.036
		(1.08)	(0.93)
Fourth Circuit		.048*	.070
		(2.25)	(1.77)
Number of Observations	926	3542	1298

Notes:

1. The dependent variable is whether the judge voted against the defendant (against = 1 and for = 0).

2. All regression coefficients are converted to marginal effects.

3. Standard errors are clustered by circuit in the death penalty regression, which includes data for all circuits except the D.C. Circuit.

4. We use robust standard errors in columns (2) and (3), which are equations limited to the Third, Fourth, and D.C. Circuits.

are consistent with the widely held belief that the Fourth Circuit was one of the most conservative courts of appeals until appointments by President Obama, not reflected in our data.

Our results suggest that court of appeals judges who have a good shot at the Supreme Court tend to alter their judicial behavior in order to increase their chances, though this is just an average tendency—we do not suggest that all court of appeals judges in what we are calling the promotion pool audition for the Supreme Court.

Auditioning for the Courts of Appeals

Compiling a list of district judge auditioners for promotion to courts of appeals is infeasible because we lack presidential short lists or (with rare exceptions) significant media coverage or scholarly analysis of federal district judges.[24] To fill the gap, we estimate a regression in which the dependent variable is whether the district judge was promoted to the court of appeals. The aim is to identify the characteristics that explain the promotion, on the theory that other judges having those characteristics had a sufficiently similar probability of being promoted to give them an incentive to try to increase their chances of promotion, assuming they wanted to be promoted to the court of appeals (not all do). For example, district judge auditioners might give criminal defendants longer sentences; a previous study found that district judges who ruled in favor of the constitutionality of the Sentencing Reform Act of 1984, which curtailed sentencing discretion and was supported by Democratic as well as Republican legislators, were more likely to be promoted to the courts of appeals than district judges who ruled against the act's constitutionality.[25]

Table 8.9 compares characteristics of district judges who were and were not promoted to courts of appeals in the period 1981 to 2010; the characteristics are the same ones that we used to predict membership in the auditioner pool for the Supreme Court. Recall from Table 8.7 that members of the Supreme Court promotion pool came disproportionately from the Second, Fifth, and D.C. Circuits. In contrast, members of the court of appeals promotion pool are concentrated in districts in the First, Second, Third, and Fourth Circuits; 35 of the 73 district judges in the pool (48 percent) came from such districts, even though these districts contained only 32 percent of the district judges confirmed since 1981. We do not have an explanation.

24. *Picking Federal Judges*, note 10 above, is an exception; it is a series of case studies of the circumstances of appointment to the courts of appeals. But the studies are illustrative rather than systematic.

25. Cohen, "Explaining Judicial Behavior or What's 'Unconstitutional' about the Sentencing Commission," note 3 above.

Table 8.9 Comparison of District Judges Promoted and Not Promoted to Courts of Appeals, 1981–2010

	Number Not Promoted	Number Promoted	Percent Promoted
All Judges	975	73	6.97
Circuit (of District Court)			
1st	36	3	7.69
2d	94	11	10.48
3rd	89	13	12.75
4th	80	8	9.09
5th	105	5	4.55
6th	94	6	6.00
7th	68	5	6.85
8th	68	5	6.85
9th	172	9	4.97
10th	57	2	3.39
11th	91	5	5.21
D.C.	21	1	4.55
Attributes			
Mean Age at Appointment	50.28	44.93	—
Year Confirmed	1995.26	1988.04	—
Appointed to District Court by Republican President	642	57	8.15
Appointed to District Court by Democratic President	333	16	4.58
Female	198	21	9.59
Male	777	52	6.27
White	809	59	6.80
Nonwhite	166	14	7.78
ABA: Well Qualified	599	35	5.52
ABA: Qualified	370	37	9.09
ABA: Not Qualified	6	1	14.29
Harvard or Yale Law School	95	12	11.21
All Other Law Schools	880	61	6.48
Mean Absolute Value of Senatorial Courtesy Score	0.34	0.31	—
Employment Prior to Promotion			
Non–Article III Federal Judge, or State Judge	445	25	5.32
Federal Government Employee	89	11	11.00
State Government Employee	34	3	8.11
Law Professor	12	5	29.41
Private Sector	395	29	6.84

Note: Senatorial courtesy scores (see http://clboyd.net/ideology.html) were not available for judges appointed after 2006.

District judges promoted to a court of appeals were, on average, five years younger when appointed to the district court than the other district judges (44.9 versus 50.3), a difference close to that between court of appeals judges who were in the Supreme Court promotion pool and those who were not (48.6 versus 53.8).

Another similarity between the two promotion pools is that judges appointed by Republican Presidents are more likely to be in the pool. Republican Presidents appointed 67 percent (699/1048) of the district judges confirmed since 1981 but 78 percent of the district judges promoted to courts of appeals (57 of the 73 judges promoted). Women and nonwhites are promoted at higher rates than males and whites, but the differences are not statistically significant.

A previous study found that for judges appointed between 1946 and 1995, the higher the ABA rating the better the odds of promotion, though this result did not hold for the judges appointed between 1981 and 1995.[26] Only seven judges in our dataset (1981–2010) received a rating of "not qualified," and just one of the seven was promoted: David Hamilton to the Seventh Circuit.[27] The other two ratings are "qualified" and "well qualified"—and oddly, judges rated "qualified" were more likely to be promoted than those rated "well qualified." This could reflect Republican Presidents' well-known mistrust of the ABA ratings (a mistrust that stems from the struggle over Robert Bork's nomination to the Supreme Court in 1987). A Republican President (or his advisers) might think that the ABA was reluctant to rate any conservative higher than "qualified" and therefore that a district judge rated "well qualified" might be a closet liberal.

As with promotions to the Supreme Court, district judges who attended Harvard or Yale law school were more likely to be promoted to a court of appeals than other district judges. Promoted judges also had a lower absolute senatorial courtesy score (.31 versus .34), suggesting they are less ideological than the other judges; but the difference is not statistically significant.

26. Elisha Carol Savchak et al., "Taking It to the Next Level: The Elevation of District Court Judges to the U.S. Court of Appeals," 50 *American Journal of Political Science* 478, 486 (2006).

27. A highly regarded judge—so much for ABA ratings!

District judges who before becoming district judges had served as federal magistrate judges, bankruptcy judges, or state judges had the lowest promotion rate (5.3 percent of the 470 judges in these groups). Former full-time law professors were promoted from the district court to the court of appeals at the highest rate of all, but the numbers are very small—5 out of 17.

Table 8.10 presents the results of logit regressions of the probability of promotion to a court of appeals. Equation (1) is based on data for 930 judges and includes two ideology variables: the party of the appointing President and the absolute value of the judge's senatorial courtesy score, which however is available only for judges appointed before 2006. Equation (2) is based on data for 1048 judges; the number is larger because it omits senatorial courtesy scores and therefore includes judges appointed since as well as before 2006.

Four variables in the table are significant predictors of the probability of promotion. Youth is one. The predicted probability (calculated from equation (2)) of promotion for a judge appointed to the district court when he is 50 is only .02 and at 60 the odds shrink almost to zero (.007), while for 40-year-olds the predicted probability is .08. The younger the age at which the judge is appointed and hence the more years he is likely to serve before he ages out of the promotion pool, the greater the likelihood of promotion. Judges appointed to the district court in 1982 had a .20 predicted probability of promotion, but the probability was only .04 for judges appointed in 1992 and .01 for those appointed in 2002. When age at appointment and year of confirmation are combined, the probability of promotion for a judge appointed at age 40 is .46 if he was appointed in 1982, .13 if he was appointed in 1992, and .02 if he was appointed in 2002. The corresponding figures for a judge appointed at age 50 are .19 in 1982, .04 in 1992, and .007 in 2002, while for a judge appointed at age 60 the probabilities are .06 if he was confirmed in 1982, .01 if in 1992, and .002 if in 2002.

Women district judges have a higher probability of promotion than men—4 percent versus 2 percent. A woman appointed in 1982 at age 40 has a predicted probability of promotion of .61, compared to .42 for a male counterpart.

The 73 judges promoted to courts of appeals in the 1981–2010 period

Table 8.10 Logit Regressions of Promotion to the Court of Appeals of District Judges Appointed between 1981 and 2010

	Equation (1)	Equation (2)
Age at Appointment	−.004**	−.003**
	(4.57)	(4.08)
Year Confirmed	−.006**	−.004**
	(5.44)	(6.10)
Party of Appointing President (1 = Republican)	−.015	−.013
	(1.16)	(1.45)
ABA Rating (1 = Well Qualified)	0.0005	.001
	(0.05)	(0.11)
Law School (1 = Harvard or Yale)	.013	.009
	(0.90)	(0.90)
Absolute Value of Senatorial Courtesy Score	−.010	—
	(0.33)	
Sex (1 = Female)	.025*	.018*
	(2.45)	(2.44)
Nonwhite (1 = Black, Hispanic, or Asian)	.015	.011
	(1.21)	(1.21)
Former Judge	.0001	.0001
	(0.01)	(0.01)
Former Federal Employee	.004	.003
	(0.25)	(0.24)
Former State Employee	.002	.001
	(0.11)	(0.09)
Former Law Professor	.049	.035
	(1.83)	(1.77)
First Circuit	.005	.003
	(0.24)	(0.21)
Second Circuit	.025	.020
	(1.59)	(1.76)
Third Circuit	.044**	.032**
	(2.88)	(2.90)
Fourth Circuit	.019	.014
	(1.23)	(1.21)
Number of Observations	930	1048

Notes:
  1. Robust standard errors.
  2. Private Sector is the omitted prior job category.

had a predicted probability of promotion of .22, compared to .06 for the other judges. Seven of the 12 district judges who had a predicted probability of promotion above .50 were promoted, compared to only 2 with a predicted probability below .02. These two were Norman Stahl and Charles Pickering. Stahl was 61 at the time of his promotion. Pickering, a

66-year-old recess appointment, retired when it became clear that the Senate would not confirm him.

Voting Behavior of Auditioners for the Courts of Appeals

To determine whether district judges in the promotion pool for the court of appeals are, like court of appeals judges in the promotion pool for the Supreme Court, tougher on criminal defendants than are non- or ex-auditioners, we created a dataset consisting of all district judges appointed between 1981 and 2010 who were promoted to a court of appeals, plus a 10 percent random sample of judges who had been appointed to the district court in the same period but were not promoted. Among judges who had served more than 16 years in the district court we distinguish between their first 16 years and their later service, since even judges who had a high probability of promotion would be unlikely to audition after 16 years because their odds of promotion would be small then, for remember that the average age of appointment to the district court is 50. This does not mean that promotion is out of the question after 16 years of service on the district court; 3 judges in our dataset of judges promoted to the court of appeals were promoted after having served that long (Gibbons, Prado, and Tinder). But it is rare. The average length of service on the district court prior to promotion is 7.4 years, with a standard deviation of 5; promotion after 16 years would be two standard deviations above the mean.

Our dependent variable in the first part of this section of the chapter is the fraction of criminal cases in which the judge had been reversed by the court of appeals. Judges who are reversed more often are likely to be tougher sentencers, because the vast majority of criminal appeals are by the criminal defendant rather than by the government, and most federal criminal appeals challenge either pro-government rulings by the district judge or the length of the sentence that the judge imposed (and often both); a reversal in an appeal by a criminal defendant is, obviously, a decision in favor of a criminal defendant.[28] We'll call district judges who are

---

28. In fiscal year 2010, 12,026 sentencing appeals by criminal defendants raised issues under the federal sentencing guidelines, compared to only 156 appeals by the government.

reversed frequently in criminal cases "harsh sentencers," but this is short-hand for judges whose rulings, not limited to sentence severity, strongly favor the government.

Our data are limited to cases that were appealed and were reported in Westlaw. But those are the cases in which district judges are most likely to audition, because they tend to be the cases with high visibility. We note, however, an important qualification: a high reversal rate may reflect not that the district judge is tough on crime but that he is a bad judge, or some combination of the two. If the bad-judge factor dominates, the reversal rate will be a poor proxy for toughness in criminal sentencing. Indeed, if bad district judges are less likely to be promoted and if reversal rates mainly reflect poor quality, judges who are promoted or more likely to be promoted will have lower rather than higher reversal rates in criminal cases.

Although our original sample contained 73 judges who were promoted to courts of appeals and 98 who were not, we can't use all these judges in our analysis of reversal rates because for some of them no appeals from their decisions are recorded in Westlaw; 12 of the 73 judges promoted, and 1 of the 98 not promoted, have no recorded appeals. The number of recorded appeals for the other judges ranged from 1 to 295; the mean was 30.7 and the standard deviation 36.5. We computed mean reversal rates, weighting the individual judge's reversal rate by the number of appeals to avoid distorting the mean.

To test the hypothesis that district judges who are tougher on criminals are more likely to be promoted, we divided the judges (both those promoted and those not promoted) into three groups: harsh sentencers, defined as judges whose reversal rate was one or more standard deviations above the mean; moderate sentencers, judges whose reversal rate was within one standard deviation of the mean; and lenient sentencers, whose reversal rate was one or more standard deviations below the mean. Since the weighted mean reversal rate is .30 and the standard deviation .11, the reversal rate is ≥.41 for a harsh sentencer,

---

U.S. Sentencing Commission, *2010 Sourcebook of Federal Sentencing Statistics,* www.ussc .gov/Data_and_Statistics/Annual_Reports_and_Sourcebooks/2010/Table57.pdf and Table 58.pdf (visited Dec. 9, 2011).

Table 8.11 Predicted Probabilities of Promotion to Court of Appeals of Harsh, Moderate, and Lenient Sentencers

Average Predicted Probability of Promotion of Auditioners (= judges in their first 16 years of tenure)	Harsh Sentencers	Moderate	Lenient
Weighted (by number of cases and judges)	.088	.074	.050
	(40)	(85)	(33)
Unweighted	.167	.115	.137
	(40)	(85)	(33)

Notes:
  1. Number of district judges is in parentheses.
  2. Because we included all the judges who were promoted but only a 10 percent sample of the others, the first row of numbers weights judges in the second group ten times more heavily than judges in the first group. The second row is an unweighted average of the predicted probabilities of promotion.

≤.19 for a lenient sentencer, and between >.19 and <.41 for a moderate one.

Table 8.11 compares the predicted probabilities of promotion (from regression equation (2) in Table 8.10) for each of the three groups. The table reveals that harsh sentencers always have the highest average probability of promotion, followed by either moderate sentencers and then lenient sentencers (weighted averages) or lenient and then moderate ones (unweighted averages). But none of these differences is statistically significant.

In Table 8.12 we analyze the data in another way. Instead of asking whether tougher sentencers have higher probabilities of promotion, we ask first whether judges who were promoted are harsher sentencers, as proxied by reversal rates, than those who are not; second, whether judges who were not promoted but had probabilities of promotion in the top 25 percent were harsher sentencers than those in the bottom 75 percent; and third, whether judges who were never promoted but had been district judges for more than 16 years were tougher sentencers in their first 16 years (the presumed auditioner years) than in the subsequent years, when our presumption is that they were ex-auditioners.[29]

The results are mixed. Contrary to our hypothesis, judges who were

29. We did not perform a similar test for judges who were promoted, because we had data on reversals before and after 16 years for only two judges.

Table 8.12   Reversal Rates for Judges Promoted, Judges Not Promoted, Auditioners, and
Non-Auditioners

| | | Judges Not Promoted | | |
| | | | Probability of Promotion | |
Average Reversal Rate	Judges Promoted	All	> .10	≤ .10
Auditioners (= judges during	.273	.308	.32	.30
their first 16 years of tenure)	(61)	(97)	(25)	(72)
Judges who served > 16 years	—			
First 16 years of service	—	.316	.31	.33
		(37)	(18)	(19)
After 16 years of service	—	.288	.24	.35
		(37)	(18)	(19)

Notes:
   1. Number of district judges is in parentheses.
   2 We weight each judge's reversal rate by the number of cases appealed.

promoted had a lower rather than a higher reversal rate than judges not
promoted—.27 compared to .31. Although the difference is not statistically significant, it suggests that quality, proxied by the reversal rate, dominates harshness in sentencing as a path to promotion.

As for the judges who were not promoted, the reversal rate was higher
(.32 versus .30) for those who had a higher probability of promotion and
for judges during their first 16 years on the bench compared to their subsequent years (.32 versus .29). This difference is even greater for the
judges who have a high probability of promotion (.31 versus .24), but it
reverses for the judges who have a low probability of promotion (.33 versus .35). None of these results is statistically significant.

We can use regression analysis to test the hypothesis that district judges
who were promoted, or had higher probabilities of promotion, were
harsher sentencers. We do not present the regression results in detail,
however, because we find no significant effects of the promotion variables
or the other judge-specific variables.

The dependent variable is the reversal rate (our proxy for harsh sentencing), and the independent variables include whether the judge was
promoted, the probability of his promotion, whether he was in the promotion pool, and the fraction of cases involving white-collar crimes. In
some regressions we added the variables from Table 8.10 (such as prior

employment, sex, and party of the appointing President) and dummy variables for the individual circuits. Except for those dummies (which were jointly significant), none of the independent variables was statistically significant. In short, introducing a number of independent variables does not change the conclusion that there is no consistent relation between tough sentencing and either promotion or predicted probability of promotion. The reason, as noted earlier, may be that a higher reversal rate may indicate not a tough sentencer but a bad judge, or both, and to the extent that it indicates a bad judge it reduces the likelihood of promotion.

We can use the recently obtained TRAC data (see chapter 5)—individual judge sentencing data—rather than a proxy for sentencing severity to obtain a sharper insight into sentencing severity as evidence of auditioning behavior. We begin by using the data to test the hypothesis that average prison sentences decline once the judge has been on the district court for more than 16 years, since after that, as our earlier analysis demonstrated, his odds of promotion are so small that we would not expect him to engage in auditioning behavior, such as being especially tough on defendants.

As in chapter 5, we use the four largest categories of offenses in the TRAC dataset: organized-crime drug offenses, other drug offenses, weapons offenses, and immigration offenses. To sharpen comparison, we initially limit analysis to sentences post-*Booker* (2006–2011) and thus exclude the 16 district judges who having been promoted to the court of appeals imposed no sentences in that period. The results are presented in Tables 8.13 and 8.14; the latter table presents regression results.

The raw sentencing data in the first table do not reveal any tendency for sentences to become shorter after the district judge has aged out of the promotion pool. But when other variables likely to influence sentence length are held constant by means of the regression analysis in the second table, the effect of length of service on all four categories of offense is statistically significant. Yet while sentences are, as hypothesized, longer in a district judge's first 16 years of service in two of the categories—organized-crime drug offenses and weapons offenses—they are shorter in the other two offense categories. As expected, sentences are longer if the judge was appointed by a Republican President or if there was a trial, and

Table 8.13   Prison Sentences Imposed by District Judges, Grouped by Length of Service, 2006–2011 *(number of sentences in parentheses)*

Sentence Length (Months)	Length of Service (Years)					
	1–5	6–10	11–15	16–20	21–25	> 25
All Judges						
Organized-Crime Drugs	103.98	103.97	96.75	97.83	99.94	102.33
	(3,677)	(7,978)	(7,148)	(6,260)	(3,449)	(3,499)
Other Drug Offenses	72.08	66.52	72.16	78.54	76.10	84.84
	(12,426)	(24,577)	(17,285)	(14,123)	(7,664)	(9,158)
Weapons Offenses	85.45	82.70	79.44	82.00	82.43	79.25
	(5,630)	(9,027)	(8,076)	(7,610)	(4,236)	(4,668)
Immigration Offenses	19.81	17.13	20.59	20.26	20.63	19.11
	(17,347)	(45,014)	(19,635)	(16,066)	(7,876)	(16,242)
All	53.81	45.98	57.24	60.63	61.99	54.08
	(39,080)	(86,596)	(52,144)	(44,059)	(23,225)	(33,567)
R Judges						
Organized-Crime Drugs	104.84	107.25	98.75	101.59	99.94	106.96
	(3,595)	(5,659)	(451)	(4,131)	(3,449)	(1,966)
Other Drug Offenses	72.05	63.18	91.72	83.33	76.10	89.38
	(12,157)	(19,799)	(984)	(9,605)	(7,664)	(4,850)
Weapons Offenses	86.62	82.31	105.79	84.75	82.43	79.30
	(5,455)	(6,843)	(505)	(5,515)	(4,236)	(2,331)
Immigration Offenses	19.92	16.32	19.27	23.48	20.63	19.34
	(16,921)	(39,409)	(895)	(9,526)	(7,876)	(8,169)
All	54.09	42.73	72.47	66.41	61.98	56.97
	(38,128)	(71,710)	(2,835)	(28,777)	(23,225)	(17,316)

D Judges

Organized-Crime Drugs	66.20	95.98	96.61	90.53	96.39	—
	(82)	(2,319)	(6,697)	(2,129)	(1,533)	(0)
Other Drug Offenses	73.81	80.34	70.98	68.37	79.74	—
	(269)	(4,778)	(16,301)	(4,518)	(4,308)	(0)
Weapons Offenses	49.04	83.92	77.68	74.77	79.20	—
	(175)	(2,184)	(7,571)	(2,095)	(2,337)	(0)
Immigration Offenses	15.56	22.84	20.65	15.56	18.87	—
	(426)	(5,605)	(18,740)	(6,540)	(8,073)	(0)
All	42.53	61.65	56.36	49.74	50.99	—
	(952)	(14,886)	(49,309)	(15,282)	(16,251)	(0)

longer also when the fraction of the judges of the court of appeals who were appointed by a Republican President is larger. With one exception —the effect of the fraction of R court of appeals judges on the sentences for weapons offenses—these correlations are statistically significant.

A weakness of the approach, and a possible explanation for the inconsistent correlation between sentence severity and judge's length of service, is that we implicitly assume that *all* district judges are in the promotion pool until they have completed 16 years of service. The assumption is false. Some district judges do not want to be court of appeals judges— they think being an appellate judge is boring. (Trials are more exciting than appellate arguments, and litigation at the trial level involves interactions with lawyers, jurors, and witnesses that some judges find more interesting, if less cerebral, than the more academic atmosphere of appellate proceedings.) And others, for various reasons, such as lack of the right political contacts or preferred credentials, know they'll not be appointed to a court of appeals and think it a waste of time to audition even if they would like the appointment. It is because not all district judges, regardless of age, are potential auditioners that earlier in the chapter we used district judges who are appointed to the court of appeals as our auditioner sample.

So let us do that now, using the TRAC data. We present the results in Table 8.15. We do not confine the data to the post-*Booker* era but instead report the post-*Booker* data in a separate row. A judge promoted since 2005 would be unlikely to have imposed many sentences since 2005, since the interval to his promotion would have been short. The TRAC data go back to 2003, and by including the pre-2005 data we increase the sample size without distorting the auditioner/non-auditioner comparison seriously, because even before *Booker* judges did have sentencing discretion, though less than since *Booker*.

We limit the comparison between auditioners and non-auditioners to judges in the same districts, to correct for possible interdistrict differences in sentencing severity; such differences might result, for example, from differences in the gravity of criminal conduct across districts.

The table reveals that the judges we classify as non-auditioners consistently give lower prison sentences than the ones we classify as audition-

Table 8.14 Regression of Prison Sentences Imposed by District Judges, Grouped by Length of Service, 2006–2011 (*t-statistics in parentheses*)

	Organized-Crime Drugs	Other Drug Offenses	Weapons Offenses	Immigration Offenses
Length of Service (1 ≤ 15 years; 0 > 15 years))	4.15**	−2.06**	3.35**	−0.72**
	(2.73)	(2.99)	(3.14)	(5.09)
Party of Appointing President(1=R; 0=D)	7.12**	4.41**	4.04**	0.96**
	(4.53)	(6.40)	(3.54)	(6.73)
Trial(1 = Trial; 0 = No Trial)	220.43**	162.21**	130.00**	34.32**
	(71.55)	(96.52)	(65.53)	(47.58)
Fraction of *R*s in Court of Appeals	56.06**	46.30**	18.56	10.90**
	(3.81)	(6.41)	(1.82)	(6.52)
District Dummies	Yes	Yes	Yes	Yes
Constant	65.87**	63.30**	45.12**	1.25
	(6.04)	(9.63)	(5.31)	(0.80)

Table 8.15   Prison Sentences Imposed by District Judges in and Not in Promotion Pool (i.e., Auditioners and Non-Auditioners), in the Same Districts, 2003–2011

	Auditioners	Non-Auditioners	Non-Auditioners with ≤ 16 Years of Service at Sentencing	Non-Auditioners with > 16 Years of Service at Sentencing
D District Judges				
Mean Prison Sentence in Months	65.39	56.41**	58.95*	46.07**
	(4325)	(3351)	(2692)	(659)
Mean Prison Sentence in Months, Post-2005	65.28	57.14**	60.80	46.07**
	(3008)	(2652)	(1993)	(659)
R District Judges				
Mean Prison Sentence in Months	87.51	74.40**	76.50**	71.52**
	(1218)	(7246)	(4180)	(3066)
Mean Prison Sentence in Months, Post-2005	85.29	73.34**	75.97*	69.88**
	(861)	(5297)	(3004)	(2293)

Notes:

1. Statistical comparisons are with the auditioners.

2. Of the auditioners, 12 were appointed by Democratic Presidents and 6 by Republican Presidents.

3. Of the non-auditioners, 63 were appointed by Democratic Presidents and 43 by Republican Presidents.

ers, and the difference is statistically significant. This is evidence of auditioning behavior, though it is not definitive, because the judges whom we are calling non-auditioners are really just judges who did not get promoted to the court of appeals. They may have wanted to be promoted, in which event they were auditioners who simply have not been promoted—yet; unless they have aged out of consideration, they may still be auditioners. So just as, in the study reported in the previous two tables, our promotion pool contained some and perhaps many non-auditioners (judges with fewer than 16 years of service who did not aspire to be court of appeals judges), so in Table 8.15 our nonpromotion pool contains some and perhaps many auditioners.

To summarize, this chapter presents evidence, though it is not conclusive, that some judges do change their behavior in order to increase their chances of promotion. This evidence supports our realistic "judge as worker" model of judicial behavior, since angling for promotion is typical behavior in labor markets.

Appendix

Court of Appeals Judges in the Supreme Court Promotion Pool, 1930–2010

	Position When Appointed to the Court of Appeals	Appointing President	Year Confirmed
st Circuit (3/23 = 13.0%) (number of judges in the promotion pool in the circuit/number of ive judges in the circuit, and former as percentage of latter)			
·yer, *Stephen G.*	Professor	Carter	1980
·ter, *David H.*	State Judge	Bush I	1990
·odbury, Peter	State Judge	F. Roosevelt	1941
:ond Circuit (15/56 = 26.8%)			
·ranes, Jose Alberto	U.S. District Judge	Clinton	1994
·ase, Harrie Brigham	State Judge	Coolidge	1929
·endly, Henry	Private Practice	Eisenhower	1959
·nd, Learned	U.S. District Judge	Coolidge	1924
·*rlan, John Marshall*	Private Practice	Eisenhower	1954
·ufman, Irving R.	U.S. District Judge	Kennedy	1961
·rse, Amalya Lyle	Private Practice	Carter	1979

	Position When Appointed to the Court of Appeals	Appointing President	Year Confirm
Marshall, Thurgood	NAACP	Kennedy	1962
Miner, Roger J.	U.S. District Judge	Reagan	1985
Mulligan, William H.	Professor	Nixon	1971
Newman, Jon O.	U.S. District Judge	Carter	1979
Oakes, James L.	U.S. District Judge	Nixon	1971
Patterson, Robert Sr.	U.S. District Judge	F. Roosevelt	1939
Sotomayor, Sonia	U.S. District Judge	Clinton	1998
Winter, Ralph K.	Professor	Reagan	1981
Third Circuit (10/56 = 17.9%)			
Adams, Arlin M.	Private Practice	Nixon	1969
Alito, Samuel A., Jr.	U.S. Attorney	Bush I	1990
Biddle, Francis	Private Practice	F. Roosevelt	1939
Chertoff, Michael	Justice Dept. Official	Bush II	2003
Davis, John Warren	U.S. District Judge	Wilson	1920
Goodrich, Herbert	Professor	F. Roosevelt	1940
Hastie, William H.	Governor of U.S. Virgin Islands	Truman	1950
Higginbotham, A. Leon	U.S. District Judge	Carter	1977
Jones, Charles Alvin	Private Practice	F. Roosevelt	1939
Lewis, Timothy K.	U.S. District Judge	Bush I	1992
Fourth Circuit (8/38 = 21.1%)			
Chapman, Robert F.	U.S. District Judge	Reagan	1981
Haynsworth, Clement	Private Practice	Eisenhower	1957
Luttig, J. Michael	Justice Dept. Official	Bush I	1991
Parker, John Johnston	Private Practice	Coolidge	1925
Widener, Hiram	U.S. District Judge	Nixon	1972
Wilkins, William W.	U.S. District Judge	Reagan	1986
Wilkinson, J. Harvie, III	Professor	Reagan	1984
Williams, Karen J.	Private Practice	Bush I	1992
Fifth Circuit (18/74 = 23%)			
Bell, Griffin	State Official	Kennedy	1962
Benavides, Fortunato	Private Practice	Clinton	1994
Carswell, George H.	U.S. District Judge	Nixon	1969
Clark, Charles	Private Practice	Nixon	1969
Clement, Edith Brown	U.S. District Judge	Bush II	2001
Garza, Emilio M.	U.S. District Judge	Bush I	1991
Higginbotham, Patrick	U.S. District Judge	Reagan	1982
Hutcheson, Joseph	U.S. District Judge	Hoover	1931
Johnson, Frank M.	U.S. District Judge	Carter	1979
Jones, Edith H.	Private Practice	Reagan	1985
Owen, Priscilla	State Judge	Bush II	2005
Prado, Edward	U.S. District Judge	Bush II	2003
Roney, Paul H.	Private Practice	Nixon	1970
Sibley, Samuel Hale	U.S. District Judge	Hoover	1931
Smith, Jerry	City Attorney	Reagan	1987

	Position When Appointed to the Court of Appeals	Appointing President	Year Confirmed
ornberry, William	U.S. District Judge	Johnson	1965
oflat, Gerald B.	U.S. District Judge	Ford	1975
ttle, Elbert P.	Treasury General Counsel	Eisenhower	1954
xth Circuit (10/58 = 17.2%)			
len, Florence	State Judge	F. Roosevelt	1934
tchelder, Alice M.	U.S. District Judge	Bush I	1991
mbs, Bert T.	Private Practice	Johnson	1967
ughtrey, Martha	State Judge	Clinton	1993
ckenlooper, Smith	U.S. District Judge	Coolidge	1928
nnedy, Cornelia	U.S. District Judge	Carter	1979
cCree, Wade H.	U.S. District Judge	Johnson	1966
erritt, Gilbert S.	Private Practice	Carter	1977
an, James L.	State Judge	Reagan	1985
wart, Potter	Private Practice	Eisenhower	1954
venth Circuit (8/45=17.8%)			
sterbrook, Frank H.	Professor	Reagan	1985
dley, Walter	U.S. District Judge	Truman	1949
nton, Sherman	U.S. Congress	F. Roosevelt	1941
sner, Richard A.	Professor	Reagan	1981
vens, John Paul	Private Practice	Nixon	1970
ne, Philip W.	U.S. District Judge	Nixon	1974
lliams, Ann	U.S. District Judge	Clinton	1999
od, Diane P.	Professor	Clinton	1995
ghth Circuit (7/48 = 14.6%)			
nold, Richard S.	U.S. District Judge	Carter	1980
ackmun, Harry	Private Practice	Eisenhower	1959
wman, Pasco M.	Professor	Reagan	1983
nyon, William Squire	U.S. Congress	Harding	1922
ne, Kimbrough	State Judge	Wilson	1916
ebster, William H.	U.S. District Judge	Nixon	1973
hittaker, Charles	U.S. District Judge	Eisenhower	1956
nth Circuit (15/87 = 17.2%)			
llahan, Consuelo	State Judge	Bush II	2003
nman, William	Private Practice	F. Roosevelt	1935
rnandez, Ferdinand	U.S. District Judge	Bush I	1989
odwin, Alfred T.	U.S. District Judge	Nixon	1971
ll, Cynthia H.	U.S. District Judge	Reagan	1984
ufstedler, Shirley	State Judge	Johnson	1968
nnedy, Anthony	Professor	Ford	1975
zinski, Alex	Other Federal Judge	Reagan	1985
cKeown, M. Margaret	Private Practice	Clinton	1998
wlinson, Johnnie B.	U.S. District Judge	Clinton	2000
mer, Pamela A.	U.S. District Judge	Bush I	1989
eed, Joseph T.	Justice Dept. Official	Nixon	1973
allace, J. Clifford	U.S. District Judge	Nixon	1972

	Position When Appointed to the Court of Appeals	Appointing President	Year Confirm
Wardlaw, Kim	U.S. District Judge	Clinton	1998
Wiggins, Charles E.	Private Practice	Reagan	1984
Tenth Circuit (5/38 = 13.2%)			
Bratton, Sam Gilbert	U.S. Congress	F. Roosevelt	1933
McConnell, Michael W.	Professor	Bush II	2002
McWilliams, Robert H.	State Judge	Nixon	1970
Phillips, Orie Leon	U.S. District Judge	Hoover	1929
Seymour, Stephanie	Private Practice	Carter	1979
Eleventh Circuit (3/24 = 12.5%)			
Johnson, Frank M.	U.S. District Judge	Carter	1979
Roney, Paul H.	Private Practice	Nixon	1970
Tjoflat, Gerald B.	U.S. District Judge	Ford	1975
District of Columbia (23/51 = 45.1%)			
Arnold, Thurman	Justice Dept. Official	F. Roosevelt	1943
Bork, Robert	Private Practice	Reagan	1982
Brown, Janice Rogers	State Judge	Bush II	2005
Buckley, James L.	Radio Free Europe	Reagan	1985
Burger, Warren Earl	Justice Dept. Official	Eisenhower	1956
Danaher, John A.	Private Practice	Eisenhower	1954
Fahy, Charles	Private Practice	Truman	1950
Garland, Merrick	Justice Dept. Official	Clinton	1997
Ginsburg, Douglas, H.	Justice Dept. Official	Reagan	1986
Ginsburg, Ruth Bader	Professor	Carter	1980
Groner, Duncan	U.S. District Judge	Hoover	1931
Mikva, Abner J.	U.S. Congress	Carter	1979
Roberts, John G., Jr.	Private Practice	Bush II	2003
Rutledge, Wiley Blount	Professor	F. Roosevelt	1939
Scalia, Antonin	Professor	Reagan	1982
Silberman, Laurence H.	Private Practice	Reagan	1985
Starr, Kenneth W.	Justice Dept. Official	Reagan	1983
Stephens, Harold	Justice Dept. Official	F. Roosevelt	1935
Tatel, David Stephen	Private Practice	Clinton	1994
Thomas, Clarence	Chairman of EEOC	Bush I	1990
Vinson, Frederick	U.S. Congress	F. Roosevelt	1937
Wald, Patricia M.	Justice Dept. Official	Carter	1979
Wilkey, Malcolm R.	Private Practice	Nixon	1970

Notes:

1. Fifth and Eleventh Circuits: Three judges (Johnson, Roney, and Tjoflat) who were appointed to the Fifth Circuit and reassigned to the Eleventh Circuit are listed twice, under both circuits. We do not include Judge Tuttle in the Eleventh Circuit list because he was a senior judge at the time of his reassignment.

2. Counts of active judges in the circuit: Two judges (John Cotteral and Robert Lewis) were appointed to the Eighth Circuit but reassigned to the Tenth. Because their reassignments came before 1930, we include them in the count of active judges on the Tenth, not Eighth, Circuit. One judge (Julian Mack) served on the Sixth and Seventh Circuits prior to 1930 and after 1930 on the Second Circuit. We include him in the count of Second

cuit judges. Eighteen judges were transferred from the Fifth to the Eleventh Circuit, but five (Jones, Morgan, es, Simpson, and Tuttle) had assumed senior status before their reassignment, so we don't count them.

3. A few judges were in other positions when they were initially shortlisted. For example, Pamela Rymer was a trict judge (not court of appeals judge) when Reagan considered her for Powell's seat. After being promoted to court of appeals she remained under consideration as a possible Republican appointment to the Supreme urt.

4. Names in italics: Nominated to the Supreme Court.

5. U.S. Attorney is the chief federal prosecutor for a federal district—more precisely, the senior Justice partment official in the district. These are the same districts to which district judges are appointed.

Conclusion

The Way Forward

WE HAVE TRIED in this book to add to the growing knowledge of judicial behavior, specifically the behavior of federal judges appointed in conformity with Article III of the Constitution (that is, district judges, circuit judges, and Supreme Court Justices). We have done this mainly by using statistical methodology to test hypotheses derived from a labor-market model of the judicial utility function—the weighted summation of a judge's preferences and aversions. We have shown, by what we believe to be a more comprehensive analysis than can be found in previous studies, that ideology influences judicial decisions at all levels of the federal judiciary. But the influence is not of uniform strength—we have found, for example, that it diminishes as one moves down the judicial hierarchy—and it does not extinguish the influence of conventional principles of judicial decision-making (what we call "legalism"); federal judges are not just politicians in robes, though that is part of what they are (in a noninvidious sense of "politician," as they are rarely partisan), owing to the indeterminate character of many cases to legalist analysis.

Moreover, ideology and a commitment (albeit qualified) to legalism do not exhaust the judicial utility function. We have found that like other workers judges exhibit in their judicial behavior leisure preference and, something that includes but goes beyond leisure preference, effort aversion—as when appellate judges yield to the views of colleagues rather than insisting on dissenting every time they hold contrary views, or dissent less frequently the heavier their caseload grows. A further example is the rules of standing that limit access to the federal courts. From the legalist standpoint that still dominates academic legal scholarship and judicial rhetoric, those rules are found in the text of Article III of the Constitution. Actually the text and the eighteenth-century practices that inform it do not dictate those rules; judges' desire to limit their workload should be taken seriously as a motivator of standing doctrine, and likewise the desire to limit types of litigation likely to conflict with a judge's ideological desires. We have also presented evidence that many judges, like many other workers, angle for promotion, that some seek celebrity status, and that such common judicial behavior as asking questions of lawyers at oral argument have more personal causes than just trying to apply "the law."

Many previous studies of judges, whether done by political scientists or by law professors, and whether conducted from a realist or a legalist perspective, have implicitly assumed that a judicial vote is costless and is therefore invariably cast in accordance with the judge's preferred outcome of the case. That is why the existence of dissent is an embarrassment for a legalist (for why cannot judges reason their way to an agreed-upon outcome, in all but the rarest cases?), while the existence of unanimity, especially in a court known to be ideologically diverse, such as the U.S. Supreme Court, is an embarrassment to the realist. More than 30 percent of Supreme Court decisions are unanimous—but by the same token, more than 60 percent have dissents, which is inexplicable except in terms of ideological division, unless one naïvely accepts that the various methodologies that different Justices purport to employ, such as originalism and "active liberty," are, though inconsistent, at least ideologically neutral.

The puzzle dissolves when effort aversion, which implies dissent aversion, is factored into the picture. It strengthens the realist approach by showing why rationally self-interested judges may often decide to mute disagreement, especially when the ideological stakes in a case are small, as they are even in a substantial number of Supreme Court cases, as we showed in chapter 3.

Although this book is the fullest statistical study of judicial behavior of which we are aware (and the only one, we believe, to consider all three levels of the federal judiciary and their interactions and to be thoroughly grounded in a realistic conception of judicial incentives and constraints), it is, unavoidably, far from comprehensive. We devote the balance of this conclusion to a discussion of promising areas for further research. We limit discussion to research that bears directly on the subject of this book—the behavior of federal judges—and disregard the many other interesting and important topics regarding judicial systems and the adjudicative process.

Particular projects to one side—we'll discuss them next—we note the utility of our datasets for further research on judicial behavior and commend them to other scholars. In collecting data for our studies we made revisions to the two most widely used datasets of judicial votes—the U.S. Supreme Court Database (the Spaeth database) and the U.S. Appeals Courts Database (the Songer database). We also updated two other databases, one for the courts of appeals, developed by Cass Sunstein and his colleagues (we also expanded the scope of that database), and another on oral argument in the U.S. Supreme Court, developed by Timothy Johnson and his colleagues. We have also created from scratch two district court datasets (see chapter 5).

Furthermore, building on existing judicial-biography datasets and adding other information gathered from a variety of sources (including the questionnaires that federal judicial nominees are required to fill out as part of the senatorial confirmation process), we have created the Database of the Federal Judiciary, containing biographical data on all Article III judges appointed between 1789 and 2010. There are other biographical datasets of judges, including one that covers all district judges who served during the period from 1789 to 2000,[1] another of all court of appeals judges appointed prior to 2000,[2] and a third of nominees to the Supreme Court.[3] The Federal Judicial Center also maintains an online biographi-

1. "District Courts Attributes Data," www.cas.sc.edu/poli/juri/attributes.htm.
2. "Appeals Courts Attributes Data," www.cas.sc.edu/poli/juri/attributes.htm.
3. "U.S. Supreme Court Justices Database," http://epstein.law.usc.edu/research/justices data.html. See also Lee Epstein et al., *The Supreme Court Compendium* (2011).

cal directory of all federal judges past and present,[4] though the biographical information contained in the directory is scanty. Our biographical dataset quantifies many personal, career (both judicial and pre-judicial), and appointment (for example, Senate composition) attributes of federal judges. And in chapter 4 we presented results from a new dataset that we have created of the ideological leanings of both Supreme Court Justices and court of appeals judges at the time of their appointment. As noted in the general introduction, all our datasets have been posted on a website[5] open to all.

Yet frequently in the book we have noted data limitations that precluded a study that we wanted to do. Recall that caseload per judge was an important independent variable in our study of dissenting behavior in chapter 6, but what we really needed was *workload* per judge, which would adjust caseload for the length or difficulty of the cases. Such adjustments are difficult to make,[6] but they are essential to the rigorous study of judicial effort aversion. We pointed out that if an increase in caseload were the result of an influx of completely meritless cases, a reduction in the dissent rate might reflect not effort aversion but merely that dissent is less likely in a case that is clearly without merit; such a case will almost certainly be decided unanimously.

We mentioned in chapter 4 the *Almanac of the Federal Judiciary*.[7] It contains a good deal of information about all federal district and court of appeals judges and many magistrate judges and bankruptcy judges as well; a worthwhile project would be coding the information in that massive sourcebook.

A difficult and time-consuming but also very worthwhile project would be to recode the Spaeth and Songer databases. They contain errors, especially the Songer database, only some of which we have been able to correct. Court of appeals opinions are more difficult to code than Supreme Court opinions because they tend to deal with more issues, and issues that arise in more fields of law. They are also much more numerous than

4. Federal Judicial Center, "Biographical History of Federal Judges," www.fjc.gov/public/home.nsf/hisj (visited Dec. 9, 2011).

5. http://widefeetdesigns.com/client/epsteinBook/.

6. See Richard A. Posner, *The Federal Courts: Challenge and Reform* 59–79 (1996).

7. Aspen Publishers Editorial Staff, *Almanac of the Federal Judiciary* (2 vols., looseleaf, updated semiannually).

Supreme Court opinions, and the Songer database contains on average only a small sample of each judge's judicial votes. The recoding of these databases should be conducted by law students at first-rate law schools under careful supervision of law professors.

We turn now to topics for future research. One set consists of extensions of specific studies reported in this book. For example, while we discussed ideological voting in federal courts of appeals at length in chapter 4, we did not consider the bearing of the following startling statistic: the percentage of court of appeals decisions reviewed by the Supreme Court fell from 1.6 percent to 0.14 percent between 1960 and 2010.[8] One would expect the courts of appeals to have become more ideological and less legalistic over this period because they have increasingly been able to get away with more; this hypothesis, derived from the notion of the judge as an imperfect agent of a diffuse principal—"the government" or "the people"—remains to be tested. Moreover, one might expect rehearings en banc in the courts of appeals to have become more frequent as review by the Supreme Court dwindled; a court of appeals judge who disagreed with a panel decision would be more likely to think rehearing en banc his last realistic hope of overturning the panel's decision.

In analyzing the courts of appeals we largely ignored three types of judge who sit on those courts besides the judges of the court who are in regular active service. All the courts of appeals have judges who have taken senior status yet sit on some or many of the court's three-judge panels. These judges generally carry a reduced workload, do not preside at oral argument or assign opinions, do not vote on whether to grant rehearing en banc, and do not participate in such a rehearing unless the judge was on the panel that heard it originally. In addition, in most courts of appeals active and especially senior district judges (whether from the same or a different circuit) sit by designation on many panels, as do visiting judges—mainly senior court of appeals judges and senior district judges—from other circuits. One would like to know whether any of these outsider

8. See U.S. Courts, "Federal Court Management Statistics, 2010," www.uscourts.gov/viewer.aspx?doc=/cgi-bin/cmsa2010Sep.pl); U.S. Supreme Court, "Granted/Noted Cases List," www.supremecourt.gov/oral_arguments/oral_arguments.aspx (both visited Dec. 9, 2011).

judges exhibit distinctive behavioral traits when serving as members of panels of courts of appeals. For example, is a visiting district judge less likely to dissent or vote to reverse than a court of appeals judge? Do visiting judges tend to defer to the views of the court's regular judges? (One study has found that panels that include a district judge are more likely to affirm than panels composed just of court of appeals judges,[9] though another study has found that the effect is not statistically significant.[10]) Do senior judges, who of course are on average older than active judges, exhibit age-related behaviors (a question we discussed very preliminarily at the end of chapter 6)? These are important questions because senior judges carry a big share of the overall workload of both the district courts and the courts of appeals—they sit on about a quarter of all court of appeals panels[11]—and so deserve study.

We did not discuss variance in dissent rates among court of appeals judges, though it is considerable, apart from the brief discussion of age and senior-status effects in chapter 6. In the Seventh Circuit, for example, which has a low average dissent rate—only 2 percent of the votes cast by the judges are dissenting votes—the dissent rate of the individual judges ranges from 1 percent to 5 percent. Why do some judges dissent five times as often as others, apart from being in an ideological minority on their court? That may well be the main reason, but it is not the only one; the variance in the Seventh Circuit cannot be fully explained by the variance in the ideology of the judges. Could it be that former academics dissent more often than other judges because they have more experience in writing? Or that former politicians dissent less often because they are good at compromise and less committed to "principle"? Might there be a distinction in this regard between judges who had been elected officials and judges who had been appointed officials? Does personality play a role in the decision to dissent? So is an aggressive judge more likely to

9. Justin J. Green and Burton M. Atkins, "Designated Judges: How Well Do They Perform?" 61 *Judicature* 358 (1978).

10. Susan B. Haire, Donald R. Songer, and Stefanie A. Lindquist, "Appellate Court Supervision in the Federal Judiciary: A Hierarchical Perspective," 37 *Law and Society Review* 143 (2003).

11. "Federal Court Management Statistics 2009: Courts of Appeals: U.S. Court of Appeals—Judicial Caseload Profile," www.uscourts.gov/cgi-bin/cmsa2009.pl (visited Dec. 9, 2011).

dissent than a timid one, or is the timid one likely to display passive-aggressive behavior and dissent more often? And could it be that the more persuasive a judge is, the less likely he is to dissent? Suppose Judge X and Judge Y are appointees of a Democratic President on a court dominated by appointees of Republican Presidents, and that when X sits with two *R*s the decision is conservative and he usually dissents, but when Y sits with two *R*s the decision is liberal because Y is persuasive even with his *R* colleagues while X is not, and so Y does not dissent. A complication is that the more persuasive judge is probably also an abler judge, and abler judges have less effort aversion and therefore find it less costly to write a dissent; they probably also write faster, further reducing their marginal cost of dissenting. By the same token, their threat to dissent is more plausible, and since we know that judges in the majority on a panel also have dissent aversion, the minority judge who can make a credible threat to dissent is more likely to get his way than a minority judge who cannot make a credible threat.

We mentioned in chapter 4 that the well-documented existence of panel composition effects in the courts of appeals might reflect the limited accuracy of the party of the appointing President as a proxy for judicial voting. We speculated that panel composition effects might be attributable to the presence of "wobblers" on many panels—judges who, though presumed conservative (because appointed by a Republican President) or liberal (because appointed by a Democratic one), really were not. They may never have been; or they might have voted differently from what would have been predicted from the ideological inclinations that they brought to the bench when they were appointed—we saw in chapter 4 that this is common.

But we didn't try to adjust panel composition data by the ex post ideology of each judge, to identify wobblers. That would require tracking judges to particular panels—a large project but a very promising one. It would involve taking a circuit (ideally, all the circuits) and classifying the court of appeals judges as liberal or conservative on the basis of their judicial votes, on the theory that the political preferences disclosed by a judge's judicial votes (that is, his ex post rather than ex ante ideology) is the best guide to whether he's a liberal or a conservative judge. Suppose a panel of two *R*s and one *D*, but both *R*s are actually liberal. Then the fact that they vote for a liberal outcome wouldn't mean they were influenced by the D. Similarly, were there two Rs and one D and one R was actually liberal, the other conservative, and the D a liberal, the conservative R, being outnumbered, might, if he was effort-averse, refrain from dissenting. Again this would not be a result of influence exerted by the D. The result of such a study might show that panel effects actually are unimportant.

Another promising study would relate changes in the ideology of court of appeals judges to the auditioning phenomenon analyzed in chapter 8. We expect less such change among auditioners than among non- and ex-auditioners. A court of appeals judge should have a better chance of being appointed to the Supreme Court by the President who had appointed him to the court of appeals, or by a future President of the same party, if he does not drift far from the ideology that he presumably shared with the President who appointed him; for a propensity to drift might carry over into the Supreme Court and make him another Blackmun—appointed by a Republican President and a great disappointment to Republicans. Other examples are Warren, Brennan, and Souter. But Blackmun, in contrast, became a disappointment to Republicans only over time.

More could be done to study ideological change in the Supreme Court. It would be interesting to see whether the change is mainly from one ideology to another (conservative to liberal, say), or whether it is from an ideological stance to a more legalistic, and therefore ideologically more neutral, stance, as the Justice's pre-judicial career recedes, especially if it was a nonjudicial career (that is, if he wasn't a judge of another court, and so probably already had a judicial philosophy, when he was appointed to the Supreme Court). It would also be worthwhile to try to disentangle ideological change from the ex-auditioner effect that we discussed in chapter 8. With no recent exceptions, once a court of appeals judge becomes a Supreme Court Justice he ceases to be an auditioner unless he aspires to be Chief Justice. If his judicial behavior changes in the direction that we predict and find for ex-auditioners in the courts of appeals— that is, if he takes a softer line on criminals once he ceases to be an auditioner—that would be evidence that he had indeed auditioned for the Court as a court of appeals judge. Thus the fact noted in chapter 3 that ideological change, when it occurs, does so soon after the Justice is appointed (we found first-term ideological differences to be highly significant predictors of ideological change starting in the Justice's second term) may be an instance of the ex-auditioner effect: the Justice becomes more himself because he has no further need to curry favor with the President and the President's advisers.

Chapters 1 and 7 discussed Supreme Court Justices' extracurricular activities, but only briefly. They are increasing in frequency, variety, and visibility and are attracting—as we noted in chapter 1—increasing, and increasingly critical, attention (at which the Justices thumb their noses, however). Those activities deserve systematic study, as do the extracurricular activities of auditioners.

For a related clue to whether a court of appeals judge is auditioning for appointment to the Supreme Court, one might ask how he treats the press, and the media more generally, in his opinions: maybe an auditioner treats them with kid gloves in recognition of their influence on the public reception of controversial nominations to high government office. And maybe auditioners have curtailed their academic or other extrajudicial writing since Robert Bork, one of the most highly qualified Supreme Court nominees in modern history, went down in flames, in part because of his paper trail of controversial utterances on matters of law and public policy.[12]

A judge's extracurricular activities have, along with a strategic dimension as elements of his or her public-relations strategy[13] or as efforts at obtaining promotion, a consumption dimension—as a form of self-expression, celebrity-status seeking, leisure preference, or effort aversion. Rather than poring over dull briefs, a judge can preside before thousands of awed admirers in a mock trial of Judas Iscariot for aiding and abetting deicide.

The growth in the amount and visibility of Supreme Court Justices' nonjudicial public activities—speeches, debates, media interviews, auto-biographies and authorized biographies, appearances at international conferences, and participation in mock trials of historical and fictitious persons and events (was the Earl of Oxford the actual author of Shake-

12. Cf. D. Scott Gaille, "Publishing by United States Court of Appeals Judges: Before and After the Bork Hearings," *26 Journal of Legal Studies* 371 (1997).

13. Jeffrey K. Staton, *Judicial Power and Strategic Communication in Mexico* (2010).

speare's plays?—a crackpot proposition endorsed by two Supreme Court Justices)—are plausibly related to the Court's decreasing workload as a result of more, and more experienced, staff, sophisticated methods of electronic search for legal materials, the cert-pool innovation (law clerks writing a memo on a petition for certiorari for most of the Justices rather than just for their own Justice, thus reducing duplication and freeing up more time for them to write or otherwise assist with their Justices' opinions), and a reduction in the number of cases in which certiorari is granted. But also contributing to that growth may be the emergence of a society-wide celebrity culture, related to the expansion of the media that has been brought about by the creation of the Internet. The reduction in the Justices' opportunity costs has increased their demand for celebrity status, and the expansion of the media has increased the supply of media venues for Justices to appear in.

Progress in scholarly analysis of the motives, scope, and consequences of judges' extracurricular activities will require the collection and analysis of systematic data concerning those activities. We made a beginning in chapter 1 with our tables of extracurricular activities of Supreme Court Justices as reported on their financial disclosure forms, which are public documents. But there is much more research to do on this subject.

More could also be done with the district judges. We focused on their decisions in cases likely to be controversial (cases decided on appeal in a published opinion), and in rulings on motions to dismiss, usually under Rule 12(b)(6) of the Federal Rules of Civil Procedure, that seek to terminate litigation at its earliest stage, before pretrial discovery. Ruling on these motions is an important part of the gatekeeping function of the district courts—a function of great importance, likely to be influenced by effort aversion and ideological bias. Gatekeeping is also performed by the courts of appeals and the Supreme Court. The Supreme Court's cert. decisions have received substantial attention in the literature,[14] but there are few empirical studies of other forms of gatekeeping at any judicial level.

Another topic that cries out for systematic analysis, though one very difficult to analyze, is the role of staff in the federal courts. This means primarily the law clerks, but in the courts of appeals it also includes staff

14. See citations in the appendix to chapter 2.

attorneys, who are law clerks to the court as a whole rather than hired by and assigned to particular judges; in some courts of appeals, staff attorneys, sometimes operating with great autonomy, handle a majority of the court's cases. (There is also heavy use of law-student interns and externs by many court of appeals and district judges.) The use of staff by judges is an increasingly important topic because of the growth of the size and quality of staff relative to the number of judges.[15] Effort aversion implies that some judges will delegate excessively to law clerks, making them in effect assistant judges; and the use of inappropriate criteria in hiring, such as personal connections and institutional loyalties (for example, to the judge's alma mater or local community), would be an unsurprising abuse of secure tenure.

It would be interesting to correlate the frequency of dissenting and concurring opinions in the Supreme Court with changes in the Court's caseload and in the size and quality of its staff. A related question for investigation is whether there are fewer dissents when the Court is less closely divided along ideological lines. Were the Court composed of, say, eight liberals and one conservative, the one conservative would have a heavy burden if he tried to dissent from every liberal decision. Similar studies could be conducted of court of appeals judges. At both levels size and quality of staff may be decisive: with enough excellent staff, that lonely conservative in our example might be able to grind out dissenting opinions effortlessly.

The main significance of the growing ratio of staff to judges (in a typical federal court of appeals, the ratio of law clerks, including staff attorneys, to judges is approximately five to one; as late as the 1960s, when there were no staff attorneys, it was one to one) is that it marks the emergence and growing dominance of a management model of the judicial workplace. The model is congenial to modern lawyers because unless they come from academia, they come from increasingly hierarchical legal institutions, such as large law firms and government agencies (primarily

15. Law clerks in the U.S. Supreme Court have received most of the scholarly attention paid to judicial staff. See, for example, Todd C. Peppers, *Courtiers of the Marble Palace* (2006); Artemus Ward and David L. Weiden, *Sorcerers' Apprentices: 100 Years of Law Clerks at the United States Supreme Court* (2006). See also Richard A. Posner, "The Courthouse Mice" (review of the Peppers and Ward-Weiden books), *New Republic*, June 5 and 12, 2006, p. 32.

prosecutors' offices). In such institutions the writing of first drafts of briefs tends to be delegated to very junior lawyers, and their drafts are then edited by more senior ones.[16] Culture is a factor here. The literary culture in America is moribund. Writing ability is not highly admired. Important people, other than academics and professional writers, are not expected to write what is published under their name.

By the time a lawyer becomes a federal judge, it may be many years since he wrote the briefs that he signs. It is natural for him to assume a managerial role as a judge. A number of appellate judges have adopted the "Becker model" (named after the late Judge Edward Becker of the Third Circuit), or a close variant of it, for organizing a judge's staff. In that model, the judge hires a former law clerk, who has additional legal experience, to be the senior clerk. The senior clerk assigns opinion writing, editing, and other duties to the other clerks in accordance with his evaluation of their strengths and weaknesses, and they report to him rather than to the judge, with whom indeed they may have little or even no direct contact. The staff may include unpaid part-time interns or externs, who report to the clerks. Sometimes the senior clerk is permanent while the junior law clerks serve the usual one-year term; sometimes some or all of the clerks are permanent.

As a result of the rise to dominance of the management model, only a few judges write their own opinions any longer. This has implications for the character of judicial opinions but also for appointments to the judiciary. Lawyers incapable of legal analysis, not needing to justify their decisions (the law clerks will do that for them), can pass as qualified judges. The result could be increased politicization, and diminished quality, of the judiciary. A partial answer is more careful and thorough screening by the appointing authorities, with the aid of the private bar—and the screening of federal judicial nominees has indeed become more careful and thorough.

The transformation of the federal judiciary from a traditional judi-

16. A clue that a senior lawyer or a judge is an editor rather than a writer is the heavy emphasis on editing in the leading legal-writing treatise by Steven V. Armstrong and Timothy P. Terrell, *Thinking Like a Writer: A Lawyer's Guide to Effective Writing and Editing* (3d ed. 2009). Manuals for law clerks assume the clerk will draft opinions. See, for example, Aliza Milner, *Judicial Clerkships: Legal Methods in Motion* (2011); Mary L. Dunnewold, Beth A. Honetschlager, and Brenda L. Tofte, *Judicial Clerkships: A Practical Guide* 91 (2010).

cial model of judges who do their own work with some assistance to a model of judges as managers of law clerk worker ants is an enormously important development that merits systematic study that it has yet to receive.

The greatest limitation of the scope of this book is that we have limited analysis to U.S. federal judges, and in fact to a subset of them. Not only have we ignored non–Article III federal judges, including not only bankruptcy judges and magistrate judges but also the judges of the Tax Court; we have ignored administrative law judges and other federal judicial officers who are not called "judge," as well as the Article III judges of an important federal court—the U.S. Court of Appeals for the Federal Circuit.[17]

By omitting these other federal judicial personnel, we reduce the variance in our data (for example, non–Article III judicial officers do not have life tenure, as Article III judges do) and thus the range of testable hypotheses that can be derived from a labor-market theory of judicial behavior. The limitation of the range of our analysis is further illustrated by our ignoring state judges and foreign judges, types of judge whose career structures differ greatly from those of Article III judges. Most state judges are elected rather than appointed (though often appointed first and only later required to undergo a retention election), and almost all are subject to mandatory retirement. These are major contrasts to the career structure of an Article III judge and to Article I judicial officers as well.

Foreign judges, especially but not only in the nations of continental Europe and in Japan—that is, civil law societies, as distinct from common law societies, which are of Anglo-Saxon origin—inhabit career structures that (except in the case of constitutional courts, largely a post–World War II phenomenon) are at the opposite extreme from our state judges. They also differ greatly from our Article III judges, who indeed in a rough way can be situated in the middle of the spectrum that extends from state judges at one end to judges of civil law systems at the other. Recruited at

---

17. Relevant empirical studies include Lawrence Baum, *Specializing the Courts* (2011); Robert M. Howard, *Getting a Poor Return: Courts, Justice, and Taxes* (2009); Lee Petheridge and R. Polk Wagner, "The Federal Circuit and Patentability: An Empirical Assessment of the Law of Obviousness," 85 *Texas Law Review* 2051 (2007); Leandra Lederman and Warren B. Hrung, "Do Attorneys Do Their Clients Justice? An Empirical Study of Tax Court Litigation," 41 *Wake Forest Law Review* 1235 (2006).

the outset of their entry into the legal profession, civil law judges are similar to conventional civil servants. They begin at the bottom rung of the
judicial ladder and, unlike most Article III judges, hold "constant hope"
of promotion to better positions over the course of their career.[18] Not only
do they start lower on the ladder than in our lateral-entry judicial system;
their ladder contains many more rungs. Japanese judges, for example, can
rise through more than 20 pay grades.[19] Foreign courts differ systematically from the courts studied in this book in other ways as well, such as in
being more specialized.

Judicial behavior is of course affected by the bar. There has, for example, been a substantial increase in the number of amicus curiae briefs filed
in the Supreme Court.[20] The increase could reduce the Court's workload
by providing more information relating to its cases and thus facilitating
decision-making and opinion writing, or it could increase the Court's
workload by increasing the amount of reading that the Justices feel obliged
to do.[21] The former effect probably dominates, because the Justices don't
actually read most amicus curiae briefs; that is done by the law clerks. But
the impact of amicus curiae participation in the Supreme Court remains
to be explored systematically.

A study of amicus curiae briefs not limited to ones filed in the Supreme
Court could help resolve some difficult coding issues concerning assessment of the role of ideology in adjudication. The economic and labor categories in the Spaeth database (see chapter 3) are too broad to allow robust inferences to be drawn about the economic ideology of Supreme
Court Justices. Business cases are difficult to code as liberal or conservative, especially when there are business firms on both sides of the case,

18. Bernard Schwartz, *French Administrative Law and the Common-Law World* 30
(2006).

19. J. Mark Ramseyer and Eric B. Rasmusen, "Why Are Japanese Judges So Conservative
in Politically Charged Cases?" 95 *American Political Science Review* 331 (2001).

20. In more than three-fourths of the Court's cases in the 1940s, no amicus curiae brief
was filed. By the 1990s that fraction had shrunk to one-tenth. Paul M. Collins, *Friends of the
Supreme Court: Interest Groups and Judicial Decision Making* 46 (2008).

21. See James F. Spriggs and Paul J. Wahlbeck, "Amicus Curiae and the Role of Information at the Supreme Court," 50 *Political Research Quarterly* 365 (1997); Karen O'Connor
and Lee Epstein, "Court Rules and Workload: A Case Study of Rules Governing Amicus
Curiae Participation," 8 *Justice System Journal* 35 (1983).

rather than a business firm on one side and a consumer, labor union, or government agency on the other. Similarly, labor cases are difficult to code when there are unions on both sides of the case or a union on one side and the National Labor Relations Board on the other. The main division between liberals and conservatives over business cases is not between liberals who dislike business and conservatives who like business; it is between liberals who favor small business over big business and conservatives who favor big business over small business when the case is between a big and a small business. In labor cases, the ideological divide is mainly between businesses, on the one hand, and unions, employees, or government agencies, on the other hand, rather than between two unions or a union and an employee. The position taken by amici curiae that have a clear ideological agenda, like the U.S. Chamber of Commerce, and commentary by business journals on business versus business cases, can reveal whether the outcome should be coded liberal or conservative. This is an important area for future research, in view of frequent claims that the Supreme Court is becoming more "pro-business."[22]

To give the reader a glimpse of what such a study might show, we present in Table C.1 the result of a pilot study based on a subcategory of Spaeth's economic category: labor cases in the 1946–2009 terms that pitted an employee, a labor union, the NLRB, or another government agency against a business firm or firms or a business association. Of the 2971 votes in orally argued labor cases in these terms, 65 involved a business on one side and either a union, an employee, the NLRB, or another government agency on the other side.

Notice how poorly business fared during the Warren Court compared not only to the Rehnquist and Roberts Courts, and to a lesser extent to the Burger Court (which was less conservative than the subsequent Courts), but also to the Vinson Court, for that was the era of backlash against the New Deal's pro-union policies, a backlash that crested with the enactment of the Taft-Hartley Act in 1948. Business did a little better

22. Adam Liptak, "Justices Offer a Receptive Ear to Business Interests," *New York Times*, December 18, 2010, p. A1; "Corporations and the Court: America's Supreme Court Is the Most Business-Friendly for Decades," *Economist*, June 23, 2011, www.economist.com/node/18866873 (visited Dec. 9, 2011).

Table C.1   Votes in Labor Cases in the Supreme Court between Business and Union,
Employee, NLRB, or Other Government Agency, for Each Chief Justice from
1946 to 2009

Business Either a Petitioner or a Respondent

Chief Justice	Business Wins (%)	Votes
Vinson	45.7	768
Warren	16.4	315
Burger	41.8	569
Rehnquist	50.2	251
Roberts	50.0	36
All	33.6	1939

Business Petitioner

	Business Wins (%)	Votes
Vinson	33.3	108
Warren	22.5	160
Burger	55.0	338
Rehnquist	57.1	126
Roberts	50.0	36
All	45.3	768

Business Respondent

	Business Wins (%)	Votes
Vinson	52.2	207
Warren	14.8	608
Burger	22.5	231
Rehnquist	43.2	125
Roberts	—	—
All	26.0	1171

Other Labor Cases

	Petitioner Wins (%)	Votes
Vinson	50.0	54
Warren	70.7	369
Burger	54.7	375
Rehnquist	43.4	207
Roberts	66.7	27
All	58.2	1032

when it was the petitioner, for we know that the Supreme Court reverses more decisions than it affirms, yet still very poorly relative to the normal reversal rate of more than 60 percent. Notice too (in the third column) the very high ratio of cases in the Warren Court in which the business party was the respondent rather than the petitioner—608 versus 160. The Court was much more likely to grant certiorari to a nonbusiness loser in the court below (and hence petitioner in the Supreme Court) than to a business loser. Notice finally that in labor cases in which there was no business party (it might, for example, be a suit by an employee against a union, or by a government agency against a union), the petitioner prevailed in 58.2 percent of the cases, which is close to the average for all cases in the Supreme Court.

It appears that a decreasing fraction of federal judges, especially at the court of appeals and Supreme Court level, are coming to the bench with substantial experience in the practice of law in business fields. The impact of a diminished understanding of business on judicial decision-making in business fields is another important area for future studies of judicial behavior.

Our last suggestion for further research is the application of computerized "sentiment analysis" (also called "content analysis," "text analytics," or "opinion mining")[23] to the content of judicial opinions. There is nothing new about using computer searches to count number of words, locate specific words, count citations, and identify or enumerate other "objective" ingredients of judicial opinions (we conduct such searches in this book)—or even to determine whether a judge is the author of his opinions or merely the editor of law clerks' opinion drafts.[24] And there is nothing new about hand coding of judicial opinions to determine more subjective characteristics, such as ideology.[25] The content analysis of oral-argument transcripts in the Supreme Court, which we cited in chapter 7,

23. See, for example, Bing Liu, "Sentiment Analysis: A Multi-Faceted Problem," *IEEE Intelligent Systems* (forthcoming); Bo Pang and Lillian Lee, "Opinion Mining and Sentiment Analysis," 2 *Foundations and Trends in Information Retrieval 1 (2008)*.

24. Jeffrey S. Rosenthal and Albert H. Yoon, "Detecting Multiple Authorship of United States Supreme Court Legal Decisions Using Function Words" (University of Toronto, May 2010).

25. Lee Epstein, William M. Landes, and Richard A. Posner, "Judicial Opinions as Text as Data" (Dec. 20, 2010), discusses some of these studies.

used hand coding. More could be done; for example, Matthew Stephenson has suggested that workload pressures could induce judges to decide more statutory cases on "plain meaning" grounds because that requires less work than digging beneath the textual surface for evidence of the purpose and likely consequences of one interpretation versus another.[26] That hypothesis could be tested by correlating workload with the frequency with which such text-oriented terms as "plain meaning" appear in statutory opinions.

What is new is using computers to determine the sentiments or attitudes expressed in a judicial opinion.[27] Yet already such searches are being conducted of consumers' online comments about consumer products in order to aid sellers in marketing. And scholars are mining blogs to determine, for example, public attitudes toward candidates for public office.[28]

Sentiment analysis seems well suited to teasing out subtle ideological signals in judicial opinions, as well as identifying other attitudinal dispositions (perhaps an ideology distinct from "conservative" or "liberal" in their usual current meanings), psychological traits (some judges may have an authoritarian personality, inclining them to punish any infraction of rules severely),[29] or intellectual characteristics, such as the size of a judge's vocabulary. A judicial opinion will identify an outcome, much as a comment by a consumer about a product is likely to state whether the consumer likes or doesn't like the product. Sentiment analysis digs beneath the "verdict" delivered by the consumer, or the judge, in an effort to identify the reasons for the verdict as well as characteristics of the opinion writer. The human reader can do this but is likely to be influenced by bi-

26. Matthew C. Stephenson, "Legal Realism for Economists," *Journal of Economic Perspectives* 191, 205 (Spring 2009).

27. We have found only one study that has tried to do this: Kevin T. McGuire et al., "Measuring Policy Content on the U.S. Supreme Court," 71 *Journal of Politics* 1305 (2009). But Ryan C. Black et al., "Emotions, Oral Arguments, and Supreme Court Decision Making," 73 *Journal of Politics* 572 (2011), studying questions asked during oral argument in the Supreme Court, seeks clues in the questioner's use of friendly and unfriendly language to Justices' leanings.

28. See, for example, Daniel Hopkins and Gary King, "A Method of Automated Nonparametric Content Analysis for Social Science," 54 *American Journal of Political Science* 229 (2010).

29. See Richard A. Posner, *How Judges Think* 98–105 (2008).

ases; the computer will be influenced by biases only to the extent that they are introduced by the programmer, and these biases can be identified by reading the program.

In this conclusion (so far), as throughout the earlier chapters in this book, our focus has been on the positive analysis of judicial behavior. We have made no suggestions for reform of any legal institutions. But it should be apparent that, at the very least, a realistic understanding of judges should spur changes in legal education, including continuing legal education (especially perhaps continuing *judicial* education), and in the practice of law, critically including preparation for trials and appeals. Litigation is an important part of legal practice; litigation in federal courts, if number of cases is weighted by their importance, has a greater impact on American society than litigation in state courts, despite the vastly larger number of state court cases; the federal judge is the decision-maker in federal litigation; and the accurate understanding of the behavior of federal judges must therefore be a central concern for litigators and their clients.

And to the extent that the incentives and constraints that shape the federal judicial behaviors explored in this book produce behaviors that are socially suboptimal, a further and vital task of normative analysis is to propose sensible reforms to the institutional structure of the judiciary—the structure that determines who is appointed to a federal judgeship; how judges are compensated and disciplined (rewarded and punished); how their incentives are aligned (or misaligned) with those of their diffuse principal, of which we spoke in chapter 1; and how they are promoted and coordinated. We have noted the anomalous combination of declining workload in the Supreme Court with increasing staff resources; could this exemplify a general tendency in the judiciary as elsewhere in government toward mindless secular expansion of bureaucracy? A tendency perhaps driven by the bureaucrats themselves, who in this instance are judges seeking to maximize their utility?

Effective reform requires empirical foundations, which we have tried to enlarge and strengthen, utilizing the methods of social science, with particular though not exclusive emphasis on economic theory and statistical analysis.

The systematic social-scientific study of judicial behavior has already resulted in the creation of a rich body of data and analysis. We hope we've added measurably to it in this book. But the best days for the study of judicial behavior may lie ahead. Continued refinement of analytic insights and tools of quantitative research, increased interest in judicial behavior by economists and other social scientists (including academic lawyers) outside the field of political science (in which the systematic study of judges began), and technical advances in the creation of datasets can open ever-wider vistas of enhanced understanding of judicial behavior.

Acknowledgments

Several chapters have evolved from previously published articles by us, though with extensive revision: chapter 1 on Richard A. Posner, "Some Realism about Judges: A Reply to Edwards and Livermore," 59 *Duke Law Journal* 1177 (2010), and "Realism about Judges," 105 *Northwestern University Law Review* 577 (2011); chapters 3 and 4 on William M. Landes and Richard A. Posner, "Judicial Behavior: A Statistical Study," 1 *Journal of Legal Analysis* 775 (2009), and Lee Epstein, Landes, and Posner, "Unanimous Decisions in the Supreme Court," *Northwestern University Law Review* (forthcoming); chapter 6 on Epstein, Landes, and Posner, "Why (and When) Judges Dissent: A Theoretical and Empirical Analysis," 3 *Journal of Legal Analysis* 101 (2011); and chapter 7 on Epstein, Landes, and Posner, "Predicting the Winner: Does the Number of Questions at Oral Argument Matter?" 39 *Journal of Legal Studies* 433 (2010).

For helpful comments on portions of the manuscript we thank participants in the Workshop on Judicial Behavior sponsored by the Searle Center on Law, Regulation, and Economic Growth of Northwestern University School of Law and the University of Chicago Law School. We also thank participants in workshops at Columbia University, Harvard University, Queen's University, Southern Methodist University, the University of Buffalo, the University of Pennsylvania, and the University of Southern California.

We thank the following students at the University of Chicago, the University of Southern California, and Northwestern University law schools for their very helpful research assistance and cite-checking: at Chicago, Clara Berestycki, Samuel Boyd, Elizabeth Chao, Ralph Dado, Gary DeTurck, Benjamin Foster, Adina Goldstein, Mark Jackson, Michael Kenstowicz, Sonia Lahr-Pastor, Xingxing Li, Ruoke Liu, Emily Rush, Linda Shi, James Shliferstein, Adam Solomon, Nathan Viehl, Steven Weisman, Li Zheng, and Michael Zhu; at the University of Southern California, Graeme Waller and Colin Shaff; and at Northwestern, Laura Baca, Rebecca Bact, Dana Brusca, Irisa Chen, Allan Chorney, Adair Crosley, Justin Ekwall, Rami Fakhouri, Zach Getzelman, Katherine Hayes, Des Kidney, Sue Landsittel, Martin Lewis-Gonzales, Angelica Lopez, Ross Neihaus, Elise Nelson, Nicole Sorell, and Brian Tweedie.

For advice and insights on various chapters we thank Micheal Giles, Linda Greenhouse, Dennis Hutchinson, Adam Liptak, Andrew Martin, Jeffrey Segal, Carolyn Shapiro, Nancy Staudt, Jed Stiglitz, Thomas Walker, Corey Yung, an anonymous reader for the Harvard University Press, and participants in the Workshop on Judicial Behavior that we mentioned. We particularly thank William Hubbard, who read and made detailed comments on the entire manuscript, impelling us to make numerous corrections in and additions to our analysis.

Finally, we thank the following scholars for making their data available and authorizing us to use those data in our statistical analysis: Christina Boyd and Marcus Hendershot (district judges); Paul Collins (amicus curiae participation); Gerard Gryski, Gary Zuk, and Sheldon Goldman (attributes of district judges); Kendall Hannon (pleadings); Timothy Johnson (oral arguments); Kirk Randazzo (district judges); Jeffrey Segal (Supreme Court); Harold J. Spaeth (same); Charles Shipan (appointments to the federal courts); Don Songer, Ashlyn Kuersten, and Susan Haire (courts of appeals); Cass Sunstein (courts of appeals); Chad Westerland (appointments to the Supreme Court); and Gary Zuk, Deborah Barrow, and Gerard Gryski (courts of appeals judges). Finally, Epstein thanks the National Science Foundation for research support.

Index